Assessing Communication Education:
A Handbook for Media, Speech, and
Theatre Educators

Assessing Communication Education:
A Handbook for Media, Speech, and Theatre Educators

Edited by
William G. Christ
Trinity University

LAWRENCE ERLBAUM ASSOCIATES, PUBLISHERS
1994   Hillsdale, New Jersey   Hove, UK

Lawrence Erlbaum Associates, Inc., Publishers
365 Broadway
Hillsdale, New Jersey 07642

Cover design by Doris Harman Lang

Library of Congress Cataloging-In-Publication Data

Assessing communication education : a handbook for media, speech,
   and theatre educators / edited by William G. Christ.
         p.   cm.
   Includes bibliographical references (p.) and indexes.
   ISBN 0-8058-1622-4 (acid-free paper). — ISBN 0-8058-1623-2 (pbk.)
   1. Communication—Study and teaching (Higher)—
Handbooks, manuals, etc. I. Christ, William G.
P91.3.A85   1994
302.2'071'1—dc20   94–20800
                                                         CIP

Printed in the United States of America
10 9 8 7 6 5 4 3 2 1

Dedicated to the memory of
David Eshelman

Contents

Preface

Accountablity. Evaluation. Assessment. Taxpayers, legislatures, and others, including academic administrators, have been asking whether a college education is worth the cost and effort. Leading the attack are critics who ask pointed questions about what faculty are teaching and what students are learning. Schools are being asked to develop measurable assessment criteria for judging success. Unfortunately for those communication programs caught in "assessment fever," there has been little written that directly applies to the complexities of most communication programs.

Within this resource handbook, we balance the philosophical implications of accountability with concrete, specific, usable assessment strategies. The aim is to provide, in one place, necessary and vital information that will help a variety of communication educators and programs.

The volume is broken into three parts. Part 1 provides background and foundational information for assessment. Rosenbaum's first chapter gives an overview of assessment and suggests how it might impact communication education. Christ and Blanchard discuss the elements of program assessment and how the linkage of mission statements with outcomes can lead to strong, innovative programs. Allison compares and contrasts the regional association requirements and ends with a section on a specific, how-to strategy for writing outcome statements.

In Part II of the book, the chapters deal with broad assessment strategies that apply to a variety of media, speech, and theatre courses and programs. Potter discusses teaching evaluation and argues that we need to identify the "what" of teaching before we try to measure the "how." Tucker looks at creative ways for formative and summative course evaluation that starts with the creation of an explicit syllabus. Orlik shows how the complex task of developing and evaluating student portfolios can be accomplished. Moore discusses the use of capstone courses as a way of evaluating not only the major but also how students have integrated their "total" educational experience. Limburg turns to internships, exit interviews, and advisory boards as important assessment strategies.

Part III stresses context-specific assessment strategies. Under the broad heading of speech education, Backlund writes about the Speech Communication Association's (SCA) oral assessment project. Morreale discusses the background and method of assessing public speaking. Hay suggests the variety of ways that interpersonal communication can be assessed and calls for future research that stresses the "knowledge" component of learning. Beebe and Barge report on a strategy for developing small group communication assessment measures. Shockley-Zalabak and Hulbert-Johnson lay out what we know about assessing organizational communication and present a variety of assessment strategies. In the area of theatre education, Malinauskas and Hunt give detailed information about how to assess theatre programs. In media education, Arnold looks at the Accrediting Council on Education in Journalism and Mass Communication (ACEJMC) accreditation guidelines as an assessment tool for individual courses, and Eastman discusses the pros and cons of exit exams for the media major.

Within this book, you will find a variety of perspectives. After Rosenbaum's overview, about half the chapters stress individual student, faculty, or course assessment (Potter, Tucker, Orlik, Moore, Morreale, Hay, Beebe and Barge, and Malinauskas and Hunt), whereas the others stress program, department, or institutional assessment (Allison, Christ and Blanchard, Limburg, Shockley-Zalabak and Hulbert-Johnson, Arnold, and Eastman). This diversity of perspectives should provide interesting and useful information to meet many of the broad assessment challenges facing communication faculty and administrators.

Assessment is an integral part of what we do as teachers, researchers, and administrators. It can be formal or informal, systematic or haphazard, harmful or rewarding. At its best, assessment can have a transforming effect on education. At its worst, it can be used as an instrument to punish people and programs. Our hope is that this book will provide media, speech, and theatre faculty and administrators with the background, understanding, and "tools" to build stronger programs and develop better courses and educational experiences for their students.

ACKNOWLEDGMENTS

This book had its genesis in a paper presented by Professor David Eshelman (Central Missouri State University) at the 1991 Broadcast Education Association (BEA) annual meeting. That paper, along with the BEA's Courses and Curricula Division's perception of a growing need for systematic information about assessment, led the editor to develop a media education assessment panel for the 1992 BEA convention. As the Program Planner for the 1992 BEA convention, Dr. Eshelman was supportive of the panel and suggested and scheduled a two-session workshop. Unfortunately, due to his untimely death a week before the convention, Dr. Eshelman did not get to see the fruits of his labor.

It became clear at the convention that many of the media assessment strategies presented at the workshop applied to all communication programs. It was decided to develop a book proposal that broadened the original concept of "media assessment" to "communication assessment." People involved with the SCA's Committee on Assessment and Testing (CAT) were contacted and agreed to write chapters. CAT, along with the SCA's newly formed Commission on Assessment and Testing, have been central in the current communication assessment movement. CAT's involvement in this project was invaluable.

I would like to publicly acknowledge the dedication and hard work of all the authors involved in this project. It was a pleasure working with them. I would especially like to thank those who allowed me to pick their brains and graciously gave me advice. These people included, in alphabetical order, Tony Allison (Cameron University), Phil Backlund (Central Washington State University), Sherry Morreale (University of Colorado-Colorado Springs), John Rosenbaum (Ithaca College), and David Tucker (University of Toledo).

From the SCA, I would like to thank Gus Friedrich (University of Oklahoma), Publications Chair, for his initial reviews and advice, and Carolyn Cooke, SCA Publications Manager, for her support. From Lawrence Erlbaum Associates, I would like to thank Hollis Heimbouch, Senior Editor, Amy Olener, Editorial Assistant, and Teresa Faella, Production Editor, for their editorial acumen. From Trinity University, I would like to thank my friends and colleagues, especially Bob Blanchard and Bill Walker, for their guidance and for helping to make my time at Trinity rewarding. Also, a special thank you to Sonya Edmondson and Delia Rios for their help in compiling the authors' index and making sure the mail ran on time.

I would also like to thank those reviewers, some whose names I do not know, who gave their time to this worthwhile project. The one "outside" reviewer I know is Jeffrey McCall (DePauw University). His timely and thorough review has made this a better book.

On a more personal note, I would like to thank the Internet, Brian Shoenberger, Ross Peterson, Ken McCullough, Sean Cassidy, Bob and Marie Christ, Nathan and Jonathan Christ, and, my true friend, Judy Christ. Thank you one and all.

William G. Christ

I

Background

1

Assessment: An Overview

John Rosenbaum
Ithaca College

The purpose of this chapter is to provide a broad context for discussions about approaches to outcomes assessment. It begins with a brief history of assessment movements in higher education since the early 1900s. Next the actors involved in five forums are examined: federal agencies, accrediting bodies, national and regional organizations, the states, and institutions. The ongoing debate between assessment's advocates, detractors, worriers, skeptics, and critics is summarized. Three alternative approaches to pencil-and-paper testing are offered: authentic, research, and quality assessment. The chapter concludes with five lessons learned about successful outcomes assessments: (a) begin by clarifying the goals and values of education, (b) analyze practices as well as performances, (c) use multiple approaches, (d) involve everyone, especially faculty, and (e) foster communication.

INTRODUCTION

What is outcomes assessment? Is it the evaluation of student learning we do every day as part of our teaching? Is it accountability for resources that we receive? Is it program review? Self-study? Accreditation? At different times, in different places, for different reasons, outcomes assessment has been all those things and more (see Banta, 1988, 1993b; Johnson, Prus, Anderson, & El-Khawas, 1991).

When the Presidential Task Force on Student Learning and Development at Kean College of New Jersey began exploring the field in the mid-1980s, it concluded that the term *outcomes assessment* has had no single, universally accepted definition (Presidential Task Force on Student Learning and Development, 1986, p. 12). The same year, administrators and faculty members at Harvard University began setting up an assessment program and concluded that outcomes assessment asks three questions: "What do students know now? How much do they gain when they're here? And how can we evaluate the effectiveness of what we do now with an eye toward constantly improving it?" (*A Conversation*, 1991).

The questions answered in assessment depend on several factors—including its purpose, the actors, the timetable, the institutional commitment, and the resources allocated—but the most important is the educational philosophy driving the enterprise. "Differences in meaning and understanding of the word *assessment* tend to be philosophical ones," according to Terenzini (1993), who explained that, "Some view assessment as a public policy vehicle, in that it provides a public accounting for the expenditure of public funds, and as having both political and educational dimensions. Others see no direct links to funding issues and consider the primary purpose of quality assessment to be the enhancement of student learning" (p. 4). On the one hand, outcomes assessment may take the form of an end product—a summative report to an outside agency with the primary purpose of accounting for allocated resources. On the other hand outcomes assessment may be approached as a process of diagnostic, formative, evaluative activities infused into all aspects of learning with the primary purpose of continuous improvement.

Whether the purpose is summative, formative, or a little of each, in planning an assessment methodology is an issue. Will it be quantitative, qualitative, or a combination of both? Will it be normative, criterion-referenced, or descriptive? Ultimately, no one approach will fit all assessments. That was the conclusion of 12 experts on outcomes assessment invited to a series of six discussions sponsored by the American Association for Higher Education (AAHE) Assessment Forum between 1989 and 1992. The participants agreed that, "There is no one best way of conducting an assessment. . .but effective practices *do* have features in common" (Hutchings, 1993, p. 6). In 1992 they issued the document *Principles of Good Practice for Assessing Student Learning* (1993), listing nine principles common to all outcomes assessment efforts:

1. The assessment of student learning begins with educational values.
2. Assessment is most effective when it reflects an understanding of learning as multidimensional, integrated, and revealed in performance over time.
3. Assessment works best when the programs it seeks to improve have clear, explicitly stated purposes.
4. Assessment requires attention to outcomes but also and equally to the experiences that lead to them.
5. Assessment works best when it is ongoing, not episodic.
6. Assessment fosters wider improvement when representatives from across the educational community are involved.
7. Assessment makes a difference when it begins with issues of use and illuminates questions that people really care about.

8. Assessment is most likely to lead to improvement when it is part of a larger set of conditions that promote change.
9. Through assessment, educators meet responsibilities to students and to the public.

Erwin (1991) pointed out that the term *assessment* was used in the fields of industrial psychology and psychometric testing before it took on a life of its own in higher education: "Out of this background, the term *assessment* has proliferated in higher education. In a sense, its meaning today depends on one's role as state official, accreditor, faculty member, student affairs staff, or student" (p. 15). In order to include all perspectives in this discussion, the term *outcomes assessment* is broadly defined. Following Erwin (1991) and Marchese (1987), as used in this chapter, outcomes assessment refers to "the process of defining, selecting, designing, collecting, analyzing, interpreting, and using information to increase students' learning and development" (Erwin, 1991, p. 15). This process includes using the information for program review and improvement, as well as to increase student learning.

The purpose of this chapter is to provide a broad context for the specific issues and various approaches to outcomes assessment that are examined in subsequent chapters of this book. The chapter begins with a brief history of assessment movements in higher education. Then it examines the actors involved, the ongoing debate, and some alternative approaches. The chapter concludes with a list of resources for additional information.

HISTORY

Outcomes assessment—whether used for summative or formative purposes—is not a recent trend in higher education. University of Virginia provost Hugh P. Kelly noted that assessment efforts began at his institution more than 150 years ago (Kelly, 1990 p. 1). Many other provosts can make the same statement, as the practice of assessment was typical in 19th-century U.S. colleges. Degree candidates routinely demonstrated their knowledge and speaking ability in senior declamations, often in public. These performances were intended to display the sum total benefit of the college experience. They were the outcomes assessment instruments of the day.

By the end of the 19th century, a combination of the elective system, the growth in the number of courses, and the larger numbers of students made it difficult to administer individual comprehensive senior exams. A typical response was to make evaluation part of each course that students took. Therefore, when students passed the required number of courses, they received their degrees without the hurdle of senior declamations. However, not everyone agreed with this change. Some educators entered the new century arguing that more than "credit" was needed for the degree.

Assessment movements in higher education since the turn of the century fall roughly into three periods: (a) 1918 to 1952, (b) 1952 to 1975, and (c) 1975 to the present. Each period has been marked by surprisingly similar expansions, complaints, demands, studies, and responses.

1918 to 1952

From 1918 to 1952 the percentage of 18- to 24-year-olds enrolled in higher education almost doubled, from 3.6% to 7.1% (Sims, 1992). This growth was accompanied by complaints about overcrowding, inadequate abilities of students, chaotic curricula, and lack of assessment. There followed the requisite studies, such as the Pennsylvania Study in 1928, the Cooperative Study in General Education from 1939 to 1944, and the Cooperative Study of Evaluation in General Education in 1950. This period saw the birth of national standardized testing by organizations such as Educational Testing Service (ETS) in 1948. Institutional responses included the revival of comprehensive exams and revised curricula, such as the General College of the University of Minnesota in 1932 and the Basic College of Michigan State University in 1944.

1952 to 1975

From 1952 to 1975 there was an even greater increase in the percentage of 18- to 24-year-olds enrolled in higher education, to about 40.5%. The number of accredited colleges and universities increased from about 2,000 to more than 3,000 (Sims, 1992).

In addition to the growth in numbers of students, another factor that made this a period of dramatic change were the new types of students attending college. The student body grew older, more diverse, and more vocal. These students demanded relevant courses and curricula. The widespread response was to reduce common core requirements and replace them with distribution requirements and elective courses. This response to student demands was influenced by a rising tide of consumerism in education and increasing competition among institutions.

This period of rapid expansion and change was accompanied by massive federal and state expenditures under programs such as the National Defense Education Act of 1957, the Higher Education Facilities Act and the Vocational Education Act of 1963, the Higher Education Act of 1965, and the Amendments to the 1965 Higher Education Act in 1972. It was common for all the federal agencies to require some form of evaluation of the projects they funded.

This activity spawned a number of assessment minimovements during the late 1960s and early 1970s. One was the *educational accountability* movement (Hogan, 1992). Bowen (1974) said the demand for accountability resulted from a lack of confidence that a college education was worth its increasing cost. Educational accountability added economic considerations—such as efficiency, cost–benefit analysis, and consumer protection—to evaluation, which primarily looked at educational effectiveness. "Accountability seems to be concerned more with end results and less with process or means, has more a financial and efficiency focus, is more of a public operation (like an audit by an external agency), and carries a greater implication of finality—of hard judgments about total programs (rather than of trying to improve on existing ones)" (Peterson, 1971, p. 16). From this point of view, outcomes assessment was a reporting instrument used only to ensure accountability.

However, it was argued that educational accountability could be more than simply an end report. Lessinger (1970), who has been called the father of educational accountability, said that, "In its most basic aspect, the concept of educational accountability is a process designed to insure that any individual can determine. . .if the schools are producing the results promised. . . .Like most processes that involve balancing of inputs and outputs, educational accountability can be implemented successfully only if educational objectives are clearly stated before instruction starts" (p. 4). I return to this discussion of accountability later in the chapter.

Another minimovement during this period was the *value-added* approach. Like educational accountability, value-added analysis derived from economics and focused on the increased value of raw materials after they go through a production process. "The notion of *value-added* derived from this model. . .involves acceptance of the production process analogy" (Ewell, 1987, p. 7). In this process "assessments needed to account for inputs (students' background, prior achievement, aptitude, and interests) and for college effects (the curriculum and extracurriculum) to determine outcomes (progress, persistence, performance, and learning)" (Ratcliff & Jones, 1993, p. 256). In value-added assessment an institution's quality was based on the degree of change that it made in its students and not on their performance level (Astin, 1987).

A different concept of assessment promoted during the late 1960s and early 1970s was *institutional vitality*. McGrath and his colleagues at Teachers College, Columbia University, defined institutional vitality as "first, *educational effectiveness* in terms of some change in the behavior of students, and second, *institutional adaptability* in terms of progressively changing rather than going through periods of reaction and reform" (Hefferlin, quoted in Peterson & Loye, 1967, p. 24). Their work on institutional vitality led to ETS's institutional self-study instrument called the Institutional Functioning Inventory.

Standardized assessment instruments proliferated during this period. For example, in the late 1960s and early 1970s ETS' Institutional Research Program for Higher Education (IRPHE) alone developed four standardized assessment instruments: College Student Questionnaires, the College and University Environment Scale, the Institutional Functioning Inventory, and the Institutional Goals Inventory. All but the last instrument have been replaced since then.

1975 to the Present

During this period there were two waves of assessment activity. The first wave took place between 1975 and 1985 when institutions began instituting assessment programs for their own purposes without external pressure to do so. Three pioneers during this period were Alverno College in Wisconsin, Northeast Missouri State University, and the University of Tennessee at Knoxville (Erwin, 1991).

The milepost for the second wave of activity during this period—and the current movement—usually is cited as the national conference on assessment held in 1985 at Columbia, South Carolina, sponsored jointly by the AAHE and the National Institute of Education (NIE). The climate for this conference had been created during the first half of the 1980s by widely discussed reports such as *A Nation at Risk: The Imperative for Educational Reform* (National Commission on Excellence in Education, 1983); *Involvement in Learning: Realizing the Potential of American Higher Education* (National Institute of Education, 1984); and *Integrity in the College Curriculum: A Report to the Academic Community* (Association of American Colleges, 1985). The latter report from a 19-member study committee asserted, "The public at large and the academic community itself are uneasy with the evidence of the decline and devaluation of the bachelor's degree in the recent past. To restore integrity to the bachelor's degree there must be a renewal of the faculty's corporate responsibility for the curriculum" (Association of American Colleges, 1985, p. 38).

This widespread criticism by government officials and educators themselves undoubtedly had a negative impact on the public's confidence in the people running U.S. higher education, continuing a downward trend that began in 1960 (McClennay, 1993). In response, there has been a flurry of assessment activity since the mid-1980s among all the actors involved with higher education.

ACTORS

The leading actors in outcomes assessment can be found in the following forums: federal agencies, accrediting bodies, national and regional organizations, states, and institutions.

Federal Agencies

The policies now guiding federal initiatives in both K–12 and postsecondary education are the eight National Education Goals listed in Appendix A.

These goals, often referred to as "Goals 2000" or the "National Education Goals," began as six goals adopted in 1990 by President Bush and the governors of the states as a "national strategy, not a federal program" (U.S. Department of Education, 1991b, p. 11) and set forth by President Bush on April 18, 1991 in *America 2000: An Education Strategy*. Each year since then legislation has been introduced that would set the six goals into law. In March 1994, the "Goals 2000: Educate America Act" was passed by Congress and signed into law. It added two new goals "encouraging parental participation and professional development of teachers" (U.S. Department of Education, 1994a, p. 2). The law will lead to voluntary national education standards approved by a proposed National Education Standards and Improvement Council.

Even as the legislation still was pending, the national goals were being implemented administratively through federal departments and agencies (National Education Goals Panel, 1991). The effort is being spearheaded by the National Education Goals Panel, formed by the nation's governors in 1990. The Goals Panel consists of eight governors, four members of Congress, and two members of the Administration. It is the driving force behind efforts to set and assess national education standards, and had already appointed a Standards Review Technical Planning Group (National Education Goals Panel, 1993). Upon the adoption of the national goals, the Department of Education's Office of Educational Research and Improvement (OERI) set up work groups to appraise the status of research for each goal.

At first the focus of the work groups was on the K–12 levels. However, the Goal 5 Work Group quickly expanded the scope beyond "postcompulsory" education. Summaries of the findings of each work group were reported in the U.S. Department of Education's (1993) series of publications *Reaching the Goals*. Goal 5 states that, "By the year 2000, every adult American will be literate and will possess the knowledge and skills necessary to compete in a global economy and exercise the rights and responsibilities of citizenship" (U.S. Department of Education, 1991a, p. 9). Goal 5 has five objectives, listed in Appendix B.

In 1992 the Goals Panel convened a Task Force on Assessing the National Goal Relating to Postsecondary Education (Goal 5) to report on the "feasibility and desirability" of standardized and comparable state reports on degree completion rates and sample-based assessment of graduates' abilities "to think critically, communicate effectively and solve problems" (Task Force on Assessing the National Goal Relating to Postsecondary Education, 1992, p. 2). The task force concluded that both reports would be feasible and desirable and recommended that a uniform format for reporting degree completion rates be adopted and a "sample-based national system of standards and assessment for postsecondary education" (p. 6) be developed for "general cognitive skills, higher order thinking skills, and occupational specific skills where appropriate" (p. 7). The task force also recommended "the creation of a separate coordinating council for postsecondary standards and assessment that parallels that recommended by the National Council on Education Standards and Testing for elementary-secondary education" (p. 8).

This shift in focus from the K–12 segment of education to higher education did not happen overnight. Its history goes back at least to 1964 and the National Assessment of Educational Progress (NAEP). In 1964 the Carnegie Corporation appointed an Exploratory Committee on Assessing the Progress of Education (Madaus & Stufflebeam, 1989, p. 225). Five years later the Department of Education instituted the NAEP program as a voluntary cooperative. Every 2 years since then the NAEP project has evaluated samples of 4th, 8th, and 12th graders and issued what has become known as "the Nation's report card." In 1988, legislation made NAEP a mandated project of the National Center for Education Statistics (NCES), as a means to "improve the effectiveness of our Nation's schools by making objective information about student performance in selected learning areas available to policymakers at the national, regional, state and local levels" (U.S. Department of Education, 1991c).

In 1990 former President Bush's Task Force on National Educational Goals called for a national assessment of postsecondary education similar to that of the NAEP. In 1991 and 1992 the NCES sponsored workshops on the feasibility of assessing higher order thinking and communication skills as part of fulfilling Goal 5, Objective 5. Following up on these workshops, the NCES funded the Center for the Study of Higher Education at the Pennsylvania State University "to provide an initial listing of higher-order thinking and communication skills" and the National Center for Higher Education Management Systems (NCHEMS) "to inventory and evaluate current indirect approaches to assessment of the skills identified in Goal 5.5" (Corrallo, 1993, p. 7). Recently the NCES announced that it is seeking proposals for a National Postsecondary Student Assessment to measure progress toward Goal 5. The NCES request for proposals said: "The contractor shall identify, define, and obtain a working consensus of the sets of skills needed for critical thinking, problem solving, and communications and the corresponding levels of achievement needed to meet the requirements of the goal" (Zook, 1993, p. A23).

Looking to the future, another initiative at the elementary and secondary levels that may be expanded to higher education is the National Board for Professional Teaching Standards (NBPTS), created in 1987 by the Carnegie Forum on Education and the Economy. The NBPTS is a 63-member board that is developing national teacher certification instruments in 38 elementary and secondary fields. It will finish the first assessment instrument in 1994, and expects to complete all 38 by 1998–1999. Like the NCES' National Postsecondary Student Assessment, down the road Carnegie's NBPTS could result in national postsecondary certification instruments beyond state certification and accreditation.

Bridging the gap between the federal and state levels has been the National Governors' Association (NGA). The NGA's education policies were spelled out in the report *It's Time for Results: Governors' 1991 Report on Education* (NGA, 1986). Although referring to the year 1991 in its title, the report actually was published in 1986. According to the preface, using a date 5 years in the future emphasized the report's future orientation.

One of the seven task forces the NGA established in 1986 was the Task Force on College Quality. It held three hearings that year (NGA, 1986). As a result, members acknowledged that assessment was being undertaken by most colleges and universities, from course exams to norm-referenced testing, but observed that the information was not being collected systematically or analyzed comprehensively: "Many colleges and universities do not have a systematic way to demonstrate whether student learning is taking place. Rather, learning—and especially developing abilities to utilize knowledge—is *assumed* to take place as long as students take courses, accumulate hours, and progress 'satisfactorily' toward a degree" (p. 20). The task force recommended that "each college and university have assessment programs in place to evaluate student, program, and institutional performance, and that information about program and institutional performance be shared with the public" (p. 21). The NGA's bottom line was that, "Parents, students, taxpayers, and state policymakers all have a keen interest in knowing that public colleges and universities are providing quality education. Assessment programs make it possible for institutions to meet this demand for consumer information with accurate, timely information on student, program, and institutional performance" (p. 21).

The NGA has played a major role on the national scene. It was the NGA's widely reported "Education Summit" with President Bush on September 27–28, 1989, at Charlottesville, Virginia, at which Goals 2000 took shape (U.S. Department of Education, 1991a, p. 73).

Accrediting Bodies

The six regional accrediting associations (see chap. 3) have been required to address the issue of outcomes assessment since both the Council on Postsecondary Education (in 1987) and the Department of Education (in 1988) mandated that information about learning outcomes must be required by the accrediting bodies (Hutchings & Marchese, 1990). Some accreditors include them as part of general standards for institutional achievement, and others have specific standards for "institutional or program effectiveness" (Ewell, 1992, p. 1). The first was the Southern Association of Colleges and Schools (SACS), which adopted standards on "institutional effectiveness" in 1986 that "were the same as those later adopted by other accreditors: develop and articulate clear goals stated in terms of outcomes, select or build appropriate local measures to gather evidence of goal achievement, and provide evidence of the ways that the resulting evidence was used to inform improvement" (Ewell, 1993b, p. 345). The largest commission, the North Central Association of Colleges and Schools, reports assessment initiatives in all the regions and all 19 North Central states.

Other accrediting bodies also have reacted to the assessment movement, and now most have policies on assessing institutional outcomes. Indeed, all 54 accreditors that responded to a 1991 survey by the Council on Postsecondary Accreditation used outcomes analysis to some extent (Council on Postsecondary Accreditation, 1992). For example, the Accrediting Council on Education in Journalism and Mass Communication cites four outcomes standards that it analyzes: Standard 3: Curriculum demonstration of learning and skills; Standard 5: Instructional/Evaluation; Standard 7: Internship and Work Experience; and Standard 11: Graduates/Alumni (Council on Postsecondary Accreditation, 1992).

National and Regional Organizations

In addition to the accrediting bodies, national and regional organizations have been involved with assessment. One example is the National Association of State Universities and Land Grant Colleges (NASULGC), which officially adopted a Statement of Principles on Student Outcomes Assessment in 1988. It "gives emphasis to developmental assessment—to the improvement of teaching and learning" (National Association of State Universities and Land Grant Colleges, 1988, p. 1). To determine the usefulness of the statement, and the status of outcomes assessment at NASULGC institutions, a mail survey was conducted in 1990. Seventy-three institutions responded. Thirty-nine had assessment programs in place, 6 were about to initiate programs, planning discussions had begun at 22, and only 6 said they had no program and no plans to start one.

Professional associations have established assessment task forces and interest groups. For example, in 1988 the Academy of Management instituted a task force on outcomes assessment (Albanese, 1988). In the field of communication, the most active group has been the Committee on Assessment and Testing (CAT) of the Speech Communication Association (SCA; see chap. 9). CAT subcommittees developed criteria for the assessment of oral communication (*Criteria*, 1991) and its members have been active in the NCES workshops on higher order thinking and communication skills (Daly, 1992). Recently, the SCA approved a Commission on Assessment and Testing.

States

Of all the external actors, the states have played the major role in shaping assessment efforts. In 1985 just 3 or 4 states were actively promoting assessment, and by 1987 the number had increased to 12 ("State Trends,"

1990). By 1990, close to 40 states were taking some legal or regulatory steps to mandate assessment ("State Trends," 1990). Ewell (1993b) reported that "all but nine states have in place a policy on assessment of some kind, affecting all but a handful of public campuses" (p. 339).

A 1989 survey of 50 states by the Academy of Management's All Academy Task Force on Outcome Measurement "indicated considerable activity at the state level," virtually all initiated since 1980 (Bernardin, 1990, pp. 3–4). However, the level of state activity varies greatly. A 50-state survey in 1987 by the Education Commission of the States found six types of state involvement: mandating statewide testing, mandating teacher education testing, employing early intervention, promoting institutional activity, using existing mechanisms, and monitoring other outcomes (Sims, 1992).

Few states mandate statewide testing. Some that do are Florida, Georgia, Missouri, New Jersey, South Dakota, Tennessee, and Texas. Florida, New Jersey, and Tennessee require entry-level basic skills tests. "Rising junior" exams are mandated in Florida and Georgia for students entering upper levels (Ewell, 1987). Missouri requires all sophomores to complete the standardized College Basic Academic Subjects Exam (CBASE; Lively, 1992). All postsecondary institutions in Tennessee must give a standardized test of generic skills to graduates and conduct a common survey of alumni (Banta, 1993b). In contrast, two states—South Dakota and Washington— tried large-scale standardized outcomes testing, and found it inadequate (Ewell, 1991). In fact, Ewell (1993b) noted that the requirements of the vast majority of states are nonprescriptive and do not require specific assessment methods or standardized instruments.

After assessment data is collected and reported, states use the assessment reports primarily for incentive/performance funding, institutional improvement, and accountability measurement.

Incentive/Performance Funding. Some states have tied monetary incentives to assessment results. Bernardin (1990) reported that at least 15 states employ student outcomes measures in the budget process.

Tennessee is noteworthy in this regard. It was the first state to adopt an outcomes assessment policy, which is the most prescriptive of any adopted since then (Banta, 1993b). In 1979 Tennessee's Higher Education Commission said a portion of state funding would be based on performance criteria, not enrollment. *Performance funding* could mean as much as 5.45% of an institution's budget for instruction (Banta, 1993b), or, for example, up to $5 million to a large institution such as the University of Tennessee at Knoxville (Hutchings & Marchese, 1990).

Incentive funding has been available in Virginia (Hutchings & Marchese, 1990); however, budget declines since 1990 have prevented the funding of all good proposals (Fuhrmann & Gentemann, 1993). Texas and Maine also are looking at performance-based funding schemes (Lively, 1992).

Institutional Improvement. About three quarters of the states polled in 1989 responded that *institutional improvement*, not *accountability*, is the purpose of their assessments ("State Trends," 1990). As put by McClenney (1993): "One of the most notable developments in the assessment movement over the past seven years has been the avoidance of the most draconian versions of state accountability policy" (p. 1). "Indeed, the primary thrust of most current state initiatives is to encourage institutions to undertake their own appropriate local assessment efforts" (Ewell, 1987, p. 25). The most widely used types of assessment instruments are not the norm-referenced, national standardized tests, but locally developed tests or exams designed by the people who "set the objectives and teach the courses" (Banta, 1993b, p. 156). One example of this approach is Virginia's plan for "discretionary institution-centered assessment" (Lively, 1992, p. A26).

Both the Association of American Colleges and the National Institute of Education discourage narrow approaches to assessment, "arguing that any assessment should instead be used as information feedback for strengthening the educational process. Emphasizing cooperation over competition, such assessment would be designed to facilitate and improve performance rather than merely to evaluate it" (Astin, 1988, p. 8).

Accountability Measurement. Few states require accountability data. Three that do are Florida, Kentucky, and South Carolina. Florida and Kentucky require reports on faculty workloads, use of classroom space, and other efficiency measures. South Carolina requires reports on 18 categories of data, including graduation and job-placement rates (Sims, 1992) and "the number of undergraduate students actively participating in sponsored-research activities" (Ewell, 1993a). In an indirect approach to accountability assessment, Ohio has mandated that public colleges and universities establish task forces to examine how they are being managed, which includes evaluating their productivity and effectiveness (Willinford & Moden, 1993).

Although few states currently require assessment data for accountability, its use for that purpose is on the rise. In part, this trend appears to be motivated by public opinion and advocacy organizations such as the Campaign for Genuine Accountability in Education, founded by the National Center for Fair and Open Testing (Fair-Test) ("State Trends," 1990). The Southern Regional Education Board, in fact, has encouraged its 15 member states to enact accountability measures (Lively, 1992).

Recognizing this trend, *Assessment Update* editor Trudy W. Banta wrote in a recent issue that, "The accountability noose is being drawn ever more tightly, and ultimately this fact will become clear to faculty throughout academe" (Banta, 1993a, p. 12). In the same issue, Ewell's (1993a) description of recent efforts by different state agencies to require graduation-rate reporting and national performance standards gave credence to Banta's metaphor: "Most emerging indicators systems, for example, contain in total some 15 to 20 distinct data items collected by the state higher education governing or coordinating body and are reported in the form of direct comparisons among institutions or sectors." (p. 12). Data being sought by states include graduation/retention rates, graduate placement, "linkage" data such as transfer rates between 2- and 4-year colleges, instructional practices, and cognitive outcomes. El-Khawas (1992) noted that although almost all respondents to the 1992 American Council on Education (ACE) survey of campus trends reported assessment activity, more than half said it has resulted in only "additional reporting requirements."

Ultimately, the bottom line may be the bottom line—such as the situation in Florida, where education officials balked at meeting expensive accountability mandates required by law when, at the same time, the lawmakers were cutting funds for resources such as libraries (Lively, 1992). The foremost example of a statewide assessment effort with more negative than positive results is the College Outcomes Evaluation Program (COEP), established in 1985 by the New Jersey Board of Higher Education. By 1990 COEP had set up a statewide assessment program—including the General Intellectual Skills (GIS) Assessment. GIS was a test of critical thinking, problem solving, reasoning, and writing skills, developed for COEP by ETS under a 2-year $1 million contract. From the onset COEP found itself embroiled in a culture of confrontation with college and university faculty who perceived COEP as a threatening top-down mandate. Abruptly, state funding for COEP was eliminated in 1991 and the program was closed down. The lesson for other states, according to Jemmott and Morante (1993), is that "costs to the institutions (related to internal structures and constituent groups) must be less than the benefits that eventually accrue" (p. 320).

Ewell (1993b) wrote that the four prominent lessons the states have learned from the last 10 years of assessment activity are:

1. Requiring assessment to stand alone results in little real impact on campus behavior.
2. Decentralized approaches, though they continue to show promise for inducing local improvement, are increasingly unsatisfactory in achieving credible accountability.
3. Decentralized approaches that preserve considerable campus initiative do work eventually to change local practice, but the process takes time and requires consistent messages and incentives.
4. Policies that act indirectly to increase the decisional discretion of institutional leaders remain the key to meaningful, long-term campus action. (pp. 352–353)

Institutions

According to ACE *Campus Trends* data, in 1988, 55% of all colleges reported assessment projects taking place on their campuses. The following year the number had grown to 67%, and in 1990 it reached 82% (El-Khawas, 1988, 1989, 1990). In 1992, 95% of respondents to a national survey of the chief academic officers of 2- and 4-year institutions indicated they were just beginning or had established assessment programs (Bradley, Draper, & Pike, 1993). According to the 1993 *Campus Trends*, a remarkable 97% of colleges and universities reported having or planning assessment programs (El-Khawas, 1993).

Some researchers have found that such high percentages do not necessarily reflect levels of activity as high as they suggest: "The overall picture. . .is best seen as one in which about one third of U.S. colleges and universities have serious initiatives directed toward student assessment and most others are experimenting with student assessment on their campuses, possibly only in discussions among a few persons or within a single department" (Johnson, quoted in El-Khawas, 1990, p. 13).

Johnson's observation is consistent with the experience of Kean College. In 1986, with a $3.9 million assessment development grant in its pocket (Boyer, 1989), the subcommittees of Kean's Presidential Task Force on Student Learning and Development went looking for comprehensive assessment programs at other institutions. They found just the three pioneers: Alverno College, Northeast Missouri State University, and the University of Tennessee at Knoxville (Presidential Task Force on Student Learning and Development, 1986, p. 3). Since then, notable assessment programs have been initiated at Harvard (the Harvard Assessment Seminars); Kings College, in Wilkes Barre, Pennsylvania (*course-embedded* assessment); the University of Virginia (*discretionary institution-centered* assessment); James Madison University (*cross-cutting* assessment); and, of course, Kean College.

Assessment also is taking place within colleges and universities—in departments, majors, libraries, student services, and other programs. Take the example of majors. Stark, Lowther, and Hagerty's (1986) survey of 12 professional majors, including journalism, found that all 12 departments were "reviewing program purposes, curricular validity, the role of foundational courses, and the volume of conceptual and technical material students must learn" (Stark et al., 1986, p. iv). In addition, all fields were questioning whether the traditional liberal arts was the best curricular vehicle in which students may achieve an understanding of the social, cultural, and economic context of their professions.

THE DEBATE

The coordinator of Assessment of Student Learning and Development at Kean College said, "The concepts of outcomes assessment are simple: determine the objectives for what you are doing, select and use instruments to get information about how well the objectives are being achieved, and use the information to approve attainment of the objectives. It's the implementation of the concepts that is not easy" (Lumsden & Knight, 1990, p. 7). That certainly is an understatement. "Advocates and practitioners of assessment in higher education are divided in their approaches to assessment by their allegiance to distinct concepts of post-secondary learning" (Presidential Task Force on Student Development, 1986, p. 12).

Although the assessment movement seems to be pervasive at all levels of higher education, not everyone has joined the program. It has its share of detractors, worriers, skeptics, and critics. Detractors argue that the process of setting goals, measuring outcomes, and making public accountability reports is a business management practice and business models do not work in the academy. Worriers fear the misuse of the information generated in outcomes assessments—that it will be used to increase workloads and faculty productivity. Skeptics assert that outcomes assessment has no value unless it is tied to rewards and incentives, such as increased funding for successful programs. Finally, critics contend that outcomes assessment is a lockstep process that cuts against the grain of individual autonomy and academic freedom—not everyone marches to the same drumbeat.

A 1986 survey of institutions by the American Council on Education identified five major obstacles to outcomes assessment:

1. Lack of funds to develop assessment procedures (71%).
2. No clear methods to evaluate (64%).
3. Fears that assessment data would be misused (60%).
4. Lack of faculty support (58%).
5. No good instruments (57%). (Sims, 1992, p. 18)

On the other hand, some argue that faculty have no choice; that they must join the program anyway for three main reasons:

1. External constituencies are mandating it through laws, regulations, and the weight of public opinion. They must be given proof that the university is delivering what it promises.
2. Faculty are already doing it anyway. Much of outcomes assessment is making explicit what faculty already have been doing, in ways that are understandable to external constituencies.
3. Used properly, outcomes assessment can contribute to the improvement of teaching and learning.

As a commentary in *The Chronicle of Higher Education* pointed out: "By choosing not to respond, we allow non-educators to set the terms of debate over the effectiveness of our work, people who most likely will turn to commercial testing agencies or other groups outside academe for answers" (Schilling & Schilling, 1993, p. A40). Some of those noneducators undoubtedly will agree with Senator Carl Parker, chairman of the Texas State Senate Education Committee, who said: "Educators need to become attuned to the fact that, whether they like it or not, they are public employees and accountable to the great unwashed" (quoted in Lively, 1992, p. A26).

ALTERNATIVE APPROACHES

If the objective is summative—to monitor, measure, and report student outcomes—conventional testing probably is adequate. Two instruments frequently employed in assessing the outcomes of general education are the ACT College Outcomes Measures Program (ACT-COMP) exam and the ETS Academic Profile. Two standardized tests frequently used to measure student knowledge in content areas are the ETS Major Field Tests (MFT) and the Graduate Record Examinations (GRE).

However, there is such a diversity of learning styles, teaching methods, and institutional goals across the nation that it is impossible for a one-size test to fit all assessments. "Study after study on campuses reveals that nationally standardized tests contain questions that cover only a fraction of the content that faculty consider important in a given domain of knowledge" (Banta, 1993b). For example, Empire State College, in New York, found that the ACT-COMP exam and other national norm-referenced tests had limited value, so they turned to locally developed instruments (Kasworm & Marienau, 1993). Another example is Kean College, where "Faculty must develop their own assessment measures and set criteria for appropriate levels of importance. Outside consultants are used to evaluate the objectives, instruments, and criteria. Faculty do not have the option of choosing nationally-normed, standardized tests" (Lumsden & Knight, 1990, p. 4).

Whether standardized or locally designed, paper-and-pencil tests will not provide adequate outcomes if the goal is to improve performance across the board. In this case, methods that more directly assess students' knowledge and skills, and their change over time, will be more useful. Three current movements in this direction are authentic assessment, research assessment, and quality assessment.

Authentic Assessment

The *authentic assessment* approach is a movement to reform assessment so there is less reliance on standardized testing. "Conventional tests are usually limited to paper-and-pencil, one-answer questions. Assessment is authentic when we directly examine student performance on worthy intellectual tasks" (Wiggins, 1990, p. 3). These tasks include activities such as researching, writing, discussing, analyzing, and debating. Assessments may take the form of oral exams, performance appraisals, performance simulations, portfolios, and self-evaluations (Johnson, McCormick, Prus, & Rogers, 1993, pp. 156–159).

The authentic assessment movement's opposition to traditional testing is not based on questions of validity: "Multiple-choice tests can be valid indicators or predictors of academic performance" (Wiggins, 1990, p. 3). However, the validity of assessment tests also should depend on how well they simulate real-world tests of ability, as done when professionals prepare for performances, reports, presentations, cases, and so on. Wiggins (1990) wrote, "A move toward more authentic tasks and outcomes thus improves teaching and learning: students have greater clarity about their obligations (and are asked to master more engaging tasks), and teachers can come to believe that assessment results are both meaningful and useful for improving instruction" (p. 4).

Research Assessment

Another departure from traditional methods is to approach assessment as research. This approach has been taken at Indiana University, which defines assessment as: "Research into the teaching-learning process which can encompass a range from the study of individuals to the study of entire programs or schools and departments or institutions" (Wolf, 1993, p. 80). The implication is that faculty are at the center of the process: "Within a course, within a program, or within a discipline, faculty are the ones who should decide the questions to be asked, the methods for data collection, *and the interpretive basis for the collected results*" (p. 5).

Research assessment in the classroom has been referred to variously as *course-embedded research, learning research, classroom research,* and *classroom assessment* (see chap. 5) All employ ongoing short-term evaluation methods as part of the teaching–learning process (Angelo & Cross, 1993). Specific techniques include goal-rankings, concept maps, 1-minute papers, interim evaluations, and student self-evaluation (Waluconis, 1993).

Essentially, the process amounts to research conducted by the teacher on-the-spot right in the classroom. "Unlike other evaluation initiatives, classroom research begins with the premise that faculty are uniquely empowered to lead the research in teaching effectiveness and, by extension, student learning" (Obler, Slark, & Umbdenstock, 1993, p. 212).

Classroom research is both formative and summative. First, it provides immediate feedback that can be used by teachers and students to make changes in teaching and learning as they are needed. This produces an active learning environment all around. Second, at the end of the course, the written records can be used as the evidence of improvement.

Research assessment may take many forms and be just as appropriate at a large institution as in a small classroom. University faculty in a discipline with quantitative research as its dominant paradigm may be receptive to a highly controlled assessment study that uses statistical measurement and analysis, which they perceive as valid. The research process—evolving from study to study as new questions arise from old answers—lends itself to the study of the constantly changing curriculum. Watt, Drennan, Rodrigues, Menelly, and Wiegel (1993) described the research approach at the University of Connecticut in its 3-year General Education Assessment Project from 1988 to 1991. From the onset the faculty were involved on a very large scale in the process. Faculty used a variety of instruments to assess different academic areas. They tailored the overall program to their specific needs and did not import a program from elsewhere. By using a research approach, "the people involved saw assessment not as a single activity, but rather as the conjunction of a number of related projects aimed at answering different questions about student education and experiences" (p. 106).

Quality Assessment

Just as earlier assessment movements adopted concepts from economics, today some educators are adopting concepts from total quality management (TQM) in business and industry. In this approach, faculty "employees" interact with student "customers" in a process of continuous improvement. The process should result in "satisfaction" as faculty and students achieve their goals. Improvement focuses on the system. Any "dissatisfaction" is said to arise from problems in the system, not the people involved. Therefore, quality improvement requires changing the system. Not all educators agree with this business metaphor. For example, Pederson (1992) contended that students are not "passive" customers and their satisfaction should not be the highest goal of education. However, other educators take the position that a number of ingredients in TQM fit the recipe for improving higher education. Krueger (1993) described four TQM "insights" that are common to education and business. First, end-product reports do not improve quality. Second, the process, not the individual, is the source of most problems. Third, to improve quality, the inadequate process must be improved. Fourth, improving quality does not necessarily mean higher costs. Some institutions that have initiated quality assessment programs are El Camino College in California, Georgia Institute of Technology, Oregon State University, and California State University, Dominguez Hills. In addition, the seven-campus Minnesota State University System has initiated a major quality assessment program called "Q-7: Quality on the Line" (p. 273)

LESSONS LEARNED

What has been learned from all the years of assessment activity in higher education? What is known about using outcomes assessment to improve the ways students learn, faculty teach, and administrators run their programs and institutions?

The first lesson is that successful outcomes assessment begins by clarifying the goals and values of education. What do we want our students to know or do? What are the missions of our departments and institutions? Indeed, what is the purpose of higher education itself? There has been no shortage of answers to these questions since the debate on the curriculum went public in the mid-1980s. One example is *50 Hours: A Core Curriculum for College Students*, which suggests 3 years of the study of cultures and civilization, 2 years of a foreign language, and 1 year each of math, natural science, and social science (Cheyney, 1989). Undoubtedly, as the NCES implements National Education Goal 5, there will be increasing pressures toward comparable national assessment standards, if not a national curriculum. The challenge to faculty and administrators will be to preserve the diversity of their goals and institutional autonomy under increasing pressures for accountability. The relationships between outcomes assessment and mission statements are examined in the next chapter.

Second, outcomes assessment should analyze practices as well as performances—the ongoing process as well as the end results. *How* faculty teach and *how* students learn need to be examined along with *what* is taught and learned (Rosenbaum, 1992). Chickering and Gamson (1989) offered seven "good practices in undergraduate education" based on a study of "50 years of research on the way teachers teach and students learn, how students work and play with one another, and how students and faculty talk to each other." The seven practices are listed in Appendix C. They are built on principles of activity, cooperation, diversity, expectations, interaction, and responsibility (p. 1). These underlying principles can be employed as indicators of educational effectiveness within the context of program improvement. The indicators will lead to answers for questions about program effectiveness such those asked by Oettinger and Cole (1978): Is the educational program achieving its objectives effectively? Are program parts equally effective? Is the program meeting goals other than those expected?

The third lesson is that multiple approaches are needed to assess the complex relationships between learning and pedagogy. Multiple approaches provide more reliable, valid, and meaningful results (Erwin, 1991). The traditional assessment tools are tests, exams, and surveys. Alternatives—including portfolios, capstone courses, oral assessments, and exit interviews—are discussed in subsequent chapters of this book. Johnson et al. (1993) suggested that existent data, such as archival records, are practical but underutilized sources of assessment information. Ewell and Jones (1993) proposed examining practices that indirectly measure student learning, such as interaction with faculty outside of class. Two other approaches are assessment centers (Millward, 1993) and coursework cluster analysis (Ratcliff & Jones, 1993). The most useful approaches will be those designed specifically to meet the unique needs of an assessment. Amiran, Schilling, and Schilling (1993) added that, "It's not simply a matter of finding what is right for each institution but also of understanding that different emphases are right for the same institution at different stages in its assessment process" (p. 85).

Fourth, outcomes assessment must involve everyone, especially the faculty, who need to take responsibility for leading and designing the assessment. Many other constituents also should be invited to participate, such as current students, administrators, graduates, employers, and external evaluators. Banta (1993b) suggested that assessment efforts should, "Build a sense of shared purpose among students, faculty, and administrators based on clearly articulated and communicated statements of mission and educational goals" (p. 365).

The fifth lesson is that outcomes assessment means communicating. Banta (1993b) pointed out, "As campus administrators—the first to feel the effects of external pressures from governments and accrediting agencies—have sought ways to encourage faculty to undertake comprehensive assessment programs, they have turned most often for leadership to good communicators within the ranks of the faculty and administrative staff" (p. 358). Clear lines of communication between all the stakeholders are important at all stages of an assessment to avoid confusion and mistrust that otherwise could arise. At the end of the process, the results must be communicated back to the people who can make best use of them for the improvement of learning; that is, the faculty and students. In the form of public information releases, the results also can be used to provide recognition for successful programs. However, Aitken and Neer (1993) suggested that in doing this, "Carefully frame assessment reports so as to guard against inappropriate use" (p. 9).

ASSESSMENT AND COMMUNICATION EDUCATION

Research has begun to show that outcomes assessment does lead to improvement in learning and teaching when designed for those purposes and conducted properly (Banta, 1993b). However, as has been suggested, not all the impact might be positive. Lumsden (1993) speculated that outcomes assessment will impact on speech communication and, it could be argued, all of communication education by (a) increasing emphasis on skills, (b) compromising objectives, and (c) motivating new approaches for instruction. He may be right. The temptation to stress skills at the expense of broader, more comprehensive objectives should be resisted. Assessment should not force us to compromise our expansive visions for the field and our students. This book, if nothing else, argues that there needs to be a balance, a range of broad and context-specific assessment strategies that address different aspects of faculty, student, course, departmental, program, and institutional success. The information in this book should enable communication faculty and administrators to take the lead in assessment and make sure that it is done right for the benefit of our students. Then, what has been called the assessment necessity will become an important and exciting opportunity. (For a list of resources see Appendix D.)

APPENDIX A: THE NATIONAL EDUCATION GOALS

By the year 2000:

Goal 1: All children in the United States will start school ready to learn.

Goal 2: The high school graduation rate will increase to at least 90%.

Goal 3: U.S. students will leave Grades 4, 8, and 12 having demonstrated competency in challenging subject matter, including English, mathematics, science, history, and geography; and every school in America will ensure that all students learn to use their minds well, so they may be prepared for responsible citizenship, further learning, and productive employment in our modern economy.

Goal 4: U.S. students will be the first in the world in science and mathematics achievement.

Goal 5: Every adult American will be literate and will possess the knowledge and skills necessary to compete in a global economy and exercise the rights and responsibilities of citizenship.

Goal 6: Every school in the United States will be free of drugs and violence and will offer a disciplined environment conducive to learning.

Goal 7: The nation's teaching force will have access to programs for the continued improvement of their professional skills and the opportunity to acquire the knowledge and skills needed to instruct and prepare all American students for the next century.

Goal 8: Every school will promote partnerships that will increase parental involvement and participation in promoting the social, emotional, and academic growth of children. (U.S. Department of Education, 1994b, p. 7)

APPENDIX B: NATIONAL EDUCATION GOAL 5
OBJECTIVES

1. Every major U.S. business will be involved in strengthening the connection between education and work.

2. All workers will have the opportunity to acquire the knowledge and skills, from basic to highly technical, needed to adapt to emerging new technologies, work methods, and markets through public and private educational, vocational, technical, work place, or other programs.

3. The number of quality programs, including those at libraries, that are designed to serve more effectively the needs of the growing number of part-time and midcareer students will increase substantially.

4. The proportion of those qualified students (especially minorities) who enter college, who complete at least 2 years, and who complete their degree programs will increase substantially.

5. The proportion of college graduates who demonstrate an advanced ability to think critically, communicate effectively, and solve problems will increase substantially. (National Education Goals Panel, 1993, p. xi)

APPENDIX C: SEVEN PRINCIPLES FOR GOOD PRACTICE IN UNDERGRADUATE EDUCATION

1. Good practice encourages student–faculty contact.
2. Good practice encourages cooperation among students.
3. Good practice encourages active learning.
4. Good practice gives prompt feedback.
5. Good practice emphasizes time on task.
6. Good practice communicates high expectations.
7. Good practice respects diverse talents and ways of learning. (Faculty inventory, 1989). Racine, WI: The Johnson Foundation, Inc. Copies are available by writing to The Johnson Foundation, Inc., Processing Center, P.O. Box 17305, Racine, WI 53217. A companion publication, *Institutional inventory: 7 principles for good practice in undergraduate education* (1989) is also available.

APPENDIX D: SELECTED RESOURCES

• ACT, 2255 North Dubuque Road, Iowa City, IA 52243, (319) 337–1136. Provides assessment instruments, including the ACT College Outcome Measures Program (ACT-COMP), ACT Activity Inventory, and ACT Alumni Survey.

• American Association for Higher Education Assessment Forum, One Dupont Circle, Suite 360, Washington, DC 20036, (202) 293-6440. Sponsors annual conferences on various aspects of assessment in higher education. Has published a directory of assessment methods and is considering an update in 1994.

•ASSESS discussion list on the Internet. To join this list send an E-mail message to LISTSERV@UKCC.BITNET that says only SUB ASSESS YOURFIRSTNAME YOURLASTNAME on the first line.

•*Assessment Update*, Jossey-Bass Publishers, 350 Sansome Street, San Francisco, CA 94104-1310, (415) 433-1767. Bimonthly newsletter on assessment in higher education.

•Clearinghouse for Higher Education Assessment Instruments, University of Tennessee, 212 Claxton Education Building, Knoxville, TN 37996, (615) 974-3748. Has a collection of assessment instruments and publications.

•EARLI-AE discussion list on the Internet. To join this list send an E-mail message to LISTSERV@HEARN.BITNET that says only SUB EARLI-AE YOURFIRSTNAME YOURLASTNAME on the first line. EARLI-AE is the European Association for Research on Learning and Instruction special interest group "Assessment & Evaluation."

•Educational Testing Service (ETS), Higher Education Assessment Program, 31-V, Princeton, NJ 08541-0001, (609) 951-6508. Provides a number of standardized assessment instruments, including the ETS Academic Profile, Major Field Tests, Graduate Record Exams, and Goals Inventories.

•ERIC Clearinghouse on Assessment and Evaluation Gopher Service provides articles about alternative assessment, descriptions of thousands of commercial and noncommercial test instruments, and the Buros Test Review Locator as searchable databases. The ERIC Gopher can be reached at GOPHER.CUA.EDU under Special Resources.

•Fund for the Improvement of Postsecondary Education (FIPSE) Comprehensive Program, U.S. Department of Education, 7th and D Streets, Washington, DC 20202-5175, (202) 708-5750. Has supported several dozen assessment-related projects since the mid-1980s ("FIPSE Connection," 1990).

•National Governors' Association, Center for Policy Research and Analysis, Hall of the States, 400 North Capital Street, Washington, DC 20001-1532, (202) 624-5300. Manages federal grants, foundation-funded activities, and state demonstration programs in education and other areas.

•Office of Planning and Institutional Improvement, Indiana University/Purdue University, Indianapolis, 355 N. Lansing Street, AO 140, Indianapolis, IN 46202-2896, (317) 274-4111. Sponsors annual international conferences on assessing quality in higher education.

•South Carolina Higher Education Assessment Network, Winthrop University, 210 Tillman Hall, Rock Hill, SC 29733, (803) 323-2341. Sponsors annual conferences on assessment in higher education.

•U.S. Department of Education, Office of Educational Research and Improvement (OERI), Department EIB, 555 New Jersey Avenue NW, Washington, DC 20208-5641. Will provide technical reports from the OERI's national goals work groups.

REFERENCES

Aitken, J. E., & Neer, M. R. (1993, May). *Using the assessment process to advance a department of communication*. Paper presented to the annual meeting of the International Communication Association, Washington, DC.

Albanese, B. (1988). Outcomes measurement: Task force forms subcommittees. *The Academy of Management News, 19*(2), 8.

Amiran, M., Schilling, K. M., & Schilling, K. L. (1993). Assessing outcomes of general education. In T. W. Banta (Ed.), *Making a difference: Outcomes of a decade of assessment in higher education* (pp. 71–86). San Francisco: Jossey-Bass.

Angelo, T. A., & Cross, K. P. (1993). *Classroom assessment techniques: A handbook for college teachers* (2nd ed.). San Francisco: Jossey-Bass.

Association of American Colleges. (1985). *Integrity in the college curriculum: A report to the academic community*. Washington, DC: Author.

Astin, A. W. (1987). Assessment, value–added, and educational excellence. In D. F. Halpern (Ed.), *Student outcomes assessment: What institutions stand to gain* (pp. 89–107; New Directions for Higher Education, No. 59). San Francisco: Jossey-Bass.

Astin, A. W. (1988). The implicit curriculum: What are we really teaching our undergraduates? *Liberal Education, 74*(1), 6–10.

Banta, T. W. (Ed.). (1988). *Implementing outcomes assessment: Promise and perils* (New Directions for Institutional Research, No. 59). San Francisco: Jossey-Bass.

Banta, T. W. (1993a). Do faculty sense the tightening of the accountability noose? *Assessment Update, 5*(4), 3.

Banta, T. W. (Ed.) (1993b). *Making a difference: Outcomes of a decade of assessment in higher education*. San Francisco: Jossey-Bass.

Bernardin, H. J. (1990). Outcomes assessment: A review of state policies toward outcomes measurement in higher education. *The Academy of Management News, 20*(1), 4–5.

Bowens, H. R. (1974). *Evaluation instruments for accountability*. (New Directions for Institutional Research). San Francisco: Jossey-Bass.

Boyer, C. M. (1989). *Improving student learning: The outcomes assessment program at Kean College of New Jersey*. Union, NJ: Kean College Press.

Bradley, J., Draper, G., & Pike, G. (1993). Assessment measures. *Assessment Update, 5*(1), 14–15.

Cheyney, L. V. (1989). *50 hours: A core curriculum for college students*. Washington, DC: National Endowment for the Humanities.

Chickering, A. W., & Gamson, Z. F. (1989). Seven principles for good practice in undergraduate education. *The Wingspread Journal, 9*(2), 1–4.

A conversation on assessment with Richard Light. (1991). Bloomington, IN: Office of Academic Affairs and Dean of the Faculties of Indiana University (videotape).

Corrallo, S. (1993). National assessment of college student learning: A status report. *Assessment Update, 5*(3), 5, 7, 11.

Council on Postsecondary Accreditation Project on "Accreditation for Educational Effectiveness: Assessment Tools for Improvement." (1992). *Accreditation, assessment and institutional effectiveness: Resource papers for the COPA task force on institutional effectiveness*. Washington, DC: Author.

Criteria for the assessment of oral communication. (1991). Annandale, VA: Speech Communication Association.

Daly, J. A. (1992, November). *Assessing speaking and listening: Preliminary considerations for a national assessment*. Paper presented to the National Center for Education Statistics workshop on the Higher Order Thinking and Communication Skills of College Graduates, Washington, DC.

El-Khawas, E. (1988). *1988 campus trends survey*. Washington, DC: American Council on Education.

El-Khawas, E. (1989). *1989 campus trends survey*. Washington, DC: American Council on Education.

El-Khawas, E. (1990). *1990 campus trends survey*. Washington, DC: American Council on Education.

El-Khawas, E. (1991). *1991 campus trends survey*. Washington, DC: American Council on Education.

El-Khawas, E. (1992). *1992 campus trends survey*. Washington, DC: American Council on Education.

El-Khawas, E. (1993). *1993 campus trends survey*. Washington, DC: American Council on Education.

Erwin, T. D. (1991). *Assessing student learning and development*. San Francisco: Jossey-Bass.

Ewell, P. T. (1987). Assessment: Where are we? *Change, 19*(1), 23–28.

Ewell, P. T. (1991). Assessment and public accountability: Back to the future. *Change, 23*(6), 12–17.

Ewell, P. T. (1992). Outcomes assessment, institutional effectiveness, and accreditation: A conceptual exploration. In Council on Postsecondary Accreditation Project on "Accreditation for Educational Effectiveness: Assessment Tools for Improvement." *Accreditation, assessment and institutional effectiveness: Resource papers for the COPA task force on institutional effectiveness* (pp. 1–18). Washington, DC: Author.

Ewell, P. T. (1993a). From the states: Performance indicators: A new round of accountability. *Assessment Update, 5*(3), 12–13.

Ewell, P. T. (1993b). The role of states and accreditors in shaping assessment practice. In T. W. Banta (Ed.), *Making a difference: Outcomes of a decade of assessment in higher education* (pp. 339–356). San Francisco: Jossey-Bass.

Ewell, P. T., & Jones, D. P. (1993). Actions matter: The case for indirect measures in assessing higher education's progress on the national education goals. *Journal of General Education, 42*(2), 123–148.

Faculty inventory: 7 principles for good practice in undergraduate education. (1989). Racine, WI: The Johnson Foundation.

The FIPSE Connection. (1990). *Change, 22*(5), 38.

Fuhrmann, B. S., & Gentemann, K. M. (1993). A flexible approach to statewide assessment. In T. W. Banta (Ed.), *Making a difference: Outcomes of a decade of assessment in higher education* (pp. 294–305). San Francisco: Jossey-Bass.

Hogan, T. P. (1992). Methods for outcomes assessment related to institutional accreditation. In Council on Postsecondary Accreditation Project on "Accreditation for Educational Effectiveness: Assessment Tools for Improvement." *Accreditation, assessment and institutional effectiveness: Resource papers for the COPA task force on institutional effectiveness* (pp. 37–54). Washington, DC: Author.

Hutchings, P. (1993). Principles of good practice for assessing student learning. *Assessment Update, 5*(1), 6.

Hutchings, P., & Marchese, T. (1990). Special report: Watching assessment—Questions, stories, prospects. *Change, 22*(5), 13–38.

Jemmott, N. D., & Morante, E. A. (1993). The college outcomes evaluation program. In T. W. Banta (Ed.), *Making a difference: Outcomes of a decade of assessment in higher education* (pp. 306–321). San Francisco: Jossey-Bass.

Johnson, R., McCormick, R. D., Prus, J. S., & Rogers, J. S. (1993). Assessment options for the college major. In T. W. Banta (Ed.), *Making a difference: Outcomes of a decade of assessment in higher education* (pp. 151–167). San Francisco: Jossey-Bass.

Johnson, R., Prus, J., Andersen, R., & El-Khawas, E. (1991). *Assessing assessment: An in-depth status report on the higher education assessment movement*. Washington, DC: American Council on Education.

Kasworm, C. E., & Marienau, C. (1993). Assessment strategies for adult undergraduate students. In T. W. Banta (Ed.), *Making a difference: Outcomes of a decade of assessment in higher education* (pp. 121–134). San Francisco: Jossey-Bass.

Kelly, H. P. (1990). *Undergraduate learning at the University of Virginia: A first report to the UVa community.* Charlottesville: University of Virginia, Office of the Provost of the University.

Krueger, D. W. (1993). Total quality management. In T. W. Banta (Ed.), *Making a difference: Outcomes of a decade of assessment in higher education* (pp. 269–278). San Francisco: Jossey-Bass.

Lessinger, L. M. (1970). Accountability in public education. In Educational Testing Service, *Proceedings, 1969 invitational conference on testing problems.* Princeton, NJ: Author.

Lively, K. (1992). "Accountability" of colleges gets renewed scrutiny from state officials. *The Chronicle of Higher Education, 38*(2), A25–A26.

Lumsden, D. L. (1993, November). *The national education goals: The challenges to communication: Contexts, issues, and implications.* Paper presented at the Speech Communication Association annual meeting, Miami, FL.

Lumsden, D., & Knight, M. E. (1990, November). *Getting started in outcomes assessment: Setting objectives, selecting instruments, utilizing findings.* Paper presented to the Speech Communication Association annual meeting, Chicago, IL.

Madaus, G. F., & Stufflebeam, D. (Eds.). (1989). *Educational evaluation: Classic works of Ralph W. Tyler.* Boston: Kluwer Academic.

Marchese, T. (1987). Third down, ten years to go. *AAHE Bulletin, 40,* 3–8.

McClenney, K. M. (1993). Assessment in an era of empowerment. *Assessment Update, 5*(1), 1–2, 4–6.

Millward, R. E. (1993). Assessment centers. In T. W. Banta (Ed.), *Making a difference: Outcomes of a decade of assessment in higher education* (pp. 231–243). San Francisco: Jossey-Bass.

National Association of State Universities and Land Grant Colleges Council on Academic Affairs. (1988). *Statement of principles on student outcomes assessment.* Washington, DC: Author.

National Commission on Excellence in Education. (1983). *A nation at risk: The imperative for educational reform.* Washington, DC: U.S. Government Printing Office.

National Education Goals Panel. (1993). *The national education goals report: Building a nation of learners: Volume one: The national report.* Washington, DC: U.S. Government Printing Office.

National Education Goals Panel. (1991). *The national education goals report: Building a nation of learners.* Washington, DC: U.S. Government Printing Office.

National Governors' Association. (1986). *Time for results: Governors' 1991 report on education.* Washington, DC: Author.

National Institute of Education. (1984). *Involvement in learning: Realizing the potential of American higher education.* Washington, DC: U.S. Department of Education.

Obler, S. S., Slark, J., & Umbdenstock, L. (1993). Classroom assessment. In T. W. Banta (Ed.), *Making a difference: Outcomes of a decade of assessment in higher education* (pp. 211–226). San Francisco: Jossey-Bass.

Oettinger, E. R., & Cole, C. W. (1978). Method, design, and implementation in evaluation. In G. R. Hanson (Ed.), *Evaluating program effectiveness* (New Directions for Student Services, No. 1; pp. 35–55). San Francisco: Jossey-Bass.

Pederson, R. (1992). The perils of Total Quality Management: Bringing business rhetoric to academe. *The Chronicle of Higher Education, 38*(5), B4.

Peterson, R. E. (1971). Toward institutional goal-consciousness. In Educational Testing Service, *Proceedings, 1971 Western regional conference on testing problems* (pp. 11–31). Berkeley, CA: Educational Testing Service.

Peterson, R. E., & Loye, D. E. (Eds.). (1967). *Conversations toward a definition of institutional vitality.* Princeton, NJ: Educational Testing Service.

Presidential Task Force on Student Learning and Development. (1986). *A proposal for program assessment at Kean College of New Jersey.* Union: Kean College of New Jersey.

Principles of good practice for assessing student learning. (1993). *Assessment Update, 5*(1), 7.

Ratcliff, J. L., & Jones, E. A. (1993). Coursework cluster analysis. In T. W. Banta (Ed.), *Making a difference: Outcomes of a decade of assessment in higher education* (pp. 256–268). San Francisco: Jossey-Bass.

Rosenbaum, J. (1992). The *what* and *how* of broadcasting curricula. *Feedback, 33*(2), 14–15.

Schilling, K. M., & Schilling, K. L. (1993). Professors must respond to calls for accountability. *The Chronicle of Higher Education, 39*(29), A40.

Sims, S. J. (1992). *Student outcomes assessment: A historical review and guide to program development.* New York: Greenwood.

Stark, J. S., Lowther, M. A., & Hagerty, B. M. K. (1986). *Responsive professional education: Balancing outcomes and opportunities.* ASHE-ERIC Higher Education Report No. 3. Washington, DC: Association for the Study of Higher Education.

State trends. (1990). *Change, 22*(5), 17.

Task Force on Assessing the National Goal Relating to Postsecondary Education (1992). *Report to the national education goals panel.* Washington, DC: National Education Goals Panel.

Terenzini, P. T. (1993). Cross-national themes in the assessment of quality in higher education. *Assessment Update, 5*(3), 1–2, 4, 13.

U.S. Department of Education. (1991a). *America 2000: An education strategy.* Washington, DC: Author.

U.S. Department of Education. (1991b). *America 2000: An education strategy: Sourcebook.* Washington, DC: Author.

U.S. Department of Education. (1991c). *National assessment of educational progress.* Washington, DC: National Center for Education Statistics.

U.S. Department of Education. (1993). *Reaching the goals.* Washington, DC: U.S. Government Printing Office.

U.S. Department of Education. (1994a). *Goals 2000: Educate America Act Supporting Systematic Education Reform Nationwide.* Washington, DC: Author.

U.S. Department of Education. (1994b). *High standards for all students.* Washington, DC: Author.

Waluconis, C. J. (1993). Student self-evaluation. In T. W. Banta (Ed.), *Making a difference: Outcomes of a decade of assessment in higher education* (pp. 244–255). San Francisco: Jossey-Bass.

Watt, J. H., Drennen, N. H., Rodrigues, R. J., Menelly, N., & Wiegel, E. K. (1993). Building assessment programs in large institutions. In T. W. Banta (Ed.), *Making a difference: Outcomes of a decade of assessment in higher education* (pp. 103–120). San Francisco: Jossey-Bass.

Wiggins, G. (1990). The case for authentic assessment. *ERIC Digest.* Report No. EDO-TM-90-10 (pp. 1–4). Washington, DC: ERIC Clearinghouse on Tests, Measurement, and Evaluation. (ED 328611)

Willinford, A. M., & Moden, G. O. (1993). Using assessment to enhance quality. In T. W. Banta (Ed.), *Making a difference: Outcomes of a decade of assessment in higher education* (pp. 40–53). San Francisco: Jossey-Bass.

Wolf, B. (1993). *Handbook on assessment strategies: Measures of student learning and program quality.* Bloomington, IN: Office of the Vice Chancellor for Academic Affairs and Dean of Faculties.

Zook, J. (1993). 2 agencies start work on national test of college students' analytical skills. *The Chronicle of Higher Education, 39*(29), A23.

2

Mission Statements, Outcomes, and the New Liberal Arts

William G. Christ
Robert O. Blanchard
Trinity University

Outcomes assessment is discussed within the context of a program assessment that takes into account both off- and on-campus realities. Challenges facing higher education suggest a New Liberal Arts for the general student that integrates traditional disciplines with professional communication perspectives.

Outcomes that stress a liberal education are developed at the program, course, and intracourse level. Assessing a program's strengths, weaknesses, and opportunities and developing mission statements, linked to outcomes, is seen as useful for establishing priorities, philosophies, and pedagogical strategies for resource allocation.

WHY ASSESSMENT?

Economic pressures, increasing competition for students, and the spread of assessment requirements and expectations, including those at the national (National Education Goals—see chap. 1; Appendix A), regional (see chap. 3), state, and university levels, continue to pressure institutions of higher learning to establish some kind of process to justify their costs (see Eshelman, 1991; Footlick, Wingert, & Leonard, 1990; Sykes, 1988; Wycliff, 1990). We believe communication educators (this includes those in journalism, mass communication, speech communication, and similar fields) are more likely to be required to justify their existence not only to outside constituencies, but primarily within their own universities and colleges. If communication education programs are seen as fragmented, peripheral, or even nonessential to the overall university mission by on-campus committees, then they are more susceptible to being downsized or eliminated.

It is prudent for communication programs to anticipate being singled out to justify their existence on their campuses. Some form of outcomes assessment, consistent with the academic traditions, practices, and ethos of their campuses, would be the best protection against arbitrary decisions. Communication programs can and should demonstrate compellingly that they are central to the mission of any institution of higher learning that professes to be offering a liberal education to students who will spend the majority of their working and living years in the 21st century.

How does a communication faculty go about establishing a system of outcomes assessment? This chapter argues that faculty should have a clear vision of a program's purpose and where it is going. Unless program assessment precedes student outcomes assessment, student assessment can be sabotaged, with faculty working at cross-purposes. Program assessment should be viewed as an ongoing participatory process. Done well, the vision or covenant that is developed among faculty can lead to a rewarding synergy. Done hastily, arbitrarily or inflexibly, the process can splinter and fragment a faculty. There is much to be learned during the ongoing give and take of faculty debates about priorities, philosophies, pedagogy, and the practical strengths and weaknesses of a school and program. Program assessment, therefore, should begin with a determination of "where are we and where are we going?"

The question, "Where are we?" needs to be answered by taking into account the situation a communication program finds itself in both in terms of off-campus forces and on-campus resources. Off-campus, there are at least three challenges communication educators need to review—historical changes facing all colleges and universities in the mid-1990s, emergent and converging communication technologies, and the philosophical and theoretical ferment within the communication discipline (see Blanchard & Christ, 1993a, chap. 1–3). On campus, the faculty should ask: (a) How and where it fits within the university—how do its mission and curriculum fit the mission, philosophy, and anticipated outcomes of the university? (b) What outcomes are appropriate for the program as a whole? (c) What courses are appropriate to match those outcomes? (d) What outcomes are appropriate within a course?

OFF-CAMPUS ASSESSMENT

Higher Education and the New Liberal Arts

There are at least two major interrelated forces impacting today on higher education: a re-emphasis on undergraduate education and a movement toward assessment. The concern about the first has lead to the second.

The critiques of undergraduate education have focused on "three, inter-related, broad criticisms: The first is that undergraduate education lacks integrity and purpose. The second is that its content, especially the liberal arts 'canon,' needs revitalization. The third is that it is too vocational, narrow and fragmented, and needs integration and unity of knowledge" (Blanchard & Christ, 1993a, p. 4). By stressing program outcomes, these three criticisms can be positively addressed. For example, outcomes help demonstrate that the so-called distinctions between professional and liberal education are not only no longer useful but also are ultimately self-defeating for the traditional liberal arts, professional education, and undergraduate education. Whether they are labeled "essential undergraduate experiences" (Boyer, 1987), or "capacities" (Association of American Colleges [AAC], 1985), or "professional preparation" (*Strengthening the Ties*, 1988), the Michigan Professional Preparation Network Report (*Strengthening the Ties*, 1988) is accurate when it wrote that "it is erroneous to view the enduring attributes of education as the sole domain of any single group of academic programs" (p. 26).

Some communication programs have historically offered a great deal to the general student. Less clear to some is the contribution that the more "professional" communication or media education programs have to offer. Students in the "information/communication" age need a cluster of experiences that integrate the knowledge of professional programs with the understanding coming out of more traditional disciplines, a New Liberal Arts. Communication education— ranging from general speech to organizational communication to media classes—has an important contribution to make to general education and the university core.

The call for assessment grows out of the concern for what is going on in higher education. Faculty are being asked to account for what and how they teach, and the impact of the educational experience. Ervin (1988), for example, identified six major recommendations from the National Governors Association that will have an impact on assessment. Many of the recommendations call for a re-emphasis on undergraduate education. These recommendations state that governors, state legislatures, state coordinating boards, and institutional governing boards should:

1. Clearly define the role and mission of each institution of public higher education in their state. Governors should also encourage the governing board of each independent college to clearly define its mission.

2. Re-emphasize the fundamental importance of undergraduate instruction—especially in universities that give high priorities to research and graduate instruction.

3. Adjust funding formulas for public colleges and universities to provide incentives for improving the learning of undergraduate students, based on the results of comprehensive assessment programs. Independent colleges and universities should be encouraged to do likewise.

4. Reaffirm their strong commitment to access to public higher education for students from all socioeconomic backgrounds. Furthermore,

5. Each college and university should implement systematic programs that use multiple measures to assess the learning of undergraduates. The information gained from such assessments should be used to evaluate the quality of the institution and of the program. Information about institutional and program quality should also be made available to the public.

6. The higher education accrediting community should require colleges and universities to collect and use information about student outcomes among undergraduates. Demonstrating levels of student learning and performance should be considered for institutional accreditation. (pp. 19–23; different order)

We think the move toward assessment can be positive if programs become more conscious about the experiences they offer their students and the kinds of outcomes they hope from these experiences.

Communication Technology and the New Professionalism

Computers, fiber optics, satellites, and even new uses for the telephone, including fax, are changing how people and corporations communicate; how they receive, process, and use information. Gone are the days when the city paper or the network affiliate held the privileged position as the only news, information, or advertising source in town; when interpersonal communication could be solely conceptualized as face-to-face communication without a mediating technology involved; when organizations could successfully function without understanding how technology impacts small group dynamics, organizational communication, and public relations. Communication educators need to account for these changes by developing programs that are fundamental, flexible, and broad based. We call this kind of integrative, broad-based approach the *New Professionalism* (Blanchard & Christ, 1993a).

If nothing else, communication programs should be studying and teaching the impact of communication technology on such issues as culture (Meehan, 1986; Thomas & Evans, 1990), texts (Banks & Tankel, 1990; Barker, 1985), politics (Armstrong, 1988; Gandy & Simmons, 1986; Lull, 1991), community (Larson & Oravec, 1987), family (Lull, 1988), privacy (Diebold, 1973; Donner, 1981), and identity (Rakow, 1988).

Ferment in the Field

The importance of the linkages and integration among various communication subspecialties has been well documented (see Ball-Rokeach, 1985; Benson, 1985; Berger & Chaffee, 1988; Delia, 1987; Dervin & Voigt, 1984; Gumpertz & Cathart, 1982; Hawkins, Wiemann, & Pingree, 1988; Levy & Gurevitch, 1993; Lowenstein & Merrill, 1990; Rogers & Chaffee, 1983; Wiemann, Hawkins, & Pingree, 1988). Not only are communication scholars investigating interactive technologies (Rogers, 1986), but also how mass media tend to impinge on face-to-face communication and how face-to-face communication impacts media use (Kubey & Csikszentmihalyi, 1990). Scholars are using variables that are normally associated with interpersonal communication research to describe and explain media use (Rubin & Rubin, 1985). For a communication program to see itself narrowly as delivering either technically trained students to shrinking industries or theoretically trained students to shrinking graduate schools is shortsighted. As Dressel (1976) suggested:

As a discipline develops, it provides:

1. Descriptions of the phenomena (subject matter) with which it deals.
2. Questions which it is to answer.
3. Procedures or tactics useful in attacking problems.
4. Methods of inquiry useful in understanding the field.
5. Concepts which give order, meaning, and structure to the objects and events studied.
6. Generalizations expressing relationships among concepts.
7. Procedures for validating generalizations and conclusions about the phenomenon studied.
8. Organized catalogs of facts, generalizations, concepts, and methods for ready use by scholars. (p. 209)

Communication and its study is too important to define it narrowly (Woodward, 1993).

So how does a communication program thrive within the changing dynamics of higher education, technological innovation, and disciplinary upheaval? Through enterprise and experimentation, programs need to expand their vision of the scope of communication studies, becoming central to the education of the nonmajor. Specifically, programs need to educate students about intrapersonal, interpersonal, small group, organizational, and speech communication, also demonstrating how communication technologies, texts, and industrial structures infuse, intertwine with, and impact their lives.

ON-CAMPUS ASSESSMENT

Situational Analysis

On campus, communication educators need to ask how and where their program can advance their university's missions and objectives. By being clear about its own mission, philosophy, and expectations or outcomes, a communication program can develop curricula and courses that position it as central to the university, its majors, and the general student (see Galvin,

1992). In many ways, this is the "antecedent of program assessment" (Hunt, 1992, p. 12).

A program should assess its strengths, weaknesses, and opportunities within the larger context of the university that houses the unit. Sims (1992) argued that in order to conduct student assessment, nine points need to be addressed. These same points need to be considered when designing, implementing, and ultimately evaluating a unit's program.

Funding. Whereas Sims discussed funding in terms of having enough money to cover student assessment evaluation, planning, and implementation, here the issue is whether there is enough money to carry out program assessment. Will outside people, for example, be brought in to help assess the program? Who will pay for these people? Who will pay for any surveys? Who will pay for locating and talking with seniors or alumni? How will the shifting of resources to assessment impact a program? Said another way, how much of a priority is the assessment?

Time. There are at least two parts to the time equation. First, who can find the time to evaluate a program? Warner (1993) argued that the "problem" with media education reform comes not from practitioners or practitioner-academic alliances, but from faculty. Faculty are, in some ways, like independent contractors hired by the university to service their students (Blanchard & Christ, 1993a). Two of the appeals of being a faculty person are the freedom in the classroom and in intellectual inquiry. For the most part, faculty have lots of leeway in how they spend their time. Unfortunately, this benefit can also lead to abuses: faculty who miss classes to do consulting; faculty who have not changed their class notes in 25 years, faculty who "mistake war stories and indoctrination for education" (Blanchard & Christ, 1993b). Those who do not care about anything but their own courses, their own narrow perspective, will be difficult to motivate to care about their program as a whole. Those who take their teaching, research, and service seriously, those who see their scholarship as central to what they do (see Boyer, 1990), also find it difficult to give any more time than they already do to the laborious task of sitting down with colleagues to hammer out ideas about their program. Even for the best of faculty it is often difficult to give up precious time to what can be perceived by some as just another series of endless meetings that may or may not have a direct impact on their own courses.

The second point to consider under time is the time line for the assessment. Programs get themselves into trouble when they try to do too much too quickly. Reflecting on the last 12 years at Trinity University suggests that changes were steady but incremental. An initial time line, however, is important. For academics, semester or full academic year milestones can prove useful. A unit might decide, for example, that they want to integrate their core courses. The expectation is that by the end of the fall semester initial objectives will be presented with the discussion about the objectives and the subsequent changes taking place over the spring semester for the following year.

Human Resources. People are at the heart of any curricular reform or assessment. Knowing the human costs of assessment and program revision is important. In other words, are the faculty, staff, and administrators in place for carrying out a program assessment? Where will the resistance come from? Again, tenured faculty are not always willing to embrace assessment unless they feel they have a stake in the outcome. Recent moves by universities to eliminate programs can be an important incentive.

Organizational Climate. This is partly a function of who called for the assessment of the program. Assessment normally has one of two functions: either for improvement (formative evaluation) or accountability (summative; Erwin, 1991). The questions that faculty tend to ask are: Is the assessment being motivated by a unit's internal need to see how well they are doing and how they can improve (formative)? Or, is the evaluation an attempt by an administrator to punish or reward certain faculty or programs (summative)? Is the need for assessment coming from an outside accrediting agency (formative and summative)? Answers to these questions will help dictate the organizational climate in which the evaluation will take place. Fundamentally, is there trust and openness among administrators, faculty, staff, students, and others (Sims, 1992)?

An argument can be made to expand the idea of organizational climate to include what Micek and Arney (1974) called five categories of the campus environment: instructional, social, organizational, fiscal, and physical (Erwin, 1991). All of these might fit into what Hunt (1992) suggested when he wrote that "the culture of the institution must help to determine the broad outline of an assessment plan" (p. 12).

The *instructional* environment tends to be organized around course work and this becomes the focus of much of assessment (Tucker, 1993; see chap. 5). One of the issues raised by looking at course work is why some students fail whereas others succeed. Bok (1986a, 1986b) suggested looking at teaching methods and how different people learn (see Potter, 1993; Potter & Clark, 1991; see chap. 4). Is the instructional environment a match for a student (see Grow, 1990, 1991)? Are students prepared for the instructional environment? What kinds of forces are working against the instructional environment? The point is that the instructional environment impacts a student's success and communication programs can have a large say in creating an instructional climate that is positive, rigorous, and rewarding for students.

The *social* environment of a campus "is its system of interpersonal influences among staff, faculty, administrators, and the students themselves" (Erwin, 1991, p. 49). Success can depend on the kinds of bridges that are built among people on a campus. Academic and personal advising, social groups like fraternities and sororities, cultural groups like the Black student unions, interest groups like the chess club, and sports can all built a sense of belonging and ultimately impact a student's success. Some communication programs have honors, preprofessional, or service clubs that also act as social clubs. Communication centers (e.g., radio station, newspaper, television production center, public relations and advertising clubs) that provide students with the chance to practice within supervised "work" environments can also provide a sense of belonging.

The *fiscal* environment, according to Erwin (1991), tends to be investigated in terms of financial aid. Erwin (1986) and Erwin and Love (1989) found that "generally, students who finance a majority of their college expenses gain more from college" (p. 50). Communication programs, through fund-raising, can be an important part of some university's strategies to enhance the fiscal environment.

The *organizational* structure includes "the student–faculty ratio, institutional rules, admissions policies, and retention policies" (Erwin, 1991, p. 50.). For the communication program, how the major, electives, general education classes, internships, and apprenticeships are structured will all impact what gets communicated to students and prospective students about what is essential and important about the discipline.

The *physical* environment "encompasses the architecture and physical design of the campus, which can influence social and personal development and learning (Moos, 1979)" (Erwin, 1991, p. 50). There are at least two points about the physical environment that should be stressed. First, where a major is housed and how its work spaces are configured can communicate a great deal about its program and philosophy. For example, in many universities, the speech program is housed literally miles away from the media studies program, or *parts* of the same program are separated from each other. In other places, it is a floor that divides the disciplines. Yet, in others, it is not a "physical" barrier, but an attitudinal barrier. These kinds of barriers are counter productive. A broad understanding of communication education that promotes integration should be encouraged, even in the configuration of the physical environment

The second point about the physical environment's impact on assessment is that, with the increased use of technology, the idea of a physical environment has changed (see Blanchard & Christ, 1993a, p. 126; Ehrmann, 1990). Communication programs, especially those with a media component, should be in the forefront of new technological ways of delivering education.

Availability of Data. Having information is an important part of assessment: "Assessment programs must not overlook readily available resources, sources of information, and opportunities" (Hunt, 1992, p. 12). Historically, how did a program develop? Who is the keeper of the institutional history? What are the graduates of the program doing now? As Sims (1992) suggested, assessment partly hinges on "availability and quality of institutional information such as records of students, departments and institutional performance, reports records; availability of students and others for providing new data through surveys, interviews and observations" (p. 117). We found, at Trinity University, one of the strongest arguments for going to a broad-based, foundational approach came when we assessed what our alumni were doing. We discovered that alumni were all over the occupational map. Those who responded included those in non-media occupations like lawyers, judges, managers, salespeople, and so forth. Those who had media jobs were working in much broader fields than what might have been expected from the narrowly focused, four-sequence major available to them years before. Our graduates were not only in broadcasting and newspaper journalism, but they held positions in advertising, public relations, cable, film, and corporate communication, to name a few fields. The point was that the information from assessing where our alumni were working helped provide ammunition for changing the organizational structure of the major. It became clear that our major was not just for journalists anymore.

Details of the . . . Program Evaluation Action Plan. What are the uni-versity's strategic plans (Hunt, 1992)? What are the assessment plans of the university? What associations accredit the university? How will these associations impact your assessment plans? How do the individual unit's plans fit into the overall plan? How detailed are the plans? What are the overall "objectives, time-table, procedures, participants, and location" (Sims, 1992, p. 117)? Obviously, communication programs will need to fit into the mission, objectives, and assessment plans of the university that houses them.

Audiences. As we discuss later in the section on mission statements, an important part of a mission statement and therefore assessment is knowing your audience or those "stakeholders" (Caywood & Ewing, 1992) who have a say in the success of your program. Where some media educators have tended to be myopic is in assuming their most important audience is the local practitioners. Students should be a program's principle clientele and audience.

Technical Ability and Feasibility. Again, assessment needs good people with good intentions. Are the technical resources available and motivated? Earlier, we mentioned the alumni information. We had to rely on the alumni office for the information. They were happy to oblige. When we asked the registrar's office, however, for specific information based on who was majoring in the department, we were told the files could not be accessed in a way that would let us answer our questions. The technical ability of the school was hindering our assessment.

Ethical Concerns. "Privacy concerns, student and institutional confidentiality, obtrusiveness, or harmful aspects of data collection and reporting" have an impact on program assessment (Sims, 1992, p. 117). If it is true, as Hunt (1992, p. 13) suggested, that "assessment models must be 'public' and the results open to 'scrutiny,'" then data should always be aggregated into a form that cannot be traced back to any one individual. Students should be notified very early about assessment plans and procedures so that they are not surprised late in their academic career.

Said another way, Erwin (1991) suggested six characteristics of successful assessment programs:

> First, successful assessment programs involve many people in the assessment process. . . .Second, there are clear, assessable educational goals and objectives. These objectives are reflected in the curricula for the undergraduate majors and for the general education programs. . . .Third, other constituent groups have been brought into the process. . . .Fourth, the data collected are meaningful, valuable, and accurate. . . .Fifth, the data are analyzed and not just tallied for compliance purposes. . . .Last, a system is established for distributing and implementing assessment results, so that the results are available to the people who can use them. (pp. 24–25)

Mission Statements

Once a program is clear about the external pressures and opportunities that provide the context for program assessment, a good place to begin the actual assessment is with its vision, its mission. In other words, what does a program say it is doing and trying to do? Where does a program see itself and what does it want to become?

All programs have missions. Some are clear, concise, and honest, whereas others are "hidden," obtuse, unarticulated, or not carefully thought out. We think it is better to be conscious, deliberate, and explicit about a mission rather than assuming that all the stakeholders (Caywood & Ewing, 1992) in the program know what is going on. "Departments might argue that they have implicit mission statements or that no matter what the mission statement says, it is the faculty, courses and facilities that define a program. Though there is merit in this argument, explicit mission statements should be at the center of curricular discussion" (Blanchard & Christ, 1993a, p. 82).

In a survey conducted by Warner and Liu (1990) of 258 member schools of the Broadcast Education Association, less than 56% of the large schools' departments and less than 50% of the medium and small schools' departments were identified as having mission statements. This is a surprisingly small number. Though trying to articulate mission statements is not easy, especially if there are disparate positions that are held by the tenured faculty, we think the debate that ensues when trying to develop statements is so important that the risks of battles and heated debate are usually worth the risk. If a program does not have a mission statement, the faculty can be asked to look at themselves, the facilities, and the courses and curricula and ask the question, "What would an external assessment group say was the mission of this media program? What is it doing?" Though coming across as a hypothetical exercise, in reality, the answer to the question, "What is your mission?" is very important to deans, vice presidents of academic affairs, and presidents. Programs need to be able to justify their existence to a wide range of people or risk losing the support of administrators or legislatures. As Galvin (1992) suggested, developing goals and mission statements can produce at least four benefits:

1. Clarifying organizational purpose.
2. Forcing consensus on what is important.
3. Creating a framework against which to evaluate resource allocation.
4. Reinforcing a commitment to student learning.

Ackoff (1986) wrote that a mission statement should have five characteristics (much of this section was first presented in Blanchard & Christ, 1993a, chap. 5). First, "*it should contain a formulation of the firm's objectives that enables progress toward them to be measured.* To state objectives that cannot be used to evaluate performance is hypocrisy" (p. 39). It is important that the objectives of a mission statement are not simply a string of "operationally meaningless superlatives such as *biggest, best, optimum, and maximum*" (p. 38).

The Missouri School of Journalism's multifaceted mission statement is an example of specific, measurable objectives (these have been abbreviated):

1. *To teach students the principles and techniques of journalism,* which we define as current, reasoned reflection, in print or telecommunications, of a society's events, needs, and values.

2. *To serve, improve, and provide leadership to both the university and the journalism, telecommunications, and advertising professions* through a variety of activities and services such as workshops and so forth.

3. *To create for the students, faculty, administration, and staff of the School of Journalism a challenging, intellectually stimulating, professionally rewarding, cooperative, participative, secure, supportive, and collegial environment* that encourages risk taking and the creation of new knowledge through research and creative activity.

4. *To be sensitive and responsive to the needs, concerns, and interests of our multiple stakeholders*: students, parents, faculty, administrators, the curators, staff, alumni, professionals, media, potential employers of students, supporters, suppliers, government, educators, and community.

5. *To maintain, enhance, and promote the reputation of the School of Journalism.* (Blanchard & Christ, 1993a, p. 82)

These five statements fit Ackoff's first mission statement characteristic because each can be used to evaluate the University of Missouri's program.

Ackoff's (1986) second point is that *"a company's mission statement should differentiate it from other companies. It should establish the individuality, if not the uniqueness of the firm"* (p. 39). The question media programs need to ask is, "What is the unique, intellectual, academic contribution of the media program to the university?" The program may be similar to other programs at other universities, but it should not be similar to other programs in the same university. Redundancy breeds contempt and an urge by administrators to merge or eliminate programs.

Ackoff's (1986) third point is that, *"a mission statement should define the business that the company wants to be in, not necessarily is in"* (p. 40). From technical schools to liberal arts and sciences colleges to research universities, from teaching programs to research mills, the "business" of education is diverse. The importance of Ackoff's third point is that mission statements should be powerful statements of vision: "Not only should they clarify a unit's objectives and distinctiveness, but they should illuminate a unit's potential" (Blanchard & Christ, 1993a, p. 83). We believe we are in the business of studying communication: its conceptualization and context; how it is produced, funded, and legislated; its impact and effects; its potential for good and ill; and, its historical, cultural, ideological, and aesthetic dimensions.

Ackoff's (1986) fourth suggestion is that *"a mission statement should be relevant to all the firm's stakeholders. . . .*The mission should state how the company intends to serve each of them" (p. 41). Missouri's School of Journalism listed 15 shareholders. Based on the school this list might shrink, expand, and change. For many public schools the "government" shareholder has mandated at least part of the mission statement. For example, Pennsylvania State University's School of Communications mission statement stated:

As an academic unit within a major land-grant university, the School of Communications has a threefold mission:

1. To educate people for careers in the media and in the academies of the Commonwealth of Pennsylvania and the nation.

2. To further research and creative work in the field of communications. The research dimension includes both professional and theoretical/critical approaches to the media, while the creative dimension includes works of the highest imaginative, artistic, and ethical standards conceived within those media.

3. To improve general understanding of the workings of modern mass media among the University community and the population of the Commonwealth

through instruction, continuing education opportunities, conferences, workshops, and publications. (Pennsylvania State University School of Communications, 1990)

Penn State's self-perception as a land-grant institution drives the thrust of its program.

The last characteristic of a mission statement, according to Ackoff, is of greatest importance: "*A mission statement should be exciting and inspiring.* It should motivate all those whose participation in its pursuit is sought. . . .It does *not* have to appear to be feasible; it only has to be *desirable*" (p. 41).

To Ackoff's list we would add a sixth characteristic: The mission statement should accurately reflect the educational philosophy of a program. Incorporating all six characteristics, and with assessment in mind, programs need to ask:

1. Who are we?
2. What needs do we address and how do we analyze or respond to those needs?
3. How do we respond to key constituents?
4. What is our philosophy or core values?
5. What makes us unique or distinctive?
6. How do we know when we are true to our mission or when we veer off course?
7. How do we create ways to readdress systematically our mission and goals? (adapted from Bryson, 1988, p. 105, in Galvin, 1992, p. 23)

Broad Program Outcomes

It is imperative that communication education programs take leadership roles in the university for what we have called the New Liberal Arts, a concept derived from the Sloan Foundation's program of that name. It was launched in the early 1980s to encourage the integration of quantitative reasoning and technology into the curricula of liberal arts colleges. This resulted in grants for pilot projects to more than 50 institutions and to the establishment of the Council for the Understanding of Technology in Human Affairs, which "promotes the development of technological literacy." The meaning of the New Liberal Arts and reports on some of the Sloan Foundation projects resulted in a variety of publications (see Kanigel, 1986; Koerner, 1984; Lisensky, Pfnister, & Sweet, 1985; Morison, 1986; Truxal, 1986; White, 1981). Although much of the emphasis in pilot projects so far has been on integration of engineering and liberal arts, we extend the concept to new communication technologies, media and information systems, and the field of communication studies that acknowledges the importance of technology.

There have always been disagreements and even confusion within the academy about what is meant by undergraduate liberal education. Most colleges or universities purport to offer their students a liberal education but, when pressed for particulars, educators provide conflicting definitions (Ahlgren & Boyer, 1981; Kimball, 1986; Rothblatt, 1976). Ahlgren and Boyer (1981) have concluded that endless faculty debates (and, we would argue, public debates) over what is a liberal arts education are not resolved because educators and others entertain fundamentally differing conceptions of liberal education.

Ahlgren and Boyer (1981, p. 180) found that some educators argue that particular courses, certain distribution of courses, or certain processes or methods taught in courses are most important for a liberal education. Others believe faculty intentions, whatever faculty "value and think the students should learn," is the measure. Others emphasize outcomes— "skills and character of the liberally educated person" as reflection in graduates of liberal arts curricula—as what counts. If it turned out that college graduates "were in no way distinguishable from those who did not attend college," we would expect content-oriented faculty to "change the measures," the outcomes faculty to "change the curriculum," and the faculty-intent proponents "perhaps not even to care."

Of the three approaches, we believe that the outcomes method is the most tangible and rational measure, and we believe it is the only measure society will ultimately accept. Outcomes are at least implied by most everyone—ranging from students and parents, admissions recruiters, those who decide how much private contributions or taxpayers' money go to higher education, to probably most faculty and administrators and scholars on the subject. Even content-oriented and faculty-intent-oriented proponents would be hard pressed to demonstrate that their philosophies do not at least imply outcomes.

In any case, faculty cannot afford the luxury of not caring. Although faculty, empowered as officers of instruction, traditionally have final say on curriculum matters, only the most reckless and monkish would make such decisions without taking note of market or political conditions of support for their institutions. This reality today is behind public outcries for accountability or assessment of academic programs. And, as we suggested, is reflected in all of the major critiques of undergraduate education.

In the context of our current political and cultural expectations, we believe that the meaning of liberal arts or liberal education will be—and perhaps always has been—defined by outcomes. Outcomes determine curricula. If current outcomes are not deemed satisfactory and changes in them are desired, then curricula will be changed to produce the desired outcomes. So what outcomes are desired in a liberal education and how are they achieved?

After comparing the AAC and Carnegie outcomes with a synthesized list of professional education outcomes, the Michigan Professional Preparation Network Report (*Strengthening the Ties*, 1988) concluded that, although there are important differences, "one cannot fail to notice that the goals of professional program educators overlap with those traditionally espoused by liberal arts educators" (p. 26). Derived from literature in various professional education fields, the professional education list bears a striking similarity to the Carnegie and ACC outcomes. This is important for those communication programs that are perceived on their campuses as being professional.

The overlap of each of the Michigan-compiled 10 potential professional outcomes with liberal education outcomes is apparent. A student pursuing a professional degree (e.g., public relations, advertising, or business communication) that exemplifies the 10 outcomes would be achieving most of the outcomes of a liberal education, as the following brief overview of the 10 professional outcomes, compared with liberal outcomes, demonstrates (*Strengthening the Ties*, 1988, pp. 23–25).

1. Communication competence: An ability to "read, write, speak, and listen and use these processes effectively to acquire, develop, and convey ideas and information." These skills, which are highly valued by most professional curricula—especially communication—are also fundamental to desired liberal outcomes of "informed citizenship and continued personal growth." This competence has also been identified as a key component of the National Education Goals: 5.5 (see chap. 1) and the Oregon Report (*Planning for Curricular Change*, 1984, p. 82). The Oregon Report suggested five kinds of media communication competencies that can be applied broadly to communication: (a) general literacy—competence in the use of the language; (b) visual literacy—understanding visual grammar and phenomena of communication; (c) computer literacy—especially a general knowledge and "hands-on" skills in computer applications; (d) information gathering—ability to systematically gather and use information for various sources; and (e) writing capability—ability to produce messages in two or more areas (news, advertising, organizational, small group, etc.). Examples: speaking, writing, production, research, design.

2. Critical thinking: An ability "to examine issues rationally, logically, and coherently"—a universally recognized and desired liberal outcome. Professional graduates seek to posses "a repertoire of thinking strategies that will enable them to acquire, evaluate, and synthesize information and knowledge." Professionals also are taught "to develop analytical skills to make decisions in both familiar and unfamiliar circumstances." This competence has also been identified as a key component of the National Education Goals: 5.5 (see chap. 1). Examples: speech; interpersonal; debate; media and organizational research; and audience, textual, and rhetorical analysis.

3. Contextual competence: "An understanding of the societal context (environment)" in which one is living and working. The liberally educated person needs "to comprehend the complex interdependence between the profession and society." Likewise, "the ability to make judgments in light

of historical, social, economic, scientific, and political realities is demanded
of the professional as well as the citizen." Examples: economic, technological,
legal, philosophical, and ethical aspects; critical and cultural studies; mass
media and society; and international and intercultural communication.

4. Aesthetic sensibility: "An enhanced aesthetic awareness of arts and
human behavior for both personal enrichment and application in the
enhancement of the profession." Example: historical, philosophical, and
ethical aspects; internships.

5. Professional identity: Concern "for improving the knowledge, skills,
and values of the profession." This "both parallels and supplements the
liberal education goal of developing a sense of personal identity." Examples: debate; communication theory; historical, philosophical, and ethical
aspects; and internships.

6. Professional ethics: Understanding and accepting "the ethics of the
profession as standards that guide professional behavior. Liberally educated individuals are expected to have developed value systems and ethical
standards that guide their behavior. . . .[T]he study of ethics provides a
context for development of professional ethics." Examples: philosophical
and ethical aspects, and internships.

7. Adaptive competence: Anticipating, adapting to, and promoting
"changes important to a profession's societal purpose and professional's
role. A liberally educated person has an enhanced capacity to adapt to and
anticipate changes in society." Examples: debate; organizational analysis;
technological, legal, and historical aspects; communication theory.

8. Leadership capacity: Exhibiting "the capacity to contribute as a
productive member of the profession and assuming appropriate leadership
roles. . . . Not only does leadership imply both functional and status
obligations, it requires the intelligent, humane application of knowledge
and skills." Examples: speech, interpersonal communication, organizational communication, debate, management, and internships.

9. Scholarly concern for improvement: Recognizing "the need to increase knowledge and to advance the profession" through both theoretical
and applied research. "The heart of the intellectual process is attention to a
spirit of inquiry, critical analysis or logical thinking." Examples: communication theory and research.

10. Motivation of continued learning: Exploring and expanding "personal, civic, and professional knowledge and skills throughout a lifetime"
are both appropriate liberal and professional outcomes. "All knowledge. .
.is liberal (that is, it enlarges and liberates the mind) when it is committed
to continuing inquiry" (Bell, 1968, p. 8). Examples: communication theory
and media studies.

The point is that these broad outcomes, coupled with a program's
mission statement, help position media programs centrally within the
university. As this is being accomplished, the needs of the communication
major must be taken into account.

Broad Course Outcomes

The preceding analysis lists broad outcomes with possible areas of study presented as examples. At the level of the communication major, it is possible to develop areas that should be covered in a curriculum. These areas suggest outcomes that would be attainable through a variety of courses or workshops. In media education, for example, the Oregon Report included eight enrichment areas in any model curriculum that suggest outcomes at the course level (*Planning for Curricular Change,* 1984). This list would need to be modified depending on the makeup of the communication program:

1. Mass communication and society—a conceptual map of the literature and documented experience that explains the relationship of media to society and to individuals in society. Dennis and DeFleur (1991) suggested a creative way of reaching the general student with this course:

> They suggested key topical essays that make linkages between the media and other key disciplines. They suggested, for example, "Noam Chomsky and Why Is He Saying Such Awful Things About the Media" to illustrate media ethics from a linguistic viewpoint. Or, "How Children Learn to Buy" to discuss advertising from a consumer behavior, sociological, and psychological perspective. Or, "The Novel as Quantitative Research" to emphasize mass communication research from an English and American literature orientation. (Blanchard & Christ, 1993a, p. 106)

2. Historical aspects—An overview both in conceptual and chronological terms; the history and traditions of mass communication; its institutions, people and enterprises, with a strong linkage to intellectual, cultural, and economic history.

3. Economic aspects—An examination of the economic basis of media activity in the United States and worldwide, and structural analysis of media institutions tied to economic history, microeconomics, and political economy.

4. Philosophical and ethical aspects—A cultural review of the values on which modern mass communication is based; theories of ethics and standards of professional practice, tying in university courses in philosophy and ethics.

5. Legal and regulatory aspects—The system of freedom of expression under which media operate; communication law, regulatory patterns.

6. Technological aspects—The relationship of mass communication to developments in communication technology; communication concerns; a contemporary portrait of new technology and its meaning for society and individualism; understanding the consequences of the new technology; how its various manifestations are related to patterns of thinking and analysis.

7. Communication theory—An advanced examination of the various theories of mass communication and the differing scholarly traditions from which they evolve. Scholarly methods and connections to other fields that study media and communication should be emphasized.

8. International communication systems—Comparison of the U.S. media system with other national systems and the emerging global system.

In speech communication programs, the enrichment areas might revolve around types of communication like persuasion and argumentation, or, they might stress context-specific aspects of communication including public, interpersonal, intrapersonal, small group, organizational, media, international, and intercultural. There are a variety of ways of organizing communication programs, curricula, and courses. What is important is that the courses and their outcomes can be rationally defended.

Broad Intracourse Outcomes

Grow (1990, 1991) proposed a model for matching student learning with teaching. He suggested that higher order skills and self-direction are what we should be aiming for in our students. Given this overall thrust to self-direction, courses tend to stress different kinds of learning (see Potter, 1993; Tucker, 1993). Looking at cognitive taxonomies (see for example Bloom, 1956; Miller, Williams, & Haladyna, 1978; Perry, 1970), for example, it is important to realize that the kinds of evaluations given to students contribute to the overall ethos, culture, or reputation of a program (Blanchard & Christ, 1993a). The following, adapted from Whitney (1970, p. 3) and Erwin (1991, pp. 39–40), demonstrates how different kinds of tests require different kinds of cognitive skills. At the intracourse level, the outcomes should move the students toward synthesis and evaluation. Media education is used as the example:

1. Knowledge: Lowest level category, involves the remembering or recall of specifics.
   Key words: To define, recall, recognize.
   Sample test plan: Define *media censorship*.
2. Comprehension: A low level of understanding, including acts of translating, interpreting, and extrapolation. Ideas are not related to one another.
   Key words: To translate, transform, state in one's own words.
   Sample test plan: Can properly interpret the use of 3-point lighting.
3. Application: The use of abstraction to perform in a new situation.
   Key words: To generalize, relate, organize, classify.
   Sample test plan: Can use the criteria of the Central Hudson Gas & Electric case to support the banning of alcohol advertising.

4. Analysis: Breaking down the elements of a situation and clarifying the rankings or relations among the elements.

    Key words: To distinguish, detect, discriminate, contrast.

    Sample test plan: Can identify differing motives of producers, advertisers, citizen groups, and audiences in the production of media texts.

5. Synthesis: Combining elements to constitute a new pattern or structure.

    Key words: To produce, modify, restructure, originate, derive.

    Sample test plan: Can develop a 1-minute news report explaining the constitutional grounds for a recent Supreme Court decision.

6. Evaluation: Using a set of criteria or standards as a basis for making judgments about an issue.

    Key words: To evaluate, judge, appraise, rate, weigh.

    Sample test plan: Can develop criteria for evaluating gender-biased reporting.

SUMMARY

Outcomes assessment should start with program assessment and that program assessment must take into account both off- and on-campus forces. Off campus, challenges facing higher education, communication technologies, and the communication discipline suggest a New Liberal Arts for the general student that integrates traditional disciplines with professional perspectives and a broad-based, functional approach to the major (i.e., a New Professionalism).

We suggest programs should begin the assessment process by developing mission statements and outcomes at the program, course, and intracourse level. Once mission statements and outcomes are in place, a program can move into strategies for evaluating the success of a program (see Appendix A).

APPENDIX A: PROGRAM ASSESSMENT AUDIT

Mission Statements

1. Does our program have an explicit mission statement?
2. When was the last time we discussed our mission and/or mission statement?
3. How well does the mission of our academic program reflect and support the mission of our institution as a whole?
4. If an outside group came to our school, what would it identify as our strengths and weaknesses?

5. How committed are we to the general education of nonmajors? What kinds of experiences (e.g., courses, apprenticeships, workshops, lecture series, and so forth) do we offer to the general student? What kind of commitment has our department made to the liberal education of all students?

6. Most of us would argue that our discipline is basic. But can we explain what is basic about our discipline? How has our program defined itself in terms of what is basic or fundamental to a liberal education and what is basic and fundamental to our discipline?

7. How is our academic unit perceived on campus by the faculty and by the administration? Are we considered intellectual leaders in communication and media studies and sense-makers of the communication/information age? Are we considered partners in the liberal arts? Do we consider it important to be considered campus leaders in communication, media studies, and/or the liberal arts? If not, what academic units on campus are providing these functions?

8. Assuming we are always in the process of developing and fine-tuning our mission does our mission statement:
   a. contain a formulation of our goals and objectives that enables progress toward them to be measured?
   b. differentiate our program from other programs at the university and possibly other universities?
   c. define the "business" we want to be in?
   d. allow us to be establish priorities that are relevant to our stakeholders?
   e. describe how we plan to serve our stakeholders?
   f. excite and inspire, especially faculty and students?
   g. reflect the educational philosophy of our program?

9. If we were not preparing students for entry-level jobs, would we still have a justification for existing?

10. What is the relationship we should foster with practitioners?

Antecedents to Program Assessment

1. Does our school have an assessment plan in place?

Where is our program in terms of:

2. Funding. Who will pay for assessment costs?
3. Time. Who has the time for assessment and how long will it take?
4. Human resources. Who supports assessment and who does not?
5. Organizational climate. What is the instructional, social, fiscal, organizational, and physical environment on campus?
6. Availability of data. Is data available about students and alumni?

7. Details of the program evaluation action plan. What are the university's strategic plans?
8. Audiences. Again, who are the stakeholders?
9. Technical ability and feasibility. Technically, what kinds of assessment are possible?
10. Ethical concerns. How open and public will the process be?

Broad Program Outcomes

How have we created an educational environment that encourages:

1. Communication competence: Ability to read, write, speak, and listen and to use these processes effectively to acquire, develop, and convey ideas and information (includes "visual literacy"; see p. 45).
2. Critical thinking: Ability to examine issues rationally, logically, and coherently—a universally recognized and desired liberal outcome.
3. Contextual competence: An understanding of the societal context or environment in which one is living and working.
4. Aesthetic sensibility: An enhanced aesthetic awareness of arts and human behavior for both personal enrichment and application in the enhancement of work.
5. Professional identity: Concern for improving the knowledge, skills, and values of the profession.
6. Professional ethics: Understanding the ethics of a profession as standards that guide professional behavior.
7. Adaptive competence: Anticipating, adapting to, and promoting changes important to a profession's societal purpose and professional's role.
8. Leadership capacity: Exhibiting the capacity to contribute as a productive member of the profession and assuming appropriate leadership roles.
9. Scholarly concern for improvement: Recognizing the need to increase knowledge and to advance the profession through both theoretical and applied research.
10. Motivation of continued learning: Exploring and expanding personal, civic and professional knowledge and skills through a lifetime, both appropriately liberal and professional outcomes.

Broad Course Outcomes

This will vary by program. In media studies, for example, do we offer courses or their equivalent that include:

1. Mass communication and society: A conceptual map of the literature and documented experience that explains the relationship of media to society and to individuals in society.

2. Historical aspects: An overview both in conceptual and chronological terms of the history and traditions of mass communication, its institutions, people, and enterprises, with a strong linkage to intellectual, cultural, and economic history.
3. Economic aspects: An examination of the economic basis of media activity in the United States and worldwide, and structural analysis of media institutions tied to economic history, microeconomics, and political economy.
4. Philosophical and ethical aspects: A cultural review of the values on which modern mass communication is based; theories of ethics and standards of professional practice, tying in university courses in philosophy and ethics.
5. Legal and regulatory aspects: The system of freedom of expression under which media operate, communication law, regulatory patterns.
6. Technological aspects: The relationship of mass communication to developments in communication technology, communication concerns, a contemporary portrait of new technology and its meaning for society and individualism, understanding about the consequences of the new technology, how its various manifestations are related to patterns of thinking and analysis.
7. Communication theory: An advanced examination of the various theories of mass communication and the differing scholarly traditions from which they evolve. Scholarly methods and connections to other fields that study media and communication should be emphasized.
8. International communication systems: Comparison of the U.S. media system with other national systems and the emerging global system.

Broad Intracourse Outcomes

Within our courses what is stressed?

1. Knowledge: Lowest level category, involves the remembering or recall of specifics.
2. Comprehension: A low level of understanding, including acts of translating, interpreting, and extrapolation. Ideas are not related to one another.
3. Application: The use of abstraction to perform in a new situation.
4. Analysis: Breaking down the elements of a situation and clarifying the rankings or relations among the elements.
5. Synthesis: Combining elements to constitute a new pattern or structure.
6. Evaluation: Using a set of criteria or standards as a basis for making judgments about an issue.

REFERENCES

Ackoff, R. L. (1986). *Management in small doses*. New York: Wiley.

Ahlgren, A., & Boyer, C. M. (1981). Visceral priorities: Roots of confusion in liberal education. *Journal of Higher Education, 52*(2), 173–180.

Armstrong, R. (1988). *The next hurrah: The communications revolution in American politics*. New York: Morrow.

Association of American Colleges (AAC). (1985, February). *Integrity in the college curriculum: A report to the academic community*. Washington, DC: Author.

Ball-Rokeach, S. (1985, October). Convention speaker questions communication theory, structure (Keynote speech, convention of the Association for Education in Journalism and Mass Communication). *aejmc News*, pp. 1, 4–5.

Banks, J., & Tankel, J. D. (1990). Science fiction: Technology in prime time television. *Critical Studies in Mass Communication, 7*(1), 24–36.

Barker, D. (1985). Television production techniques as communication. *Critical Studies in Mass Communication, 2*(3), 234–246.

Bell, D. (1968). *The reforming of general education: The Columbia College experience in its national setting*. New York: Columbia University Press.

Benson, T. W. (Ed.). (1985). *Speech communication in the 20th century*. Carbondale: Southern Illinois University Press.

Berger, C. R., & Chaffee, S. H. (1988). On bridging the communication gap. *Human Communication Research, 15*(2), 311–318.

Blanchard, R. O., & Christ, W. G. (1993a). *Media education and the liberal arts: A blueprint for the new professionalism*. Hillsdale, NJ: Lawrence Erlbaum Associates.

Blanchard, R. O., & Christ, W. G. (1993b). A symposium challenge: The new professionalism and the iron triangles. *Feedback, 34*(1), 5–8.

Bloom, B. (Ed.). (1956). *Taxonomy of educational objectives (Vol. 1): Cognitive domain*. New York: McKay.

Bok, D. (1986a). *Higher learning*. Cambridge, MA: Harvard University Press.

Bok, D. (1986b, May–June). Toward education of quality. *Harvard Magazine*, pp. 49–64.

Boyer, E. L. (1987). *College: The undergraduate experience in America*. New York: The Carnegie Foundation for the Advancement of Teaching, Harper & Row.

Boyer, E. L. (1990). *Scholarship reconsidered: Priorities of the professoriate*. New York: The Carnegie Foundation for the Advancement of Teaching, Princeton University Press.

Bryson, J. M. (1988). *Strategic planning for public and nonprofit organizations*. San Francisco: Jossey-Bass.

Caywood, C. L., & Ewing, R. P. (1992). Communications strategies and tactics: All the stakeholders. In C. L. Caywood & R. P. Ewing (Eds.), *The handbook of communications in corporate restructuring and takeovers* (pp. 223–238). Englewood Cliffs, NJ: Prentice-Hall.

Delia, J. G. (1987). Communication research: A history. In C. R. Berger &. S. H. Chaffee (Eds.), *Handbook of communication science* (pp. 2–98). Newbury Park, CA: Sage.

Dennis, E. E., & DeFleur, M. L. (1991). A linchpin concept: Media studies and the rest of the curriculum. *Journalism Educator, 46*(2), 78–80.

Dervin, B., & Voigt, M. J. (Eds.). (1984). *Progress in the communication sciences*. Norwood, NJ: Ablex.

Diebold, J. (1973). *The world of the computer*. New York: Random House.

Donner, F. J. (1981). *The age of surveillance: The aims and methods of America's political intelligence system*. New York: Vintage.

Dressel, P. L. (1976). *Handbook of academic evaluation*. San Francisco: Jossey-Bass.

Ehrmann, S. C. (1990). Reaching students, reaching resources: Using technologies to open the college. *Academic Computing, 4*(7), 8–14, 32.

Ervin, R. F. (1988). Outcomes assessment: The rationale and the implementation. In R. L. Hoskins (Ed.), *Insights* (pp. 19–23). Columbia, SC: Association for Schools of Journalism and Mass Communication.

Erwin, T. D. (1986). Students' contribution to their college costs and intellectual development. *Research in Higher Education, 25,* 194–203.

Erwin, T. D. (1991). *Assessing student learning and development.* San Francisco: Jossey-Bass.

Erwin, T. D., & Love, W. B. (1989). Selected environmental factors associated with change in students' development. *NASPA Journal, 26,* 256–264.

Eshelman, D. (1991, April). *Outcome assessment strategies: Implications for broadcast education curricula.* Paper presented at the 36th annual Broadcast Education Association Convention, Las Vegas, NV.

Footlick, J. K., Wingert, P., & Leonard, E. A. (1990, December 10). Decade of the student. *Newsweek,* pp. 70, 72.

Galvin, K. N. (1992). Foundation for assessment: The mission, goals and objectives. In E. A. Hay (Ed.), *Program assessment in speech communication* (pp. 21–24). Annandale, VA: Speech Communication Association.

Gandy, O. H., Jr., & Simmons, C. E. (1986). Technology, privacy and the democratic process. *Critical Studies in Mass Communication, 3*(2), 155–168.

Grow, G. (1990, August). *Enhancing self direction in journalism education.* Paper presented at the Association for Education in Journalism and Mass Communication, Minneapolis, MN.

Grow, G. (1991). Higher-order skills for professional practice and self-direction. *Journalism Educator, 45*(4), 56–65.

Gumpertz, G., & Cathart, E. (Eds.). (1982). *Inter/media: Interpersonal communication in a media world.* New York: Oxford University Press.

Hawkins, R. P., Wiemann, J. M., &. Pingree, S. (Eds.). (1988). *Advancing communication science: Merging mass and interpersonal processes.* Newbury Park, CA: Sage.

Hunt, G. T. (1992). The antecedents of program assessment. In E. A. Hay (Ed.), *Program assessment in speech communication* (pp. 12–13). Annandale, VA: Speech Communication Association.

Kanigel, R. (1986, March–April). Technology as a liberal art: Scenes from the classroom. *Change, 18*(2), pp. 20–27, 30.

Kimball, B. A. (1986). *Orators and philosophers.* New York: Teachers College Press.

Koerner, J. D. (1984). *The new liberal arts program—A status report.* New York: Alfred P. Sloan Foundation.

Kubey, R., & Csikszentmihalyi, M. (1990). *Television and the quality of life: How viewing shapes every day experiences.* Hillsdale, NJ: Lawrence Erlbaum Associates.

Larson, C. U., & Oravec, C. (1987). "A prairie home companion" and the fabrication of community. *Critical Studies in Mass Communication, 4*(3), 221–244.

Levy, M. R., & Gurevitch, M. (Eds.). (1993). The future of the field I. *Journal of Communication, 43*(3).

Lisensky, R. P., Pfnister, A. O., &. Sweet, S. D. (1985). *The new liberal learning: Technology and the liberal arts.* Washington, DC: Council of Independent Colleges.

Lowenstein, R. L., & Merrill, J. (1990). *Macromedia.* New York: Longman.

Lull, J. (1988). The family and television in world cultures. In J. Lull (Ed.), *World families watch television* (pp. 9–21). London: Routledge.

Lull, J. (1991). *China turned on (television, reform, and resistance).* London: Routledge.

Meehan, E. R. (1986). Conceptualizing culture as commodity: The problem of television. *Critical Studies in Mass Communication, 3*(4), 448–457.

Micek, S. S., & Arney, W. R. (1974). *Inventory of institutional environment variables and measures.* Boulder, CO: National Center for Higher Education Management Systems.

Miller, H. G., Williams, R. G., & Haladyna, T. M. (1978). *Beyond facts: Objective ways to measure thinking.* Englewood Cliffs, NJ: Educational Technology Publications.

Moos, R. H. (1979). *Evaluating educational environments: Procedures, measures, findings, and policy implications*. San Francisco: Jossey-Bass.

Morison, E. E. (1986). The new liberal arts: Creating novel combinations out of diverse learning. *Change, 18*(2), 7–8.

Pennsylvania State University School of Communications. (1990). *Curriculum guide for students/advisors 1990–1991*. University Park, PA: Author.

Perry, W. G., Jr. (1970). *Forms of intellectual and ethical development in the college years*. New York: Rinehart & Winston.

Planning for curricular change in journalism education. (1984). (Project on the Future of Journalism and Mass Communication Education). Eugene, OR: The Oregon Report.

Potter, W. J. (1993, April). *Faculty evaluations*. Paper presented at the annual meeting of the Broadcasting Education Association, Las Vegas, NV.

Potter, W. J., & Clark, G. (1991). Styles in mass communication teaching. *Feedback, 32*(1), 8–11.

Rakow, L. F. (1988). Gendered technology, gendered practice. *Critical Studies in Mass Communication, 5*(1), 57–70.

Rogers, E. M. (1986). *Communication technology: The new media*. New York: The Free Press.

Rogers, E. M., &. Chaffee, S. H. (1983). Communication as an academic discipline: A dialogue. *Journal of Communication, 33*(3), 23–25.

Rothblatt, S. (1976). *Tradition and change in English liberal education*. London: Farber & Farber.

Rubin, A. M., & Rubin, R. B. (1985). Interface of personal and mediated communication: A research agenda. *Critical Studies in Mass Communication, 2*, 36–53.

Sims, S. J. (1992). *Student outcomes assessment*. New York: Greenwood.

Strengthening the ties that bind: Integrating undergraduate liberal and professional study (Report of the Professional Preparation Network). (1988). Ann Arbor: The Regents of the University of Michigan.

Sykes, C. (1988). *ProfScam: Professors and the demise of higher education*. WA: Regmery Gateway; WI: Reardon & Walsh.

Thomas, S., & Evans, W. (Eds.). (1990). *Communication and culture: Language, performance, technology and media*. Norwood, NJ: Ablex.

Truxal, J. G. (1986). Learning to think like an engineer: Why, what, and how? *Change, 18*(2), pp. 10–19.

Tucker, D. (1993, April). *Course evaluations*. Paper presented at the annual meeting of the Broadcast Education Association, Las Vegas, NV.

Warner, C. (1993). Response. *Feedback, 34*(2), 3.

Warner, C., & Liu, Y. (1990). Broadcast curriculum profile (A freeze-frame look at what BEA members offer students). *Feedback, 31*(3), 6–7.

White, S. (1981). Comments. In J. D. Koerner (Ed.), *The new liberal arts: An exchange of views* (An occasional paper from the Alfred P. Sloan Foundation). New York: Alfred P. Sloan Foundation.

Whitney, D. R. (1970). Improving essay examinations: I. Writing essay questions. *Technical Bulletin No. 9*. Iowa City: Evaluation and Examination Service, University of Iowa.

Wiemann, J. M., Hawkins, R. P., &. Pingree, S. (1988). Fragmentation in the field—and the movement toward integration in communication science. *Human Communication Research, 15*(2), 304–310.

Woodward, W. (1993, April). *Lecture*. Trinity University. San Antonio, TX.

Wycliff, D. (1990, September 4). Concern grows on campuses at teaching's loss of status. *New York Times*, pp. A1, A9.

3

Regional Accrediting Association Requirements and the Development of Outcomes Statements

Tony M. Allison
Cameron University

All six regional accrediting associations and many state legislatures are mandating some form of program assessment. Even though these regional accrediting associations are providing general guidelines, the problems that many universities are encountering are centered around specific instructions in preparing appropriate and acceptable assessment strategies. This chapter first examines the requirements for program assessment of the six regional accrediting associations.

Second, it provides a cost-effective "how-to" assessment strategy for writing student outcomes statements for mass communication and speech communication programs.

INTRODUCTION

Academic program assessment is fast becoming the major agenda of almost every university in the country as each institution prepares for evaluation by its respective regional accrediting association or by having a mandate from its respective state legislature (see Appendix A). Hunt (1992) stated that "as many as 37 states have some type of mandate for the assessment of student learning" (p. 12). All six of the regional accrediting associations now require assessment of institutional effectiveness.

For many years colleges and universities viewed accreditation as a process of completing successful self-studies and external reviews that were conducted periodically (in many cases every 5 to 10 years) by a regional accrediting association in order to maintain accreditation. These periodic reviews, although examining every aspect of a university, have "traditionally focused on resource measures such as number of library holdings, amount of funding, number of faculty, proportion of faculty holding doctorates, etc." (Southern Association of Colleges and Schools Commission on Colleges [SACS], 1992b, p. iii). In recent years the six regional accrediting associations have added a new focus or criterion to the accrediting process. Colleges and universities are being required to systematize an institutional assessment program that examines continuously the effectiveness of the institution by first comparing its performance to its goals, and second, evaluating its performance to implement improvements in its academic programs (SACS, 1992b). By adding the emphasis on assessment and institutional effectiveness to the accrediting process, the self-examination of an institution has been expanded from a periodic event to a continuous process (SACS, 1992b).

SOUTHERN ASSOCIATION OF COLLEGES AND SCHOOLS

In the late 1970s, the leadership of the Southern Association began to reexamine standards and procedures for accreditation. In a 1980 survey of its membership, Rogers stated that "while the members were satisfied with the current standards and with the self-study process, they were clearly interested in a stronger emphasis on the results of the education process" (Rogers, 1990, p. 397). In 1983, subcommittees worked on the revision of standards, which led to the development of the *Criteria for Accreditation*. In December 1984, the SACS adopted the new emphasis on the assessment of institutional effectiveness (Rogers, 1990). This new emphasis established "an internal planning and evaluation system through which institutional self-examination becomes a continuous process rather than a periodic event" (SACS, 1992b, p. iii).

According to Wolff (1992) of the Western Association of Schools and Colleges, "among the regionals, the Southern Association took the lead by adopting a major new standard on institutional effectiveness as part of an effort to more consciously link outcomes assessment to the accrediting process" (p. 39).

The Southern Association in its *Criteria for Accreditation* (SACS, 1992a) identified six units that concern accreditation for its member institutions:

Section I: Principles and Philosophy of Accreditation
Section II: Institutional Purpose
Section III: Institutional Effectiveness
Section IV: Educational Program
Section V: Educational Support Services
Section VI: Administrative Processes

It is Section III, Institutional Effectiveness, that emphasizes the assessment process. In addition to the *Criteria for Accreditation*, the Southern Association approved the *Resource Manual on Institutional Effectiveness* in June 1987, which provides member institutions additional information in formulating assessment programs. Even though the *Resource Manual* does not prescribe a "cookbook" approach to assessment, it does offer many useful examples that could assist institutions in developing their own programs. The Southern Association identified 18 institutional operations as focal points for assessment:

Admissions	Student Development Services
Completion Requirements	Intercollegiate Athletics
Curriculum	Organization and Administration
Instruction	Institutional Advancement
Continuing Education	Financial Resources
Faculty	Physical Resources
Library	Externally Funded Grants and Contracts
Instructional Support	Related Corporate Entities
Institutional Research	Computer Resources and Services
(SACS, 1992b, p.13)	

The Southern Association requires that institutions establish adequate procedures for planning and evaluation: "The institution must define its expected educational results and describe how the achievement of these results will be ascertained" (SACS, 1992a, p. 16). It recommends that the planning and evaluation process should involve participation by faculty, staff, students, and administration. In assessing each institutional operation, Southern Association recommends that "planning and evaluation" utilize four steps:

1. State institutional purpose/mission.
2. Define goals/results.
3. Describe means of evaluation.
4. Describe use of evaluation results (SACS, 1992b, pp. 4–13).

The Southern Association suggests that the goals should be stated as simply and clearly as possible and that the goals be linked to the statement of institutional purpose. It also suggests that institutions should strive "to specify appropriate time frames, to address both minimum standards and target standards for excellence, to indicate at what level the assessment will be conducted and used, and to designate responsibility for implementing evaluation and for ensuring appropriate use of evaluation results" (SACS, 1992b, pp. 9–10).

The *Resource Manual* provides a collection of examples of the "planning and evaluation" process. One example provided in the *Resource Manual* that applies to assessment of an academic program concerns program completion requirements for a psychology program:

Statement of Purpose (Excerpt): Graduating students will demonstrate competence in their major fields.

Expected Results: In psychology, each senior will: 1) when presented with a report of a psychological experiment, critique the experiment in terms of its research design, analysis, conclusions and application; 2) when presented with a specific psychological topic, write a comprehensive review of published research on that topic, demonstrating mastery of the literature resources and effective written communication of scientific findings useful for a reader who is not a psychologist; and 3) take a nationally standardized, comprehensive examination covering the generally accepted components of an undergraduate major in psychology.

Assessment Procedures: For 1) and 2) above, each critique and review of research will be evaluated by one local faculty member and two faculty members from other institutions using a common rating form. For 3) above, a nationally standardized, comprehensive examination such as the Graduate Record Examination's Psychology Subject Test will be administered to all graduating seniors.

Administration of Assessment Procedures: Seniors will be enrolled in a one-semester course in which they will write the required papers and take the comprehensive examination.

Use of Assessment Findings: The department chair will summarize the jury evaluations of the critiques and literature reviews and produce a composite profile of the senior's performance on the comprehensive examination. This information will be presented to the faculty at its annual planning retreat and used as a basis for improvement in curriculum and/or instructional methodology. (SACS, 1992b, pp. 30–31; reprinted by permission.)

This provides an excellent example of utilizing the Southern Association's four steps of the planning and evaluation process of assessment. The *Resource Manual* is an excellent reference for any institution that is in the early stages of developing an assessment program.

NORTH CENTRAL ASSOCIATION OF COLLEGES AND SCHOOLS

The North Central Association (NCA) has developed a very broad approach to the assessment of institutional effectiveness. It has taken the position that the institution should develop an ongoing program of evaluating and assessing its effectiveness in almost every area of the institution. It suggests that the assessment program should provide continuous information that assists in developing plans and making improvements in the institution. The assessment information becomes a very crucial part of an institution's self-study.

The NCA has developed four criteria for accreditation of colleges and universities:

Criterion #1:   The institution has clear and publicly stated purposes, consistent with its mission and appropriate to a postsecondary educational institution.

Criterion #2:   The institution has effectively organized adequate human, financial, and physical resources into educational and other programs to accomplish its purposes.

Criterion #3:   The institution is accomplishing its purposes.

Criterion #4:   The institution can continue to accomplish its purposes. (NCA of Colleges and Schools Commission on Institutions of Higher Education, 1992b, p. 9)

In addition to the criteria, the association also "identifies specific general institutional requirements related to mission and authorization, educational programs, institutional organization, financial resources, and public disclosure that must be met by member institutions" (Thrash, 1990, p. 385).

It is the third criterion, "Is the institution accomplishing its purpose?" that involves the assessment of institutional effectiveness. North Central goes beyond the assessment of student outcomes and academic achievement by listing nine possible areas to be included in the self-study for institutional assessment:

Special Constituencies	Student Academic Achievement
Student Development	Public and Community Service
Program Quality	Institutional Climate
Faculty Accomplishments	Equity and Diversity
Research and Development	
(NCA, 1992b, pp. 17–19)	

North Central also suggests assessing the effectiveness in other areas of the institution:

Administrative and Support Programs: (e.g., personnel, planning, public relations, institutional development and fund-raising, accounting, budgeting, maintenance, risk management, faculty and staff development).

Student Services: (e.g., advising, placement, counseling, health services, and housing), of academic support (advising, developmental services, library and learning resources, and computing). (NCA, 1992b, p. 19)

Assessing Student Academic Achievement

One of the nine suggested general areas to be included in the assessment of "institutional effectiveness" is assessing student academic achievement. It is this particular area that academic programs and departments want to closely examine.

The NCA in 1989 adopted the "Statement on Assessment and Student Academic Achievement," which clarifies the Association's position on documenting student academic achievement (NCA, 1992b). Besides considering a broad range of approaches to assessing institutional outcomes, North Central stated that documenting student achievement at the undergraduate and graduate levels "is a critical component in assessing overall institutional effectiveness" (NCA, 1992b, pp. 19–20). North Central does not dictate a specific approach to assessment. It suggests "that determination should be made by the institution in terms of its own purposes, resources, and commitments" (NCA, 1992b, p. 19).

North Central's *Guide to Self-Study* (1992b) also suggests that assembling an assessment plan is crucial for an institution. The assessment plan should include the following five components:

1. The plan is linked to the mission, goals, and objectives of the institution.
2. The plan is carefully articulated and is institutionwide in conceptualization and scope.
3. The plan leads to institutional improvement.
4. The plan is being implemented according to a timeline.
5. The plan is administered. (p. 21)

Like the recommendations made by the Southern Association, this assessment plan should become an ongoing program that has the flexibility to adapt to change and growth. North Central expects assessment programs will change over time as institutions learn more about collecting and analyzing information. Even though North Central does not dictate a specific method of assessing academic achievement, it does expect the program to be institutionwide and systematic. It does not expect the institution to "collect identical information about all its programs. Invariably, some of the information collected may be objective and quantified, some more subjective and qualitative" (NCA, 1992b, p. 21).

North Central cautions institutions about assessing everything concerning student academic achievement. It views it as "impractical." It further stated, "What matters most is that the information is sufficiently diverse and detailed for the institution to use it to enhance student learning and improve educational programs" (NCA, 1992b, p. 21).

North Central suggests in Appendix B of its *Guide to Self-Study* (1992b) 10 major characteristics of an assessment program. A program to assess student academic achievement should:

1. Flow from the institution's mission.
2. Have a conceptual framework.
3. Have faculty ownership/responsibility.
4. Have institutionwide support.
5. Use multiple measures.
6. Provide feedback to students and the institution.
7. Be cost-effective.
8. Not restrict or inhibit goals of access, equity, and diversity established by the institution.
9. Lead to improvement.
10. Include a process for evaluating the assessment program. (pp. 47–50)

North Central emphasizes the importance that the assessment program should be built around a conceptual framework that flows directly from the published mission of the university. North Central stresses the need for faculty responsibility and participation in the design, implementation, and evaluation of an assessment program. It is also crucial that institutions use multiple measures in assessing student outcomes: "No one instrument is sufficiently complex to capture the range of student achievement necessary for the institution to make a judgment regarding how well it is fulfilling its purposes in a particular area" (NCA, 1992b, p. 49). The use of multiple measures in assessing an academic program has significant impact on the development of an assessment program. It may be necessary for some programs to assess student achievement with multiple measures at various stages to show appropriate progress.

Besides providing feedback to the institution, assessment programs should also provide feedback to the students. Concerning cost-effectiveness, North Central suggests that "monetary and human resources be prudently and effectively deployed" (NCA, 1992b, p. 49). Assessment programs should not restrict goals of access, equity, and diversity. It is also important for institutions to show improvements being made in the academic program as a result of an ongoing assessment program. Finally, North Central suggests that the assessment program itself should also be assessed or evaluated for effectiveness.

North Central placed considerable importance on the assessment of student academic achievement. It is allowing much freedom and flexibility for institutions to develop their own assessment programs that apply to the individual situation of each campus.

WESTERN ASSOCIATION OF SCHOOLS AND COLLEGES

In 1988 The Western Association of Schools and Colleges (WASC) adopted a revised set of accreditation standards that added a major emphasis "calling on institutions to focus on assessment as a means to assure institutional and program quality and effectiveness" (Wolff, 1990, p. 401). The WASC allows institutions the freedom to develop whatever assessment approach best suits the institution's character. The association seems to be very protective of institution autonomy. The Western Association identifies assessment activities in the following standards of accreditation:

Standard 2.C   Institutional Effectiveness
Standard 4.B   Evaluation of General Education
Standard 4.F.5   Program Review
Standard 7.A   Co-Curricular Educational Growth
(WASC Accrediting Commission for Senior Colleges and Universities, 1992, pp. 12–21)

Standard 2.C on institutional effectiveness provides overall direction for an institution's assessment efforts. Institutions should develop the following:

1. An overall plan, or set of plans, that includes a census of what data are collected and how they are to be disseminated and used, and also establishes the working definition of assessment to suit institutional needs and interests.
2. A visible, regular, and technically sound array of mechanisms for gathering evidence about issues of importance at the institution.
3. A process for involving faculty, particularly in designing assessments related to student learning and achievement.
4. A visible and meaningful link between the collection of evidence and institutional decision making. (WASC, 1992, p. 12)

General education programs are also to be a part of the assessment program. Institutions are expected to "periodically evaluate the extent to which general education goals are being achieved" (Wolff, 1990, p. 406).

Program reviews are essential to the accrediting process. Assessment of student outcomes is to be incorporated into program review procedures. The Western Association suggests that assessment procedures for program review "should 1) cover knowledge and skills taught throughout the program's curriculum, 2) relate to the goals specified for the program, 3) involve multiple judgments of performance, 4) provide information on multiple dimensions of performance, and 5) involve more than simply a self-report" (WASC, 1992, pp. 20–21).

The final standard pertaining to assessment for the Western Association deals with assessing the cocurricular programs of the institution. It suggests that assessment can be instrumental "in determining the quality of student experience at the institution" (Wolff, 1990, p. 407).

Even though much of the Western Association's language concerning assessment is the same as the other regional accrediting associations', Western claims some difference in the application of the assessment process. Ralph Wolff, Associate Executive Director of the Western Association, stated that "the Commission has indicated that it has purposely chosen not to join or give special priority to any particular facet of the national assessment movement such as testing, value-added approaches or comprehensive institutional goal setting" (1990, p. 405). It prefers to have institutions develop "substantive evidence of effectiveness without dictating a particular form of assessment as the best or most appropriate means" (p. 404). The concern for the autonomy of the institution is central. Wolff stated that assessment should create a "culture of evidence" in which the institution "welcomes critical questions about institutional performances and uses data in responding to such questions" (Wolff, 1992, p. 41).

Wolff (1992) cautioned institutions in several areas of the assessment topic. He suggested that the definition of assessment should include all parts of an institution and not just student achievement. He suggested there are some who define assessment as all testing and evaluation activities and some who define it as discovering information about student learning or student achievement. Wolff believed that assessment encompasses a collection and analysis of evidence of effectiveness for all parts of an institution. He also cautioned institutions against relying only on goal-oriented models for assessment. He contended that a goal-oriented model "is essentially hierarchical, linear, and deductive" (1992, p. 43). He believed it is only one way to approach assessment.

Wolff (1992) recommended that "goal-free models can be built on inductive approaches to assessment that generate data around questions of importance. . . .From such questions specific data can be collected and analyzed, and insights drawn about institutional goals. In other words, the derivation of institutional goals becomes the last rather than the first step in the process" (p. 44).

Wolff also cautioned institutions on comprehensive assessment. He believed it would be better for institutions to start small with pilot programs and build from those experiences. Initially, comprehensive assessment may be beyond the technical and financial resources of many institutions. Wolff (1992) stated: "There is simply no point in asking institutions to undertake assessments for which they lack the resources, experience, and sophistication" (p. 45). The freedom of an institution that is a member of the Western Association to choose its own particular assessment approach is apparent. The association offers sound advice in starting small and building from a base of experience.

MIDDLE STATES ASSOCIATION OF COLLEGES AND SCHOOLS

According to Mayhew and Simmons (1990), the Middle States Association of Colleges and Schools formed a Task Force on Outcomes Assessment in

December 1988. They also indicated that Middle States had been stressing the necessity for institutions to provide evidence of a connection between stated goals and actual learning outcomes since the mid-1950s. It was "the rebirth of the outcomes assessment movement in the 1980s, fueled by a growing public awareness of the crisis in nationwide higher educational effectiveness, that provided impetus to the Commission's inquiry" (Mayhew & Simmons, 1990, p. 375). After long deliberations the Task Force on Outcomes Assessment developed a manual entitled *Framework for Outcomes Assessment* to assist institutions in developing their own assessment programs.

The Middle States Association (MSA) defined outcomes assessment in *Framework* as a "process by which evidence for congruence between an institution's stated mission, goals and objectives, and the actual outcomes of its program and activities is assembled and analyzed in order to improve teaching and learning" (MSA of Colleges and Schools Commission on Higher Education, 1990, p. 4). The MSA identified a hierarchy of goal categories:

Institutional Goals
- Common to many institutions
- Specific to a particular institution

Program Goals
- Content related and program specific
- Skill related and program specific
- Related to general education

Course Goals
- Content related and discipline specific
- Skill related and discipline specific

(MSA, 1990, pp. 7–8)

Middle States stresses the importance of linking program and course goals with institutional goals. *Framework* focuses on three questions: "What should students learn? How well are they learning it? How does the institution know?" (MSA, 1990, p. 11). Middle States describes a teaching/learning/assessment/improvement loop model. Each component of the model influences the next and then cycles back to improve teaching. The model shows a commitment to an improvement-oriented role for outcomes assessment (MSA, 1990).

Because teaching and learning is the focus of outcomes assessment for the Middle States Association, it recommends three areas that should be assessed by institutions. First, it suggests that an assessment program be designed for general education, including information literacy (the ability to retrieve and use information). Second, it recommends that academic programs be assessed. Third, it suggests that individual course offerings be assessed (MSA, 1990).

Concerning the assessment of an academic program, it suggests that the program review process would be enhanced by the appointment of an institutionwide committee of faculty and administrators. This committee should become a part of the permanent governance structure of an institution for the ongoing or cyclical task of program review. Middle States suggests that this committee should: "1) articulate goals and objectives of program review at the institution, 2) write general and specific charges to the individual units under assessment, 3) ask for outside validation of the program, and 4) review unit reports and the outside evaluations and make recommendations for change" (MSA, 1990, p. 19).

Middle States encourages the use of "multi-dimensional evaluation of scholastic achievement using qualitative and quantitative measures" (MSA, 1992, p. 18). Even though institutions have the freedom of selecting particular measures to be employed, the use of multiple measures is recommended. Middle States surveys some of the major categories of measures. First, it identifies proxy measures, which in one sense are related to resources or inputs of an institution. Examples given include "number of books in library, credentials of faculty, facility and equipment resources" (MSA, 1990, p. 23). This was once a major method in evaluating institutions and programs. Middle States suggests using outcomes-related proxy measures in addition. Examples given include "retention and graduation rates, passing rates on licensing examinations, transfer and job placement rates" (MSA, 1990, p. 23). *Framework* provides an example of proxy input measures and proxy output measures.

I. Proxy Input Measures
   Resources
   • Credentials of those teaching in the undergraduate program (e.g., percent of faculty with PhDs; number of faculty with publications/year);
   • Faculty/student ratios in the major courses in the program;
   • Facilities/equipment/learning resources available to students in the program;
   Student Preparation and Demand
   • Percent of entering class needing remediation; average SAT scores, average high school rank, etc.;
   • Five-year trends in applications, breadth and depth of applicant pool, competing programs, etc.
II. Proxy Output Measures
   Program Outcomes
   • Percent of entering students completing program;
   • Percent of graduates placed in program-related jobs or accepted into next degree level at outstanding colleges and universities;
   • Student performance in the next level program (i.e., GPA, completion rates, etc.);

•Student opinion surveys on the quality of program, courses and faculty;
•Employer surveys on their perceptions of the preparation of program graduates.
(MSA, 1990, pp. 25–26)

A second major measure category is *direct assessment of learning*. It is important for programs to specify learning objectives based on knowledge and skills of the program. When objectives are specified in this manner it is easier to assess learning and make improvements. Middle States allows the freedom for institutions and programs to choose what instruments are to be incorporated into the assessment program.

A third major measure category is the use of *value-added* measures: "The value-added approach involves a pre-assessment as well as post-assessment phase, and typically uses the same instrument for both activities" (MSA, 1990, p. 28). The primary goal of the value-added approach is to measure the difference in student achievement occurring between the first testing and the last testing. One excellent instrument for this approach is portfolio assessment (see chap. 6).

Finally, Middle States requires that outcomes assessment, whether it is for general education, academic program reviews, or individual courses, must be part of an ongoing institutional activity in order to be successful. It suggests that the institution "may wish to devise a cycle of activity where some institutional, program and course objectives are assessed in one year, some in others" (MSA, 1990, p. 33).

NORTHWEST ASSOCIATION OF SCHOOLS AND COLLEGES

The Northwest Association of Schools and Colleges updated its standards for accreditation when member institutions approved revisions in December 1991. Margaret Kaus, Assistant Director of the Northwest Association, stated that a standing committee examined the standards for accreditation and the committee "has updated 'Standard V—Educational Program and Its Effectiveness' with renewed focus on assessment of educational outcomes, and in addition has prepared a policy statement (#25) on educational assessment" (M. Kaus, personal communication, November 10, 1992). Northwest's "Policy Statement (#25) on Educational Assessment," which was approved in December 1991 and incorporated in its *Accreditation Handbook*, provides a multipage document that details a recommended assessment process for academic programs and student outcomes.

The Northwest Association (NWA), cognizant of the wide diversity of institutional missions, "emphasizes the necessity of a continuing process of academic planning, the carrying out of those plans, the assessment of the outcomes, and the influencing of the planning process by the assessment of activities" (NWA of Schools and Colleges Commission on Colleges, 1992, p. 47). In addition to evaluating the institution as a whole, Northwest requires that each institution "will need to direct each internal academic unit, program, major or concentration, as part of the self-study process, to conduct a separate study concerned with its role and development in terms of the mission of the entire institution, including general education/related instruction" (NWA, 1992, p. 48).

In evaluating the effectiveness of academic programs institutionwide, Northwest offers some illustrations:

a. Assess the effectiveness of student learning during the previous 5 years.
b. What percentage of graduates in recent years continued their education in senior colleges, graduate, or professional schools?
c. What results have been learned from studies conducted of recent graduates who entered occupational or professional careers? What is the level of employer satisfaction?
d. What has been learned about educational effectiveness of the various instructional programs from former students who left before completing their programs of study?
e. How satisfied are alumni with their education after 5, 10, 15 years away from the institution? (NWA, 1992, p. 50)

Northwest also offers suggestions for the "internal academic unit" to be considered in evaluating an academic program. Among some of these are the following: demonstrating that the unit's objectives are being realized, showing how majors reflect the purposes of the units, and evaluating the institution's general education requirements as they relate to the unit. Concerning the evaluation of students within the academic unit, Northwest suggests the consideration of the following five questions:

a. Compare the number of student majors over the last five years. What differences in quality does the faculty note?
b. What evidence is there to demonstrate the quality and achievement of former students?
c. What evidence is there of student growth in their capacities to solve problems, analyze, synthesize and make judgments?
d. What evidence is there of student growth in reasoning and communicating?
e. What evidence is there to demonstrate student growth in reasoning skills and knowledge, and as to such values as integrity and objectivity? (NWA, 1992, p. 51)

Northwest also encourages the appraisal of courses offered in the academic unit as well as evaluating faculty and methods of teaching.

In its "Policy Statement on Educational Assessment," Northwest stresses that "outcomes assessment is an essential part of the ongoing institutional self-study" (NWA, 1992, p. 54). This ongoing assessment process of evaluating educational programs should be based on a variety of data sources: "The more data sources that contribute to the overall judgment, the more reliable that judgment would seem to be" (NWA, 1992, p. 54). Northwest offers a list of outcomes measures that could be used by institutions:

a. Student Information
b. Mid-Program Assessments
c. End of Program Assessments
d. Program Review and Specialized Accreditation
e. Alumni Satisfaction and Loyalty
f. Dropout/Non-completers
g. Employment and/or Employer Satisfaction Measures (NWA, 1992, pp. 55–57)

Concerning end-of-program assessment, Northwest offers several questions that could be considered in developing an assessment program.

> What percentage of those students who enter an institution graduate from it over time? Is the percentage increasing or decreasing? Why? What is the mean number of years in which students graduate over time? Is that mean increasing or decreasing? Why? What are the criteria for these judgments? What is the several year retention pattern from one class to the next, such as freshman to sophomore? If patterns reflect significant losses between one level and another, what are the reasons? Similar questions may be asked by gender and/or ethnic background. If the institution or program requires a capstone experience at the end of the curriculum, are present students performing better or worse than their predecessors? What are the reasons? What are the bases for the judgments? (NWA, 1992, pp. 55–56)

The Northwest Association's approach to assessment is very similar to those of the other regional associations. It allows freedom to develop unique institutional assessment programs built around ongoing multiple measures, both quantitative and qualitative.

NEW ENGLAND ASSOCIATION OF SCHOOLS AND COLLEGES

The New England Association of Schools and Colleges (NEASC, 1992) in its *Standards for Accreditation* describes 11 standards that institutions must document in order to receive accreditation. These standards are the following:

1. Mission & Purposes
2. Planning & Evaluation
3. Organization & Governance
4. Programs & Instruction
5. Faculty
6. Student Services
7. Library & Information Resources
8. Physical Resources
9. Financial Resources
10. Public Disclosure
11. Integrity (NEASC Commission on Institutions of Higher Education, 1992, p. i)

Assessment is encompassed in New England's Standard 2: Planning and Evaluation:

2.4 The institution evaluates the achievement of its mission and purposes, giving primary focus to the realization of its educational objectives. Its evaluative procedures are appropriate and effective for addressing its unique circumstances. To the extent possible, evaluation enables the institution to demonstrate through verifiable means its attainment of purposes and objectives both inside and outside the classroom.

2.5 The institution systematically applies information obtained through its evaluation activities to inform institutional planning, thereby enhancing institutional effectiveness, especially as it relates to student achievement.

2.6 The institution determines the effectiveness of its planning and evaluation activities on an ongoing basis. Results of these activities are used to revise and further enhance the institution's implementation of its purposes and objectives. (NEASC, 1992, p. 3)

These three items in Standard 2 set up the foundation for assessment activities. New England does not provide a "resource manual" on assessment, but it does provide an attached document to the *Standards for Accreditation* titled "Policy Statement on Institutional Effectiveness," that gives further details concerning assessment. The policy statement includes some of the typical characteristics of assessment. It uses the same description of assessment as the Middle States Association: "The assessment process requires the gathering and analysis of evidence of congruence between an institution's stated mission, purposes, and objectives and the actual outcomes of its programs and activities" (NEASC, 1992, p. 18).

New England "prescribes no formula that an institution must use for measuring or demonstrating its effectiveness" (NEASC, 1992, p. 18). Because institutions differ in mission and resources available, institutions are free to develop their own assessment programs. New England emphasizes that "assessment is not a one-time activity; rather, it is evolutionary, ongoing, and incremental" (NEASC, 1992, p. 18). It acknowledges that institutions may proceed in stages in designing assessment programs, starting on a limited basis and then eventually developing a more comprehensive and systematic program. New England requires that assessment activities utilize both qualitative and quantitative measures. It also states that "assessment does not require standardized or even professionally developed instruments or complicated methods of statistical analysis" (NEASC, 1992, p. 18).

New England is very concerned about preserving institutional autonomy. Although it does not dictate specific procedures in conducting assessment activities, it does provide a mandate for assessment to be included in the accrediting process.

OVERVIEW OF REGIONAL ASSOCIATIONS

The six regional accrediting associations have many similarities. Each regional association appears to share the same goal of outcomes assessment, which is to measure institutional effectiveness by conducting "ongoing" self-evaluations that provide data to determine if the institution is meeting its stated goals and to help make better decisions and improve its educational programs. There is no attempt to make outcomes assessment punitive for an institution in any way. The emphasis is on improvement of educational programs.

It will be important for academic programs to link intended outcomes to the mission of the institution as the academic unit attempts to document achievements (see chap. 2). The goal-oriented model approach to developing an assessment program was endorsed by all six of the regionals, though the Western Association suggested that a goal-free model approach could also be utilized (Wolff, 1992).

Examining regional accrediting association documents, there seem to be four major reasons why the associations provide a "general framework" approach to assessment instead of a "prescriptive cookbook" approach:

1. The regional accrediting associations recognize assessment is still in the developmental stage. There will be changes and revisions for many years.
2. The regional accrediting associations recognize that diversity among institutions is important and freedom should exist to support the institutional character.
3. The regional accrediting associations recognize that the autonomy of an institution should be protected. They want the institution and faculty to realize ownership of the assessment process.

4. The regional accrediting associations recognize that flexibility in developing an assessment program is critical.

The regional associations should be commended for allowing this flexibility. Although they encourage the freedom of building individualized programs, they do insist on the use of multiple measures (both qualitative and quantitative) in documenting intended outcomes. These multiple measures could involve a whole range of possible instruments.

To what extent will the entire operations of the institution be assessed? This will depend on the institution, the stage of development of the assessment plan, and the regional association. The documents of both the Southern Association and the North Central Association are very clear that almost every operation of the institution should be involved in an ongoing assessment activity. The Western Association cautions institutions against developing comprehensive assessment programs too quickly (Wolff, 1992). It suggests moving slowly to build assessment programs on experience.

The focus of outcomes assessment is on educational programs. It is apparent that institutions assess general education programs as well as each academic program in an institution. The Middle States Association (1990) also requires assessment of individual course offerings, and the Western Association (1992) requires assessment of cocurricular educational growth.

The concern of academic departments is the documenting of student achievements in each academic unit, major, or concentration (see Sims, 1992). Although the emphasis of most assessment programs of academic units seems to be on exit assessment, it will become increasingly important for departments to examine the merits of pre-assessment and mid-assessment. Currently, language in the documents of the regional associations does not mandate either pre-assessment or mid-assessment. These are only options. Departments may want to show progress of students as they advance through an educational program. In order to document student progress in a value-added approach, all three levels of assessment (pre-, mid-, and exit) could be utilized.

What will happen to assessment data? The intent of the regional associations is to allow universities to use assessment results to revise and improve educational programs. It will be important for institutions to document improvements of academic programs that are initiated because of assessment data.

Assessment Challenges

Assessment practices will be in a state of change for many years. This writer feels institutions will be faced with many challenges:

1. Institutions will be challenged to develop comprehensive assessment programs that do not drain financial and human resources.
2. Institutions will be challenged to develop an assessment program that will meet the approval and positive interpretation of a visiting accrediting team. The problem of a broad framework of criteria is specific interpretation by all parties (see the following).
3. Institutions will be challenged to inform and train faculty quickly on assessment practices.
4. Institutions will be challenged to win support of faculty and staff to actively participate in assessment activities and feel ownership of the assessment process.
5. Some institutions will be challenged to develop an assessment program that meets not only the regional accrediting association requirements but also the mandates of state legislatures.

The North Central Association released comments in December 1992 of its first Assessment Plan Review panels. Twenty plans were reviewed by panel members. Some of the typical criticisms of the submitted plans were:

- Not articulating a rational conceptual framework for the plan.
- Omitting detailed and clear descriptions of assessment activities.
- Failing to address some critical educational goals.
- Involving only the assessment committee in planning and failing to involve the rest of the institution in planned assessment activities.
- Failing to inform students about not only what would be assessed, but why those assessments were useful.
- Providing vague information on the "mechanism and responsibility lines" for review and dissemination of the data or for the improvement process itself.
- Ignoring improvement as a goal of assessment.
- Failing to provide a specific timetable.
- Providing a plan with unrealistic deadlines within which it would be impossible to accomplish the planned program.
- Providing vague information about the administrative process or charges to the parties listed and how they would interact with one another to achieve the end product. (NCA, 1992a, p. 8)

The response of institutions to assessment challenges will no doubt be varied for the next decade. Regional accrediting associations have set into motion criteria for accreditation that will have long-lasting effects, and they have probably taken one of the most significant steps in improving higher education in this century. An institution would be well advised to review the supporting material from all of the regional accrediting associations (e.g., the Southern Association and the North Central Association have published some excellent documents). Although some regional associations have provided more material than others, all six associations have seriously addressed the issues involved in outcomes assessment. To obtain material from the associations, see the addresses in Appendix B.

DEVELOPING OUTCOMES STATEMENTS

The last section of this chapter examines student outcomes statements in the context of the entire assessment process. Developing these outcomes statements may be one of the most crucial aspects of the assessment process.

Faculty Participation

It is imperative for program supervisors and department chairpersons to recruit active participation from the faculty in defining assessment procedures. The attitude and motivation of the faculty will affect the assessment program. Several of the regional associations advocate faculty involvement and ownership of the assessment activity. Besides documenting accountability for the academic unit, the faculty should view assessment as a method of improving the academic program, as an opportunity for dialogue toward professional growth in excellence. Assessment for improvement (formative evaluation) and assessment for accountability (summative evaluation) both serve two central purposes of the assessment process (Erwin, 1991). Christ and Blanchard (1993) raised questions that faculty may ask. "Is the assessment being motivated by a unit's internal need to see how well they are doing and how they can improve (formative)? Or is the evaluation an attempt by an administrator to punish or reward certain faculty or programs (summative)? Is the need for assessment coming from an outside accrediting agency (formative and/or summative)?" (p. 11). Even though the language in the regional accrediting association documents emphasizes assessment for academic program improvement, accountability is still a factor in the assessment process.

Program supervisors and department chairpersons will be challenged to convince faculty members to approach assessment with a positive attitude. Supervisors may meet with resistance. Some faculty members may view assessment not only as additional workload, but also as a threat, because assessment costs will be competing for scarce department financial resources. Still others may fear unfavorable assessment results could bring punitive measures—poor faculty evaluations and fewer salary increases and promotions. But the academic program self-improvement process demands faculty support if it is to become a reality. Wise program leaders should insist on all faculty members participating in cooperative processing during every phase of planning, beginning with formulating a mission statement. The time spent will increase departmental unity and trust, making a successful implementation of the assessment process much more likely.

Mission Statement, Goals, and Objectives

The regional associations have suggested that departmental assessment plans should be linked or related to the mission statement of the institution. Most institutions should have a well-defined mission statement (institutional purpose statement) accompanied by general goals and objectives (see chap. 2). Even if department programs also have clearly articulated mission statements, goals, and objectives, a department will want to re-examine them before it advances much further in developing an assessment plan because it is essential for each academic unit or department to define its own role. Galvin (1992) stated that "effective departmental assessment depends on the level of clarity and consensus reflected in a department's statement of mission and in its goals and objectives which operationalize the mission" (p. 21).

Erwin (1991) classified objectives into two broad categories: learning objectives and developmental objectives. "Learning objectives are cognitively oriented objectives, including subject matter knowledge and skills. For instance students can learn basic principles and theories of a discipline, or they can learn skills such as writing or computing. Developmental objectives typically include cognitive and affective dimensions" (p. 10). Erwin (1991) stated "Cognitive developmental objectives are descriptions of higher-order thinking skills, including critical-thinking skills. Affective developmental objectives refer to attitudinal, personal, and social dimensions nurtured through the college experience" (p. 39).

Gardiner (1989) identified three types of goals and objectives: inputs, processes, and outcomes. Input goals and objectives involve "faculty members, campus facilities, finances, and campus psychological climate" (p. 49). Process goals and objectives involve "programs, services, and activities to be offered in attempting to fulfill the mission using the resources (inputs) available" (p. 49). These processes could include planning, courses, and cocurricular activities. Outcomes goals and objectives involve "the desired or intended achievements that will result from the processes" (p. 49). These outcomes goals and objectives are what departments should develop for assessment. As departments fine tune their goals and objectives for assessment purposes, they would be well-advised to focus on student outcomes in constructing objectives. The terms objectives and outcomes are often used interchangeably.

Defining Outcomes Statements

According to Spady (1992), "an outcome is a demonstration of learning that occurs at the end of a learning experience" (p.1). The Southern Association

(1992b) in its *Resource Manual* used the term *expected results* for intended outcomes. Spady (1992) also referred to an outcome as a result of learning, an observable demonstration of knowledge, skills, and attitude. James Nichols (1991), Director of University Planning and Institutional Research at the University of Mississippi, said that "statements of intended student (educational) outcomes are descriptions of what departments intend for students to know (cognitive), think (attitudinal), or do (behavioral) when they have completed their degree programs, as well as general education or 'core' curricula" (p. 17). Astin (1993) classified "student outcomes into two broad domains: cognitive (sometimes called intellective) and affective (sometimes called noncognitive)" (p. 43). Cognitive deals with knowledge, and affective deals with student attitudes. These broad areas could serve to group outcomes statements. Thus outcomes statements answer the questions: What must a graduate of the program know? What must the graduate be able to do? What attitudes must the graduate show if the student is to be successful in the real world beyond this program? Assessment statements answer the question: How will the student demonstrate success in these areas? Criteria answer the question: What constitutes a successful demonstration?

Gardiner (1989) identified two types of outcomes: outputs and impacts. "Output outcomes are 'first-order consequences' or direct end products" (p. 50) such as student achievements, competency in particular skills, and so on. "Impact outcomes are 'second-order consequences' or indirect products" (p. 50), such as a graduate getting and maintaining a job or success of a student in a graduate school. A department will want to develop both types of outcomes statements.

Measuring Outcomes Statements

Because student outcomes must be measured, it will be helpful to know which instruments are the most feasible for the department as each outcome statement is being written. The regional associations suggest using multiple measures, both qualitative and quantitative, in assessing student outcomes. Qualitative measures, which tend to address holistic approaches to evaluation, will be able to utilize portfolios, internships, public performances, senior interviews, and so on. Quantitative measures tend to use such instruments as standardized achievement tests, entrance examinations, licensing examinations, charts of the number of graduates going to graduate school or getting employment in discipline-related fields, and attitudinal questionnaires such as senior exit surveys and alumni surveys. Whatever measures or assessment instruments are incorporated in an assessment plan, tests of validity and reliability may need to be applied to those measures or instruments.

Limiting Outcomes Statements

The number of outcomes statements needed will vary between departments and universities. Nichols (1991) strongly advised developing no more than three to five statements of intended outcomes/results. He stated:

> For every intended student outcome, there will need to be developed at least one means of assessment to determine its accomplishment. Hence, the identification of intended student outcomes forms the framework around which the assessment plan must be constructed. If a large number of intended student outcomes are identified, then a larger and elaborate (expensive) assessment mechanism will be necessary. (p. 20)

In order to limit the number of outcomes statements, it may be necessary to formulate statements that include concepts of several courses or subareas in a program rather than writing a separate statement on each course. Having a lengthy list of outcomes to assess annually would be difficult. Possibly, some of the areas that do not get attention in an annual assessment program could be scheduled on a 3-year cycle. For those who are starting assessment programs, it may be best to take the advice of Wolff (1992), who encouraged starting small and building an assessment program on experience. There will always be time to add to the assessment program later or revise it. Current assessment practices are encouraging ongoing revisions not only of academic programs but also of assessment plans.

Criteria to Determine Success

Assessment planners should also define what constitutes a successful outcomes demonstration. Program supervisors and department chairs should be cautious about having expectations that are too low or too high. The percentage of graduates scoring in a certain percentile on standardized exams and the percentage of graduates getting jobs in discipline-related fields should be closely examined before committing the department to specific numbers in documenting success (Nichols, 1991).

SAMPLE MODELS OF ASSESSMENT

Two models are provided to offer a practical guide to creating an assessment plan. Both models were created by the author to serve as examples of radio/television and speech communication assessment plans.

Assessment Model 1: B.A. in Communication (Radio/Television Concentration)

The following assessment model for a broadcast program combines the Southern Association's suggestions and Nichols' suggestions in formulating an assessment plan. It includes an institutional mission statement, department mission statement, and adds criteria for success. Much of this model would be best implemented in a capstone course during the senior year (see chap. 7).

Institutional Mission Statement (Excerpt): The university provides curricular programs in undergraduate education that prepare students for competency in career-related fields.

Department Mission Statement: The Communication Department provides curricular programs to prepare speech communication and radio/television (R/TV) students with a high level of competency concerning knowledge and skills in career-related fields.

Program Goal: To equip broadcast students with the knowledge and skills necessary for careers related to radio and television or entry into a graduate school.

#1 Intended Outcome/Objective/Expected Result: Graduating R/TV students will be able to demonstrate knowledge of the broadcast discipline.

Assessment Procedure and Administration: All graduating seniors will take a locally developed criterion-referenced test based on broadcasting courses taken at the university. An assessment committee of faculty will score the exam.

Criteria for Success: Eighty percent of the students should score a grade of 80% or above.

#2 Intended Outcome/Objective/Expected Result: Graduating R/TV students will be able to demonstrate competency of audio and video skills.

Assessment Procedure and Administration: Each graduating senior will submit a portfolio containing samples of the student's audio and video projects. The portfolio will contain the following:

- a 3–5 minute telescoped air check with live commercial and/or news
- a 30–60 second radio commercial with script
- a 30–60 second live talent TV commercial with script
- a 2–4 minute television news package with at least two sound bites with script
- a video or audio project of student's choice

A Radio/TV faculty committee will evaluate portfolios based on published criteria of the department. Every 3 years portfolios will be selected at random and sent to outside evaluators from other institutions to be evaluated using the published criteria.

Criteria for Success: Eighty percent of the graduating seniors should have an average rating of satisfactory or better on the audio and video portions of the portfolio (ratings: excellent, satisfactory, and unsatisfactory).

#3 Intended Outcome/Objective/Expected Result: Graduating R/TV students will be able to demonstrate writing and research competencies related to broadcasting.

Assessment Procedure and Administration: Each graduating senior will submit a portfolio containing samples of writing and research projects. The portfolio will contain at least two writing projects that demonstrate the student's writing and research skills in broadcasting; one of the projects must have been written during the senior year. A faculty committee will evaluate portfolios based on published criteria of the department. Every 3 years portfolios will be selected at random and sent to outside evaluators from other institutions to be evaluated using the published criteria.

Criteria for Success: Eighty percent of the graduating seniors should have an average rating of satisfactory or better on the writing and research portion of the portfolio (ratings: excellent, satisfactory, and unsatisfactory).

#4 Intended Outcome/Objective/Expected Result: Graduating seniors will be prepared for employment in radio, television, communication-related fields, or admission to graduate studies.

Assessment Procedure and Administration: Graduating seniors will be given an attitudinal questionnaire annually. Alumni will be surveyed for information on graduate school admission or employment in broadcasting/communication-related fields. Employers and intern sponsors will be surveyed on performance of graduates. Both the alumni and the employer/intern sponsor surveys will be administered every 3 years. A faculty committee will evaluate the results of the surveys.

Criteria for Success: Eighty percent of the graduating seniors should respond positively regarding training and education received at the university. A majority responding to the alumni surveys should report successful employment in broadcasting/communication-related fields or successful entrance into graduate school. Eighty percent of employers and intern sponsors responding to the survey should give a favorable evaluation of the graduate.

Use Of Assessment Findings: The assessment committee will meet annually with the department chair to examine all assessment data and make recommendations for program improvements. Assessment results and recommendations for program improvements will be reported to the dean and the university assessment director. All graduating seniors will be given their assessment results.

Assessment Model 2: B.A. in Communication (Speech Communication Concentration)

The following assessment model for a speech communication program also integrates many of the Southern Association's and Nichols' suggestions for developing an assessment plan.

Institutional Mission Statement (Excerpt): The university provides curricular programs in undergraduate education that prepare students for competency in career-related fields.

Department Mission Statement: The Communication Department provides curricular programs to prepare speech communication and radio/television students with a high level of competency concerning knowledge and skills in career-related fields.

Program Goals:

I. To provide speech communication students with an opportunity to acquire a high level of skills and knowledge of both oral and written communication.

II. To prepare speech communication students for graduate school and/or professional careers in education or positions where superior communication skills are mandatory.

#1 Intended Outcome/Objective/Expected Result (Program Goal I): Students completing the baccalaureate program in communication with a concentration in speech communication will be able to demonstrate effective oral communication skills. The student will demonstrate effective skills in analysis, critical thinking, and problem solving.

> *Assessment Procedure and Administration:* During the senior year the student will submit a portfolio containing video samples of the student's oral presentations. The portfolio must contain a 5–10 minute persuasive or informative speech (on videotape) that the student delivered in the last three semesters at the university. The student's presentation should demonstrate skills in analysis, critical thinking, and problem solving. A faculty committee will evaluate the portfolio based on published criteria of the department. Every 3 years portfolios will be selected at random and sent to outside evaluators from other institutions to be evaluated using the published criteria.
>
> *Criteria for Success:* Eighty percent of the graduating seniors should have an average rating of satisfactory or higher on the video/oral portion of their portfolio. (Ratings: excellent, satisfactory, and unsatisfactory). Eighty percent of students should have an average score of satisfactory or higher in all eight public speaking competencies as identified by the Speech Communication Association's Committee on Assessment and Testing.

#2 Intended Outcome/Objective/Expected Result (Program Goal I): Graduating speech communication students will be able to demonstrate knowledge of the speech communication discipline.

Assessment Procedure and Administration: All graduating seniors will take a locally developed criterion-referenced test based on speech communication courses taken at the university. An assessment committee of faculty will score the exam.

Criteria for Success: Eighty percent of the students should score a grade of 80% or above.

#3 Intended Outcome/Objective/Expected Result (Program Goal I): Graduating speech communication students will be able to demonstrate effective written communication skills. The student will demonstrate an understanding of the theory and process of communication as well as demonstrating effective skills in analysis, critical thinking, problem solving, and evaluation.

Assessment Procedure and Administration: During the senior year the student will submit a portfolio containing writing assignments the student has collected over the 4 years at the university. These writing samples should demonstrate cognitive knowledge in the theory and process of communication as well as analysis, critical thinking, and problem solving. One of the writing assignments included in the portfolio must be a 3–5 page written critique evaluating a speech given by someone other than the graduating senior. A manuscript or video copy of the speech being critiqued should be included in the portfolio. A faculty committee will evaluate writing documents and the 3–5 page critique evaluating a speech based on published criteria of the department. Every 3 years portfolios will be selected at random and sent to outside evaluators from other institutions to be evaluated using the published criteria.

Criteria for Success: Eighty percent of the students should score a rating of satisfactory or higher on the writing and research portion of the portfolio (ratings: excellent, satisfactory, and unsatisfactory).

#4 Intended Outcome/Objective/Expected Result (Program Goal II): Speech communication students will be prepared for either employment or admission to graduate studies.

Assessment Procedure and Administration: Graduating seniors will be given an attitudinal questionnaire annually. Alumni will be surveyed for information on graduate school admission or employment in communication-related fields. Employers and intern sponsors will be surveyed on performance of graduates. Both the alumni and the employer/intern sponsor surveys will be administered every 3 years. A faculty committee will evaluate the results of the surveys.

Criteria for Success: Eighty percent of the graduating seniors should respond positively regarding their training and education received at the university. A majority responding to the alumni surveys should report successful employment in a communication-related field or successful entrance into graduate school. Eighty percent of employers and intern sponsors responding to the survey should give a favorable evaluation of the graduate.

Use of Assessment Findings: The assessment committee will meet annually with the department chair to examine all assessment data and make recommendations for program improvements. Assessment results and recommendations for program improvements will be reported to the dean and the university assessment director. All graduating seniors will be given their assessment results.

FINAL NOTE ON ASSESSMENT

Developing clearly articulated statements of intended student outcomes/expected results is a significant step in the assessment process. The regional accrediting associations realize that the assessment process is relatively new. Because they are not mandating a specific formula in how to develop an outcomes assessment program, they are providing much flexibility at the present time. As assessment procedures improve with experience, higher education will benefit.

APPENDIX A: GENERAL FRAMEWORK FOR AN ASSESSMENT PROGRAM

1. The assessment program should be a systematic plan based on a conceptual framework that links program goals to the institution's mission statement.
2. The assessment program should be an ongoing continuous self-evaluation process and not a periodic self-study that takes place every 5 to 10 years.
3. The assessment program should have institutionwide support and involve faculty participation and ownership.
4. The assessment program should be cost-effective.
5. The assessment program should articulate clear statements of intended student outcomes (expected results) that are clearly linked to program goals.
6. The assessment program should describe the procedures to be used to assess these intended outcomes and to show that goals are being met.

7. The assessment program should use multiple measures, both qualitative and quantitative.
8. The assessment program should show who will administer the assessment procedures and how the program will be administered.
9. The assessment program should show how assessment findings will be used for planning and making improvements in the academic program. Feedback should be provided to the institution and the student.
10. The assessment program should include a process for evaluating the assessment program itself.
11. The assessment plan should provide a specific time table.

APPENDIX B: ADDRESSES OF THE SIX REGIONAL ACCREDITING ASSOCIATIONS

Middle States Association of Colleges and Schools
Howard L. Simmons, Executive Director
Middle States Association of Colleges and Schools
3624 Market Street
Philadelphia, PA 19104
(215) 662-5606, Fax: (215) 662-5950

New England Association of Schools and Colleges
Charles M. Cook, Director
New England Association of Schools and Colleges
209 Burlington Road
Bedford, MA 01730
(617) 271-0022, Fax: (617) 271-0950

North Central Association of Colleges and Schools
Patricia A. Thrash, Executive Director
North Central Association of Colleges and Schools
159 North Dearborn Street
Chicago, IL 60601
(312) 263-0456, Fax: (312) 263-7462

Northwest Association of Schools and Colleges
Joseph A. Malik, Executive Director
Northwest Association of Schools and Colleges
3700 University Way, N.E.
Seattle, WA 98105
(206) 543-0195, Fax: (206) 685-4621

Southern Association of Colleges and Schools
James T. Rogers, Executive Director
Southern Association of Colleges and Schools
1866 Southern Lane
Decatur, GA 30033-4097
(404) 679-4500, Fax: (404) 679-4558

Western Association of Schools and Colleges
Stephen S. Weiner, Executive Director
Western Association of Schools and Colleges
P.O. Box 9990
Mills College
Oakland, CA 94613-0990
(510) 632-5000, Fax: (510) 632-8361

REFERENCES

Astin, A. W. (1993). *Assessment for excellence: The philosophy and practice of assessment and evaluation in higher education.* Phoenix, AZ: Oryx.

Christ, W. G., & Blanchard, R. O. (1993, April). *Mission statements, outcomes, and the new liberal arts: Assessing the new professionalism.* Paper presented at the annual meeting of the Broadcast Education Association, Las Vegas, NV.

Erwin, T. D. (1991). *Assessing student learning and development.* San Francisco: Jossey-Bass.

Galvin, K. (1992). Foundation for assessment: The mission, goals, and objectives. In E. A. Hay (Ed.), *Program assessment in speech communication* (pp. 21–24). Annandale, VA: Speech Communication Association.

Gardiner, L. F. (1989). *Planning for assessment: Mission statements, goals, and objectives.* Trenton: New Jersey State Department of Higher Education Library.

Hunt, G. T. (1992). The antecedents of program assessment. In E. A. Hay (Ed.), *Program assessment in speech communication* (pp. 12–14). Annandale, VA: Speech Communication Association.

Mayhew, P. H., & Simmons, H. L. (1990). Assessment in the Middle States Region. *NCA Quarterly, 65*(2), 375–379.

Middle States Association of Colleges and Schools Commission on Higher Education. (1992). *Characteristics of excellence in higher education: Standards for accreditation* (Rev. ed.). Philadelphia, PA: Author.

Middle States Association of Colleges and Schools Commission on Higher Education. (1990). *Framework for outcomes assessment.* Philadelphia, PA: Author.

New England Association of Schools & Colleges Commission on Institutions of Higher Education. (1992). *Standards for accreditation.* Winchester, MA: Author.

Nichols, J. O. (1991). *The departmental guide to implementation of student outcomes assessment and institutional effectiveness.* New York: Agathon.

North Central Association Commission on Institutions of Higher Education. (1992a). Assessment: Comments from the APR process. *Briefing, 10*(3), 8.

North Central Association Commission on Institutions of Higher Education. (1992b). *A guide to self-study for commission evaluation 1992–93.* Chicago, IL: Author.

Northwest Association of Schools and Colleges Commission on Colleges. (1992). *Accreditation handbook.* Seattle, WA: Author.

Rogers, J. T. (1990). Assessment in the Southern Commission on Colleges. *NCA Quarterly, 65*(2), 397–400.

Sims, S. J. (1992). *Student outcomes assessment.* New York: Greenwood.

Southern Association of Colleges and Schools Commission on Colleges. (1992a). *Criteria for accreditation* (8th ed.). Decatur, GA: Author.

Southern Association of Colleges and Schools Commission on Colleges. (1992b). *Resource manual on institutional effectiveness* (3rd ed.). Decatur, GA: Author.

Spady, W. G. (1992). *It's time to take a close look at outcome-based education.* Unpublished manuscript, The High Success Network, Eagle, CO.

Thrash, P. A. (1990). Assessment in the North Central Region. *NCA Quarterly, 65*(2), 385–391.

Western Association of Schools and Colleges Accrediting Commission for Senior Colleges and Universities. (1992). *Achieving institutional effectiveness through assessment: A resource manual to support WASC institutions.* Oakland, CA: Author.

Wolff, R. A. (1992). Assessment and accreditation: A shotgun marriage? In Western Association of Schools and Colleges Accrediting Commission for Senior Colleges and Universities. *Achieving institutional effectiveness through assessment: A resource manual to support WASC institutions* (pp. 39–48). Oakland, CA: Western Association of Schools and Colleges.

Wolff, R. A. (1990). Assessment in the Western Accrediting Commission for Senior Colleges and Universities. *NCA Quarterly, 65*(2), 403–413.

II

Broad Assessment Strategies

4

Teaching Evaluation

W. James Potter
Indiana University

The primary challenge of faculty evaluation is to provide clear criteria for performance, especially in the area of teaching. The key to developing these clear criteria is to examine carefully the academic culture and the expectations (or learning styles) of students. In assembling this information into a definition of good teaching, three strategies can be used: (a) match strategy (assuming that student expectations are primary, the key is to maximize student satisfaction by matching students' learning styles to corresponding faculty strengths), (b) canon strategy (believing that certain knowledge and skills must be taught, the key is matching faculty strengths with certain kinds of information), and (c) liberal strategy (recognizing that a full learning experience requires a kaleidoscope of experiences for the student, the key is to provide students with the fullest range possible).

INTRODUCTION

In general, evaluation essentially involves three tasks: (a) setting the criteria, (b) gathering evidence, and (c) comparing the evidence to the criteria. If the first two of these tasks have been performed properly, the third task is very simple. With the evaluation of teaching in higher education, the persistent problem has been the setting of clear criteria. This chapter is designed to help faculty think through that problem and move toward a clearer statement about what quality teaching means (or should mean) to the decision makers at academic institutions.

This chapter exhibits three characteristics as it addresses the problem of developing good teaching criteria. First, there is a focus on the *what* of teaching evaluation, rather than the *how*. The *how* has been addressed well in other books. For example, scholars have written about the techniques of student rating forms (Doyle, 1975; Seldin, 1980; for a lengthy annotated bibliography on the early research on this topic see Miller, 1974), examination of course materials (such as syllabi, handouts, tests, etc.; Seldin, 1991), analysis of grading patterns and/or student learning, and colleagues observing teaching (for example, see Centra, 1979b; Cohen & McKeachie, 1980; French-Lasovik, 1982; Hoyt, 1982; Lewis & Barber, 1986). Much has been written about the strengths and weaknesses of each of these, and the general conclusion is that it is best to use a combination of methods (Centra, 1979a; French-Lasovik, 1982; Fuhrmann & Grasha, 1983; Grasha, 1977; McKeachie, 1978). These writings provide clear guidance into the technology of data gathering, but they do not help one to determine what should be the criteria for quality teaching.

A second characteristic of this chapter is its mid-level approach to teaching criteria. Almost all of the criteria statements about teaching are either very general or very reductionistic. Although both of these types of criteria statements are better than no criteria, they each have serious problems. General statements are good for providing a broad philosophical perspective on teaching, but they are usually unmeasurable, because they are too abstract. To illustrate, in most schools there is a general definition of good teaching that is displayed in tenure/promotion guidelines. It usually reads something like: "Faculty should deliver quality teaching." Because this is very general it is not of much help to faculty. Some statements may elaborate a bit, such as: "Quality teaching helps students understand the beauty and complexity of the world in which they live." Again this is very general. Although general statements like these allude to very worthy teaching goals, they are impossible to measure and therefore trigger frustrating debates about whether faculty member X has achieved the goal, and if so, has she achieved it "enough" to warrant tenure and promotion? Or, has she achieved it better than faculty member Y, and if so, who gets merit raises and how much?

In contrast to these general perspective statements as teaching criteria are lists of specific behaviors. These have the advantage of providing detailed guidance to faculty as well as decision makers. They are relatively easy to measure, but they fail to capture the real essence of teaching. For example, faculty members might meet all their classes, hold office hours, give out study guides, have the correct number of tests and papers, *but* still be regarded by students and faculty as poor teachers. Quality teaching is not something that can be adequately captured in a reductionistic list of behaviors. There is a synergy in the teaching enterprise that makes quality inexplicable at this reductionistic level. This is why a higher order approach to determining criteria is needed. But to move to a level too abstract to measure is also a mistake. Therefore this chapter focuses on mid-level type criteria.

A third characteristic of this chapter is its focus on practical information. The intention is to present useful perspectives that will help faculty develop their own criteria for their own particular setting, whether it be a department in a large university, a small liberal arts college, a division within a community college, or even for themselves. This chapter does not argue for a single predominant prescription for excellence in teaching. Excellence comes in many forms and grows out of the values of each institution.

This chapter is organized into four sections. The first section deals with level of criteria ranging from institutional goals to student learning. The second section, which presents a variety of student expectations and personalities, shows that the consideration of student learning styles is a very important part of the mix of information that must be considered when developing criteria. The third section presents examples of criteria that will result from using this method, and the fourth section discusses the use of criteria in summative and formative contexts.

LEVEL OF CRITERIA

Faculty have two teaching constituencies that they must satisfy: the institution and the student. The institutional expectations are foundational in the sense that they must be met first. But even if they are met, this does not guarantee that the higher level expectations will also be met. For example, institutions have clearly stated expectations about when classes should begin, what grading procedures are acceptable, when grades should be filed, and behaviors that faculty are not permitted to exhibit in the classroom (racial/gender slurs) or outside the classroom (dating students). There are also unwritten expectations about how faculty members should dress, how much work should be assigned, and the like. These elements, especially the unwritten rules, are produced by the culture of the organization. An exercise in criteria writing must be sensitive to these elements (see chap. 2).

Besides institutional expectations, there are student expectations which have the components of satisfaction and learning. Student satisfaction goals are rarely stated explicitly. The feeling is that the more students are satisfied with a course, the better it is. But rarely is there careful thinking concerning *what* about the course students should be satisfied with, or *how* satisfied they should be in order for the course to be considered "good." Instead, there is a backwards reasoning process from data on course evaluation forms to criteria. For example, there are operational definitions of good teaching embedded in student course evaluation instruments. Rarely do faculty have any input into the design of these. Sometimes they can add their own supplementary items on a course-by-course basis, but this piecemeal process does not address the problem of a lack of front-end thinking about the nature of student satisfaction with courses. Instead, it continues to reify the partial definitions that can be handled in optscan computer programs. As if the reductionistic definitions are not problem enough, the interpretation of the computer printouts offers an opportunity for even more serious abuse. In many departments, the interpretation creates a specious competition among faculty where decision makers ignore what the numbers mean in terms of student input and instead compare all courses in the department to a mean rating. This guarantees that half the courses will be rated below the mean, and these submean courses are interpreted as poor ones, even though students may have been very satisfied with all the courses in the department. In short, students might have thought all courses in a department were very good, but this system of interpretation would result in half the courses being regarded as below average by decision makers. This shift in meaning invalidates the data.

Student learning is usually considered the ultimate goal of a course. No one would argue this point, but there is a wide range of opinion concerning what learning is. Should the memorization of info-bits be considered learning? Or should we limit our focus to higher level skills such as analysis, synthesis, and problem solving? What about the skills of writing, speaking, arguing, questioning, quantitative reasoning, mechanical ability, and compositional spatial ability? In communications, all of these things are important—sometimes in the same course (see chap. 5, 6, and 7).

What further complicates this problem is that learning is not linear. Especially with skills, students must "pay a lot of dues" before they begin to see the payback. Teachers of introductory classes might do an excellent job of getting students to pay their dues, but there is not much payback in terms of sophistication of reasoning. Then later, a teacher doing a poor job in an advanced seminar sees students far out on the learning curve performing very well; should this later teacher get credit for the obvious learning that students are demonstrating even though the learning is much more a product of earlier dues paying in rigorous introductory courses?

Exercise: Addressing Issues About Level of Criteria

To get a full picture about what the teaching criteria are at your institution, perform the following exercise. Start by making a grid on a piece of paper (see Appendix A). Create three horizontal and three vertical blocks on the page. Label the three rows: Institutional Goals, Student Satisfaction Goals, and Student Learning Goals. Label the three columns: Goals, Written Criteria, and Unwritten Criteria. Now fill in the six blocks with all the information about teaching criteria that you can find. Look at written materials, such as memos, bulletins, catalogs, accreditation guidelines, evaluation reports, faculty contracts, and so on. Interview faculty, administrators, and students, and observe behaviors.

In gathering this information, you will need to be an ethnographer. Because the environment you will be studying is your own, you must be careful that you do not overlook the important elements in your culture that you have come to take for granted. The challenge is to become more sensitive to your surroundings and to organize your perceptions into patterns.

When you feel you have gathered all the information you can, study the patterns on the grid. Are some of the boxes empty and others overflowing? Is there more in the unwritten criteria column than in the written criteria column? The pattern of information will tell you a lot about what is valued (and what is ignored) in your academic unit.

Label this grid *Information about Teaching Criteria,* and on another sheet of paper create the same three-line (institutional goals, student satisfaction goals, and student learning goals) by two-column (written criteria and unwritten criteria) grid. Label this second grid *Ideal Teaching Criteria.*

The next step in this exercise can be done individually, but it is more useful to undertake it as a group discussion. Look at your information grid and think about what you feel should be changed in order to provide a stronger set of guidance about teaching goals. Are there too many unwritten rules? If so, should they be formalized as written rules or should they be eliminated? Is there too much focus at one level (such as institutional goals) and not enough at another (such as student learning)?

The purpose of this exercise is to become more sensitive to what Blanchard and Christ (1993) called a "unit's culture"(pp. 99–100). They pointed out that what we use as our operating assumptions about what we do is not always the same as what others perceive. This is why it is important to both: (a) gather information from the total array of sources, and (b) discuss this information openly so that people can compare their perceptions to those of others. This process results in the development of a better set of criteria reflected on the Ideal Teaching Criteria sheet. What makes this set better is that it is the product of a conscious process of confronting the values embedded, and often hidden, in the environment. Even if there are no changes felt warranted (where Ideal Teaching Criteria sheet replicates the same points on the Information sheet), the resulting articulation of teaching criteria is still better, because you and your colleagues will gain a higher level of awareness of the criteria as well as the rationale that support them.

STUDENT LEARNING STYLES

No one would argue that students are not an important part of the instructional process or that their input should be excluded from the evaluation of teaching. However, what is largely ignored is the fact that students exhibit widely differing expectations for their education, their courses, and their instructors. When student input is solicited, it is usually measured through course rating forms. Sometimes the forms will allow special questions to distinguish among courses, such as large lecture courses, labs, and seminars; *but all these forms are based on the assumption that all students are alike*. But there are far more profound differences among students than there are among courses.

Students differ from each other in terms of skills, motivations, background information, and in many other ways. The differences that are most relevant for our discussion of teaching criteria are in the area of instructional expectations. These expectations have been shown to be related to how a student reacts to a course in terms of satisfaction and learning (see Emanuel & Potter, 1992; Potter & Emanuel, 1990).

Listed on the following pages are 16 student learning styles that are grouped into five categories: Dependent, Independent, Competitive, Participant, and Avoidant (see Appendix B). The 16 profiles illustrate the differences in general expectations students have for education, and these expectations can be translated to reactions for individual types of courses and faculty. The styles focus on student expectations for instructional situations and as such are reflected in expectations for faculty, assignments, tests, pace of course, types of projects, and students' own work habits.

The Dependent Styles

Dependent students seek direction from authorities such as professors and texts. Course content is a commodity to be acquired, and the best professors are those who provide the greatest amount of this commodity at the lowest cost to the student. There are four types: the Achiever, the Emulator, the Consumer, and the Hopeful Sponge.

Achievers have very clear goals and know how to reach them successfully. Achievers enmesh themselves strongly in the campus and value it highly. They see college life as a platform for achievement, so they contribute whatever they can to strengthen that platform that supports them. They also know that college is the foundation for a career, so they make the most of college opportunities.

They are opinion leaders. They do not create new trends, but because they are astute observers of dress and behavior, they have the ability to popularize those trends.

In the classroom, they are spotted by the professor and the other classmates as the good students. This can lead to a halo effect, with which professors and students still perceive achievement even on those days when they are unprepared for class. Although they have this leadership power, they do not exploit it in class. There is a temptation to take over the class, but they usually resist, unless they feel that the course is not providing a proper challenge. Then they will try to do things to change the course but do them in a constructive manner rather than making a power play.

Emulators want to be Achievers but can never quite make it. They work hard (or think they are working hard), but they miss getting the rewards that the Achievers do. The reason for this is that they are missing a key ingredient (IQ, study skills, background knowledge, motivation, proper guidance, direction, or some important personality trait). Sometimes their college careers follow the structure of a tragic play, where a fatal flaw presents itself as an insurmountable barrier as they work even harder to achieve a goal that they can never attain. However, few Emulators are truly tragic. They have flaws, but the really damaging factor that prevents them from achieving more is usually a faulty perception of themselves.

Consumers regard courses as tangible products. The facts within the courses are commodities. Consumers focus on getting the highest value from their college experience. They define value in basic economic terms of getting the most in return for the least.

What do Consumers want to get from their college experience? There are several major commodities, and Consumers differ in terms of which commodity they are buying. These commodities are listed in a roughly descending order in terms of their present popularity to Consumers: positioning for a good-entry level job on an exciting and rewarding career path, a prestigious degree, high grade point average (GPA), and knowledge.

For Consumers, course effort is the major factor in the value equation. It is the factor they must face everyday, and it is very concrete. Course effort includes all of the following and more: going to class, taking class notes, reading the text, going to the library and getting reserve materials, organizing notes, studying for exams, and so on. If there is a term paper, it also includes thinking up a topic, tracking down books in the library, taking notes, arranging thoughts, writing the paper, editing, typing, copying, and so on. It might also include group projects, simulations, field trips, an internship, and so on.

Consumers are motivated to increase the value of the course. This can be done in several ways. During registration, they seek to enroll in the most stimulating and exciting courses. In a practical sense, this means the courses that interest them the most, so it will not be a drag to go to class. Also, it could mean taking courses given by those professors who are the most skillful at making otherwise boring classes interesting and informative. After students are enrolled in their courses, they decide what grade they want, then regulate their effort to achieve that grade. If they feel that they are not getting enough value out of the course (too much work for the grade), then they seek to reduce their costs. When there is a high gap (lots of work required with little interesting information coming back), they are strongly motivated to cut their costs by waiting until the last minute to cram for a test.

Hopeful Sponges are very passive students in class, where they sit quietly hoping to absorb all the information needed in order to do well in the course. For them a good course is one where they are not bored by class and where they can listen and pick up all the information they will need to do well on tests.

They hate group projects, primarily because they must work outside of class, and this exposes their nonperformance to other students who work hard. They also do not like research papers, because searching for information and then organizing it is hard work. If the professor passes out examples of good papers, then they are happier because then they can reduce the exercise of writing a paper to a "fill in the blanks" task. In essence they can copy the examples in form and structure and merely fill in their own information and opinions in the appropriate places.

The Independent Styles

Independent students take great pride in determining their own goals and taking responsibility for their own learning. The best professors are those who allow freedom for students to follow their own course and help them develop their own strategies for success. There are three types: the Searcher, the Pathfinder, and the Stimulate-Me.

Searchers are rugged individualists. They like the challenge of discovery and are not afraid to take big risks in the searching. Searchers do not follow the syllabus. They abhor written exams, preferring instead to have their skills tested in real-life experiences. They will read the texts and other materials, but will do so selectively. Their focus is on what interests them. Professors who look for student dedication, enthusiasm, energy, and self-starting ability will be impressed with Searchers, but professors who grade students on their inventory of knowledge within the core material will find Searchers at the very low end of the grading distribution.

They do not have formal goals for their search; there is no destination for this journey. The searching itself is what is valued. Instead of goals, they reach plateaus. A plateau is a place in the searching where students feel that the searching is worth it as they survey the territory they have covered. The plateau is not a pinnacle in the sense that it is an end point to the journey or a finishing of a task. Rather it is a place of reward and satisfaction along the journey.

Pathfinders are very much like Searchers, but there is one major difference. Pathfinders have a very clear idea about what goals they want to achieve. Like Searchers, Pathfinders want to find their own way. They do not want someone else to tell them what path to take. Their independence is rooted in a distrust for the effectiveness or efficiency of existing methods. They feel they can find a better way. Given a free reign they could accomplish amazing feats of learning and creativity.

They also feel that they can learn much better when they figure something out for themselves. In this way, the knowledge is made a part of them because it was gained through a struggle rather than simply handed to them.

The *Stimulate-Me* students appear to be independent on the surface, because they do not appear to be highly engaged in the course. In fact, they take a very skeptical view that the course can provide them anything of value. They sit back and wait to be aroused. When they find an interesting element of information in a course, they use it as a door into an adventure and quickly exit through that door off onto a tangent that they pursue with great enthusiasm. They will learn more about that element than anyone else in the course, even far more than the professor. However, in doing so, they will ignore all other topics in the course.

They attend class in a search for stimulating ideas. They may take many courses without hearing anything that stimulates them. However, when they do get stimulated, they come alive and work hard—not necessarily on the projects the professor has put into the course. They stay with the idea that stimulated them and work with it to push it and expand on it as long as it excites them. This may take them on their own journey to the library, to experts, and to special projects of their own.

The Competitive Styles

Competitive students regard the elements of the course as playing pieces in a game. The best professors are those who set up an interesting and challenging game, then carefully enforce the rules so the best players win. There are three types: the Gamer, the High Roller, and the Small Changer.

Gamers regard college (and most of life) primarily as a contest. In the early stages of any experience (college, a particular course, a relationship, etc.), Gamers are quiet as they carefully observe everything in an effort to figure out the rules. Once they feel they have a handle on how things operate, they will begin testing the rules to determine if they really hold. When they are satisfied they know the real rules, they will begin playing. Their goal is playing to win and making sure others know they are winning.

Their first task in a course is to identify the rules. Some of these rules are formal and easy to spot. For example, professors will list rules for class attendance, for earning points on tests and papers, and so on. But, in each class, there are also many other unwritten rules, such as how to act around the professor, how to work around deadlines, how many classes can be cut, and so on. Once they understand the rules, they begin to play the game. If acquiring knowledge is required to get points, then Gamers will go for a lot of knowledge. But they will not be afraid to cash in some knowledge for something else that will get them more points. While they are playing, they see themselves on a stage along with the other players. As they make a particularly good play, they expect praise (or at least a look of fear or respect in the eyes of other players). If they do not get these minirewards while they are playing, the game will lose its excitement for them.

The *High Roller* students appear like Gamers in their fundamental view of education. They look for the rules then seek to experience college primarily as a game. However, unlike the Gamer, High Rollers are attracted to big risks. Whereas Gamers are driven by a need to play the game, High Rollers are motivated by a need to feel risk—the bigger the better, so High Rollers will not play just any game. They are looking for the big game, such as seeing if they can get an A out of a professor after cutting almost all the classes.

The *Small Changer* students are like Gamers, but they are usually very risk averse. They focus on the reward side of the equation, and avoid the risk or work side. Like Gamers and High Rollers, they observe situations to try and figure out the rules, then they begin playing by the rules. If they are able to identify the correct rules and if they are able to play the game well, then there is no problem. However, Small Changers usually put only average (or below-average) effort into a course. When they get behind in a course, they look for an easy way out rather than working harder. They look for loopholes in the rules. When they cannot find loopholes or ways around the rules, they seek to change them, usually by trying to lower the standards of grading or by reducing the amount of work in the course. Their game then shifts to making small changes in the course so they can be more successful. Sometimes they will be forced to take a risk because they are bored, run out of time, lack motivation, and so on; but these risks are always small.

The Participant Styles

Participant students enjoy being a part of a system of activities that requires their time and energy in return for contact with others. The best professors are those who offer a lot of class activities to involve students. There are four kinds: the Networker, the Intellectual Partier, the Social Partier, and the Altruistic Hero.

Networkers focus on people. They like being around other people and having lots of things to do. But they are not just social party animals; they also like being around others in class and in campus organizations. Being with others in all sorts of situations keeps them stimulated and feeling good. They do not make a sharp distinction between their studies and their social life; it is all part of the same pattern. In class, they interact with other students with ease, much like at a party. At a party, they feel comfortable discussing a wide range of experiences including what is happening in classes.

They judge success in college by the number of people they know and are known by. They feel connected when they know a wide range of people. What they are connected to is less important to them than that the feeling that those connections are many and strong. This is why they join lots of clubs and organizations, and why they go to class and talk a lot before and after class. They intuitively know that people will help them get ahead in classes and in life. Through their interactions, they find the courses they want to take and get practical information about how to do well in the courses. They also make contacts for jobs after graduation. But they are not motivated by the end rewards; that is, they are not calculating in determining to meet only those people who can help them the most. Instead, they are motivated merely to increase their contacts among all kinds of people.

They are what psychologists would label extroverts, because they feel energy flow from others when they are in social situations. Whereas many people might get exhausted by talking to different kinds of people all day, Networkers feel depressed and exhausted when they are cut off from others.

The *Intellectual Partier* students, like Networkers, love being around other people. On the surface, they might look like a Networker, because they participate in lots of different kinds of groups. But their reasons for participation are very different. Intellectual Partiers are looking for a certain type of person—someone who loves to discuss and argue. They try to build a group of these people.

When they get together, it is a party. It might not have all the trappings of a party (music, dancing, etc.) but it is a party nonetheless, because it is a social activity that is play for the participants. These parties are often late-night bull sessions or discussions over coffee in the commons.

They are bored by listening to people recite facts or definitions. They want to see positions debated and ideologies espoused or demolished. In class they want their minds engaged in a running debate with their professors. They do not like courses where the information is reduced to simple facts. Instead they like courses where great ideas are rolled out and rotated through various interpretations. This freedom to interpret engages their minds and hearts.

Social Partiers focus on other people in a nonserious context. They feel a sense of accomplishment when meeting new people and keeping many friendships going. College excites them, because there are so many people their own age with similar lifestyles to their own.

They like going to class, not because they might acquire facts in the course, but because they will see their friends and can make plans for after class. During class, they find it hard to concentrate on the professor or the material. Instead, they are watching other classmates and are actively processing information about how people look, what they are wearing, and how they act. To them a good class does not mean the professor has conveyed interesting information to them. Instead, a good class is one where they have observed some interesting things about their classmates and have engaged their imaginations.

The *Altruistic Hero* students define themselves in terms of helping others. They love to tutor, not to impress others or to have more friends, but because they simply get satisfaction out of helping others. It makes them feel a central part of the general mission of higher education. They like being around other people a lot, because they feel people are more important than buildings or courses or facts. But they are not like the Intellectual Partiers, who often put down others so they can feel good. And they are not like the Social Partiers, who want lots of friends and therefore assemble a large entourage to build a more fun environment. Altruistic Heroes do things for other people, and that makes them feel good. However, the service they provide to others is not a calculating tactic designed primarily to give them pleasure. They do not feel pleasure unless the person they are trying to help truly benefits. In sharing their notes, their time, and their sympathetic ear, they feel that they are making other people better and this makes the college a little better.

In class they often ask questions of clarification. They rarely challenge a professor. When they do, it is because they feel a great sense of injustice committed against the class or one of its members. The Altruistic Hero will step into the situation with a righteous innocence believing that merely pointing out the wrong to the professor will bring about an immediate change. But speaking up often puts the student in great danger if it results in the professor being embarrassed. However, the Altruistic Hero does not consider this. If the injustice hurts, then no risk is too great to bring about a change.

The Avoidant Styles

Avoidant students dislike their courses and seek to reduce their contact and involvement. The best professors are those who ask as little as possible. There are two kinds: the Sprinter and the Clueless Marginal.

The *Sprinter* students hate everything about college. However,they have a very strong motivation. Their clear goal is to beat the place and graduate rather than allowing the place to beat them, and they want to achieve this goal as quickly as possible. There is no joy or excitement to their learning.

They will take outrageously heavy loads of easy courses, and be angry when they have to do any work for the course, trying instead to get reductions in assignments. When necessary, they will do the work, but resent it and get it done as quickly as possible.

They interact with other students as little as possible. When they do talk to other students, they ask about shortcuts to work. They do not want to make friends, because they do not want to develop any reason to stay around longer than the absolute minimum. Also, friends would require their time, and they feel very overworked and exhausted most of the time.

Clueless Marginals are in colleges because someone forced them to be there. They stay because they do not know what else to do or because it is a lesser evil than the alternatives. They have no goals and no motivation. They usually do not last very long unless they can evolve into a different style. On the surface they may appear somewhat like the Independent style types, because they do not engage in the course. They look like they may be seeking their own path. But unlike the Independent styles, they are not looking for a point of departure from the course where they will fashion their own learning path. Instead, they are looking to get out of the course as quickly as possible.

There is no motivation here. If they had clear career goals and college was preventing them from getting on with their career, then they should be advised to drop out of college. Their motivation would then take them into their career path where they would finally be able to work on something they want. But that is not the case with Clueless Marginals. They do not have an alternative that is more attractive than college, and college is very *unattractive* to them. Typically, they end up failing courses and dropping out. Then they get a job, but do not feel very motivated to work hard and soon leave for something else.

They often cut classes. When they attend a class, they usually sit in an inconspicuous place while their minds wander. They may fantasize about sports, music, or parties. But with sports, they are frustrated because they do not have the talent or drive to really play and the same is true for music. They like to go to parties, but they are passive and have a hard time enjoying themselves.

Exercise: Addressing Issues About Student Styles

The task of addressing student styles has two components. First, faculty must identify what styles are most prevalent in their academic unit. Second, faculty must decide what to do about the student profiles that are identified.

The first task of identifying the student styles is the easier of the two. Student styles are easy to identify by simply observing the way students behave in and out of class.

Communication students exhibit different styles in general compared to students with other majors, and even within communication, there is a variety of profiles (see Potter & Clark, 1991). For example, students interested in technical areas such as law or research are more likely to have Dependent-type styles; students in more creative areas such as writing and production are more likely to be Independent; students in advertising, more Competitive. There are, of course, students who are exceptions to the dominant profile within each type of communication subtrack. Therefore, it is important not to take style stereotypes for granted and instead to assess the student styles periodically in courses and across the instructional unit (for a summary of styles see Appendix B).

TEACHING STRATEGIES

Once the dominant styles have been identified, there is a more philosophical question that must be addressed: How do faculty respond to the information about the dominant style and the other styles exhibited in their department or academic unit? Working toward an answer to this question illuminates faculty values in the academic unit, especially if faculty engage in a discussion with their colleagues. There are three perspectives on teaching and curriculum development that can be used as strategies in addressing this question: (a) match strategy (striving to meet student satisfactions by giving the students what they want), (b) canon strategy (being guided by the importance of certain traditional bodies of knowledge), and (c) liberal arts strategy (recognizing that a full learning experience requires a kaleidoscope of instructional challenges, so the key is to provide students with the fullest range possible). Each of these perspectives is very different in terms of implications for teaching evaluation. Each perspective and its implications are explored in the following sections.

Match Perspective

The essence of match perspective is reducing the gap between students' expectations and faculty performance. If students request more specific guidance (Dependent style), then faculty should provide it. If students want more flexibility and freedom (Independent), then faculty should provide that. And if students want less work (Avoidant), then faculty should cut back the course requirements. When faculty respond as students want, there is a match and student satisfaction is maximized. However, this satisfaction might or might not lead to higher levels of learning.

Faculty who operate under a match perspective have one of three tactics available to them to achieve a successful teaching environment. First, faculty can convert to the students' position. This is the consumer marketing tactic. Faculty who find that students expect something different from the course than they had planned will find out what those student expectations are and seek to fulfill them. A second tactic is to achieve a match by converting students to one's own way of thinking. This is the educational evangelical tactic, in which faculty will seek to change student expectations. Once students are converted, they experience a match between their new expectations and what is delivered in the course. The third tactic is one of negotiation. This tactic is the one used most often because of its moderate and flexible nature. To apply this tactic well, faculty must continually monitor the attitudes of students and continually assess performance in meeting their needs (see chap. 5).

Canon Strategy

Canon strategy is the belief that there is a core of knowledge and skills at the center of one's discipline. The faculty have spent years learning this canon and it is their primary task to pass it along to the next generation. A college education is synonymous with learning this canon across all the relevant disciplines. Students may or may not like having to learn all of the canon, but their attitudes are not relevant and do not influence the canon.

Many critics of higher education point to the breakdown of the canon idea as the major problem with education (Bloom, 1987; D'Souza, 1991; Hirsch, 1987). When education is defined in terms of a canon, pluralism becomes a problem, not a strength. The culture is weakened when education does not make the next generation literate in a core set of ideas.

Among students, the Intellectual Partier along with the Dependent styles feel most comfortable with the canon perspective. However, if professors can engage the Competitive and Independent students, this could result in high levels of learning and satisfaction, but it presents much more of a challenge to faculty.

Liberal Education Perspective

The liberal education perspective is the belief that higher education offers a kaleidoscope of knowledge, skills, and experiences. As for knowledge, students should sample from the range of courses across the university. Only in this way can they develop their analytical skills in determining what are the common themes and the rich uniqueness that define human endeavor. In short, the greater the diversity in the mix, the richer the learning environment. For a good discussion of differing views on a liberal arts education, see the first chapter of Blanchard and Christ (1993).

Teaching itself should be part of this mix. It follows then that teaching should be experienced in a variety of formats and that even exposure to bad teaching can be beneficial, because it would force students to engage their analysis of the educational experience itself to the deepest level. This is not to say that departments should seek out bad teachers and hire them to strengthen their programs. Instead, faculty should attempt to do the best they can, but because there are so many different styles and perspectives on teaching, some styles will seem as bad to certain students in certain situations. In these instances, a broad perspective on education would allow students, faculty, and administrators to see the variety as a strength, because the worst that happens in such a situation is that students learn something new about themselves and about the educational enterprise. Even if they do not learn much of the course content, they will still be sharpening their skills of perception, analysis, and argumentation. They are developing a point of view, and that is one of the aims of *higher* education. The liberal arts perspective should allow for the widest range of teaching styles.

EXAMPLES OF CRITERIA

Given the perspectives already mentioned, there are many teaching criteria statements that could be developed. To illustrate some of these, three situations are presented as examples. These examples do not represent the most typical criteria, but instead illuminate interesting points in the range.

Example 1

Let us say your department is part of a state university system where the legislators feel that the needs of the students are primary. Your department has been losing enrollment over the years, so the faculty believe it is essential to maximize student satisfaction. Given these characteristics in the environment, you feel it is best to use a match perspective. You examine the styles of the students that take courses in your department (especially those who are majors) and find that there is a dominant profile, which is in the Competitive family. Therefore the goal of your criteria is to direct faculty to focus on increasing satisfaction among competitive students.

You write a set of student satisfaction criteria that could include some of the following statements. In all courses, faculty should instill a spirit of healthy competition by: (a) designing projects where students need to compete for resources and rewards with other students, (b) providing continual feedback to all students so they always know where they stand relative to other students, (c) maximize the range of rewards so all students have a good chance of being rewarded, and (d) making the presentation of rewards as public as possible so all students can learn from the successful examples. Faculty must grade all work fairly and always make standards explicit so that even the impression of favoritism is always avoided. Faculty should design competitive projects so that students learn to compete both as individuals and as part of a team. Because team-based competition develops the skills of cooperation and leadership, faculty should seek out competitions outside the department in order to: (a) provide students with the experience of competing in wider and more challenging arenas, and (b) increase the visibility and reputation of the department.

Example 2

In this next example, let us say your department is part of a small, religious liberal arts college where the students have a solid academic background. The faculty members in your department, and the institution itself, strongly believe in a canon of knowledge. Your examination of student behaviors convinces you that there is a dominant style and that it is in the Dependent family; that is, students are very goal directed, but they need faculty to tell them what those goals are and how to achieve them. Therefore the goal of your teaching criteria is to direct faculty to focus on guiding students toward a mastery learning of each element in the canon.

You write a set of student learning criteria that could include some of the following statements. Students will learn _____ (fill in the blank with learning objectives from the curriculum and course syllabi). Students will develop an appreciation for the principles embodied in their courses and will begin to model their behavior throughout life on those principles. Students will develop an interest in exposing themselves to works outside the canon and be able to apply critical abilities to see how they either contribute to the ideals in the canon or how they exhibit elements inferior to those in the canon.

Example 3

In this last example, let us say your department includes many subtracks of communication (journalism, rhetoric, interpersonal, advertising, and theatre). The faculty regard this diversity within one department as a real strength and have designed the curriculum to require students to take several courses in each of the component areas so as to receive a broad-based, liberal education. This is what Blanchard and Christ (1993) advocated as a blueprint for what they call the *new professionalism*. In order to avoid fragmentation in the curriculum, Blanchard and Christ (1993) proposed an enriched major that would consist of a conceptual core, a linkage to "broader ethical, social, economic, and political contexts" (p. 49), and a "hands on" component that provides experience using the media. Such a curriculum most likely would attract students with many different learning styles. The conceptual core would attract dependent students, the linkage component would attract independent students, and the experiential component would attract collaborative and participative students. None of these styles would be the predominant learning style. In such a case, there would be a temptation to compartmentalize the department into tracks where each track has its own unique set of criteria and therefore an appeal for only a certain type of student. But compartmentalization would go against the grain of the new professionalism as advocated by Blanchard and Christ (1993). Instead, they wrote that there should be a unification of purpose within a department. This suggests a single set of criteria for all students majoring in the department. Let us say you decide to write a single set of teaching criteria for the entire department. Such a set would include statements such as the following: Students will learn to appreciate all the diverse facets within the broader field of communication. Students will become expert in one area, and literate in all. Students will be able to compare and contrast viewpoints across the different areas. Then part of a student's education will be to learn how to interact with other types of students.

The criteria in all three examples aim for the middle range; that is, they avoid the extremes of being too general to be measurable and of being too reductionistic to miss the essence of teaching excellence. They attempt to provide clear guidance to the faculty about what will be rewarded, and each encapsulates a unique departmental vision that grows out of the existing needs and culture in the academic unit.

There is no warehouse of teaching criteria where successful lists can be ordered and transplanted into any environment. By looking at the three examples given, it should be clear that good teaching criteria must come from the culture of the institution and from an understanding of the students. When this is realized, the development of teaching criteria can be more successful. Because the development of criteria for teaching excellence begins with a stronger foundation, the resulting criteria have a greater chance of being useful to faculty, administrators, and students.

The examples should also make it clear that there is a wide range of criteria for excellence in teaching. There is not one single definition and there is no best formula. Teaching excellence means something very different in the three examples. If the criteria in the first example were applied in the second or third examples, the results would be disastrous.

SUMMATIVE AND FORMATIVE CONTEXTS

Teaching criteria are typically used in a summative context; that is, they are used as standards against which our performance is judged for the purpose of making some kind of a decision, such as merit raises, promotion, or tenure. Under the match perspective, faculty members who give the students what they want would be the best teachers. Because most students are dependent, what students want is clear and entertaining lectures requiring little work from them, plenty of well-organized handouts indicating exactly what will be on tests, and no group projects that require them to work around other students' schedules and through their personalities. However, faculty members who challenge dependent students to stretch their minds in new directions and regard learning as hard work where students are required to carry most of the burden will be regarded as terrible teachers by those dependent students. With such a teacher, negative opinions will predominate on the typical student evaluation forms, and if those forms are read uncritically (without an understanding of the teaching criteria context), decision makers could make the wrong interpretation. For example, student dissatisfaction in a department with a match perspective should lead to a conclusion that the teacher is doing a poor job. However, student dissatisfaction in a department with a liberal arts perspective *might* mean that the teacher is excellent. Let us examine this latter conclusion more closely.

We must be careful not to conclude that student dissatisfaction automatically leads to excellence in teaching; there are too many reasons for student dissatisfaction, such as the teacher being unprepared for class, the teacher not being knowledgeable in the subject matter, or the teacher appearing to hate teaching and thus avoiding students. If any of these reasons are the cause of student's dissatisfaction, then it would be very difficult to make a case for even adequate teaching, much less excellence. However, students could also be dissatisfied that the teacher has high grading standards, requires students to work hard to stretch their minds beyond their previous limits, or that the teacher does not digest difficult concepts for the students, preferring instead to require the students to work through difficult interpretations on their own. If these are the causes of student dissatisfaction, then the teacher might really be excellent if the teaching criteria allow for it; that is, allow for a focus on something beyond levels of student satisfaction. Of course, if we were operating under a match perspective, then student satisfaction would be a primary criterion. But if we were operating under a canon perspective, then many students will be forced to expose themselves to topics (many of them very difficult) for which they have no natural interest or background. With this perspective on teaching criteria, a very high level of student satisfaction might be evidence of poorer teaching than lower levels of satisfaction.

Departments operating under a liberal perspective, such as that envisioned by Blanchard and Christ (1993), would attract many different types of students. Dependent students would feel most at home in the core courses, independent students would be attracted by the ability to take a wide range of courses in related departments, and participative and collaborative students would like the hands-on experiences of working with equipment and engaging in internships. Because all these types of students would be required to take courses in all three areas, there would be some high levels of student dissatisfaction with most courses. However, if the decision makers realize the mix of student learning styles in the department, they will be able to make better interpretations of those expressions of dissatisfaction. In short, the decision makers will be able to partition the dissatisfaction into two categories: problems with the teacher and problems with the student expectations. If the problems are with student expectations, then decision makers should not rule out the possibility that the teacher may be very good. But if the problems are with the teacher (such as lack of preparation, lack of organization, no feedback to students, poor attitude, and the like), then this type of dissatisfaction reflects poor teaching practices of a generic nature.

In addition to summative evaluation, there is formative evaluation, which has its focus on diagnosing strengths and weaknesses so that individual teachers can improve. What does it mean to improve? The general answer is that improvement comes when a teacher narrows the gap between teaching criteria and teaching performance. Some teachers have a seemingly natural ability to do well from the beginning, but others need to analyze their abilities to determine where their shortcomings are.

Again, we can make a distinction between teaching problems of a generic nature and those problems that can be traced to student expectations. Generic problems (such as a failure to present an organized syllabus, missing classes, not giving students clear and timely feedback, etc.) reflect a fault in the basics of quality teaching. A discussion of this type of problem is beyond the scope of this chapter (see McKeachie, 1978).

Problems that are traceable to student expectations reflect a lack of fit between students' own styles and the instructional styles of their teachers. Just as students have learning styles, teachers have teaching styles (Christ, 1990; Grow, 1990; Potter, 1993). For example, Christ (1990), used four metaphors for teaching: teacher as server, teacher as technician, teacher as gardener, and teacher as guide. Students who are dependent would be most satisfied with a teacher as a server or technician, whereas independent students would be dissatisfied with these types, preferring instead teachers who serve as gardeners to their personal growth or guides to their own special journeys.

There are several strategies that can be used in a formative plan to address the problem of low student satisfaction. Our starting place again is with the overall teaching perspective in the department. If the perspective is a matching one, then faculty should be assigned to particular courses on the basis of their own instructional styles and the styles of students in those courses. If a problem arises with a lack of a match, it is the administration's fault as much as the faculty for failing to recognize the mismatch. If a department does not have a range of styles in its faculty, then the administration needs to encourage certain teachers to broaden their styles so that they will be able to fit better with certain instruction situations and student expectations.

If a department instead has a liberal perspective, then there is no need to match certain instructors with certain types of students so as to maximize the fit in expectations. Instead, a faculty member's content area becomes the sole criteria for assigning courses—style considerations are not important in the assignment. However, these style considerations should become important as contexts for interpretation in the evaluation phase.

SUMMARY

The purpose of this chapter was to demonstrate that academic units need to conduct a careful examination of the teaching values and student expectations in their own cultures, then to develop their own special criteria out of that knowledge. This is an exercise in self-discovery and self-definition. After the criteria have been developed they should be made explicit to all faculty, students, and administrators. Once the philosophical task of determining the *what* of teaching evaluation is completed and shared, it is a relatively simple matter to undertake the technical task of *how*.

APPENDIX A: EXERCISE: ADDRESSING ISSUES ABOUT
LEVEL OF CRITERIA

Goals	Written Criteria	Unwritten Criteria
Institutional Goals		
Student Satisfaction Goals		
Student Learning Goals		

APPENDIX B: STUDENT LEARNING STYLES

Dependent Styles

Students seek direction from authorities such as the professors and texts. Course content is a commodity to be acquired, and the best professors are those who provide the greatest amount of commodity at the lowest cost to the student.

1. *Achievers* are the most successful students from an institutional point of view, because they carefully seek out the rules and norms of the institution and diligently follow them.
2. *Emulators* are inspired by the example set by achievers, but something prevents them from being as successful.
3. *Consumers* are shoppers for the best courses and professors, where "best" is regarded in economic terms of the most value for the effort.
4. *Hopeful Sponges* passively sit through courses hoping that they will absorb enough information to pass.

Independent Styles

Students take great pride in determining their own goals and taking responsibility for their own learning. The best professors are those who allow freedom for students to follow their own course and help them develop their own strategies for success.

5. *Searchers* are rugged individualists who are motivated by the challenge of personal discovery.
6. *Pathfinders* distrust instructional formulas, the status quo, and other people's vision for what they should be or do.
7. *Stimulate-Me's* are skeptical about structured education, and they attend class waiting to be "struck by the lightning" that would motivate them.

Competitive Styles

Students regard the elements of the course as playing pieces in a game. The best professors are those who set up an interesting and challenging game then carefully enforce the rules so the best players win.

8. *Gamers* translate their experiences into competitions then become motivated to play for the purpose of winning.
9. *High Rollers* seek the big game rather than many small ones as Gamers do.
10. *Small Changers* like competition but only when the risks are small and the gains are big.

Participant Styles

Students enjoy being a part of a system of activities that requires their time and energy in return for contact with others. The best professors are those who offer a lot of class activities to involve students.

11. *Networkers* need to be around other people to feel stimulated and to have a purpose.
12. *Intellectual Partiers* like to be around other people, because they are stimulated by discussion and argumentation.
13. *Social Partiers* like to be around other people, because social experiences provide good times.
14. *Altruistic Heroes* strive to help others, and this makes them feel useful and good.

Avoidant Styles

Students dislike their courses and seek to reduce their contact and involvement. The best professors are those who ask as little as possible.

15. *Sprinters* dislike the college experience, and they try to get through as quickly and as painlessly as possible.
16. *Clueless Marginals* have no sense of drive or purpose about college and continue only because external factors force them to be there.

REFERENCES

Blanchard, R. O., & Christ, W. G. (1993). *Media education and the liberal arts: A blueprint for the new professionalism.* Hillsdale, NJ: Lawrence Erlbaum Associates.

Bloom, A. (1987). *The closing of the American mind.* New York:Simon & Schuster.

Centra, J. A. (1979a). *Determining faculty effectiveness,* SanFrancisco: Jossey-Bass.

Centra, J. A. (1979b). Evaluation of colleagues. In J. A. Centra (Ed.), *Determining faculty effectiveness* (pp. 99–112). San Francisco: Jossey-Bass.

Christ, W. G. (1990, August). *How shall I teach thee? Let me count the ways.* Paper presented at the annual meeting of the Association for Education in Journalism and Mass Communication, Minneapolis, MN.

Cohen, P. A., & McKeachie, W. J. (1980). The role of colleagues in the evaluation of college teaching. *Improving College and University Teaching, 28,* 147–154.

Doyle, K. O., Jr. (1975). *Student evaluation of instruction.* Lexington, MA: Lexington.

D'Souza, D. (1991). *Illiberal education: The politics of race and sex on campus.* New York: The Free Press.

Emanuel, R., & Potter, W. J. (1992). Do students style preferences differ by grade level, orientation toward college, and academic major? *Research in Higher Education, 33,* 395–414.

French-Lasovik, G. (Ed.). (1982). *New directions for teaching and learning: Practices that improve teaching evaluation* (No. 11). San Francisco: Jossey-Bass.

Fuhrmann, B. S., & Grasha, A. F. (1983). *A practical handbook for college teachers.* Boston, MA: Little, Brown.

Grasha, A. F. (1977). *Assessing and developing faculty performance: Principles and models*. Cincinnati, OH: Communication and Education Associates.

Grow, G. (1990, August). *Enhancing self direction in journalism education*. Paper presented at the annual meeting of the Association for Education in Journalism and Mass Communication, Minneapolis, MN.

Hirsch, E. D., Jr. (1987). *Cultural literacy: What every American needs to know*. Boston: Houghton Mifflin.

Hoyt, D. P. (1982). Using colleague ratings to evaluate the faculty member's contribution to instruction. In G. French-Lasovik (Ed.), *New directions for teaching and learning: Practices that improve teaching evaluation* (pp. 57–72). San Francisco: Jossey-Bass.

Lewis, S., & Barber, L. (Eds.). (1986). *Improving your own instruction: Self-assessment and peer review*. Bloomington, IN: Phi Delta Kappa.

McKeachie, W. J. (1978). *Teaching tips: A guidebook for the beginning college teacher*. Lexington, MA: Heath.

Miller, R. I. (1974). *Developing programs for faculty evaluation*. San Francisco: Jossey-Bass.

Potter, W. J. (1993, April). *Instructional styles and student learning styles*. Paper presented at the annual meeting of the Broadcast Education Association, Las Vegas, NV.

Potter, W. J., & Clark, G. (1991). Styles in mass media classrooms. *Feedback, 32*(1), 8–11, 24.

Potter, W. J., & Emanuel, R. (1990). Students' preferences for communication styles and their relationship to achievement. *Communication Education, 39*, 234–249.

Seldin, P. (1980). *Successful faculty evaluation programs*. Crugers, NY: Coventry.

Seldin, P. (1991). *The teaching portfolio*. Boston, MA: Anker.

5

Course Evaluation

David E. Tucker
University of Toledo

The primary purpose of this chapter is to examine how classroom assessment might best be accomplished by the communication professor. Classroom assessment can be viewed on three different levels: formal procedures, informal procedures, and classroom research. This chapter gives examples of all three and how they can be used in specific communication classes. A secondary purpose of this chapter is to show the actual need for such procedures. Good classroom assessment should be the base of the assessment pyramid, not merely an afterthought.

It is expected that this chapter will be most useful to graduate students and faculty just beginning their teaching careers.

INTRODUCTION: THE PROBLEM

Much has been written since the early 1980s about assessment. Two major issues have involved how to best accomplish assessment and deciding at what level assessment should occur. With accrediting agencies, state legislatures, and taxpayers all clamoring for accountability and educational costs climbing universities are examining ways to answer these questions. Within 5 years of the publication of *A Nation at Risk* (National Commission on Excellence in Education, 1983) there were hundreds of task forces and more than 60 major reform reports issued (Cross & Angelo, 1989) calling for standardized testing, exit exams, curricular evaluations, and other forms of outcomes assessment procedures (see chap. 1). The problem, as Cross and Angelo (1989) stated it is, "none of the people writing reports, making recommendations, passing legislation, and devising new measures of accountability affect directly what students learn in college. The quality of education depends largely on what happens when teachers meet students in college classrooms" (p. 23). The assumption has been that class-room assessment, usually in the form of a grade, has accurately taken place, or that such assessment is covered when the entire program or college is reaccredited (Cross, 1987). That may be a rather large assumption.

Only one half of all teacher education programs in the United States require a class in measurement for initial certification (Schafer, 1991). Al-though these results are for programs training elementary and secondary teachers, there seems little reason to believe that graduate programs do a better job in preparing college professors and, in all likelihood, require less. Stiggens (1991b) went so far as to label us a "nation of assessment illiterates" (p. 7).

The assumption is made time and again that because an individual has obtained a PhD in a discipline such as communication, they can therefore teach that discipline to others. Although broadcast communication profes-sors were very upset when *The Roper Report* failed to differentiate between the skills necessary to be a good broadcaster and those skills necessary to be a good broadcast professor (Tucker, 1990) these same professors should be upset when PhD programs fail to differentiate between those skills necessary to obtain a PhD in communication and those skills necessary to teach broadcasting, journalism, theatre, or speech communication. Al-though we spend a great deal of effort in evaluating the research capabilities of PhD students, we spend almost no effort at determining whether they can teach (Bok, 1991). Ernest Boyer (quoted in Bok, 1991) president of the Carnegie Foundation for the Advancement of Teaching, described college teaching in the following manner: "With few exceptions, when we visited classes the teacher stood in front of rows of chairs and talked most of the forty-five or fifty minutes. Information was presented that often students passively received. There was little opportunity for positions to be clarified or ideas challenged" (p. 236). Yet these individuals are expected to properly assess the students in their classroom.

Many reasons have been given for the problems. Schafer (1991) believed it is because those who teach classes in measurement and assessment have not made clear the relationship between such classes and effective teaching and evaluation of students. Stiggins (1991a) believed that teachers and administrators view systematic assessment of the achievement of their students as risky. Hills (1991) believed that teachers do not learn the technical skills involved in testing, evaluation, and grading because their colleagues and supervisors are apathetic about evaluation. He continued by stating that he doubted a single teacher in the United States has had his or her career adversely affected by an ignorance of these skills. Although Hills was speaking of elementary and high school teachers, it is easy to extrapolate to college-level teaching. Skills are learned that will help in tenure and promotion. Such skills have generally been in the area of research and not in assessment. Whatever the reason, formal training in classroom assessment seems to be missing.

And what about those teachers who actually have been exposed to some form of assessment procedures? Have they benefited? Stiggens (1991a) did not think so. He believed that those teachers who actually do get some limited classroom assessment training find that it is primarily in the large-scale, standardized, paper-and-pencil test format. Gullickson, in a 1986 survey (cited in Linn, 1990, p. 427), found a large disparity between what professors thought they should teach in a class on assessment and what teachers felt they should be learning in such a class. The three areas that teachers felt were most important were (a) using test results for instructional planning and formative evaluation, (b) using test results for summative evaluation purposes, and (c) employing nontest evaluation devices. These areas were hardly touched by professors. Professors were more interested in comparing and interpreting statistical data. In other words, professors were more interested in discussing reliability, validity, and standard deviations, than in what the teachers expected or believed they needed from such a class.

CLASSROOM ASSESSMENT: A DEFINITION

At its most basic level classroom assessment asks, "Did I accomplish in this class what I set out to do?" If such a question is asked at the end of each lecture, or at the end of a section and an answer sought, then the instructor is engaging in formative assessment. Such an evaluation collects data with the intention of improving the learning process (Cross, 1987). If the instructor is evaluating students at the end of the course or at the end of their collegiate career, then the assessment procedure is summative. Stating the definition of classroom assessment a little more formally, "the evaluator must decide what kind of information is needed, how the information should be gathered and how the information should be synthesized to support the outcome" (Ebel & Frisbie, 1991). This definition implies a basic teaching model that has five steps: (a) instructional objectives, (b) entering behavior, (c) instructional procedures, (d) performance assessment, and (e) a feedback loop (Ebel & Frisbie, 1991). The model requires that the professor have a clear understanding of where the class is headed, be willing to measure the level of achievement that students have brought with them to class before the first lecture is given, have clear instructional procedures, be willing to accurately measure student performance, and then analyze what worked and what did not.

Planning the Course: Developing a Syllabus

If the material already presented seems a bit overwhelming, there are course planning models available. Frye's (1989) model contains three levels. It begins with the catalog description, from which is written broad course objectives. His second level suggests determining the order and the extent to which various topics will be covered. A course outline is then developed, which is segmented into units. Units are differentiated through conceptually consistent content, length suited to the level of the learner, and then conclude with evaluation or feedback. Unit goals should be written by the professor. These goals should support at least one of the course objectives written for Level I. All Level I objectives must be supported by at least one unit goal. Frye's third level specifies desired student competencies that satisfy the Level II goals. Lesson plans are then developed that will lead the learner to achieve the Level III objectives. These are performance objectives. They are observable and hence measurable.

Greive (1989) created a somewhat different model for course planning, but it essentially includes the same elements of course description, course goals, student outcomes or objectives, teacher activities, student activities, student feedback, and evaluation as Frye (1989). The names are slightly changed but the major goal is the same—a well-organized classroom.

By following these course planning procedures, the instructor should then be able to develop a comprehensive syllabus for the class. Instructors may use a variety of techniques to communicate to students what the expectations are for the course, but a syllabus provides a written document of those expectations. Although such documents may vary to some degree in form and content, there are some basic elements that should be contained in all of them (Ryan & Martens, 1989). Every syllabus should include: information about the instructor (office hours, phone number(s), any other means of communication), course title, credit hours, catalog description, prerequisites, and the types of students for whom the course is intended. Most importantly, the syllabus should outline course goals and objectives as developed by the instructor utilizing a solid course planning procedure. In addition the syllabus should contain a full description of the assignments and their particular weight in the grading scale. Class attendance and participation should be spelled out as well as any external field trips or laboratory time. Other items generally included are absence and excuse policies, make-up exams, and any flexibility regarding any of the items listed in the syllabus and how to negotiate them with the professor. The syllabus may also include the relation of the course to student development, program goals, general education requirements, and even the mission of the university. Ryan and Martens (1989) believed that a well-organized and comprehensive course syllabus gives the students confidence that the instructor knows what is supposed to happen and this, in turn, benefits the students. Returning to the rather broad definition of classroom assessment used earlier, "Did I do what I set out to do?," course planning and an accurate, complete syllabus are major prerequisites to determining the answer to that question.

CLASSROOM ASSESSMENT: THREE LEVELS

Classroom assessment can actually be viewed on three different levels: formal procedures, informal procedures, and classroom research. These distinctions are somewhat arbitrary and overlapping, but hopefully useful for the following discussion.

Level 1: Formal Procedures

Turning first to formal procedures used in classroom assessment, they include such items as test design, statistics, textbook exams, standardized tests, and so on. It is the kind of information that would be gathered from a high-quality course in measurement and evaluation, or from a good textbook on the subject. Several authors believe the "cure" for the problem of classroom assessment lies in this area. Curtis (1918, cited in Nitko, 1991, p. 2) prescribed his cure in the following way:

1. Teachers should realize how important measurement is to education and should desire to become proficient in its use.
2. Teachers should acquire knowledge of a wide range of tests, their advantages, and their limitations.
3. Teachers should develop skills in elementary statistical methods (making and graphing distributions, calculating means, medians, standard deviations, and correlations) and in using educational assessments in a consistent manner.
4. Teachers should develop the ability to use educational assessments to solve instructional problems.

Schafer (1991) expanded on this list, defining different content areas that he believed anyone entering a classroom should know. Ideally, these content areas would be covered in a class on measurement and subsequently reinforced through workshops. The next section of this chapter examines those areas and how they might specifically apply to communication. (Linn, 1990, has a comparable list and this author recommends reading both.)

Schafer's (1991) first content area is *basic concepts and terminology of assessment*. The goal is to understand the language used in classroom assessment. It is the prerequisite for understanding assessment techniques. For instance, what is the difference between formative and summative assessment, or norm-referenced and criterion-referenced assessment? What are the precise definitions of reliability, validity, relevance, and objectivity? Such knowledge is necessary to be able to evaluate assessment procedures. The ability to evaluate standardized tests or those that accompany textbooks is dependent on a working knowledge of the language of assessment. Making the assumption that because an exam appears in print that it is, therefore, either a reliable or valid exam is wrong. Learning the language is the first step (Ebel & Frisbie, 1991; Mitchell, 1992; Swezey, 1981).

Schafer's (1991) second content area is *uses of assessment*. Our assessment techniques in various classes have to be consistent with the needs they are addressing. In the case of formative assessment it can be used as an aid to instruction. By assessing students as the class progresses, it is possible to determine which teaching techniques are working and which are not. If an assessment procedure follows a particularly difficult topic and shows the students failed to grasp the information, then the professor may wish to return to the topic and review the material. Perhaps the material should be presented in a different fashion altogether. Why wait until the final exam to discover students do not understand? It is a little late at that point to help anyone.

The summative evaluation should present a fairly clear picture of what students have learned after the class is over. Summative assessments must be fair and geared to what the student truly needed to gain from the class in order to succeed in subsequent classes or after graduation. In other words, why are we teaching this class? Once we know the basic objectives of a class and how that class is supposed to fit into the curriculum, then it is possible to develop assessment procedures fitting the purpose. For instance, if the class is Introduction to Communication, and the student must obtain a C or better to continue on in the program, then the objectives of the class would be to, in some way, prepare the student for the remainder of the curriculum, and the assessment procedures should predict the student's success in that curriculum. Put in a negative light, if 50% of the final exam asks the student to identify individuals in communication and yet the remainder of the curriculum contains primarily performance or writing classes, then the objectives of the class and the assessment procedures used do not justify it as a gatekeeping class.

Schafer's (1991) third content area is *assessment planning and development*. This content area involves the choosing of what test or type of test to administer. There is the whole issue of norm-referenced versus criterion-referenced tests. A norm-referenced test compares one student against another, whereas a criterion-referenced test compares the student against some general standard. There are times when one or the other is the more appropriate choice. Other issues might include deciding when a paper-and-pencil test is a good way to assess achievement in a public speaking class. What about performance assessments, standardized tests, group assessments, or oral questions, and how do these various test types relate to the behavioral objectives developed before the class even began?

Linn (1990) believed that one of the real weak points in classroom assessment is the inability of teachers to know whether they or someone else has developed a good exam. Many teacher's manuals include tests (Alexander & Hanson, 1993; Felsenthal, 1987; Whittiker, 1993; Willis & Aldridge, 1992; Zettl & Hopkinson, 1992). The tests vary from definition, to fill-in, to multiple choice, to possible essay or discussion questions. An understanding of what makes a good test question is central to determining the worth of such exams. Although this chapter is not designed to compare the quality of various test types or to prescribe which type to use in which situation, several broad statements are relevant. First, the test must answer the behavioral objectives stated in the syllabus and developed for each unit in the course (Hudson, 1973). The professor must be able to defend the method of assessment based on the stated goals in the syllabus. It all connects. Second, the professor must determine the content to be covered, the level of difficulty, the number and type of items, and the purpose of the test (Ebel & Frisbie, 1991). There are several excellent texts on the development and use of tests (Ebel & Frisbie, 1991; Heywood, 1989; Hudson, 1973; Mitchell, 1992).

Some professors believe that once the test has been taken and graded that it is time to move on to the next unit. The graded exam can provide another learning situation for the students as well as for the professor (Ebel & Frisbie, 1991). Classroom discussion of an exam can help those students who did poorly to understand how the proper answer was arrived at by some students and help the professor determine where the presentation of material may not be as strong as he or she would like it to be. Also, analyzing the test item by item can help to reveal flaws in the specific questions and hence improve subsequent tests (Ebel & Frisbie, 1991).

Ebel and Frisbie (1991) developed a list of characteristics used in determining the quality of a norm-referenced achievement test. They include relevance, balance, efficiency, specificity, difficulty, discrimination, variability, and reliability. *Relevance* is judged by examining each item for content appropriateness, taxonomic level, and extraneous abilities. *Balance* is a judgment on how well the ideal specifications were achieved in terms of content representativeness and cognitive abilities. If the professor determines prior to the class that one entire period will be spent lecturing on television programming in the 1990s and only one half of a period will be spent lecturing on radio programming in the 1990s, did the test reflect that balance? *Efficiency* is judged by comparing the test you used with other hypothetical tests that could have been used. Efficiency relates to maximizing the amount of information about achievement that may be obtained during the test period. *Specificity* relates to how well the test measured information that could only be obtained through this particular course. If a testwise individual who is not in the class can take the exam and do well above the chance level, then the test lacks specificity. Test *difficulty* relates to the purpose of the test and the test type. If a test is too easy or too difficult then the score distributions will be skewed at one end or the other and thus make it impossible to determine who the true achievers are in a particular class. A norm-referenced test must be able to *discriminate* between high and low achievers and should be able to do so on an item-by-item basis. Thus a test must be difficult enough to discriminate between the good and bad students. In terms of *variability*, the larger the standard deviation of an exam, the more successful the test constructor has been in differentiating between high and low achievers. Finally, the instructor should measure the *reliability* of the exam. Has the same exam given over several semesters yielded similar results?

In addition, the professor needs to be able to decide what type of assessment procedure fits a particular situation. The objectives outlined in the syllabus should help dictate what type of assessment procedures are most appropriate for the class. If, for instance, one of the objectives is for the student to exhibit an understanding of the theatre preproduction planning process, then an essay asking for such information might be appropriate (see chap. 14). However, it might be just as appropriate to assess such knowledge through observation. On the other hand, if the class is a television production course that stresses operation of the equipment, then criticizing the student for failure to plan a production is not an appropriate means of assessment.

Portfolios, essay exams, term papers, individual observations, oral questioning, and informal inventories all have a place depending on the objectives developed prior to the class and illuminated in the syllabus. Descriptions and suggestions for their use are available in Hudson (1973), Swezey (1981), Greive (1989), Ebel and Frisbie (1991), and Mitchell (1992).

Schafer's (1991) fourth content area is *interpretation of assessments*. The instructor needs to have an understanding of error, confidence intervals, limitations of specific measurement methods, and bias in assessment. Does a particular type of assessment technique favor a particular type of student? Some students do well in performance settings, whereas others do well with paper and pencil and 3 hours to take a final exam. Still others do well when given work to take home. Again, it is necessary to refer back to the class objectives. For example, in an advanced public relations class, if one of the objectives discusses writing under time constraints, then a perfectly acceptable assessment measure would be a timed writing assignment done within the classroom setting.

Schafer's (1991) fifth content area is *the description of assessment results*. It is at this point the instructor should understand measures of central tendency, standard deviations, correlations, bar graphs, and other descriptive statistics. Assume that over time you are the only instructor to teach a particular class (e. g., Human Communication). Keeping track of test results on similar exams across several semesters would provide invaluable information. The instructor would begin to get a sense of where the students truly are when they enter the class and what can actually be expected of them. Instead of merely having anecdotal information describing your students, you would have actual data. It would then be necessary to know how to display and interpret that data so that it would become useful for both assessment and instructional purposes.

Schafer's (1991) sixth area is *evaluation and improvement of assessments.* The instructor should be able to determine if the assessment instrument has met the goal of evaluating the student properly on the class objective. Again, the concepts of reliability and validity are important here. How good is a standardized test and how useful the scores?

Schafer's (1991) seventh content area is *feedback and grading.* Assessment provides both formative and summative information to the student. A formative assessment is basically how the student has done to that point. It can be a daily, weekly, or other type of assessment. The summative assessment tells students how they have done over the entire class. What have they mastered and what have they not mastered? To be effective, assessment results must be clear to the student as well as the teacher. What do the comments mean? What does a C mean in an introductory communication class? Does it mean I should not go on? Giving a summative assessment at the end of the semester is required but if the student never revisits the professor to discuss what the grade really means and how it was arrived at then the assessment has not achieved the full extent of what assessment should be designed to do. Instead of the professor merely asking the question posed earlier in this chapter, "Did I do what I set out to do?" students must also be taught that they have the burden of asking, "What did I really achieve by taking this class?" Perhaps the best example is the term paper.

This author has always assigned a major paper in the seminar titled Broadcast Ratings. It is a major piece of work involving ratings interpretation, mathematics, interviews with station personnel, and so on. What good does it do? Very little if the students never pick up the graded paper, read the comments, or discuss the paper with the professor. It is essential if assessment is to mean anything to the student that some sort of feedback be built into the system. Perhaps an addition to the syllabus describing what the professor believes a B represents would be helpful, or passing out next semester's office hours along with an invitation to come in to discuss the previous semester's grade.

Schafer's (1991) eighth and final area is *ethics of assessment.*" To what end is the assessment being used? Any time an instructor assesses a group and makes a judgment, there can be both positive and negative results of the assessment. Tests are used to determine who goes on and who stays behind. The students and professors involved in such a situation have an obligation to each other that such assessment procedures are fair and impartial. The whole procedure is defeated if one student has been given an unfair advantage over another. Assume an introductory communication class is being used as a screening class for entry into the major. Only one in four students will be allowed into one of the communication sequences. The assessment procedures in such a class must be clear, fair, and unimpeded by personal likes and dislikes. Students must be allowed a level playing field. Each year's tests must resemble in some way previous years' evaluations or you will have been unfair to students from the year before. There must be consistency within the instruction or again, some students will have gained an unfair advantage.

Schafer outlined a substantial amount of work for the average college professor. This is especially true if the professor has never taken an assessment or measurement class. This is where a university has the responsibility of helping faculty with assessment, without that help seeming punitive.

Level 2: Informal Procedures

Informal assessment includes those techniques that teachers have developed to help them determine how the class is faring on a day-to-day or topic-to-topic basis. Informal assessment is practically always formative in nature. These informal classroom assessment techniques (referred to as CATs by Angelo & Cross, 1993) are specific feedback devices designed to give faculty immediate responses to very specific questions. They are techniques designed to help improve student learning.

Angelo and Cross (1993) developed a quick three-step technique for "beginners" in classroom assessment techniques. They suggest picking one class in which to do your first CAT. It should be the class that you are most comfortable teaching and in which you have the most experience. Then pick one of the simpler CATs, such as: The Minute Paper, The Muddiest Point, or the One Sentence Summary. The Minute Paper asks students to respond to two questions: (a) What was the most important thing you learned today, and (b) what questions remain as we conclude this class? The Muddiest Point is similar to the Minute Paper in that it asks students, "What was the muddiest point in my lecture today?" The One Sentence Summary asks students to summarize what the lecture was all about.

The second step (Angelo & Cross, 1993) is implementing the procedure. Make certain students are clear about what you want them to do. Make certain you have allotted enough time so that students do not feel rushed in completing the procedure. Then, read the responses as soon after class as possible. In this way your lecture and their responses are still fresh in your mind.

The third step suggested by Angelo and Cross (1993) is responding. All of these steps require teachers to be willing to respond to the students' comments about their teaching. The feedback loop is essential. The students must feel as if they are truly a part of the process.

Using the Muddiest Point assessment technique and taking an example from an Introduction to Broadcasting lecture on the Sixth Report and Order, the professor might find the following problems: students failing to comprehend the difference between UHF and VHF television, or what you really meant by intermixture, or what the difference is between frequency and channel.

A couple of caveats are in order here. First, informal classroom assessment techniques are designed as aids to instruction. The whole idea is to find out during the process what students do not know rather than after the process is over. As Hills (1991) noted, this can be risky. It is easier for all of us to assume that material has been covered, if not brilliantly, then at least adequately, and the reason students have failed to do well is they are not studying hard enough, or they just do not care, or they were not prepared properly in high school for college. Although all of this may be true in some cases, it is also possible that the lecture was so dull that it is now being used by the local sleep disorders clinic, or that it was so unintelligible that if Edwin Howard Armstrong were in the audience even he would not know who invented FM. Teachers who ask need to be really interested in knowing the answer and be willing to change.

Angelo and Cross (1993) gave over 50 classroom assessment techniques. They gave five suggestions for someone just starting to use as aids to their teaching. First, if the idea of classroom assessment does not appeal to your intuition or professional judgment as a teacher, do not do it. Second, do not turn assessment into a chore or a burden. Third, do not ask students to use a classroom assessment technique that you have not tried. Fourth, allow more time than you think you will need to carry out and respond to the assessment. Fifth, make sure you close the loop. Let students know that if they participate in these techniques, that you will respond to what they say. Remember, the goal is to improve your teaching and their learning.

Level 3: Classroom Research

The third area of classroom assessment falls under the title of classroom research. Teacher research is, "systematic, intentional inquiry by teachers about their own school and classroom work" (Lyle & Cochran-Smith, quoted in Pine, 1992, p. 657). Its purpose (Cross & Angelo, 1989) is "to improve the quality of learning in college classrooms by improving the effectiveness of teaching" (p. 24). Although this latter sentence sounds a bit like the classroom assessment techniques of Angelo and Cross (1993) described earlier, classroom research is more than that. *Systematic* is the key word. Perhaps *consistent* would also apply. These are questions formulated by teachers that go beyond the immediate. They ask more than, "Did this lecture achieve what I wanted it to?" For instance, a teacher might compare various techniques used to teach the same material. This could be done across several quarters. Many and Russell (1993) designed a writing feedback tool that students are given every time a writing assignment is turned back to them. In Many's class the students are asked to review the professor's critique of the assignment, make corrections, and then explain which particular journalistic rule they broke that then required the correction. The goal is to improve students' ability to learn and retain a particular journalistic style. Using Many and Russell's (1993) approach, teachers would be able to compare student performance both with and without the use of this feedback tool. In other words, did this particular teaching device make a difference in the classroom?

Another possibility is to analyze the exam. Ebel and Frisbie (1991) have developed a six-part procedure for doing this. First, arrange the scored test papers in order from highest to lowest. Second, separate the highest 25% from the lowest 25%. Third, for each test item count the number of examinees in the upper group that chose each response alternative. Do the same tally for the lower group. Fourth, record the results for each item on a separate copy of the exam. Fifth, add the two counts for the keyed response and divide this by the total number of students in the combined upper and lower groups. Multiply by 100 to gain a percentage. The result is an estimate of the index of item difficulty. Sixth, subtract the lower group count from the upper group count for the keyed response. Divide this difference by the number of examinees in one of the groups. The result is the index of discrimination.

This technique alone will help to differentiate between good and bad items on objective tests. But, if the professor keeps attendance and lecture dates, the professor will not only know what percentage of the class missed particular questions but also be able to cross-tabulate that information with how that material was presented in class with an eye toward altering the lecture material if necessary. This method is extremely useful the longer it is used. The professor begins to gather a data test bank containing questions that reflect what is being taught and truly discriminate between low- and high-achieving students.

In task analyzing exams several things may become apparent. First, it is quite possible that some questions have limited value. They assess the student's ability to retain information and little else. For example if 30 students take an exam and 15 miss a particular multiple-choice question, the professor should first examine the question. How was the question worded? Was it misleading? Was it typed correctly? Then the professor should examine the way that particular piece of information was communicated to the student. Was it an offhand comment? What did that particular lecture emphasize? If 50% of the students missed the question, there was a failure to communicate at some point.

Essay questions can be dealt with in a number of ways. It is possible to take the total number of points available to the class (e. g., 30 students times 25 points each equals 750 possible points) and determine the percentage of points the class achieved. It is also possible to percentage each student score, add those, and take an average. Using either method will once again lead the professor to ask the set of questions: Was the question worded properly, and did the method used to communicate this information adequately accomplish that task?

Other possibilities for classroom research may include a comparison of test style or class size across semesters. Perhaps for a specific class there is an optimal size and test style. The professor might wish to compare student performance on exams the professor devises versus those that come in teacher's manuals. Or, it is possible to compare those questions the instructor writes with those taken from a manual and do so on the same exam. There are many ways to present the same material. Comparing student learning across these various techniques seems a fruitful way of learning which techniques work best with you and your particular student type.

Cross and Angelo (1989) believed that "inquiry and intellectual challenge are powerful sources of motivation, growth, and renewal for college teachers, and that classroom research can provide that challenge" (p. 23).

CLASSROOM ASSESSMENT: UNDERSTANDING THE PROCESS

Given this information, here are several suggestions. First, find a good text on formal classroom assessment. Ebel and Frisbie's (1991) *Essentials of Educational Measurement* is one. The fifth edition of their text covers much of what Schafer (1991) and Linn (1990) outlined in their discussion of formal classroom assessment. Two more are Hudson's (1973) *Assessment Techniques: An Introduction,* and Heywood's (1977) *Assessment in Higher Education.*

Second, the instructor should begin a course-by-course evaluation of what he or she teaches. Perhaps the best way to begin this is with the Angelo and Cross (1993) Teaching Goals Inventory. This is a self-administered questionnaire that forces the instructor to realistically assess what the instructor's goals are for the class. Only when you know what you think the class is going to achieve can you devise adequate assessment techniques for that class. Then, drawing on one of the teaching models described earlier, the instructor's evaluation should include, but not be limited to the following:

1. *Course objectives.* The student must understand at the beginning of class what that class is supposed to achieve, and how these objectives coincide with other classes. Classes are not taught in a vacuum, but should be dependent on what is taught in other classes. The objectives should reflect this. The objectives must be realistic. They must take into account the facilities available, the type of student enrolled in the course, and the curricular aims of the course.

2. *The pretest.* A technique used by some instructors, the idea is to get a preliminary reading on where the students are in your class as regards the material you are going to cover. In this manner it will then be possible to say how far they have come. Some groups of students will have different

starting points than others. Also, it is impossible to say how much learning has occurred if you do not know at what point the student was when he or she entered your classroom. One way to do this would be to give the class your final exam on the first day and then repeat the test during the final exam period.

3. *Instruction*. The professor should also test the class to determine how the class learns best (see chap. 4). An assessment of the class' learning modalities will help with the method of instruction and also with the method of testing. Students fall into three broad categories: auditory, visual, and tactile. Knowing how your students learn is important to how the classroom materials are presented and how the students are tested.

4. *Assessment/Grading*. The test should relate directly to the class objectives. There should be feedback that actually gets to the student. In the best of all worlds, the instructor would hold private meetings with each student after each form of assessment to discuss the outcome of the assessment. In a performance class such as Television Directing or Public Speaking, a private critique session of the student's efforts would be in order. Please remember that any assessment procedure, whether it is a test, or other type of written assignment, is not a contest to see how many students will fail. Rather, it is an estimate on how far they have come and hence a direct reflection on you.

5. *Feedback*. There must be a feedback loop that is nonthreatening to both parties. The students must be able to critique the assessment procedures without being intimidated by the instructor. One suggestion is to allow students to examine their efforts along with the instructor's comments and then to write their own critique of the exam or other assessment procedure.

When using any assessment technique it is necessary to articulate the particular reasons for using that particular assignment. Each assignment (term papers, short essays, speeches, directing projects, etc.) must have an easily understood reason for being a part of the classroom assessment procedures. The instructor should also be able to articulate why the assignment was given, why it was given a particular percentage, and how it fits with the larger picture of both that particular class and the curriculum as a whole. For example, let us assume the instructor in an introductory class has two short writing assignments during the quarter. The assignments should be assessing particular goals stated in the syllabus and elaborated on in the course design. Has the professor analyzed the results of such written work? What types of errors are most common? How many of the students have had Basic English or a comparable composition class? Did the students improve from the first essay to the second? What kind of instructions were given with each assignment? What kind and how extensive was the feedback given on the written work? How was it graded? What percentage did grammar count versus content? Was this communicated to the student? Merely to grade the written work and then complain that "students can't write as well as they used to" is not adequate. The goal is learning.

CLASSROOM ASSESSMENT: SUMMARY

There are at least two things that are important to remember in terms of classroom assessment. The first is that most college teachers have little background in assessment. The second is that they are not likely to take several classes to make up for that deficiency. Until colleges provide more than lip service to the importance of teaching, most instructors will spend their time doing research because that is what gains tenure and promotion at a majority of institutions. However, there are informal procedures that are relatively easy to implement that have proven valuable to classroom teaching. The teachers will then know that they are doing a better job in the classroom and such knowledge can in and of itself provide a boost to their teaching. In order to aid teachers and universities, a referral program has been developed by the Speech Communication Association's Committee on Assessment and Testing (CAT).(For further information call the SCA national office at (703) 750-0533.)

APPENDIX A: COURSE EVALUATION QUESTIONS

Course Planning Procedure

A. What is the plan? (Questions based on Ebel & Frisbie, 1991; Frye, 1989; Grieve, 1989):

1. What are your course objectives? What are your instructional objectives? Do your broad course objectives fit the catalog description?
2. What does a pretest tell you about the level of student achievement and ability coming into the class? Do you know "where the students are" in terms of performance?
3. How do your students learn? What instructional procedures have you developed? What topics need to be covered? What are the goals of the units that develop each topic? Does each goal support at least one course objective?
4. What is your assessment/grading plan? Does your course outline "make sense" in terms of the topics that need to be covered, the broad course objectives, and the catalog description? What are the desired student competencies?
5. Is there a well-established feedback loop?

B. What does your syllabus look like? Does it contain information about (based on Ryan & Martens, 1989):

1. The instructor—office hours, phone number(s), and any other means of communication?
2. Course title, credit hours, and catalog description?
3. Prerequisites?
4. Types of students for whom the course is intended?
5. Course goals and objectives?
6. A full description of the assignments and their particular weight in the grading scale?
7. Class attendance and participation policy?
8. External field trips or laboratory time?
9. Absence and excuse policies?
10. Negotiating room with the professor?
11. Relation of the course to student development, program goals, general education requirements, and the mission of the university?

Formal Evaluation Procedure (based on Schafer, 1991):

1. Do you understand the language of assessment?
2. Do you know the uses (strengths and weaknesses) of assessment?
3. Do you know which tests or types of tests work best with what you are trying to assess?
4. Do you know how to interpret test scores?
5. Do you know how to present the assessment information?
6. Will you know if your assessment instrument is meeting the goal of evaluating the student properly on the class objective?
7. How much feedback are you giving during the course?
8. How will the assessment be used beyond the classroom?

Informal Evaluation Procedures (based on Angelo & Cross, 1993):

1. What are the strategies you use to evaluate classes on a daily or weekly basis? Do you ask your students: What was the most important thing you learned today? What questions remain as we conclude this class? What was the muddiest point in my lecture today? How would you summarize, in one sentence, what the lecture was all about?
2. Are you clear with your students why you are evaluating the course on a regular basis? Have you allotted enough time so that students do not feel rushed in completing the evaluation procedures?
3. Do you communicate back to the students what you found out in your assessment?

Classroom Research

1. Have you experimented with different types of tests and testing procedures to see which actually does a better job of measuring achievement?
2. If you are looking for class differentiation, do your tests differentiate in a meaningful way?
3. How well do your students, and tests, perform over semesters and across different student populations and class sizes?

REFERENCES

Alexander, A., & Hanson, J. (1993). *Instructor's manual for taking sides* (2nd ed.). Guilford, CT: Dushkin.

Angelo, T., & Cross, K. P. (1993). *Classroom assessment techniques* (2nd ed.). San Francisco: Jossey-Bass.

Bok, D. (1991, Winter). The improvement of teaching. *Teachers College Record, 93*(2),236–251.

Cross, K. P. (1987, March). The adventures of education in wonderland: Implementing education reform. *Phi Delta Kappan, 68*(7), 496–502.

Cross, K. P., & Angelo, T. (1989). Faculty members as classroom researchers. *AACJC Journal, 59*(7), 23–25.

Ebel, R., & Frisbie, D. (1991). *Essentials of educational measurement* (5th ed.). Englewood Cliffs, NJ: Prentice-Hall.

Felsenthal, N. (1987). *Study guide for broadcasting in America* (5th ed.). Boston, MA: Houghton-Mifflin.

Frye, B. (1989). Goals and objectives for college courses. In D. Grieve (Ed.), *Teaching in college: A resource for college teachers* (pp. 153–167). Cleveland, OH: Info-Tec.

Greive, D. A. (1989). Planning model for college faculty. In D. Grieve (Ed.), *Teaching in college: A resource for college teachers* (pp. 117–152). Cleveland, OH: Info-Tec.

Heywood, J. (1989). *Assessment in higher education* (2nd ed.). New York: Wiley.

Hills, J. (1991, March). Apathy concerning grading and testing. *Phi Delta Kappan, 72*(7),540–545.

Hudson, B. (1973). *Assessment techniques: An introduction.* London: Methuen.

Linn, R. L. (1990, Spring). Essentials of student assessment: From accountability to instructional aid. *Teachers College Record, 91*(3), 422–436.

Many, P., & Russell, C. (1993). *Fix-it sheet.* Unpublished manuscript. Department of Communication, University of Toledo, Toledo, OH.

Mitchell, R. (1992). *Testing for learning.* New York: The Free Press.

National Commission on Excellence in Education. (1983). *A nation at risk: Ther imperative for educational reform.* Washington, DC: U.S. Government Printing Office.

Nitko, A. (1991, Spring). Editorial. *Educational Measurement: Issues and Practice, 10*(1), 2.

Pine, N. (1992, Summer). Three personal theories that suggest models for teacher research. *Teachers College Record, 93*(4), 656–672.

Ryan, M. P., & Martens, G. G. (1989). *Planning a college course: A guidebook for the graduate teaching assistant.* Ann Arbor: University of Michigan.

Schafer, W. (1991, Spring). Essential assessment skills in professional education of teachers. *Educational Measurement: Issues and Practice, 10*(1), 3–6.

Stiggins, R. (1991b, Spring). Relevant classroom assessment training for teachers. *Education Measurement: Issues and Practice, 10*(1), 7–12.

Stiggins, R. (1991a, March). Assessment literacy. *Phi Delta Kappan, 72*(7), 534–539.

Swezey, R. (1981). *Individual performance assessment: An approach to criterion-referenced test development.* Reston, VA: Reston.

Tucker, D. (1990, January). A response to the Roper Report on electronic career preparation. *ACA Bulletin, 71,* 23–29.

Willis, E., & Aldridge, H. (1992). *Instructor's manual with tests for television, cable, and radio.* Englewood Cliffs, NJ: Prentice-Hall.

Whittiker, R. (1993). *Instructor's manual to accompany television production.* Mountain View, CA: Mayfield.

Zettl, H., & Hopkinson, M. (1992). *Instructor's manual for television production handbook* (5th ed.). Belmont, CA: Wadsworth.

6

Student Portfolios

Peter B. Orlik
Central Michigan University

Creative portfolios have long been a fixture in the business world as a means of demonstrating their preparer's artistic, design, or writing abilities. In many ways, the use of the portfolio instrument as a self- or programmatic assessment mechanism is simply an evaluative extension of this practice. Instead of merely showcasing what the author believes to be his or her best work, the *assessment* portfolio provides a panoramic view of that person's professional development experiences—and thereby also serves to measure the contribution to those experiences made by the educational institution from which that individual hopes to graduate.

There is a wealth of trade press guidance on how to prepare creative portfolios, and there is a burgeoning body of academic literature on the use of portfolios as student and programmatic assessment devices. In one short chapter, we cannot even attempt to survey this vast field. Instead, our main purpose here is to focus exclusively and pragmatically on how to structure a portfolio to meet the specific assessment needs of a communication studies curricula.

It should be kept in mind, however, that no student-generated programmatic assessment instrument will succeed if it does not clearly serve the needs and gratifications of its preparer. Therefore, it is an underlying tenet of our discussion that the demonstrable *student* benefit accruing from portfolio preparation must be *at least* as great as the evaluative benefit received by that student's sponsoring department.

INTRODUCTION

The Roots of Assessment Portfolios

Many of the insights that underpin assessment portfolio theory were derived from advances in the field of experiential learning. In 1971, The

Commission on Non-Traditional Study (a cooperative effort of the College Entrance Examination Board, the Educational Testing Service, and the Carnegie Corporation) was formed as one response to the demand for more learner-centered educational delivery systems. In its report 2 years later (Commission on Non-Traditional Study, 1973), the Commission's recommendation 47 asserted that: "New devices and techniques should be perfected to measure the outcomes of many types of nontraditional study and to assess the educative effort of work experience and community service" (p. 125). As a result of this recommendation, several higher education institutions joined with the Educational Testing Service in 1974 to undertake the Cooperative Assessment of Experiential Learning Project. Funding was provided by the Carnegie Corporation.

Though the Carnegie grant was only short term, the project that it underwrote did much to validate the whole concept of prior learning assessment. Building on this foundation, the nonprofit Council for the Advancement of Experiential Learning (CAEL) was created in 1976 to further develop responses to the original Non-Traditional Education Commission's proposals. Out of this concern for the proper recognition of education outside the classroom grew new assessment mechanisms—one of the most prominent of which became the *prior learning portfolio.*

As the name implies, the prior learning portfolio allows students to focus on experiences previous to their current educational endeavors. These experiences may have occurred in the workplace, the home, community and recreational organizations, and training venues beyond the boundaries of the conventional college course. Within the prior learning portfolio's pages, the students describe each experience, isolate the specific learning that flowed from it, and then provide clear evidence of their participation in this education-deriving event. The sponsoring collegiate institution must then translate these described experiences into appropriate academic credit, discriminating those situations in which real college-level competencies have been attained from those in which the student has failed to apprehend higher learning outcomes.

Obviously, the prior learning portfolio places a great deal more burden on the educational institution than does a volume prepared within the more conventional and circumscribed environment of a communication studies department. For in prior learning assessment, students are not only seeking to describe what they have learned, but also to achieve educational credentialing for experiences that may be far removed from the campus structure and the departmental major.

Nonetheless, by employing some of the mechanisms found to be successful in *prior* learning assessment, the communication studies unit (and those who evaluate it) achieve a far more comprehensive picture of student learning and the many paths that might lead to the same educational goal. This can only improve our instructional performance. Ultimately, we need to become less concerned with *where* a student developed a learned competency and more concerned with validating that the competency has, in fact, been attained.

Through portfolio facilitation, a curricular unit may discover that, though its exiting students have acquired the desired skills and insights, many of these competencies did not flow from the course work intended to teach them but rather, from other classes or experiences to which students fortunately (and perhaps accidentally) have been exposed. Two positive outcomes result from such a revelation: (a) the unit does successfully demonstrate that students are, in fact, graduating with mastery of the desired competencies; (b) the unit can strengthen and further support those activities that actually are generating such competencies and modify or delete those that are not fulfilling the task they were supposedly servicing. Scarce instructional resources therefore can be reapportioned to make successful activities stronger and to address competency shortfalls in other areas.

Unlike prior learning vehicles, the primary task of the communication studies department's portfolio process is not to take a vast spectrum of noncampus learning and assign equated college credit to it. Instead, in a much more narrow-gauge way, the portfolio that capstones our students' course of study examines experience that often *already has been transcripted* in order to:

1. Ratify what each student *individually* has achieved.
2. Compare this to what other students exposed to the same curricular structure have learned.
3. Validate that each student possesses the fundamental skills and insights necessary to the initiation of a successful communication career.

The outcomes that each communication department identifies and mandates for its students will vary from unit to unit, of course. A theatre program will exhibit a different focus than a speech communication or telecommunications sequence, and all three may be further subject to divergent requirements laid down by state authorities. Other chapters in this book deal with the selection and construction of such outcome statements. Our point here is simply that, as a means of determining curricular efficacy, *any* student's self-generated portfolio can, if its structure is well designed, be benchmarked against the minimal competencies that we require of *every* student in a particular communication major.

Fundamental Learning Philosophy

In designing a discriminating portfolio structure, it is essential to recognize that *experience* and *learning* are not the same thing. Learning can only flow from experience—but all experience does not result in learning, or at least, in college-level learning. In other words, real comprehension does not flow from "just being there." If, as filmmaker/comedian Woody Allen once said, "Eighty percent of life is just showing up," then all of our learning comes from the other 20%.

When it comes to the translation of experience into learning, portfolio composition must take two outcome realities into account: (a) some people never really "learn" a competency—even after repeated experiences germane to that competency's application, and (b) two perceptive persons sharing the same experience may learn quite different things from it.

At some time in your life, you may have performed alongside someone for whom each day was a reinvention of the wheel. They never seemed able to reduce the job to its key components, never were capable of modifying the task so that needless or repetitive elements were eliminated. They *did* the job, day after day—but never really *learned* its essence so as to be able to refine and streamline it. This is very much like the student who "works" the audio console in the lab but is incapable of translating this experience to other audio consoles because he or she has not *learned* the basic functions common to every console's design. It is also like the extemporaneous speaking student who wrestles with each new topic without the capability to select from and apply fundamental rhetorical structures. True learning, in short, is the isolation of the most important and generalizable from the peripheral and specific.

Our second outcome reality—that different people can learn different things from the same experience—becomes more and more likely as the experience becomes (a) more complex, and (b) less structured. Thus, the more we move from the tightly controlled progression of the lecture course to the less rigid progression of the seminar or studio, the more we advance from the simple world of pushing buttons or delivering lines to the complex environment of directing people who speak or button push, the greater will be the likelihood of a learning divergency.

The writer recalls evaluating the graduate-level prior learning portfolios of two Defense Department district audit supervisors. Both had progressed from the same accounting training through the same series of junior/senior auditor positions, to identical supervisory roles in different parts of the country. The length of time each spent at the various stages of the career ladder was also very similar. Yet, as evidenced by their portfolio exhibits, the two had learned quite different things from their current position.

Auditor A's discussion demonstrated that he was a master of work flow planning. He could take the most complex systems audit and estimate almost to the hour how long it would take a team of his accountants to complete the task. However, the individuals under his direction were apparently perceived as little more than interchangeable cogs in a well-oiled machine.

Conversely, Auditor B had become an adept personnel manager and career programmer. His observations indicated that he knew how to detect and productively utilize work style differences among his subordinates and could bring this knowledge to bear in selecting and pairing different people for different types of assignments. His group's audits were being completed—but not with the time line precision common to his colleague.

Both of these students were experiential *learners*. Both had honed their competencies to a high level. Yet, because each selected for attention different elements from the complex web of real-life immersion, each had acquired different competency strengths, and cognitive weaknesses. Sensitive portfolio instruments can detect these differences in a prescriptive way for the student (What do I still have to learn?) and in a descriptive way for the department (What are we actually teaching and where?).

Any assessment portfolio, therefore, including those used in communication education evaluation, must accommodate learner distinctiveness through scrupulous attention to *self-assessment*, and must identify and gauge the sources of learning through rigorous standards of *documentation*. Putting the matter most succinctly, documentation evidences the *doing*, whereas self-assessment validates the *learning*. Because self-assessment and documentation are the twin pillars by which the entire portfolio process is supported, let us take a moment to examine each.

SELF-ASSESSMENT

A precise portfolio self-assessment mechanism forces students to convey the essense of the experience together with what they learned from it, *in their own words*. Self-assessment probing is based on two primary assumptions. If a person has really learned something, they should be able to (a) isolate its most important elements, and (b) explain the essential characteristics of these elements in language that is discernible to a reasonably educated lay person. As previously discussed, different people learn different things from the same experience. The more complex the experience, the greater the variety of learned competencies likely to be derived from it—and therefore, the greater dissimilarity of student self-assessment statements about it. Thus, it is to be expected that a supervisory position at the department's radio station or as captain of the debate squad may produce a wider spectrum of articulated competencies among students who performed these functions than would their mutual exposure to the instructor-structured world of a basic lecture class.

From an individual student standpoint, self-assessment allows us to ascertain just what was gained from a given experience, without prejudging as to whether or not this is what our department *wanted* or expected the student to learn in this activity. Unlike a classroom test where we often seek a commonality of responses, the self-assessment questions posed in each portfolio exhibit should be structured to permit divergence. We encourage the student to describe what they *really* learned from a given experience.

Then, taking the portfolio as a whole, we evaluate whether key competencies have been attained by the student as a sum total of all the experiential events that portfolio chronicles.

From a programmatic standpoint, of course, our primary interest is whether this sum total reflects the competency attainment that we mandate for each of our graduates. This is also the concern of those external agencies to which we are accountable. But in addition, an open-ended self-assessment mechanism also facilitates *internal* review of all of the components that make up our curriculum and its cocurricular and extracurricular enterprises. If several student self-assessments are isolating the same learning outcome for a given activity—and that outcome substantially departs from the activity's "official" reason for existence—we can take two courses of action: (a) If the learned outcome is important to our mission, we can modify the activity to more directly support that outcome, and look for another course or planned experience to teach our originally intended subject matter; or (b) if the learned outcome is peripheral or irrelevant to our mission, we can downgrade or delete the experience altogether. Either way, student self-assessment has helped to refine our program by distinguishing what learning is really occurring from the learning that we *thought* was occurring. The more "historic"the curriculum, the more graphic this dichotomy is likely to be evidenced in our students' self-assessments.

To be sure, self-assessment requires deep reflection on the part of each learner. However, through careful formulation of framing questions, a portfolio format can encourage students to engage in the process in a way that is revealing both to them and to the communication studies program in which they are enrolled. These positive results are enhanced by requiring that self-assessment responses be expressed in the student's own words. Portfolio preparation instructions must establish that the parroting of catalog and syllabus course descriptions is prohibited; that the mimicking of internship and cocurricular objectives and mission statements is not allowed. In short, it must be made clear that the only wrong answers to the portfolio's self-assessment questions are those that do not flow from the student's own articulated observations.

DOCUMENTATION

As was previously stated, self-assessment validates the learning, whereas documentation proves the doing. In other words, documentation serves two functions: (a) It establishes that the student actually participated in the experience; and (b) it evidences the breadth and depth (the scope and length) of that experience. Documentation authoritatively places the student in a situation that possesses the potential for generating college-level competencies. Although the type of learning (as revealed via self-assessment) may vary substantially from student to student, the dimensions of a common experience are much more uniform. Proper portfolio documentation assures that a student participated in a complete experience, and establishes that this experience was of sufficient duration, intensity, and sophistication to carry the likelihood of the attainment of college-level competencies.

In the sample portfolio packet found in the following section of this chapter, several types of appropriate documentation are listed. For a conventional course offered within a communication studies department, documentation is obviously a much easier task than for a hobby or other life experience that takes place totally outside any structured class or workplace. Yet, even for a regular course, proper documentation is more than the mere attachment of a grade report. It must also encompass specific evidence of the kinds of learner performance that resulted in that grade.

A SAMPLE PORTFOLIO PACKET

Appendix A contains a prototype portfolio packet that can be implemented by a communication studies program. Following the cover sheet (configured to reflect institutional identity and format requirements), the first form in the packet provides key information about the student. Just as important, it requires this student, as author, to attest to the accuracy of all of the exhibits that are to follow. Depending on the role of the portfolio in fulfilling graduation requirements, this certification statement could be strengthened into a formal affidavit complete with notarized signature and specification of penalties for willful deception.

The next page, the portfolio table of contents, inventories all of the exhibits to be found in the book, together with the documentation that accompanies each. This contents list may extend to several pages, depending on the breadth of experiences that the communication studies unit wishes to encompass in the portfolio development project.

Part One, *Learning from Work Experiences,* is a two-sided form designed for the discussion of a single job. The student would use a separate form for each work experience included in the portfolio. Because we are interested in identifying the student's learned competencies rather than their financial status, unpaid practica, performances, and internships are usually treated like any remunerated employment.

All work situations share a fundamental commonality. At least as compared to classroom experiences, the progression of an occupational activity (paid or unpaid) is relatively unstructured and capricious. To learn from it, the employee/participant must bring careful perception and organized reflection to bear. There is no instructor or coach to provide continuous focus and development. Even if the supervisor is a skilled trainer, the bulk of an employee's time is still spent in self-learning—in trying to pull coherence from a mass of simultaneous, repetitive, and sometimes conflicting tasks. An appropriately organized portfolio packet recognizes this commonality by grouping all on-the-job experiences in the same section, with the same self-assessment measurements applied to each.

Thus, after providing basic time and place specifics, our prototype form asks the student a series of three leading questions, the answers to which will comprise the exhibit's self-assessment component.

In responding to the central "What have you learned?" query, it often is useful for students to engage in the continuous self-critiquing exercise of asking themselves: "So what?," "Why is this important?," and "What's the underlying principle?" These questions will help the portfolio writer to move beyond mere experience description to genuine learning isolation:

"I learned to write and deliver short, persuasive sales pitches."

SO WHAT?

"This taught me the value and power of proper word selection and arrange-ment in successful communication. I now take a great deal more care in my choice of words and progression of ideas in everything that I write."

"I can now manipulate a studio camera with confidence that I will deliver the required shot."

WHY IS THIS IMPORTANT?

"To direct viewer attention to the pictorial center of interest, I found that you must not only know the equipment, but also understand visual planes and aesthetic framing."

"This internship allowed me to see that traveling theatre companies must learn to adapt to many staging limitations."

WHAT'S THE UNDERLYING PRINCIPLE?

"I learned that artistic flexibility is at least as important as role preparation in successfully bringing the theatre experience to a variety of publics."

These questions assist students in transcending the actual experience to recall what learning theorist David Kolb labeled the *Reflective Observation* that should have taken place as a proximate *result of* the experience. If true learning has occurred, the student should then be able to employ this observation to reach Kolb's third stage of *Abstract Conceptualization*, which can then be extended to cope with future situations as *Active Experimenta-tion* (Kolb, 1984).

If, on the other hand, the student's self-assessment remains stuck at the "traveling theatre is harder to do" stage, we might seriously question whether true college-level learning has taken place. And if most students coming out of this particular job placement exhibit a similar cognitive limitation, we might want to distance our program from any formal rela-tionship with this employment provider—or reconfigure the experience if the department itself is providing it. Perhaps the available job tasks are just too rudimentary ever to result in broader ranging college-level learning.

In any case, the work experience form would be followed by appropriate pieces of documentation that authoritatively place the portfolio author in this employment/participant setting and evidence the level of success that was attained there. The documentation must demonstrate that the situation provided the kinds of experience that could potentially stimulate the claimed learned competencies.

Part Two, *Learning from Professional Training Experiences*, pertains to course-type settings. Though the precise questions asked are somewhat different from Part One's forms, these exhibits are structured in a very similar way. The request for time and place data is followed by queries about the class content, scope, level, and evaluative mechanisms. Then, the crucial self-assessment response is requested (to which students should apply the same self-critiquing questions that were suggested to help shape job-derived self-assessments).

As in the previous section, the student typically would complete a separate Part Two form for each training experience. However, depending on the precise purposes the portfolio is intended to serve in a given communication studies curriculum, it may be more logical to group sequence courses together on a single form. Alternatively, certain introductory or core courses may be omitted altogether from the portfolio process to allow it to concentrate on more high-level or specialized offerings. This decision hinges, of course, on the outcomes we are trying to measure—and for whose scrutiny. This context will also determine whether training experiences completely external to our curriculum and campus are to be included in the portfolio's purview. Whatever exhibits are encompassed, each form is then followed by documentation relevant to the experience or experience cluster.

Part Three, *Learning from Hobbies and Other Life Experiences*, is largely optional. If the portfolio process is deployed to reflect only what occurs under the direct sponsorship of the communication studies unit, few if any Part Three experiences will qualify for inclusion. If, on the other hand, we are interested in chronicling the total spectrum of students' college-level learning, regardless of source, this section adds an essential dimension to the process. In other words, if the portfolio is intended solely to measure the efficacy of our curriculum, Part Three is irrelevant. But if the portfolio is designed, even in part, to be a student self-appraisal or job-hunting vehicle, then hobbies and other life experiences that have resulted in professionally relevant competencies should probably be included. The Part Three form requires an articulation of this relevance along with responses similar in thrust to what was requested in the previous two sections' exhibits. Multiple forms may be required to complete Part Three as well.

For organizational clarity and to further emphasize the distinctions between these three sections, it is advisable to print their forms on differentcoloredstock. *Learning from Work Experiences* may be reproduced on yellow paper, for example, with the *Training Experiences* form printed on pink and the *Other Experiences* documents rendered in blue. Students would obtain as many of each as necessary in order to construct the number of exhibits entailed by their learning background. Once the forms are completed and assembled with their supporting documentation, the pages can then be hole-punched and placed in a three-ring binder for submission.

Although they would not be submitted in the finalized book, the initiating portfolio packet should also include additional pages of instructions, definitions, and student encouragements. The instruction sheets we have included in our prototype clearly pertain to a portfolio that is as much a student-promoting "achievement book" as it is an accountability instrument for the sponsoring communication studies program. Whether you wish your portfolios to serve one or both purposes is an issue that should be faced in the earliest stages of process implementation.

PORTFOLIO BENEFITS FOR THE STUDENT

The concluding comments in the preceding section notwithstanding, it is difficult to conceive of a successful portfolio process that does not, at least in part, serve the self-interests of the students who will be preparing these books. This is a tenet we expressed at the very beginning of the chapter. Portfolio systems that are constructed solely to protect or enhance the parent department's interests with external authorities are unlikely to motivate students to engage in enthusiastic book preparation. The real purpose of these volumes will become far too obvious, and artificially tying their completion to course or graduation requirements scarcely adds to their student appeal.

Conversely, the portfolio instrument designed to accommodate students' twin desires for self-concept support and a job-seeking tool will be embraced much more readily. The portfolio structure we suggest simultaneously meets both of these student needs—in addition to servicing programmatic accountability mandates.

In the rapidly changing and intensely competitive communication and theatrical professions, graduates need the initial assurance that they possess the competencies required for success. Once we have ensured that our curriculum provides these competencies—and credentials only those students who have been able demonstrably to attain them—it is essential that we help to convey this sense of valid accomplishment to those graduates. The process and result of portfolio completion ratifies for its author the learning that has occurred. It concretely demonstrates: "I have done a lot. I already have achieved a number of goals to get myself ready for the career ahead." Adults tend to define themselves in terms of their past experiences. The assessment portfolio focuses this definition on the experiential outcomes most relevant to professional stature and growth.

In addition, with little or no modification, the assessment portfolio provides a potential employer with tangible evidence of the assets that this applicant immediately can "bring to the party." It can work in conjunction with a *creative* portfolio or serve as a stand-alone vehicle in the case of students who are not seeking writing or visual design positions. Although few corporate or institutional interviewers may read the book in its totality, even a cursory skimming of a well-ordered portfolio will plant specific and applicant-advantageous impressions.

PROGRAMMATIC EVALUATION OF THE PORTFOLIO

In utilizing the portfolio to determine the efficacy of our curriculum, we must derive a consistent means for book appraisal. A portfolio does not determine a department's instructional outcomes, of course. Rather, it is a vehicle for analyzing whether or not your students are reaching the learning goals you have separately and previously isolated.

Each communication school or department must set its desired instructional outcomes *before* it deploys a portfolio system. Otherwise, in the words of an old advertising industry conundrum, "If you don't know where you're going, you're likely to end up somewhere else." Outcomes isolation is a topic that has been addressed in previous chapters of this book, so for the purposes of our discussion here, we restrict our focus to the subsequent portfolio evaluation procedures.

First of all, it is suggested that the unit develop a master *outcomes nomenclature template* that inventories the total range of competencies that we wish to detect in our students. For purposes of illustration, Table 6.1 constitutes a very comprehensive template developed by Central Michigan University's Prior Learning Assessment Team. Because this team seeks to identify learned competencies evidenced from the student's total range of experiential learning, without regard to departmental affiliations, this instrument is much broader than one fashioned for use by a communication studies department. We can, however, develop a similar matrix to survey our curricular purview in a more narrow-gauge way.

A communication department's Level 1, for example, might list competencies in Station Management, Theatre Administration, or Corporate Communication Direction. Its Level 2 might encompass such titles as Studio Control, Speech Activities Coordination, Discussion Leadership, Campaign Organization, or Rehearsal or Tournament Planning. Finally, a communication department's Level 3 could isolate such task-specific competencies as Small Group Facilitation, Basic Audio Production, Scene Design, or Newswriting Practices. No matter how the nomenclature template is originally designed, it should then be subjected to continuous refinement

TABLE 6.1
Outcomes Nomenclature Template Developed by Central Michigan University's
Prior Learning Assessment Team, College of Extended Learning

Level 1

Administration: Broad applications of planning, implementation, and control. The general term *administration* would be used when the student has demonstrated that these competencies go across divisional lines.

Specific Administration Competencies

Accounting/Auditing	Human Resource Administration	Operations Administration
Administration	Logistics Administration	Program Administration
Communications Administration	Maintenance Administration	Production Administration
Facility Administration	Marketing Administration	Public Administration
Fiscal Administration	National Security Administra-	Purchasing Administration
Health Care Administration	tion	Resource Administration

Level 2

Primary responsibility for carrying out one or more parts of the administrative process. This will usually entail the responsibility for supervising others in carrying out these tasks.

Controlling	Community Leadership	Land-Use Planning
Control Analysis	Educational Leadership	Long-Range Planning
Cost Control	Industrial Leadership	Operations Planning
Fiscal Control	*Organizing*	Product Planning
Health Systems Control		Program Planning
Inventory Control	Organizational Psychology	Scheduling
Operations Control	Organization Therapy	Strategic Planning
Production Control	Organizational Development	Work Flow Planning
Quality Control	*Planning*	*Supervision*
Coordination	Administrative Planning	Clinical Supervision
	Contract Planning	Educational Supervision
Educational Coordination	Database Planning	Laboratory Supervision
Instructional Coordination	Facility Planning	Office Supervision
Operations Coordination	Fiscal Planning	Operations Supervision
Leadership	Forecasting and Planning	

Level 3

Responsibility for carrying out a specific task. The focus of the individual is on a task rather than the supervision or coordination of others carrying out these tasks.

Communication	Traffic Operations	*Financial Methods*
Business Writing	Inventory Control	Auditing
Creative Writing	Warehousing	Budgeting
Editing	Wholesaling	Cost Accounting
Fund-Raising	*External Relations*	Cost Analysis
Interviewing		Cost Estimation
Journalism	Campaigning	Credit And Collections
Photojournalism	Community Services	Financial Accounting
Public Relations	Community Development	Income Tax Theory and Prepara-
Public Speaking	Contractor Relations/Procedures	tion
Publication	Customer Relations	Investments
Report Writing	Fund-Raising	Tax Accounting
Technical Writing	Lobbying	*Health-Care Operations*
Telecommunications	Political Action	
Distribution	Supplier Relations	Clinical Measurement
	Vendor Relations	Emergency Medical Technology

Gerontological Health Care
Health-Care Practices
Health-Care Services
Inhalation Therapy
Laboratory Instrumentation
Nutrition

Human Resources

Affirmative Action/Race Relations
Career Programming/Counseling
Collective Bargaining
Employee
  Compensation/Benefits
  Development
  Evaluation/Appraisal
  Recruiting
  Relations
  Training
Industrial Relations
Interview Techniques
Labor Relations
Performance Appraisal
Personnel Services
Union Relations
Wage and Salary Administration

Information Systems

Computer Applications
Computer Concepts
Computer Systems
Data Systems
Management Information Systems
Records Systems
Systems Analysis
Systems Development

Instruction

Curriculum Development
Instructional Aide
Instructional Strategies
Learning Theory
Religious Instruction
Student Assessment
Training and Development
Visual Aid Construction
Vocational Education

Internal Relations

Client Services
Scheduling
Traffic Operations
Work Flow Planning

Manufacturing/Operations

Computer-Assisted Design
Computer-Assisted Manufacturing
Industrial Engineering
Industrial Safety
Numerical Control Systems
Product Design
Production Control
Production Control Analysis
Quality Assurance
Quality Control
Robotics
Shop Methods
Statistical Process Control
Time and Motion Study

Office Systems

Applied Secretarial Skills
Clerical Practices
Keyboarding/Typing
Office Management
Office Practices
Office Procedures
Office Systems
Record Keeping
Records Systems
Word Processing

Politics

Campaigning
Legislative Process
Lobbying
Local Politics
Party Politics
Practical Politics

Professional Development

Purchasing

Inventory Control
Logistics
Negotiations

Procurement
Supplier Relations
Vendor Contracting

Real Estate

Real Estate Principles
Real Estate Sales

Research Areas

Analysis
  Cost
  Data
  Fiscal Control
Evaluation
Forecasting
Marketing
Performance
Quality Control
Work Flow Measurement

Quantitative Methods

Analytical Skills
Computer Applications
Computer Concepts
Computer Programming
Data Processing
Economic Analysis
Library Resource Skills
Microcomputers
Operations Research
Software Design
Software Use (specify)
Statistics

Small Business

Small Business Administration
Small Business Practices

Social Services

Alcohol Counseling
Client Counseling
Community Development
Community Services
Family Relations
Public Safety
Recreation Services
Social Work
Substance Abuse Counseling
Youth Activities

as the unit and its faculty have the opportunity to examine and process more and more portfolios.

Consistency in the assessment of portfolios begins with a common nomenclature template. But this consistency actually is operationalized by faculty who have a common understanding of the unit's assessment process. One practice that has proven effective in experiential learning circles is the use of the team approach. Two faculty, for example, would independently evaluate a student's portfolio, identifying the competencies from the template that are persuasively present in it. These two separate evaluations would then go to the team coordinator, who also reads the portfolio, and then reconciles differences between the two original evaluators to arrive at the final competency assessment determination. If the discrepancy between the two evaluators is wide, the coordinator can also meet with them to resolve the discrepancy and to address the possible assessment misapplications that caused it.

In such a system, the coordinator reads every portfolio submitted. (In large, multifaceted departments, separate coordinators could be appointed for Theatre, Radio-Television, Speech Communication, etc.) This not only assures a consistency of evaluations, but also identifies "deviant" faculty evaluators who require additional training in the assessment process. Because of the scope of the coordinator's duties, the person fulfilling this function should be (a) interested and committed to the assessment process, (b) a respected senior colleague who therefore is not politically dependent on evaluators, and (c) the recipient of a substantial "released time" allocation in recognition of these responsibilities. All members of the department may be required to serve as initial evaluators as part of their ongoing contractual tasks. Alternatively, a smaller team of more skilled assessors may be assembled with their advising or other loads reduced accordingly to support their involvement with a greater number of portfolios.

In reaching their assessment decisions, faculty evaluators must not only detect competencies, but also the depth of these competencies as evidenced in a given portfolio. They therefore must come to common understandings as to five variables:

1. *Time.* What is the minimum length of time necessary to achieve the competency in a course, work, or other life experience?
2. *Level.* Is this experience one that feasibly and demonstrably leads to more comprehensive, directorial competencies (Levels 1 and 2 on the nomenclature template) or more narrow, task-oriented (Level 3) competencies?
3. *Complexity.* Does this experience appear to lead to a single competency, or a cluster of a primary and one or more secondary competencies (such as a mastered class in Theatre or Media Management in which the student also attained secondary competencies in Budgeting and Publicity)?
4. *Relevance.* Is this learned competency of importance to the student's plan of study and career goals? Does it pertain to outcomes encompassed by the department's mission?
5. *Progression.* Was this competency built on earlier learning—or is it a replicative or regressive experience as compared to previous activities and achievements?

Once some general understandings and guidelines pertaining to these variables have evolved, the portfolio evaluation process can move from its trial to its fully functioning phase. It must be stressed once again, however, that portfolio evaluation will only be successful to the extent that the sponsoring department has clearly and conscientiously identified its own mission and desired student outcomes.

THE PORTFOLIO OUTLOOK

Whether or not we choose to (or are required to) utilize an assessment portfolio in our own communication studies program, it seems clear that the portfolio mechanism is becoming a fixture in many academic sectors. Several colleges of education now tie portfolio preparation to the selection and career preparation of teacher candidates. Even more broadly, the K–12 accountability movement has injected portfolios into many public school systems. As just one example, on July 16, 1992, the Governor of Michigan signed into law a statewide portfolio mandate (Legislative Service Bureau, 1992). Section 104 of Public Act 148 specifies that, "To receive state aid, each district must: provide and maintain a student portfolio until the pupil graduates or leaves the district" (p. 619). The Act phased in the requirement to apply to all ninth graders in 1993–1994 and all students beginning the eighth grade in 1994–1995. It further specified that each portfolio have at least four major sections containing: (a) records of academic and nonacademic plans that the student intends to follow, (b) records of academic achievement, (c) records of career and job preparation, and (d) records of recognitions, accomplishments, and community service.

Derived from a 1987 survey of state employers and piloted in 22 Michigan districts during 1991–1992, this portfolio system reflects a nationwide concern about employability skills and an insistence on tighter linkages between the education and business communities. It is a trend that communication educators cannot afford to ignore—if only because we are far more likely than most disciplines to profit from it. With so much of our curriculum devoted to preprofessional training, it makes sense to participate in a process designed to enhance and credential career preparation.

As more and more of our students are initiated to portfolio building in their earlier schooling, it should become easier for us to adopt higher level portfolio strategies that directly reflect and identify professional communication competencies—and demonstrate all that we are doing to foster them.

APPENDIX A: ORGANIZATIONAL PACKET AND INSTRUCTIONS

Cover Sheet:

THE COMMUNICATION STUDENT'S
COMPETENCY PORTFOLIO

Organizational Packet and Instructions

Communication Studies Department
Multiplex University
653 Reputable Hall
Stubblefield, MI 48859

KEY INFORMATION ABOUT THE PORTFOLIO AUTHOR

Name:
Present Address:

Permanent Address:

Preferred Phone Number:
Alternate Phone Number:

Degree Being Completed:
Major:
Area(s) of Concentration:
Minor(s):
Previous Post-Secondary Schools Attended:

Previous Post-Secondary Degrees and Diplomas Received:

AUTHOR CERTIFICATION

I affirm that the information submitted in this portfolio is true and accurately presented.

_____   _____
(author signature)   (date)

PORTFOLIO TABLE OF CONTENTS

Instructions: This page should catalog all of the exhibits (sections) included in your portfolio. Each exhibit is identified by a hyphenated part and order number. Thus, the first (most recent) work experience/exhibit is labeled I-1, the first training experience/exhibit is labeled II-1, and the first hobbies and other life experience/exhibit is labeled III-1. Use as many pages as necessary to complete this table of contents.

Number	*Title of Experience*	*Documentation List*
I-1		

PART ONE: LEARNING FROM WORK EXPERIENCES
(Including practica and internships)

Instructions: Use the front and back of this page to describe what you learned in each single position. All related documentation should be placed in your portfolio immediately behind this page. Begin with your most recent (current) work experience and proceed backward in reverse chronological order—most recent to least recent. Use as many sheets as you need. Include precollege work *only* if you believe the experience resulted in the acquisition of *college-level* competencies.

Dates of Employment (month, year)

From: *To:*

Full-time or part-time?

Average number of hours per week:

Exact Title of Position:

Name and Address of Employing Organization:

Name and Title of Immediate Supervisor:

Supervisor's Address & Phone Number:

What were the primary RESPONSIBILITIES assigned to you in this position? (Describe in your own words.)

(Two queries below would be printed on the back of this sheet.)
What have you LEARNED as a result of your performance in this position? (Do not forget to include technical skill development as well as knowledge acquisition.)

Did you accomplish any special tasks that attracted commendation while functioning in this position? (Special achievements must be documented as well as described.)

PART TWO: LEARNING FROM PROFESSIONAL TRAINING EXPERIENCES

Instructions: Use the front and back of this page to describe each single training experience (class) that resulted in learning directly applicable to the performance of professional tasks within the communications industries. All related documentation should be placed in your portfolio immediately behind this page. Begin with your most recent training experience and work your way back in time. Use as many sheets as you need. Do *not* include secondary school coursework.

Title of Class or Session:

School/Organization Providing the Training:

Dates of Training (month/year)

From: *To:*

In-Class Clock Hours:

Brief description of the course and its major units (in your own words):

Describe the amount and type of course preparation required outside of class:

What were the prerequisites for admission to this course?

(Two queries below would be printed on the back of this sheet.)
By what means was your performance evaluated, and how frequently?

In the space below, discuss in your own words the specific knowledge and competencies you gained from this training experience. Do not just repeat the offering organization's course description.

PART THREE: LEARNING FROM HOBBIES AND OTHER LIFE EXPERIENCES

Instructions: Complete this part if you have attained college-level competencies from activities outside of conventional work and training experiences—such as hobbies, travel, and community/social service endeavors. All related documentation should be placed in your portfolio immediately behind this page. Begin with the most recent experience and work your way back in time. Use as many sheets as necessary, but remember, each experience described should have resulted in the acquisition of knowledge and competencies directly applicable to your career as a communications professional.

Activity Title/Brief Description:

Dates of Activity (month, year)

From: *To:*

Organization (if applicable):

Approximate hours per month spent on this activity during the specified period:

What tasks did you complete during your participation in this activity?

What was your primary responsibility or focus during your participation in this activity?

(Two queries below would be printed on the back of this sheet.)
Describe the activity in detail:

What specifically did you learn? What is the relevance of this learning to your anticipated career as a communications professional?

ADDITIONAL CONSIDERATIONS AND INSTRUCTIONS

(Do NOT include this sheet in your completed portfolio)

Work Experiences

Learning from a work experience differs in nature and kind from learning acquired in a class/training experience. For example, classroom learning is much more focused and concentrated than "real life." In a work experience, *you* must isolate what is important. Different people often learn/emphasize substantially different things from the "same" job. There seldom is an instructor figure to distill and organize the experience to make the learning uniform in topic and depth. Consequently, it usually takes longer to acquire a competency through a work experience than it does through a training experience. And the competencies attained by two persons in similar positions may be radically different. In short, describe and detail what *you* learned—not what someone else may have learned from the same job.

Training Experiences

Similarly, course outlines and objectives set forth instructor/institutional goals for a class. They seldom correspond exactly to what an individual student learns from that class. Thus, be certain to isolate what *you* personally achieved from this training rather than what a course bulletin or syllabus indicates you should have achieved.

Hobbies and Other Life Experiences

Sometimes a hobby or community service activity can result in competency attainment that is directly relevant to your career. For example, you might learn the rudiments of facility management by scheduling ice time for the teams in your youth hockey league. You might acquire principles of budgeting and/or accounting as treasurer of a club or sorority. Or perhaps you've attained the ability to select and edit commercial music beds as a by product of piano study or playing in a band. Do not overlook sources of learning outside the obvious situations of the workplace and college classroom.

Documentation

For all three categories of learning experiences, you must provide tangible evidence of your participation and level of attainment in each activity. Documentation typically consists of such items as the following:

Work Experiences

Performance evaluations by your supervisor, official job descriptions, awards, letters of commendation/congratulation for high performance, evidence of promotion, samples/excerpts of work produced, evidence of suggestions adopted, or special projects/innovations that you organized or created.

Training Experiences

Course descriptions, syllabi, or outlines; official transcripts/reports of grades received; samples of assignments you completed; written instructor comments on your work; licenses or certificates earned; written evidence of class preparation required; official statement of qualifications necessary for admittance to the class.

Hobbies and Other Life Experiences

Copies of publications, writings, or drawings; newspaper articles describing your proficiency or contribution; letters confirming your participation with service organizations; commendations, recognitions, and awards received; photos of items you built/created together with certifications that the item pictured was your work.

In Summary

A well-structured portfolio constitutes a detailed assessment of your competencies and achievements. It is not a pile of random observations or claims. Instead, it serves as an integrated and documented album of the knowledge and skills that you are ready to bring to bear in taking your place as a successful communications professional. The conscientiously prepared portfolio not only showcases your competencies to others, but also functions as a *personal* reminder/reassurance of what you have already accomplished.

APPENDIX B: RECOMMENDED READINGS

Dewees, P. (1986). *The assessment of prior learning: A critical adult learner service.* Athens, OH: Project Learn.

Fugate, M., & MacTaggart, T. (1983). *Managing the assessment function: Cost effective assessment of prior learning* (Vol. 19, pp. 27–43). San Francisco: Jossey-Bass.

Keeton, M. (Ed.). (1976). *Experiential learning: Rationale, characteristics and assessment.* San Francisco: Jossey-Bass.

Keeton, M., & Tate, P. (1981). *Learning by experience —What, why, how.* San Francisco: Jossey-Bass.

Knapp, J. (1977). *Assessing prior learning.* Columbia, MD: Council for Advancement of Experiential Learning.

Knapp, J. (1981). *Financing and implementing prior learning assessment.* San Francisco: Jossey-Bass.

Kolb, D. (1976). *Learning style inventory: Technical manual.* Boston: McBer & Company.

Kray, E., & Hultgren, L. (1976). *Implementing and financing portfolio assessment in a public institution.* Columbia, MD: Cooperative Assessment of Experiential Learning.

Mandell, A., & Michelson, E. (1990). *Portfolio development and adult learning: Purposes and strategies.* Chicago: Council for Adult and Experiential Learning.

Rydell, S. (Ed.). (1982). *Creditable portfolios: Dimensions in diversity.* Columbia, MD: Council for Advancement of Experiential Learning.

Simosko, S. (1985). *Earning college credit for what you know.* Washington, DC: Acropolis.

Simosko, S. (1988). *Assessing learning: A CAEL handbook for faculty.* Columbia, MD: Council for Adult and Experiential Learning.

Warren, J., & Breen, P. (1981). *The educational value of portfolio and learning contract development.* Columbia, MD: Council for Advancement of Experiential Learning.

Whitaker, U. (1990). *Assessing learning: Standards, principles and procedures.* Philadelphia: Council for Adult and Experiential Learning.

Willingham, W. (1977). *Principles of good practice in assessing experiential learning.* Columbia, MD: Cooperative Assessment of Experiential Learning.

Yelon, S., & Duley, J. (1979). *Efficient evaluation of individual performance in field placement.* East Lansing: Michigan State University.

REFERENCES

Commission on Non-Traditional Study. (1973). *Diversity by design.* San Francisco: Jossey-Bass.

Kolb, D. (1984). *Experiential learning: Experience as the source of learning and development.* Englewood Cliffs, NJ: Prentice-Hall.

Legislative Service Bureau. (1992). *Public and local acts of the legislature of the state of Michigan.* Lansing, MI: Author.

7

The Capstone Course

Robert C. Moore
Elizabethtown College

The capstone course is an opportunity for students to demonstrate that they have achieved the goals for learning established by their educational institution and major department. The course should be designed to assess cognitive, affective, and psychomotor learning and to do so in a student-centered and student-directed manner that requires the command, analysis, and synthesis of knowledge and skills. The capstone course described in this chapter integrates learning from the courses in the major with the courses from the rest of the academic experience. It is a multifaceted course that requires the application of knowledge to course requirements that serve as instruments of evaluation in all three modalities of learning. The course fosters interdisciplinary partnerships among university departments and helps cultivate industry alliances and cooperation. The chapter outlines a rationale for the capstone course and a review of the course design that involves four different capstone experiences.

EVALUATION AS A TRADITION

In examining a basis for the existence of a capstone experience, the literature in the field of education, specifically curriculum and instruction, provides some direction. From a wide variety of definitions for curriculum, one definition seems particularly useful because it specifies the elements of curriculum:

> A curriculum usually contains a statement of aims and of specific objectives; it indicates some selection and organization of content; it either implies or manifests certain patterns of learning and teaching, whether because the objectives demand them or because the content organization requires them.

Finally, it includes a program of evaluation of the outcomes. (Oliva, 1982, p. 7)

These elements are not mutually exclusive. Their integration should result in a positive and successful learning experience. The critical last element, evaluation, not only validates the learning, but also enables faculty to revise and refine courses or curricula to attain desired outcomes. Just as curriculum development is a systematic process, curriculum evaluation is a systematic process by which the student's total education is weighed.

Student achievement traditionally has been assessed by examination. Although applicable as a tool of evaluation, the test usually measures one's cognitive ability to recall and understand knowledge. Another important method of evaluation may be the student project that allows for the application of learning. Such projects are usually limited in scope and are closely related to competency in a single course. The testing method of evaluation is normally formative. That is, it is assessment used during actual instruction designed to track progress and understanding. It is a measure of the teaching and learning process. The project is summative evaluation; that is, its role is to assess learning and skills generally mastered in a course or the achievement of course goals.

By its very nature, the capstone course is a method of summative evaluation. It not only assesses previous cognitive learning in the major, but also provides a forum that allows an instructor to assesses the student's overall collegiate learning experience. Because in addition to cognitive skills, learning can occur in two other domains (affective and psychomotor), a capstone course allows for a mix of evaluative styles that assess the broad range of the students' past experiences (Kemp & Smellie, 1989, p. 20). This approach also allows students, who perhaps excel in one area more than another, to demonstrate the strengths of their learning. Achievement in the cognitive domain is usually represented by an ability to recall, understand, and apply knowledge. Evaluation of affective learning is characterized by expression of feelings, values, and attitudes (especially regarding events, issues, and topics related to, or impacting, the students' field of study). Finally, psychomotor learning is evaluated by the application and performance of skills. Ideally, a student's competence will be demonstrated in all three learning modalities.

In a summative evaluation of the students' experience in the university curriculum, a capstone course is an instrument used to measure the attainment of curricular outcomes. It is an in-depth opportunity for the student to demonstrate accomplishment of the full spectrum of that learning. It is, therefore, critical that the capstone course contain a wide and balanced variety of expectations. The student is given the opportunity to analyze and apply the accumulated learning and display creative products and solutions to requirements presented by the course. A useful model for such expectations is Bloom's Taxonomy of Educational Objectives (Bloom, 1956) as applied to the final course. These progressive levels of objectives are: recall of knowledge, comprehension, application, analysis, synthesis, and evaluation. The last three levels are higher order intellectual activity. They are concerned more with the how and why of learning rather than the what.

Affective learning has been referred to by Bloom (1971) as the implicit curriculum. It is made up of attitudes, interests, values, and feelings derived by the student through learning and by interaction with other learners and professors. The affective domain of learning advanced by Krathwohl consists of five levels: receiving, responding, valuing, organization, and characterization of a value complex. This final level, the highest order, indicates that one's beliefs, ideas, and attitudes have been integrated into a total philosophy (Kemp, 1975).

Psychomotor learning is an ongoing refinement process. Such learning is assessed as units and courses are completed. Often, new courses bring with them different and unusual forms of learning. For example, an oral performance course may develop voice delivery to a more refined stage, whereas a course in interpretation may require a new application of that previously learned skill. A course in video production may require the development of an unfamiliar combination and synchronization of finely coordinated movements. Psychomotor learning encompasses gross bodily movements, finely coordinated movements, nonverbal communication, and speech behaviors (Kemp, 1975).

The capstone course expectations should be a display of a mastery of learning and the ability to apply it to new, unusual, and integrated project requirements. Table 7.1 specifies the progressive levels of achievement in each of the learning modalities and the expectations of student performance in a capstone course.

Other learning theories have been advanced that present reinforcing views of the three domains of learning. Gagné, clarifying the hierarchical structure of learning, also noted that learning is a "cumulative process. Basic information or simple skills . . . contribute to the learning of more complex knowledge and skills. He identified five categories of learning: verbal information, intellectual skills, cognitive strategies, motor skills, and attitudes . . . . These fall into three phases of learning advanced by Bell-Gredler: preparation for learning, acquisition and performance, and retrieval and transfer" (of knowledge, attitudes, and skills; Kemp & Smellie, 1989, p. 16). Merrill classified outcomes of learning in two dimensions. First, content is drawn from advancing levels of facts, concepts, procedures, and principles. The second outcome of learning is performance characterized by remembering, using, and finding a generality (Kemp & Smellie, 1989).

These approaches to learning provide a basis for course design and evaluation. Learning expectations of students should increase with their advancement through a curriculum. A capstone course might be designed that makes use of the increasing complexity of student learning when the end of the process of instruction is reached. The course uses cumulative

TABLE 7.1
Learning Expectations in a Capstone Course

Cognitive Learning	Course Expectations
Recall of Knowledge Comprehension Application Analysis Synthesis Evaluation	Students are presented with a problem and draw on their knowledge and research to weigh and select various data leading to a solution of the problem that is workable and intellectually defensible.

Affective Learning	Course Expectations
Receiving Responding Valuing Organization Value complex	The approach and decisions made reflect attitudes, values, feelings, and beliefs characteristic of the discipline and the profession.

Psychomotor Learning	Course Expectations
Gross bodily movements Finely coordinated movements Nonverbal communication Speech behaviors	The production of a project solution to a problem and the oral and visual presentation of it, reflects a degree of skill competency as a communicator.

learning, after all previous courses and objectives have been met, to relate to more than single concepts; the course draws on the whole of the learning experience and applies it in a meaningful way.

OUTCOMES ASSESSMENT AND THE CAPSTONE COURSE

For too long, university curricula have seemed to be too specialized and fragmented. More often than not, students plodded from one course to another and often were provided little opportunity to link the relevant content and skills across the various courses. The role of the capstone course is to draw all of that learning together and to provide a single opportunity or experience during which students demonstrate that they have accomplished or achieved the university and department educational goals as represented by the various courses taken and the appropriate mission statements.

Unfortunately, faculty also often see few links between their courses and those of colleagues in other departments. The learning acquired by students in nonmajor courses is rarely applied to major courses in a meaningful manner. Curricula lack integration of the total college academic experience. It is no wonder, then, that parents, legislators, and other publics are demanding accountability. They demand proof that the education being provided is both sound and produces the desired learning in students.

The reality of higher education today is that students' major programs cannot exist in isolation from the rest of their education. Although knowledge- and discipline-specific skills are important, more universities' educational goals are embracing those outlined by the Carnegie Report (Boyer, 1987) and by the Association of American Colleges (AAC, n.d.). Schools are recognizing that they "should be accountable not only for stating their expectations and standards, but for assessing the degree to which those ends have been met" ("The Growth of a Model College," 1986, p. 31). As Blanchard and Christ (1993) stated, "the outcomes method [of assessment] is the most tangible and rational measure [of learning]" (p. 13). They cited the Michigan Professional Preparation Network Report and its listing of 10 potential professional/liberal outcomes as a framework that can be used to ascertain if students have satisfactorily met the goals of their education. As an overall statement of the goals of learning, these outcomes provide a unifying strategy for the students' entire curriculum as well as an excellent framework for the major. The 10 outcomes listed by the Michigan report are:

1. Communication competence is the ability to read, write, speak, and listen, and to use these processes effectively to acquire, develop, and convey ideas and information.
2. Critical thinking is the ability to examine issues rationally, logically, and coherently.
3. Contextual competence is an understanding of the societal context or environment in which one is living and working.
4. Aesthetic sensibility is an enhanced aesthetic awareness of arts and human behavior for both personal enrichment and application in the enhancement of work.
5. Professional identity is a concern for improving the knowledge, skills, and values of the profession.
6. Professional ethics is an understanding of the ethics of a profession as standards that guide professional behavior.
7. Adaptive competence is anticipating, adapting to, and promoting changes important to a profession's societal purpose and the professional's role.
8. Leadership capacity is exhibiting the capacity to contribute as a productive member of the profession and assuming appropriate leadership roles.
9. Scholarly concern for improvement is recognizing the need to increase knowledge and to advance the profession through both theoretical and applied research.
10. Motivation of continued learning is exploring and expanding personal, civic, and professional knowledge and skills through a lifetime. (Blanchard & Christ, 1993, pp. 15–16)

TABLE 7.2
Integrating Expected Outcomes With the Modalities of Learning

	Cognitive Learning	Affective Learning	Psychomotor Learning
Communication competence	X		X
Critical thinking	X	X	
Contextual competence	X	X	
Aesthetic sensitivity		X	
Professional ethics		X	
Adaptive competence		X	X
Leadership capacity		X	
Scholarly concern for improvement	X		
Motivation for continued learning	X		

Using the outcomes specified in the Michigan report, it is possible to show (see Table 7.2) how the intent of each of the expectations can be categorized into one or more of the modalities of learning previously discussed.

If seen as a blueprint for higher education, each of the 10 outcomes of the Michigan report provides a benchmark by which institutional and departmental mission statements might be measured. In turn, those mission statements provide the organizational plan for a curriculum and are the benchmarks by which a capstone course should be designed and outcomes measured.

The Carnegie Foundation recommends three instruments for measuring such outcomes in a capstone course. These include: a senior thesis (which draws on the historical, social, and ethical perspectives of the major), an oral presentation of the thesis with peer critique, and preparation of a portfolio (see chap. 6; "Prologue and Major Recommendation," 1986).

Curriculum evaluation is not new; neither is testing and measuring students' knowledge and demonstration of key skills. However, the capstone course provides the opportunity for faculty to assess student learning not only in relation to content- or skill-specific areas but also within the context of universally applied expectations of the educational experience. In short, the capstone course links or integrates the rational expectations of society for education with the mission of the university and the mission of a major program of study: "Even the most traditional colleges expect their graduates to move on to careers" (Boyer, 1987, p. 109). A multifaceted capstone course integrating expected outcomes can demonstrate that the student has learned what the school has established as its goals and can show the acquisition of skills and the development of a career identity for eventual employment and a promise for continued learning.

MISSION STATEMENTS AND THE CAPSTONE COURSE

The course is the singular opportunity to determine if the student has assimilated the various goals of the total education. The course can be a self-directed, integrated learning opportunity with goals established on several levels. The first and most global in nature are the general goals of higher education that have been represented here as those articulated by the Michigan report. They tend to be written as societal goals for higher education. Based on these broad statements of outcomes, the university and department design their mission statements using the philosophical approach to education most congruent with the campus culture and direction of that particular department. These statements of outcomes are the linchpin on which courses are taught. They provide the focus for expectations in the capstone course. (A sample institutional mission statement for Elizabethtown College can be found in Appendix A.)

Each academic department, in successfully integrating itself into its institution at large, must embody the basic mission statement. Yet, given the varied focus possible in any discipline, especially communications, the institutional perspective is extended in a departmental mission statement. (The mission statement of the Department of Communications at Elizabethtown College is in Appendix B.) Articulation of goals at this level is vital. Here, the profile of the educated individual is specified. It is that profile, and the level of attainment of it, that is critical in an outcomes assessment, in particular, the capstone course.

Bohn (1988), commenting on the characteristics of the mission of the School of Communications at Ithaca College, provided a good example of desired outcomes for a capstone course. He wrote:

> The core of the discipline of . . . communication is process . . . (it is) . . . to ground students in the theory, history, criticism, economics, ethics, policy, and practice of communications; to prepare them to participate as people of both competence and conscience in their future communication careers. (A) school (or department) works to achieve this mission through a program both integrative and holistic—one which introduces students to the intellectual traditions and disciplines of communication and links these traditions and disciplines to the rest of higher education and to contemporary communications practice in society and the communication professions . . . (A school or department of communications) anticipates [technological advancement and new economic realities] not simply to teach entry-level job-related skills but to provide students with the ability to understand both the context and text of . . . communication; to conduct coherent and probing inquiry, to propose, analyze, and evaluate strategy, and to express themselves in oral, written, and mediated language. . . . Students will comprehend the unique interdisciplinary nature of communications. [They] will learn to recognize communication issues, concerns, and content within larger cultural, economic, artistic, ethical and social contexts. (p. 18)

This mission statement makes an attempt to draw into its goals those of higher education and those of the educational institution. It is clear that communication is a process and that process consists of several key areas: acquisition of knowledge, application of knowledge in a meaningful way, ability to display critical thinking skills, adaptiveness in terms of context of performance, and continuance of learning as part of one's professional identity. Each of these key areas become a focus for capstone course goals.

DESIGN OF THE COMMUNICATIONS CAPSTONE COURSE

The foundation for the curriculum is in the integration of the discipline and the liberal arts. A student as a "compleat" communicator must be able to write well, speak and listen intelligently, communicate through media, develop a sense of aesthetics, and demonstrate creative expression. If skills development is a part of the curriculum, demonstration of abilities must go beyond "nuts and bolts." Faculty expectations are that students will use their knowledge and the information gathered to plan, design, and produce original projects that integrate the various types of expression. Such expectations provide a basis, indeed a mandate, for a capstone course that can adequately assess such learning. Blanchard and Christ (1993) called this approach "cross-training. . . a flexible, fundamental, integrated approach to media education" (p. 32).

Learning, not teaching, is at the center of such experiences. Student expression is critical to demonstrating successful achievement of capstone course objectives. The professor should be a mentor and guide, a consultant or counselor. Such courses are student-centered and seldom resemble those in traditional classrooms. The capstone course is driven by problem analysis, information sharing, creative solutions, and projects.

The capstone course, as presented here, is based on applied research. Students presented with a new problem must utilize their knowledge, experience, and abilities to plan and research various solutions to the problem and then correctly apply the chosen solution as an effective way to meet the purpose and goal of the problem. Multifaceted problems present challenges to the student that require the use of knowledge gained in divergent courses. Focusing that knowledge in a single capstone course provides the opportunity for applied research to meet varied demands. Additionally, in professionally oriented programs, when "real-world" problems are presented, then it is valuable that students will work with "real-world" clients in developing solutions. This component of experiential learning presents the opportunity for the student to work outside the classroom and campus (see chap. 8). It allows the student to begin to develop a sense of identity by working with individuals already in the field and jointly developing a meaningful project. For students moving on to graduate school, systematic research and its application provides excellent background and experience. The course begins a transition from school to an eventual career as the students work closely with clients and actively draw on past learning. The benefits of such an evolution include the practice of adaptive competence, establishment of the beginnings of a professional identity, observation of professional ethics, and utilizing learning within the context of one's living and working environment—all key outcomes listed in the Michigan report.

THE CAPSTONE COURSE GOAL

The departmental and institutional mission statements, incorporating various elements and the spirit of the Carnegie report, the Michigan report, and others, provide a basis for the direction and development of curriculum at the institutional and departmental level. They also provide for a basis on which a capstone course goal might be formulated. One such goal statement for the course might be:

> The capstone course integrates course work, knowledge, skills, and experiential learning to enable the student to demonstrate a broad mastery of learning across the curriculum for a promise of initial employability and further learning and career advancement.

In order to achieve this goal, a wide variety of skills might be focused on that will allow the student to demonstrate the level of achievement reached with regard to key areas of learning. Kings College lists these as *transferable skills*. They are the skills students master throughout their learning and through which they communicate attainment of the course goal. They are: "critical thinking, creative thinking and problem solving strategies, effective writing, effective oral communication, quantitative analysis, computer literacy, library competency . . .(and mediated communication)" ("The Growth of a Model College," 1986, p. 23). Portions of a communications capstone course syllabus, including goal and objective statements, course requirements, grading expectations, and thesis and project proposal guidelines appear in Appendix C. This capstone course, from Elizabethtown College, is broader than courses with similar purposes at other institutions. Depending on the nature of those communication programs, capstone courses may be more or less specialized in order to provide an outcomes assessment appropriate to the school's mission. At Elizabethtown College, the attainment of many institutional goals (Appendix A) is incorporated into the course expectations, as are the goals and objectives of the departmental mission statement (Appendix B). Although not all of these outcomes may be appropriate in all communication curricula, four course requirements of the capstone course provide a means by which a faculty member may judge a student's performance against those outcomes.

THE CAPSTONE COURSE REQUIREMENTS

Based on the recommendations of The Carnegie Foundation, a portfolio, a senior thesis or project, and an oral presentation are suggested as the key instruments to measure achievement of outcomes at the capstone level.

The Senior Thesis

The thesis examines the history, values, ethics, and social perspectives of the discipline related to a particular problem or issue. The research study extends the prior knowledge of the student through the conduction of a literature review. The student then proceeds to conceptualize the study, develop procedures, analyze the data, and make recommendations regarding the topic.

The Senior Project

Students in professional or performance-based curricula might be required to produce a project specifically tied to the thesis. The purpose of the project is to provide an opportunity for the research work to actually be a workable solution to the problem presented. Production or performance at this level not only demonstrates applied skills and abilities but also allows for practically applied research (see chap.14).

The projects that are selected "follow three major guidelines. First, the student should believe that there is a substantial need for the project. Second, the project must be approachable through recognized communications knowledge and techniques. Third, the project must be feasible within the time limits of the course" (Wallace, 1988, p. 36).

In addition, "using projects as part of the content of such a course offers several advantages. First, this format provides for close contact with faculty. . . . It provides practical career-related experiences . . . (and) offer(s) the student a sense of accomplishment as they serve . . . in a quasi-professional, practical capacity" (Wallace, 1988, p. 35). Specifically, a client project is a collaborative effort at problem solving; it develops interpersonal skills and uses evidence as a support for plans and decisions. Additionally, the concept of deadlines, persuasive argument, and personal responsibility are developed. Certainly, the project assists in establishing better corporate–institutional relationships and possibly creates partnerships among a school's various departments.

The project demonstrates the level of achievement reached by the student in communication and production skills. It also, as an experiential project, requires the student to interact on a close, personal, and regular basis with a client. The integration of this internship-type experience is a key element in helping the student learn contextual and adaptive competence and develop a professional identity (Moore, 1987).

The Oral Presentation

The content of this performance is based on the integration of the thesis and the project. It is a presentation of the research study; it allows for a summarization of the literature review, discussion of its procedures, data, and recommendations. It also can review the project, exhibit the production or performance, and discuss its results applicable as a solution to the problem. As a public performance, likely with peer review, oral and nonverbal expression can also be assessed.

The Portfolio

A formal collection of works that covers the full collegiate career of the student, the portfolio provides the evidence, documentation, and best samples of various types of creative expression and skills learning. Options exist for this portfolio to be submitted as evidence of learning or as a tool to be used in an employment search. In either case, the portfolio should show that specific aims of the curriculum have been mastered (see chap. 6).

APPLIED RESEARCH

The senior thesis and accompanying project require the student to engage in intellectually productive research for a client. Typically referred to as *applied communications research*, the goal of the work is to solve problems and bring about change (Moore, 1988). O'Hair, Kreps, and Frey (1990) listed the various characteristics of a definition of applied research. Generally, applied research is the practical design of a workable solution for a real-world problem designed specifically for a particular client.

Using the terminology for the stages of applied research as identified by O'Hair and Kreps (1990, p. 25), Table 7.3 lists and relates them to the capstone course requirements that incorporate the senior thesis and the accompanying senior project. The course requirements follow the systematic development of the research and literature review and integrates them with the project as a workable solution to a problem. Finally, and perhaps most importantly, it specifies as a final stage the process of evaluation of the solution.

Each of the course requirements, or learning measurement instruments, provides for individual differences in learning and permits demonstrated achievement in areas in which the student excels. In Table 7.4, each instrument is related to the specific type of learning modality applicable to it.

These course requirements enable the student to address and demonstrate achievement of the various outcomes statements, goal of the course, and skills expected of graduates of the curriculum by the institution. By integrating the Michigan report, the recommendations of the Carnegie Foun-

TABLE 7.3
The Applied Research Model for the Senior Thesis and Project

Problem identification	Client interviews, project selection, research question and analysis.
Conceptualization	Literature search: informal and institutional sources, library and database sources, interviews.
Operationalization	Transform the research findings into concrete approaches to solving the problem. Select project strategies based on evidence, credibility, and audience.
Measurement	Preproduction strategies, data gathering, observations, interviews relevant to the production of the project.
Analysis	Project production. Analysis of techniques, approaches, results of the project.
Recommendations	Discuss the ways in which the solution solved the problem: successes, weaknesses, suggested revisions.

TABLE 7.4
Outcomes Instruments as Related to Learning Modalities

Instrument	Cognitive Learning	Affective Learning	Psychomotor Learning
Senior thesis	X	X	
Senior project	X	X	X
Oral presentation	X	X	X
Portfolio	X	X	X

dation report, and mission statements similar to those in Appendix A and B, Table 7.5 summarizes and integrates those various aims of education within applicable learning styles and course requirements.

The capstone course is the sole learning experience that has the ability to draw together all of the elements of prior learning. When the demonstrable course requirements are completed and the faculty member has assessed student learning and performance as having satisfactorily met the expected outcomes, then student achievement of the curriculum plan has been successful.

ADVANTAGES AND CHARACTERISTICS OF THE CAPSTONE COURSE

Ward (1987) outlined the goals of curriculum reform at the University of Minnesota. With each somewhat applicable to the capstone course, one in particular seems to summarize the value of the course rather well: "[It] connect(s) the message-making work of mass communicators with the cultural and historic traditions we all share, helping students to synthesize

TABLE 7.5
Aims Achieved by the Evaluation Instruments

	Thesis	Project	Presentation	Portfolio
Cognitive learning	Scholarly concern for advancing the profession through research.	Creative thinking and design of solutions: organization, treatment, production.	Understanding of the communication/present ation process: informative, narrative, persuasive, and so on.	Works exhibit a broad range of abilities.
	Improve one's knowledge of the profession or discipline.	Discrimination between concepts, applying relevant approaches to the problem.	Use of supporting strategies and information: nonverbal communication, imagery, visual support, ethos-pathos, questioning, presentation of proof or reinforcement.	Shows an understanding of the responsibilities amd attributes of a communicator.
	Ability to acquire, develop, convey, and integrate knowledge and information.	Adaptive competence in relating knowledge to a project.	Strategy for organization: comparison/contrast, problem solving, etc.	Shows imagination, concept development.
	Critically examine issues.	Advancing the profession through applied research.	Understanding the audience, shaping of ideas appropriately.	
	Evaluation of data collected and conclusions related to issues of thesis.	Leadership capacity to initiate, manage, and carry a project to conclusion.		
	Quantitative/qualitative data analysis.			
Affective learning	Understand the societal context of learning.	Applying knowledge, skills, values of profession or discipline to a new or unique problem.	Assumption of a proper professional identity appropriate for delivery of the thesis or project.	Professional value and interest is evident in preparation of the work.
	Convey professional values and ethics.	Assume a professional identity and exhibit professional responsibilities.	Display an attitude for performance that indicates mastery of verbal techniques: clarity, relevance, effectiveness.	Presentation of work represents a professional identity.
	Show motivation for continued learning.	Shows aesthetic sensibility.	Creative planning and presentation of thesis or project.	Creative approach to the display of work.
Psychomotor learning	Competence in reading, writing, research.	Mastering the skills of the profession and application of them to a project.	Performance skills: nonverbal communication, oral communication, mediated presentation.	Collection of mastered skills and abilities.
	Computer literacy.	Design, writing, scripting, visual representation and production.	Presentation skills and organization.	Technical acumen evident in displayed work.
	Library competency.		Production and use of supporting materials.	

their other liberal arts studies with their communications studies" (p. 4). Even for those programs that do not include the mass communication element, the course can be "a clear link between knowledge in . . . communication and the rest of [a student's] education" (Dennis & DeFleur, 1991, p. 78).

Although the position presented in this chapter and the examples provided have focused on the integration of writing, speaking, and communicating through media, it has also incorporated the need for a sense of aesthetics, creative expression, and experiential learning. The nature of differing curriculums in communications, especially those without a professional focus, requires the flexible application or alteration of capstone course requirements as necessary in order for the assessment provided by the course to be faithful to the specific mission statements of that department and institution.

The following list of advantages and characteristics of a capstone course are a summary of the educative value of such an experience for students presented in this chapter.

The capstone course:

• Allows for the *adoption and integration* of institutional mission statements, departmental and school mission statements, and course objectives to the general goals of higher education.

• Is a *broad-based course* drawing together disciplines across the university. This allows for unique partnerships to develop between departments, resulting in a greater integration of them in the university fabric.

• *Allows conclusions to be drawn from student performance* regarding the level of involvement in the liberal arts versus professional training. It also enables faculty to address perceived weaknesses in a curriculum. Ongoing assessment in the capstone course allows for continual evaluation and development of the curriculum so that students are demonstrating that they are learning what faculty think they are teaching.

• As curricula and expectations change, the course *can address and incorporate new approaches and objectives.*

• *Can be tailored to measure outcomes in any of the various divisions or configurations of the communications field.* Research projects can be applied to a wide variety of interests, issues, or professional settings.

• *Places expectations on students so that they become independent learners.* The course is student centered and self-directed, allowing students to work at a pace with which they are most comfortable and in a direction suitable to career aspirations.

• *Requires students to perform at higher levels of learning* by requiring a student to engage in analysis, synthesis, and evaluation of past learning and apply it to new experiences.

• As a summative tool, provides the *opportunity to evaluate students at the end of their major program of study.*

•Is a *multifaceted instrument of assessment*. It goes beyond examinations and simple projects by integrating various assessment strategies. These include a senior thesis, an applied project for the thesis, public oral performance, and a portfolio.

•Allows *students to perform and excel in those learning modalities most appropriate* to them.

•*Integrates skill demonstrations into objectives* of an experiential nature, providing a real opportunity for business and industry alliances.

DISADVANTAGES OF THE CAPSTONE COURSE

Although one generally might not argue against the evaluation of learning or against the summative evaluation of the entire learning experience, capstone course experiences do have several limitations. As such, the departmental faculty need to be satisfied that this level and type of assessment is adequate for drawing conclusions about student achievement and the curriculum.

The capstone course:

•*Evaluates students' knowledge, identity, and skills* subjectively.

•*May allow less motivated and goal-oriented students too much flexibility* by focusing on independent and self-directed learning.

•*Can be too unfocused* unless faculty monitor departmental curricular expectations as they evolve and adjust the course.

•*Requires faculty to depart from self-serving or specialized agenda* and focus on an integrated experience where the "compleat" communicator is more important than the specialist.

•*Places great demand on student time, learning, and performance.* Many students may not be up to the task.

•May allow a student to excel in a favored learning modality but *does not easily assist students who perform in an average way, or below, in other modalities.* There is typically no course of remediation for problems and failures.

• Allows a student to approach the goal of curricular integration but does not always specify to what level that occurs. It also *does not specify how various levels of success can be quantified and translated into a summary of positive performance* of attaining the curriculum's mission.

All four instruments (thesis, project, portfolio, and presentation) of evaluation are strengths in the course. They draw their success from their variety of approaches and the way in which each of the course requirements integrates with the others to create a complete picture of student achievement. Yet, that variety and sheer workload are very demanding in terms of faculty commitment and time. Although tempting to make the course less time consuming, elimination of any one of the instruments weakens the course because each in isolation cannot be the summative tool of assessment that they are when integrated. Any one of the instruments does not allow for written, oral, and mediated expression in all three modalities of learning.

CONCLUSION

Communications programs have evolved greatly in the past century. Having originated from programs like English, curriculums gradually became more specialized and moved further away from the core program of the university. In the more recent past, the field became fragmented and more vocational (Rowland, 1992, pp. 1–3). Today, the debate has brought us back to our roots, to the liberal arts. The "new professionalism" positions the communications curriculum at the center of the university program. Driven by intellectual pursuit, the program espouses integration of learning, linkages between departments, and, perhaps most importantly, the elevation of the message to all-important status.

The diverse fields that make up the discipline of communication are blending. Yet, the one unchanging element in the mix is the message: "Creation of the message, regardless of the medium, always has been at the core of communication education. This is a distinction that critics of the discipline have long failed to understand: What is most central to our curriculum is not the how of communicating messages—what buttons to push or writing or speaking style to affect—but the what of message content" (Pease, 1992, p. 9).

Such is the focus and the value of the capstone course. The capstone course is the curricular embodiment of convergence. The course is the single opportunity for all of the knowledge and skills to be drawn together. The course ties knowledge and experience together, from the totality of the student educational experience requiring a critical assessment and unique application of 4 years of learning to the successful completion of course requirements. Drawn into the mix are the course expectations that university core courses, and those from any configuration of courses selected, will be drawn on to demonstrate a command of knowledge and ability. The course defines a basic education, a basic expectation; it outlines a level of academic and professional performance that fosters criticism and creativity. The capstone course draws together the expected outcomes of higher education, the institution, and the department into one educational experience so that those who graduate from our programs have shown that they possess more than a sheepskin.

They are "well-informed, inquisitive, open-minded young people who are both productive and reflective, seeking answers to life's most important questions. . . who not only pursue their own personal interests but are also prepared to fulfill their social and civic obligations" ("Prologue and Major Recommendations," 1986, p. 16).

APPENDIX A: ELIZABETHTOWN COLLEGE MISSION STATEMENT

Founded by members of the Church of the Brethren in 1899, Elizabethtown College aims to develop sound intellectual judgment, keen moral sensitivity and an appreciation for beauty in the world. This educational process fosters the capacity for independent thought and commitment to personal integrity. In keeping with its historical and religious tradition, the College affirms the values of peace, justice and human dignity, striving to achieve a distinctive blend of the liberal arts and professional studies. This union of the world of spirit and the world of work is expressed in the College motto, "Educate for Service," and on its seal, *Deus Lux et Veritas*.

The College fulfills this mission by:

Striving to attain a diverse academic community.

Promoting cultural pluralism and international understanding in a collegial community.

Creating an environment that encourages the spirit of free inquiry, stimulates intellectual curiosity, and cultivates academic achievement.

Developing the skills for critical analysis and effective communication.

Designing programs that foster maturity, leadership, and responsible citizenship.

Providing campus-wide support services necessary for the development of mind, body, spirit.

Serving as a learning resource and cultural center for society at large.

The institutional goals for the academic program at Elizabethtown College, in outline, reflect this general statement of educational philosophy:

1. A threefold purpose in the education of students:
   a. A general education (core) requirement, developing analytical and relational process of thought, clear and coherent means of self-expression, and a growing understanding of self and environment through distributional and integrative requirements in the liberal arts.
   b. A specific education requirement or major, preparing the student for advanced studies and/or career opportunities by adding the different experience of specialized in-depth knowledge to the breadth of the general educational requirements.

    c. A body of electives ensuring flexibility in each student's program that will best suit individual needs and interests, whether in general or major areas of study.

2. Response to contemporary needs for greater international understanding, by providing general education in intercultural studies and languages.

3. Provision of support in both general education and major programs for cross-disciplinary and interdisciplinary education.

4. For major disciplines of study, inclusion of opportunities in most of the liberal arts traditions of sciences, fine arts, humanities, and social sciences, and in the professional areas; while maintaining balance between professional and liberal arts programs of study for majors.

5. Provision for adult educational opportunities in a variety of traditional and nontraditional modes, integrated as far as possible with the regular educational program and faculty.

6. Fostering an environment supportive of faculty research and professional development.

7. Supporting as a part of its regular educational program quality experiential-learning programs such as clinical experiences, supervised internships, field study and other off-campus courses, and similar activities.

8. Continuing to support or to develop as appropriate, strong cooperative programs with other institutions of high learning.

(Elizabethtown College academic program: Educational philosophy and objectives, 1993)

APPENDIX B: ELIZABETHTOWN COLLEGE DEPARTMENT OF COMMUNICATIONS MISSION STATEMENT

The Department of Communications and its faculty strive to provide an educational environment wherein students analyze the theories and concepts of communication, consider its history and impact, and develop a level of expertise in production and performance. The Department ensures students the opportunity and educational foundation to consider societal implications and ethical considerations of communication practices, procedures, policies, and issues. It is important that students acquire craft and skill in designing and developing messages from a variety of perspectives, gaining and exhibiting communicative and technological acumen. In addition, the Department seeks to foster aesthetic awareness and encourage creative expression from Communications students. Development of professional expertise, critical judgment, and individual creativity are all essential to the liberal education provided by the Department of Communications and Elizabethtown College.

Objectives

Developed in the context of the broader baccalaureate curriculum provided through the all-college core, the department course of study is designed to:

• Encourage students to foster the liberal education programs of the College by advising students to explore a variety of disciplines, participate in and lead cocurricular activities, and to expand and broaden their interests.

• Create an atmosphere wherein students examine the importance of Communications in the study of the Humanities, Sciences, Arts, and Social Sciences, and to encourage the use of elective study in these areas.

• Build upon the clearly interdisciplinary nature of Communications by promoting the pursuit of complementary second majors and minors.

• Encourage Communications faculty to promote responsibility, leadership, and service by encouraging students to participate in, and apply their specialized knowledge to problems and opportunities within the College and the broader community.

• Promote a balance among personal expectations of the student, theoretical and pragmatic expectations of the faculty, those of the communications profession, and the spirit and tradition of a liberal educational experience.

• Recognize and foster the value of Communications as a basis for further study in a variety of graduate programs. It is part of the mission of the department to encourage students to view the Communications program in the perspective of a lifelong learning process.

(Department of Communications literature, n.d.)

APPENDIX C: ELIZABETHTOWN COLLEGE DEPARTMENT OF COMMUNICATIONS COMM 485—COMMUNICATIONS SEMINAR

Course Description

At Elizabethtown College, Comm 485, Communications Seminar (3 semester credits) is the final or capstone course required of all majors. The course is intended to provide an opportunity for an integration of previous courses in and outside of the major. The student will be expected to analyze and synthesize past learning and relate it to issues and problems in Communications. Course requirements are able to be tailored to meet a student's specific career plans or focus. The course is intended to not only permit the integration of oral, written, and visual projects, but also to provide the opportunity to research and plan a major study or produce a major project and make a public presentation to the campus community. Class meetings focus on assisting students in establishing a professional identity, whereas individual conferences routinely discuss project planning, progress, and problems.

Goal

The capstone course integrates course work, knowledge, skills, and experiential learning to demonstrate mastery of learning for initial employability and a promise for further career development.

Objectives

The capstone course is designed to help the student achieve the following outcomes:

- Enables students to work independently.
- Enhances students' skills in written, spoken, and visual communication.
- Makes available a variety of quality experiential learning opportunities, on and off campus, that provide a basis for professional expertise and identity.
- Provide the means for student acquisition of management abilities and acuity pertaining to the communications professions.
- Enable students to evaluate and process learning: find similarities, draw distinctions, synthesize concepts, be flexible, and create new ideas.
- Enable students to develop an informed sense of design and production and to use a variety of forms of mediated communication effectively.

Course Requirements

Shortly after the beginning of the semester, each student selects an off-campus client with whom they will work, for the entire semester, on developing and producing a major project for use by the client. Contacts, selection of a client, and topic of the project, are the individual responsibility of the student. Possible client leads are maintained by the professor, but formal contact and interviewing is required in order for the student to be "hired" to produce the project. Final approval of the client and project rest with the instructor.

This project becomes the focus of the course for each individual student and provides the basic framework for a rather significant literature search to be done in advance of the project. This research paper is submitted at midterm.

Having developed a research-based foundation for the project, the production process begins as the student develops, in parallel, a more significant research paper. The senior thesis demands that the student demonstrate a high level of communication competence, especially in reading and writing.

The formal written document, submitted with the project, at the end of the semester, consists of six sections or chapters: (1) An introduction to, and description of, the client and the project. Here the student explores the problem presented by the client and articulates the goal of the project. (2) A rewrite of the midterm literature search perhaps addressing deficiencies in writing, the addition of material to fill in gaps in the research, or to provide for new directions to the literature review. (3) A section of analysis and description of the actual project based upon the review of literature. The focus is on preplanning of the project. (4) This chapter provides documentation of the how's and why's of project production. Specific attention is paid to the concept, decisions made, and focus of the project. (5) The final chapter of the paper is made up of a summary and conclusion. The project is evaluated. Assessments are made as to the level of success, achieved, possible revision, and future considerations or plans as a result of the project. The follow-up to the literature review and the adapting of information to the actual project shows not only critical thinking abilities, but also a capacity for using or applying scholarly research to an immediate problem and creation of a solution that is useful and effective in meeting its goal. (6) An appendix section includes previously required progress reports, journals, treatments, scripts, logs, meeting notes, and so forth. All of this material was evaluated throughout the semester and now provides a historical record for the entire experience.

The research paper and project are also presented in public performance during the final week of the semester. Students are required to give an oral performance of 20 minutes minimum with a project presentation or selected screening at a maximum of 10 additional minutes. This presentation is generally a review of related literature with an in-depth focus on the project as a solution to the client's key problem or goal. Students must select appropriate media to support and enhance the presentation.

In preparation for the oral defense, the student will present an in-class 10-minute summary review of the literature search. This speech provides an opportunity for an advanced peer critique of content and delivery technique. The oral presentation, along with the display or screening of the project, allows the student to convey ideas and information in a speech and also in a mediated presentation. The development of poise and effective delivery in this setting enables the student to assume his or her professional identity and to demonstrate that a transition is taking place from student to professional communicator.

All students must formally plan and prepare a professional résumé. The résumé is a result of an introspective analysis of learning and skills drawn from the curriculum. The résumé provides for an articulation of a professional identity and direction for pursuit of a career after graduation. The résumé, a product of introspection and a review of learning, projects a character or identity as a total professional. It targets a specific identity with which the student is comfortable and provides the grounding for further development of a lifelong career.

Each student, based upon course background and experiences in and out of the classroom, will prepare a comprehensive portfolio of their professional strengths and expertise. The portfolio is the collection of the student's best work that specifies those varied skills and abilities developed in the past 4 years. It is a physical representation of the student's professional identity and a validation of the level of skills achieved by the student.

Grading

In grading all of the course requirements, the instructor's focus is on the display of a high level of knowledge and the application of it to a high level of professional production and performance. Societal implications and ethical considerations are addressed in evaluations, as are the craft and skill in designing and developing messages. Superior students bring to the course knowledge and information from a multitude of disciplines and show the application of that learning to their particular problem.

Each of the requirements are weighted differently in calculating the final course grade. The project, research paper, and oral defense make up 50% of the grade. The remaining portion of the grade is drawn from the midterm literature review, the portfolio, and two small requirements: the résumé and a mini-oral presentation.

Guide for Senior Project Proposal

Overview

- Background of client (name, location, type of business, etc.).
- Current status of a problem, issue, or concern that is to be addressed by the project.
- Goal: The single most important goal or solution to the problem. The client's stated purpose for the project. The reason why the client wants the project to be done and the expected outcome or solution desired.

Objective

Several independent items that the client has established as things to be addressed in meeting the project goal; that is, specifics that the project will do that, when accomplished, will effect the solution to the problem as stated.

Preproduction Strategies

Specific elements or approaches to the project that, when completed, will achieve each of the objectives and in turn effect the solution to the problem. The areas addressed here are planning, data gathering, and project design necessary to begin production.

Production Activities

Detailed list of all of the production planning and activities that must be done in order to complete each objective (and therefore meet the client's goal for the project).

Evaluation

Planned activities to be undertaken to determine the appropriateness and success of the project. These often will be long-term plans that cannot be completed in the time frame of the course. In that case, identify specific evaluation plans for the short term—to evaluate the effectiveness of the project production and the suitability of the strategies.

Guide for the Research Plan (Thesis)

Subject

A written statement describing the client's problem in its simplest terms. What is the problem to be addressed by the project? Who is it for (audience)? What is its goal or purpose?

Area of Study

Generally refers to the student's concentration or area of study in the major. This provides the focus or angle to the project and sets the tone for the research.

Topic

Drawn from the previous two items, this is a statement that specifically indicates the areas of literature to be investigated. Functionally, the topic is narrowed at this stage.

Research Question

A question that integrates the previous information and the goal of the research. What one expects to learn from the research study. The question sets a theme for the research that helps the student focus only on key elements related directly to the problem.

Research Components

A prioritized listing of from three to five key elements, drawn from the research question, that must be researched for a complete inquiry. They include: discipline-related material, project management and design literature, specific production materials, and project distribution/implementation literature, including planned evaluation.

Thesis

An integrated statement that indicates the specific nature and direction of the research. The statement cites the problem and the key areas of research that will lead to the conceptual design and production of the project.

(*Course syllabus, Comm 485, Communications Seminar,* 1993).

REFERENCES

Association of American Colleges. (n.d.). *A search for quality and coherence in baccalaureate education.* (Project on redefining the meaning and purpose of baccalaureate degrees). Washington, DC: Author.

Blanchard, R. O., & Christ, W. G. (1993). *Media education and the liberal arts.* Hillsdale, NJ: Lawrence Erlbaum Associates.

Bloom, B. S. (1956). *A taxonomy of educational objectives: Handbook I, The cognitive domain.* New York: Longman.

Bloom, B. S. (1971). Affective consequences of school achievement. In J. H. Block (Ed.), *Mastery learning* (pp. 13–28). New York: Holt, Rinehart & Winston.

Bohn, T. W. (1988). Professional and liberal education. *ACA Bulletin, 64,* 16–22.

Boyer, E. L. (1987). *College: The undergraduate experience in America.* New York: Harper & Row.

Course syllabus, Comm 485, Communications Seminar. (1993). Elizabethtown, PA: Elizabethtown College, Department of Communications.

Dennis, E. E., & DeFleur, M. L. (1991). A linchpin concept: Media studies and the rest of the curriculum. *Journalism Educator, 46*(2), 78–80.

Department of Communications literature. (n.d.). Elizabethtown, PA: Elizabethtown College, Department of Communications.

Elizabethtown College academic program: Educational philosophy and objectives. (1993). Elizabethtown, PA: Elizabethtown College.

Kemp, J. E. (1975). *Planning and producing audiovisual materials* (3rd ed.). New York: Crowell.

Kemp, J. E., & Smellie, D. C. (1989). *Planning, producing, and using instructional media* (6th ed.). New York: Harper Collins.

Moore, R. C. (1987, February). *A hierarchical program of experiential learning opportunities in communications education.* Paper presented at the AECT Convention, Atlanta, GA.

Moore, R. C. (1988, January). *The role of applied research in undergraduate communications education.* Paper presented at the AECT Convention, New Orleans, LA.

O'Hair, D., & Kreps, G. L. (1990). *Applied communication theory and research.* Hillsdale, NJ: Lawrence Erlbaum Associates.

O'Hair, D., Kreps, G. L., & Frey, L. R. (1990). Conceptual issues. In D. O'Hair & G. L. Kreps (Eds.), *Applied communication theory and research* (pp. 3–22). Hillsdale, NJ: Lawrence Erlbaum Associates.

Oliva, P. F. (1982). *Developing the curriculum.* Boston, MA: Little, Brown.

Pease, E. C. (1992). Defining communication's role and identity in the 1990's: Promises and opportunities for journalism and communication studies. In R. Wells (Ed.), *Insights* (pp. 6–10). Columbia, SC: ASJMC.

Prologue and major recommendations for Carnegie Foundations report on colleges. (1986, November 5). *The Chronicle of Higher Education,* pp. 16–22.

Rowland, W. D., Jr. (1992). The role of journalism and communications studies in the liberal arts: A place of honor. In R. Wells (Ed.), *Insights* (pp. 1–9). Columbia, SC: ASJMC.

The growth of a model college (A report of the President, Kings College). (1986). Wilkes-Barre, PA: Kings College.

Wallace, R. C. (1988, January). A capstone course in applied sociology. *Teaching Sociology, 16,* 34–40.

Ward, J. (1987). Developing journalism curriculum in the information age. In R. O. Blanchard (Ed.), *Partial proceedings from the second ASJMC Administrators Workshop* (pp. 3–5). Columbia, SC: ASJMC.

8

Internships, Exit Interviews, and Advisory Boards

Val E. Limburg
Washington State University

The three functions identified for this chapter are those elements of an education that serve as links to the profession, and for the student, "job getting." Without a proper understanding of various facets, advantages, and disadvantages of internships, exit interviews, and advisory boards, neither the faculty member nor the student will be able to bring to full circle the critical tasks of education—assessment and application.

INTERNSHIPS

Why Internships?

Before even entering a communication program, students often learn that they cannot enter the profession without experience. This may be why they have chosen a program: It offers experience. Their attempts to jump from high school to a "boss jock" in the city's radio station, or anchor at the local TV station, or any responsible positions in public relations or advertising are met with knowing nods and the simple admonition: "Get your college degree." Then, after grinding through all the demanding courses, with degree in hand, the graduate is told, "Sorry, we can't hire you without experience." It is frustrating for the student to learn that the degree is, in a pragmatic sense, worthless, and discouraging for faculty to see that it is so perceived (Meeske & Sullivan, 1989; Renz, 1988). This is a basic reason that programs in communication have established professional internships. At the same time, a true liberal arts education need not be overlooked (see Blanchard & Christ, 1993a, 1993b; Durham, 1992; Eastman, 1987, 1993;

Parisi, 1992; "Planning for Curricular Change," 1987; Rosenbaum et al., 1992, Warner, 1993; Wood, 1993.)

Definition and Characteristics

An internship is professionally supervised training in preparation for a career with demands for specific tasks, abilities, or knowledge. It is the practical application of the concepts, principles, and skills learned in the classroom. It could also be considered the final test for a sound curriculum in preparing the student for a profession. Many of the traits of an internship present problems or dilemmas for those involved. (Good preliminary discussions are found in Gross, 1981; Hilt, 1991.) Such problem-generating traits are identified in the following:

Prospective Sites

What kinds of places, organizations, or sites are possible for serving an internship? Generally, any organization large enough to be able to use the labor and offer the guidance and tutoring for an intern offers the potential for an internship. A student or supervising faculty member may wonder where to begin. A survey of library resources on internships offers directories and information on the following kind of internships: public service, working in state government, education/teaching, education/administration, pharmacy, environmental science, adult and continuing education, minority management, work with the Smithsonian Institute, the FBI, and even the White House. Many of these need interns with specialized kinds of training and interests. Some of these offer administrative, organizational, or public relations opportunities.

In the area of communication, for example, there is Fry's (1990) Directory in an *Internship* series. This particular one includes thousands of internships at hundreds of major ad and public relations agencies, research firms, corporations, and associations throughout the United States and Canada.

All levels of internships can be found. Even for the academic who seeks to keep professional ties, some associations make this possible. For example, the Broadcast Education Association worked for years to link college faculty with stations that were willing to take them on during the summer, offering an updating of their knowledge of the industry, and an opportunity to keep in touch with the profession generally. (In this case, it was finally determined that interested faculty could as easily set up their own arrangement.)

Credit

Generally, interns receive credit from an educational institution, which means that a faculty member works together with a professional in approving the work done by the intern. It also means that the credit received allows the work to be done without complaints from labor unions about the hiring of free or cheap labor to displace their existing work force.

In a discussion of the "zero-hour internship," Blanchard and Christ (1993a) explained that such an arrangement may offer opportunities for experience without overweighing internship credits in the student's program. Such internships can even accommodate registration at many schools, thus avoiding the requirement by some organizations that those who intern with them need to be college enrolled.

Amount of Credit

Some institutions allow students to enroll for as much credit as any other one course would allow, perhaps 3 semester hours. The student may then regard such internship experience as another course—to spend 5 to 10 hours per week in the required setting. This is feasible if the school is located near the internship site.

However, if the school is located in a more rural setting, or in a "college town," it may not be possible for the student to commute between school and the internship site. In such a setting, the school may make provisions to allow the student to engage full time in the internship experience, living near the site, and focusing entirely on the professional internship experience. This would seem to have advantages for both the intern and the professional alike, because it allows for full engagement in the experience, rather than a more casual requirement of a few hours a week. The problem here, however, is that of credit. If students take a full semester out of school, or at least off the campus, they must either sacrifice significant credit, or ask for a semester's worth of credit for the full-time internship. Schools may offer such credit, but doing so presents a curricular dilemma: It gives more than the conventionally allowable credits under accreditation. Thus, the school in the setting away from a metropolitan area may actually be at a disadvantage in seeking accreditation, that is, if the program has a high priority on internships. (The Accrediting Council on Education in Journalism and Mass Communications restricts the number of hours that can be in the major; many hours for an internship could actually prohibit many regular courses from the student's program; *Accredited Journalism and Mass Communications Education 1990-1991*, 1991). No solution to the dilemma is offered here, but the problem is one of the inherent evils in attempting to design a strong curriculum in good faith.

Paid or Unpaid

For many students, the prospect of working for nothing is not very exciting, but may be compensated by the fact that they are gaining important experience in preparation for a career. And, in order to receive college credit for the internship experience, the student will usually have to pay some form of tuition or fees. In the past, labor unions have objected to the use of interns as "free labor" to replace their own members. In 1973, the U.S. Department of Labor ruled that interns were not employees (Barnes, 1973). The skepticism by some unions about internships remains.

For the employer or professional internship supervisor, the intern offers "free labor," or reduced expenditures for labor. But it may also mean time taken away from important tasks by those who must attend to the proper training of the interns (Ladone, 1990).

Some professionals insist on paying their interns. It may be minimum hourly wages, or in the form of a stipend to help pay expenses or tuition. Sometimes such stipends will come at the end of the internship where responsible work has been demonstrated. In some cases, the internships with higher stipends become a prize, or an award given to the better students in the program.

For the professional, paying an intern may assure two other things: (a) obtaining an intern when one could really be used, as the professional competes with scores of other professionals in vying for competent students. Generally, there are more internship sites then there are qualified students to serve in those positions. (b) The best students will apply for those internships that give stipends or some monetary incentives. Some colleges may even have an application process and award the paid internships to those who are the most qualified. For the professional and the student alike, this is a rewarding advantage.

A "Legitimate" Educational Experience

Most institutions of higher education will insist that in order for a student to receive credit, there must be some "education," some legitimate learning associated with the credit. Thus, an internship where the student simply answers the phone, or serves as "go-fer" to fetch coffee may not be considered legitimate; there is little real learning that takes place. Such learning or educational requirements should be made clear, up front, by the faculty member arranging the internship (see, for example, Kamalipour, 1992).

Often, there may be a form or contract that incorporates an agreement by both parties (the faculty and the professional) about what the agreed upon tasks will be during the internship (Kramer, 1988). Often, it could be detailed enough to include how many hours or weeks will be devoted to each specific function or task (see Appendix B).

Who Carries the Initiative?

College or university programs concerned with a legitimate, independent, or accreditable experience for their students will be concerned about arranging the internship (see Appendix B). If the student arranges the internship, it may not meet the expectations of the program (e.g., the agreement of assigned tasks *before* the internship commences). On the other hand, if the faculty member arranges the internship, it may not satisfy the specific interest of the student. It seems, then, that there must be a joint effort in making the arrangement (Ware, 1975). This can be done by an application form (see Appendix A) that asks the student to identify:

1. Preferred site or location. Sometimes it is easier for a student to work in a setting convenient to his or her residence.
2. Basic nature of an internship. A student preparing for an internship in TV news may not be happy being assigned to a weekly newspaper.
3. The organization. A student's principles may allow him or her to be happier doing public relations work for an environmental organization than a Fortune 500 company.
4. Grades and demonstrated preparation. This can be translated as incentives for good work. If the organization has a reputation for providing its responsible interns with good job leads or a cash stipend, a good student may opt for that situation.

The supervising faculty member may then match student applications with a form from the professional who specifies the kinds of tasks offered and something about the setting of the internship site.

There are other ways of working the application process. One is simply to have students investigate and line up the internship on their own. However, in a college setting where the key responsibility for a student's education rests on the shoulders of the faculty and the carefully designed curriculum, such "on your own" exploring flies in the face of a carefully directed program. Some would argue for a middle ground: Allow the student to find internships that they want. Then, armed with the right information, or some leads, the faculty member can give sanction to the site.

The problems:

1. To what extent should the student be able to dictate the terms of the internship? Is the application merely preference that may or may not be met?
2. What happens when a match cannot be made?
3. To what extent might a professional supervisor be able to reject the candidate matched by the faculty member?
4. To what extent may the professional supervisor change the kinds of tasks agreed upon earlier?

Who Is the Teacher? Who Is the Evaluator?

It should be evident that during the internship much of the day-to-day instruction is done by the person working with the intern in the professional setting. Some may argue that the real control of instructional design is lost when the faculty member, carefully and systematically chosen by the educational institution, does not have direct control of what the student learns. There is no institutional evaluation of the professional supervisor in a conventional sense—no annual review or no demonstration of scholarly activity (Association of American Colleges, 1985).

Others would argue that this is exactly what a good teacher should be judged on—a focus on productivity and outcomes, and avoidance of those things that distract from the practical tasks (Christ & Blanchard, 1993).

In the end, however, the faculty member and the professional evaluator work together as a team. Both evaluate (see the Intern Evaluation form, Appendix C). It could also be argued that although this professional will evaluate the work of the intern, it is still the faculty member that will determine the granting of credit. This is where final control remains. It is a matter of shared teaching and shared evaluation. Still, some faculty perspectives may have trouble with that concept.

It could be argued that if most of the student's instruction is controlled by the faculty, what is the harm of professionals sharing that limited role when getting students ready for specific professional roles?

Who Qualifies?

Should any or all students in the major be qualified for an internship? Or should students be required to earn a minimum grade in a qualifying course? For example, a student may be a communication major, having to earn a high grade point average in order to certify, but earns a C– in the TV News course. Should the student then be allowed to serve an internship in TV news? It could be argued that such a student has demonstrated she or he is not suited for such a professional calling. On the other hand, the student may need the internship to polish the skills that were only crudely developed in the classroom. Some people are simply slow starters, but may turn out to be the most competent.

Many programs have qualifications for internship credits (Kamalipour, 1993; Meeske, 1988). Most commonly, this would include upper-class standing, usually senior. Also familiar in the list of prerequisites are grade point average and a good grade (B or better) in the qualifying course. Such criteria may depend greatly on the philosophy of the curriculum design.

The Reporting Process

"The job's not done until all the paperwork is completed." This expression hits the target for the closure of the internship experience, especially if there is credit to be earned. Some faculty may regard the full reporting process as the real element that earns the credit. Some programs require a simple completion of a form (see Appendix D). Others require comprehensive and detailed descriptions of the day-to-day experience.

What are the kinds of things that might be included in the reporting system?

• A diary, journal, or calendar of events listing or describing the experience on a day-by-day or week-by-week basis.

• A description of the tasks learned. This may be the formal tasks (working with equipment) or informal (responsibility and dress codes).

• An evaluation by the intern of whether the experience was worthwhile. Did the professional supervisor take the time to train and explain what was to be learned? Would the intern recommend that this internship be retained for future interns?

• With hindsight, what courses and experience in the college curriculum were the most valuable in preparing for the internship? Describe which classes and which faculty member's demands were most in conformity with professional expectations. Were there any weaknesses in the curriculum design—things for which the classes did not provide preparation? What things would you do differently in both college course work and at the onset of the internship?

Such internship reporting could also be given in a postinternship seminar, as suggested by Garrison (1981).

It would be assumed, then, that this information could be used as feedback for the redesigning or refinement of the internship component of the curriculum.

Evaluation of Student Performance

The evaluation team of the faculty and the professional together look at the internship performance. First, the professional could either complete a form (such as the one found in Appendix C), or otherwise communicate with the faculty member responsible for giving the credit. The faculty member then: (a) decides whether to grant credit (for a credit-bearing internship), (b) puts the professional's evaluation and other relevant materials into the student's portfolio, (c) uses the material for the exit interviews (see next section), (d) communicates with the student about the level of his or her performance.

EXIT INTERVIEWS

Definition

The term *exit interviews* implies an assessment of the students as they leave the program and enter the professional setting or practice. In a broad sense it is not limited to a sit-down interview with the advisor or department chair during the week before graduation. It can and does involve other kinds of assessment. As part of the definition of *exit interviews*, here are some of the patterns of assessment:

Assignments from Key Courses. If professional preparation is the objective of a course, there will be professionally oriented assignments required in the course. A Public Relations Campaigns course, for example, demands application of the components of a campaign. If a student does not know how to apply the principles taught, or prepares the assignment half-heartedly or poorly, this can reveal as much as any in-depth exit interview might.

Often, senior level courses have term projects that require the application of many levels of information. The outcome is supposed to be equivalent to a formal proposal in a professional setting. What better way to assess students' readiness as they are about to exit the program?

There may be a consistent pattern of poor preparation of important assignments in key courses. The impression from collective assignments can reveal a lot about individuals as they exit to the real world.

It may be necessary for a curriculum to identify those key courses with assignments that are central to student performance assessment. Most programs have required courses in the curriculum. Are these the ones with such assignments? Are the required courses those with demanding instructors? To what extent can the faculty agree on a curriculum that would serve assessment functions with its instruction?

Direction of Work Quality. Some students enter college poorly prepared or unmotivated. Their initial work or their work in general university requirements may be minimal. Some such students, after a poor start, may work with great enthusiasm and attain good grades after entering the major, however. Has the work improved, especially during the senior year? Is a maturation evident in this person? There should be consideration for such scholastic upward mobility.

Improvement is a quality that should be evident from a quick look at the student's transcript. It might also be apparent to those who have worked with the student over the program. In large programs, however, such close attention may be overlooked. Often, faculty may see a student in only one class, and if that is at the beginning of a program, the improvement factor may not be assessed.

Student Portfolio. Increasingly, students are being asked to keep some kind of portfolio that reflects career preparation (see chap. 6). The nature of the portfolio differs, depending on the student's professional direction. A student in broadcast news may keep a résumé tape with pieces of stories or reporting efforts. A student in advertising may keep pieces of creative work, layout, or media placement proposals. A journalist would keep a clip file of stories that had been used by newspapers, including student papers, and so on. A faculty advisor may then sit down and confer with a student as to whether such portfolios are suitable, of professional quality, or missing key elements.

Perhaps no other tangible element of a student's education is more practical and useful in the actual job-getting process than is this portfolio. For that reason, it should be assembled with the specific job or professional position in mind.

Internship Evaluations. As explained in the preceding section, professional work for credit, when carefully and properly evaluated, serves as an important evaluative factor as the student exits the program. It is here that the professional strengths become evident. For some professionals, an evaluation by a peer professional means more than one by a faculty member. Some students with good evaluations may wish to make them part of their portfolio used in the actual job search.

Letters of Recommendation. Perhaps the bottom line in any kind of exit interview is the piece of paper the student carries away from such closing evaluations. Faculty members involved with senior-level or professional-oriented courses should expect requests for letters of recommendation. There are a few rules for the student and evaluator or reference to keep in mind:

1. Students should ask for recommendations only from those who know of the work they want recommended. It makes no sense to ask for a letter from the instructor who teaches the theory course if the employer is not interested in what the student knows of theory, but rather how that theory is applied in the media campaigns course.

2. Students should ask for recommendations only from those who can give positive and good assessment. Someone who does not know the characteristics or, worse still, someone who sees the work as having been poorly produced, should not be asked to provide an assessment. Although such assessment from both the positive and negative sides of the student's work would give a more accurate picture, expectations of recommendations are that they will be positive and can speak of specific qualities in a positive manner. Sometimes an honest, thorough evaluator will mention weaknesses in a way that puts them in an overall context that subordinates their gravity. Employers seeking more than the conventional compliments of recommendations may do their own detective work in finding evaluators who will be honest in revealing weaknesses as well.

3. Students and evaluators alike usually realize that the recommendations encompass both specific professional abilities and personal characteristics, such as initiative, responsibility, punctuality, and so on. This should

serve as a critical clue for students entering a program that their style of work, as well as their end product, are all assessed.

4. The best recommendations or evaluations are those that are directed to a specific individual concerning a specific professional position. Less effective is the generic letter ("To Whom it May Concern") describing the student's ability only in general terms, applicable to a vast array of positions.

5. As an extension to this last idea, the ideal reference may be that person who is in a position to have contacts with professionals or potential employers, both for the sake of hiring, and for knowing others who may be hiring. Most reputable programs whose influence reaches into the professions through their alumni have a professional liaison. Without that, the program may remain an academic ivory tower, or at the very least, a program that puts students completely on their own in initiating the career path.

Involvement in Extracurricular Activities. Some programs and many professional employers want detailed information about the student's involvement in extracurricular activities. Was there involvement in a service group? An honorary group? A student production competition team? Student government or leadership? Work for on-campus quasi-professional organizations?

Who Assesses? When there is an actual exit interview, it may be done by the department chair, in schools whose programs make such an assignment feasible. In larger programs, such an interview may fall to the faculty member who serves as advisor, or the person who serves as the specialist in the focus of the student's program. In some programs, there may be a central office that tracks the graduates and keeps an alumni file. Such exit records may be part of this exit interview process. Unless the department is committed to the success and career paths of its students, there may not be reward or even provision for such an exit interviewing process. If there is any priority placed at all on such a process, there should be provisions for reward or reinforcement in the faculty reviewing process, because this interviewing is an arduous task.

The kinds of questions asked or information communicated in the exit interview will differ from one program to the next. Generally, however, it may contain the kinds of information found in Appendix E, the Exit Interview Checklist.

The student who can earn good grades in course work and at the same time demonstrate quality efforts in some experience-earning activity is likely to have an advantage over the one without some parallel extracurricular activity.

In summary, the exit interview is much more than the term implies. It is often a series of assessments from a number of different activities, often by a number of different people. The more comprehensive and inclusive the assessment at exit time, the better the picture a future employer will have of the prospective employee at the onset of the career path. Assessment, after all, can be a win–win–win situation for the student, department, and employer.

ADVISORY BOARDS

A discussion of advisory boards perhaps begs the question, "Should a communication program (or any college curriculum) have an advisory board?" But such a question still needs to be asked. If a faculty assiduously develops a curriculum with a broad liberal arts base, as well as a professional orientation, is the perspective of the professionals needed? Could there not be singular proprofessional bias, one that lacks the critical look at the problems of some professional practices? Would an advisory board interfere with true academic freedom? On the other hand, without such advice, the curricular design could come from the Never-Never land of the Ivory Tower. The dilemma seems to have no easy solution, but maybe there is one.

Note that the term is *advisory* board. The idea and usual design is to give advice or input, not dictate the terms. It is, perhaps, possible that a faculty allows itself to be manipulated and have the design of its program dictated by a professional advisory board. At the other extreme, it would be somewhat hypocritical for the school to have a professional board in theory only, where the real advice is illusory and never implemented. Ideally, there will be a golden mean where the input of the board is taken seriously, but still subject to the final judgment of the faculty. The board is *advisory*, not executive.

Creating an Advisory Board

The first step is for the school or the faculty to make the decision to have such a board. If so, there can be an early design or agreement as to its function and boundaries. Usually, professionals are flattered to sit in on such an advisory board, and would not dare to be so presumptuous as to start off its advisory function in dictating the terms of its power or of any of its functions such as the curricular design.

Why Have an Advisory Board?

There are probably more compelling reasons to seek an advisory board than to argue against one. The board obviously attracts attention of the professions to the school's program. If, however, the program is weak, such attention may be unwelcomed. A strong program should welcome such a gaze and may even think of this as an important promotional activity.

Secondly, the input, whether the program is weak or strong, can lead to greater strengths or new ideas to be introduced into the curriculum. Who is afraid of new ideas, or shuns input? Such people should probably be involved neither in advisory boards, nor higher education (Limburg, 1993).

A third point is that the professional members of the advisory board can serve as important reference points for students breaking onto the career path. They can be mentors. They know the people who are hiring if they themselves are not. They are in the network of professionals in an area (Ramsey, 1988).

There are other reasons, of course (see the next section). However, these three should speak for themselves as to the potential importance of an advisory board.

When the school decides to begin the process of creating an advisory board, what are some of the guidelines that might be helpful?

1.   Allow the composition of the advisory board to represent the various components or sequences of the program. If a school has programs in public relations, advertising, film production, print journalism, speech communication, corporate communication, TV news, or radio programming—each of those professional orientations ought to be represented. It may be a good idea to have more than one representative for each professional orientation.

2.   Be creative and diverse in finding professionals. For example, a speech communication graduate working as a consultant for a corporation's internal communication structure could be a valuable asset.

3.   Search for professionals who are willing to volunteer time, service, and help to the institution. Perhaps they are alumni who are willing to give something extra for the alma mater.

4.   Membership of the board should include those not currently employed by the school. A renewable term with an expiration, such as 3 years, could be designated.

5.   The selection process could be formalized. For example, new board members could be selected by current board members and school faculty, with a two-thirds vote by that combined body for approval for board membership.

6.   Board leadership, or chair of the board, could serve a specified term in office (e.g., renewable 3 years). That person would preside at board meetings and coordinate the activities of the board.

7.   Meeting times and places could also be designated to assure that there would, in fact, be meetings with goals, agenda, and accomplishments.

8.   Finally all these functions and structuring should be drafted into a charter and by-laws. That way, there is foreknowledge and an agreed on set of expectations.

Activities, Goals, and Functions

Contributions ought to include a variety of practical services in support of the school's program. These could be developed at the onset of the board's organization, or as supplement to existing boards. Advisory requests from the board could include:

1. Suggestions for improvement in the curriculum to make it more responsive to the communication professions.
2. Advice on faculty recruitment, including interviewing finalists for positions.
3. Assistance for the school in fund-raising activities, including assistance for all extramural funding.
4. Helping the school in acquiring instructional equipment.
5. Aiding the school in providing professional development opportunities for faculty (e.g., faculty internships, summer temporary work in keeping current in the profession, etc.).
6. Assisting the school in providing internships for students.
7. Aiding the school in student recruitment, including any and all enhancements of the school's reputation among potential students.
8. Assisting the school in sponsoring special events—speakers, symposia, programs, and so on (see Ramsey, 1988).
9. Working as mentors for students aspiring to their professional area; advice could be personal and may include helping graduates with job leads or other employment helps.
10. Providing funding for scholarships. This could be in conjunction with the school, or independent as a professional organization.
11. Assisting with accreditation; generally work with the academic establishment in gearing up for a respectable program at the school.[1]

There may be other functions, of course. However, it should be evident that the advisory board is not merely a group of myopic professionals insisting that a course in which it is interested be taught. The contributions of this proactive board are really vital to a successful program.

Problems

What happens when the advisory board does not work? Here are a number of potential problems with possible solutions:

Problem: A heavy-handed advisory board member insists on certain measures, such as curricular reform.

Solution: Ask other board members for their ideas. Often group opinion tempers a strident voice. Discuss in an open, frank manner the problems in

---

[1]Thanks to Alex Tan, Director of the Edward R. Murrow School of Communication at Washington State University for much of this list.

implementing certain ideas. Or, agree to *try* the idea, with the provision that several other factors come into play and may change the outcome.

Problem: The board tries to posture itself as a legislative, law-making body rather than an advisory board.

Solution: From the onset, make sure that the understanding is that the board is *advisory* in nature. If necessary, go back to those initiating arrangements and express appreciation for the members' input. (*Input* implies giving advice, as opposed to constructing reality.)

Problem: The board does not seem to understand the bureaucratic and complicated procedure in getting ideas into action at an institution of higher education.

Solution: Take the time and effort to educate the board members. Explain processes of approval, time frames, and so forth. Have board members attend faculty meetings, curriculum committee meetings at the university level, and so forth.

Problem: The advisory board just will not work!

Solution: Take a positive, proactive stance. Convey the attitude that it is working. Take time to make the measures that ensure success. Most successful professionals understand such an approach.

SUMMARY

It should be clear from these descriptions that the internships, exit interviews, and advisory boards all serve to give the program distinct advantages. They serve to give assessment and input, both to students, as part of their education, and to the program, which prides itself on a professional education.

These functions may be especially critical for those programs that think they do not need it. Many strong programs have one or more of these three elements. Those with the fastest growing reputations in their field are conscious of finely tuned assessment tools from both faculty and professionals. These accept the contributions of their professional counterparts, whether from internship evaluation, or on advisory boards. For them, there is no question of the advantage of internships, exit interviews, or advisory boards.

APPENDIX A: APPLICATION FOR PROFESSIONAL INTERNSHIP

Name: ID:

Campus Address:

Phone:

Home Address:

City: State/Zip:

Phone:

Request for internship for   semester/quarter, 19   .

Indicate courses taken in program and grade:

Overall GPA: Comm GPA:

Total credit hours, end of this semester:
Expected graduation date:

You are a certified major?

Indicate professional position or area in which you prefer internship:

Location preference: (specific sites or organizations may be identified)

Attestation: I agree that I will perform in a professional manner and will follow the instructions and policies of the organization where I will be interning. I understand that I will submit a written report describing my activities and evaluating my off-campus experience at the conclusion of my internship. This must be done in a satisfactory manner before credit may be granted. I understand that I must enroll for credit with the school and if I drop or fail to pay my tuition fees, I will be dismissed from the internship program and the on-site supervisor will be notified that I am no longer with the university.

Note any special information:

Signature: Date:

APPENDIX B: INDUSTRY AGREEMENT

Date

In agreement with: (School),
our organization agrees to use an intern during:

Fall semester   Spring semester   Summer term

The following tasks would be assigned to the intern:

It is agreed that the intern will be provided with supervision and training
in exchange for the labor provided. It is further agreed that contact will be
maintained with the school's internship coordinator, and that at the end of
the internship, the school will be provided with an evaluation reflecting the
intern's work.

Name:

Title:

Company:

Address:

City/State/Zip:

Phone:

Signature:

Return this form to:

APPENDIX C: INTERN EVALUATION

Intern   Site
                   Excellent   Good   Fair   Poor   Not applicable

WORK TRAITS

Personality

Appearance

Dependability

Initiative

Takes direction

Accepts criticism

Applies criticism to work

Handles pressure

Contributes

WRITING

Clarity

Grammar

Spelling

Turnaround time

Accuracy

SPECIFIC TASKS

Preparation of materials

Understanding of equipment, facilities

Understanding/use of resources

Other:

APPENDIX D: INTERNSHIP PROGRESS REPORT

Intern: Date:

Location:

1. Attach with this report an organization profile. This should include as much information as you can gather concerning the organization, its goals, its market, its clients/audience, personnel policies, practices, and so on.

2. Attach with this report a weekly log or some systematic description of your professional training experience during the internship.

3. Attach with this report an evaluation of the school's curricular prerequisites preparing you for the internship.

4. Briefly list or outline each of the tasks performed to date for your internship.

5. Did your supervisor(s) provide you with learning opportunities, or make an effort to train you? Explain.

6. Do you feel satisfied with the variety and nature of experience on your internship? Explain. Would you recommend that this organization be retained as a participant in the internship program? Why or why not?

7. Briefly evaluate your internship to date.

Submit this report by:

APPENDIX E: EXIT INTERVIEW CHECKLIST

Student:

A. Academic

Curriculum Specialization:
Grade Point Average:
Overall   Major
Awards, scholarships, honorariums, recognition:

Thoroughness of preparation for area of specialization:

Projects, achievements in key courses:

B. Extracurricular

Campus: Departmental:

Organization membership:

Curricular activities:

Leadership positions:

Skills, special talent:

C. Personal Characteristics

Responsibility, dependability:

Preparation for career track:

Initiative:

Working with others:

Takes direction:

Appearance, dress, mannerisms:

D. Evaluations and Recommendations (may be attached)

Advisor: Instructors
Professional references   Personal references

REFERENCES

Accredited journalism and mass communications education 1990–1991. (1991). Accrediting Council on Education in Journalism and Mass Communications. Lawrence: University of Kansas.

Association of American Colleges. (1985). Integrity in the college curriculum: A report to the academic community. In C. F. Conrad & J. G. Haworth (Eds.), *Curriculum in transition: Perspectives on the undergraduate experience* (p. 65). Needham Heights, MA: Ginn.

Barnes, A. M. (1973, July–August). Federal rule specifies intern is not employee. *PNPA Press,* p. 14.

Blanchard, R. O., & Christ, W. G. (1993a). *Media education and the liberal arts: A blue-print for the new professionalism.* Hillsdale, NJ: Lawrence Erlbaum Associates.

Blanchard, R. O., & Christ, W. G. (1993b). The new professionalism and the iron triangles. *Feedback, 34*(1), 5.

Christ, W. G., & Blanchard, R. O. (1993). The new professionalism means integration. *Feedback, 34*(2), 7.

Durham, F. (1992). Cultural history of a curriculum: The search for salience. *Journalism Educator, 46*(4), 14.

Eastman, S. T. (1987). A model for telecommunications education. *Feedback, 28*(2), 21.

Eastman, S. T. (1993). Theme-based curricula: A response. *Feedback, 34*(2), 4.

Fry, R. W. (Ed.). (1990). *Internships.* Hawthorne, NJ: Career Press.

Garrison, B. (1981). Post-internship seminar can solve academic credit, grading problems of internship programs. *Journalism Educator, 36*(1), 14–17, 48.

Gross, L. S. (1981). *The internship experience.* Belmont, CA: Wadsworth.

Hilt, M. L. (1991). Improving broadcast internships. *Feedback, 32*(1), 6.

Kamalipour, Y. R. (1992). Broadcast education vs. vocational education. *Feedback, 33*(1), 2.

Kamalipour, Y. R. (1993). Internship procedure, performance and assessment. *Feedback, 34*(3), 25–26.

Kramer, T. (1988). Internship liability: Protecting the student, the university and the host organization. *Feedback, 29*(4), 35.

Ladone, K. (1990, May 23). Summer interns: Slave labor. *New York Times,* p. A17.

Limburg, V. E. (1993). 'Yes' to the new professionalism; 'No' to the pseudo reasons for its need. *Feedback, 34*(2), 3.

Meeske, M. D. (1988). Broadcast internships: Results of a national survey. *Feedback, 29*(4), 37.

Meeske, M. D., & Sullivan, M. (1989). A survey of broadcast job placement. *Feedback, 30*(1), 13.

Parisi, P. (1992). Critical studies, the liberal arts, and journalism education. *Journalism Educator, 46*(4), 4.

Planning for Curricular Change in Journalism Education (2nd ed.). (1987). (Project on the Future of Journalism and Mass Communication Education). The Oregon Report. Eugene: School of Journalism, University of Oregon.

Ramsey, R. T. (1988). The guest speaker as an agent of socialization. *Feedback, 29*(2), 3.

Renz, B. (1988). Broadcasting industry perceptions of the relative value of college majors for entry-level employment. *Feedback, 29*(2), 8.

Rosenbaum, J., Moore, R. C., Quenzel, R., Yancy, T. L., Limburg, V. E., Craig, J. R., & Wood, D. N. (1992). What should the mass media core curriculum be like? *Feedback, 33*(2), 14.

Ware, P. D. (1975, November). *Broadcasting student internships: Put them in writing.* Paper presented to the Western Speech Association Convention, Seattle, WA.

Warner, C. (1993). Response. *Feedback, 34*(2), 3.

Wood, D. N. (1993). Higher education and crap-detecting. *Feedback, 34*(2), 2.

III

Context-Specific Assessment
Strategies

9

Oral Communication Assessment: An Overview

Philip Backlund
Central Washington University

Since the early 1980s, the Speech Communication Association and its Committee on Assessment and Testing have attempted to clarify the issues surrounding development of effective techniques for assessing oral communication. The chapter summarizes many of those efforts.

To that end, the chapter is organized into five parts: (a) background to oral communication assessment; (b) the need for clear objectives; (c) criteria commonly used to select an assessment instrument or procedure; (d) issues of reliability, validity, and bias; and (e) general procedures of assessing oral communication. The goal of this chapter is to supply a working knowledge of assessment methods and procedures in oral communication and identify resources for further information.

BACKGROUND TO ORAL COMMUNICATION ASSESSMENT

The point of any assessment program is student learning. To put this point into question form, how do we know whether students know (or can do) what we want them to know (or do)? When students are engaged in a program of instruction, whether it is television production or public speaking, teachers need to know a number of things about the effect of instruction. Teachers need to know: (a) whether the instruction has had any effect, (b) how the skills and knowledge levels of their students compare with predetermined optimum levels, (c) whether their students are learning some aspects of the curriculum faster than they are learning others, and (d) how their students compare in ability to other students in similar classes.

Teachers need to be able to provide answers to these questions in a systematic fashion with confidence that the answers are both reliable and valid. Answers to these questions form the basis of an effective program assessment with the focus of the assessment clearly on student outcomes. After all, the ultimate goal of any assessment program should be better instruction.

In many ways, assessment of oral communication is unique in higher education. Methods of assessment used in other academic areas cannot always be adapted to oral communication. To understand the impact of this, we must consider three points: (a) how oral communication assessment compares and contrasts with assessment in other academic areas, (b) the general purpose of such assessments, and (c) typical situations in which skills are assessed.

Comparing Oral Communication Assessment

First, in comparing oral communication skill assessment with assessment in other academic areas, certain distinctions can be made. For example, in most areas of education, testing uses such methods as aptitude tests, achievement tests, inventories of interests, and personality characteristics, and objective and subjective tests of content. As Mead (1982) argued:

> For many academic areas traditional testing methods made a lot of sense. A great deal of the educational experience involves acquiring knowledge for some unknown application later in life. For instance, most students who take science in school do not intend to become scientists. It is probably not necessary to measure these students to see how well they handle laboratory equipment. It does make sense to see how well these students grasp the basic vocabulary, concepts, and process of science. There are, however, certain academic areas that should be assessed using methods that tap competence directly, rather than indirectly. Oral communication is one of these areas. Like reading and writing, speaking and listening are used to accomplish a host of purposes. They are process skills. It does not make as much sense to assess students' knowledge about how they should communicate as it does to assess students' communication performance in real situations. Thus, oral communication skills have generally been assessed with performance measures. Students typically have been asked to present a speech or to listen to material, not to answer knowledge questions about oral communication. (p. 2)

Due to the unique nature of communication, assessment of oral communication performance encounters certain limits and problems. Oral communication is an interactive process. Thus, its correctness is generally based on the situation, with usually more than one "correct" answer. Each person in the situation is commonly both speaker and listener. In these situations, meaning is exchanged not only through verbal modes—that is, through words—but also through nonverbal modes such as tone of voice, facial expression, posture, gestures, eye contact, and so on. Finally, evaluation of a communicator depends on criteria that are culturally and situationally based. For example, whereas talking is a very appropriate social behavior at a cocktail party, it is very bothersome in a library reading room (Mead, 1982). Cultural evaluations become even more problematic. These factors make the assessment of oral communication more difficult—not impossible—than some other academic subjects.

All these aspects of oral communication help to make it unique among academic areas as far as testing is concerned. Although these features create some problems affecting the purpose and type of the test selected to assess students' oral communication skills, the problems are not insurmountable. It is possible to define in clear, behavioral terms both nonverbal and verbal aspects of communication (such as the amount of eye contact and desired language patterns needed in a given situation). Criteria of competence that take cultural and situational differences into account must and can be identified, because a communication behavior might be "right" in one situation and not in another. Because communication is shaped by culture, this danger of rater and test bias is substantial. Methods that assess performance consistently and accurately need to be developed through efforts to increase reliability and validity. If developed effectively, these methods can work in a variety of situations with a variety of raters. Finally, some objections can be (and have been) raised regarding assessment feasibility. This can be a problem if expensive equipment, extensive training of raters, or multiple ratings are required. Any assessment procedure needs to be developed with an eye to practicality. In some cases, these feasibility issues can be a greater deterrent to the implementation of an oral communication assessment program than any other assessment problem. Whereas some of these issues resemble those in other academic areas, others do not. Each must be dealt with if a systematic program of oral communication skill assessment is undertaken. It is possible to develop an effective program that accounts for each of these issues.

The Purposes of Assessment

Second, if such a program is undertaken, what purposes can it be expected to serve? The goal of all testing programs is to improve the education of students. To this end, oral communication skills can be assessed in a number of different places for a number of different purposes. One such purpose is testing for basic skills. A motivating force in the early 1980s for assessing oral communication skills was the basic skills movement. In 1978, the federal government included oral communication in its definition of basic skills. Other agencies, commissions, and educational institutions endorsed the idea that the ability to listen and speak effectively is basic to effective functioning in society. These endorsements served to place oral communication on the same level as reading, writing, and mathematics.

For years, English and math placement tests have helped colleges to place students in remedial or normal classes. Now, placement tests for speaking and listening are in use at some schools and under development at others. Not all students enter college with similar levels of ability in oral communication. Testing for basic skills can lead to testing for many types of placement purposes. In addition to basic skills, testing and assessment can be used to generate program-related information. An assessment program helps a college to fit the most appropriate instruction to the greatest need. Thus, assessment can take place at entrance to college, to chart progress during instruction, and at exit to determine whether a student has acquired the desired level of skill. In addition to student-centered assessment, testing of oral communication also can serve the needs of program assessment.

Typical Situations

Third, typical situations for assessment flow from the purposes of the assessment. Assessment methods are used not only for program assessment, but most obviously in the classroom. Here again, assessment is focused both on performance and on knowledge. In the classroom, teacher-constructed procedures are far more common than standardized tests. Teacher-constructed procedures have the advantage of a close match with instructional objectives, but they may lack reliability and validity. Such procedures are commonly used in interpersonal communication, small group communication, public speaking, oral interpretation, listening, and other performance classes. Standardized tests are often more reliable and valid, but they must be selected carefully if they are to align with the purpose of the testing program. An effective integrated assessment program incorporates and aligns classroom educational objectives together with general instructional program objectives. By considering classroom and program goals, an assessment process can be developed that gives feedback not only about the student, but the educational program as well. However, clarity of goals is a major stumbling block to many assessment programs. Some individuals begin by seeking the instrument. This usually is an ineffective strategy, as it is difficult for someone to know what instrument to select until the objectives are identified.

· THE NEED FOR CLEAR OBJECTIVES

For any testing program to work, it must be based on a clear set of educational objectives. One cannot decide to test speaking and listening skills and begin by looking for a test. There are simply too many available. If a decision is made to test oral communication skills (or any academic learning), the most critical step is to pinpoint the objectives and skills that you wish the students to possess. Curriculum objectives in speaking and listening were slower to develop than in those areas such as reading and writing. However, much progress has been made in the past few years. The Speech Communication Association has published two guides for developing programs in speaking and listening. These include: *SCA Guidelines: Essential Speaking and Listening Skills for Elementary School Students (6th Grade Level)* (1985), and *SCA Guidelines: Speaking and Listening Competencies for High School Graduates* (1982). Both sets of objectives were developed through discussions with public school teachers and experts in speech communication. Examples of the skills identified in these two documents include (these are drawn from the lists at random): (a) speaks clearly and expressively through appropriate articulation, pronunciation, volume, rate, and intonation (sixth grade); (b) uses nonverbal cues that emphasize meaning (sixth grade); (c) seeks to influence others' beliefs and actions and reacts to others' persuasion (sixth grade); (d) uses spoken language creatively to enjoy and participate in imaginative situations (sixth grade); (e) describes others' points and recognizes how they differ (sixth grade); (f) listens effectively to spoken English (high school); (g) identifies main ideas in messages (high school); (h) distinguishes between informative and persuasive messages (high school); (i) organizes messages so that others can understand them (high school); and (j) can give accurate and understandable directions (high school). Similar sets of skills have been developed for students at the college sophomore level (SCA Guidelines: *Can your students communicate effectively*, 1985, and for public school teachers (SCA Guidelines: *Communication competencies for teachers*, 1988).

Clear objectives are the first step in developing a successful testing program. If the objectives are not clear, nothing else will make sense.

One excellent example in speech communication exists that demonstrates this point. Listening is an important skill, yet researchers have disagreed about virtually every aspect of the listening process—definition, dimensions, methods of assessment, and methods of improving listening ability. Thus, validity is one of the greatest difficulties posed by listening tests. Because there is no agreement about what listening is, researchers cannot be certain that listening tests actually measure listening. For example, definitions of listening have ranged from the ability to respond appropriately when "Fire!" is shouted in a school to the ability to accurately gauge the internal emotional state of the speaker. That covers quite a range. The problem of assessing listening ability is compounded by the fact that most tests depend on the expressive abilities of those individuals tested. This is not to say that tests of listening are useless. They are highly useful. The key is the match between the objectives and the test. If the listening objectives are clearly defined, then a listening test can be selected that taps those objectives (see chap. 11).

Clear objectives is a critical first step to developing an effective assessment program.

CRITERIA USED TO SELECT AN ASSESSMENT PROCEDURE

There are a great many tests and assessment procedures for assessing oral communication skills. Various compilations list well over 100 procedures that tap some aspect of oral communication behavior (Backlund, Gurry, Brown, & Jandt, 1982; Larson, Backlund, Redmond, & Barbour, 1978; Rubin & Mead, 1984). The lists do not include the wide range of teacher-constructed procedures used in countless classrooms across the country. In selecting the best or most appropriate procedure to fit a particular need, certain criteria can be followed to ensure an effective choice. The criteria presented here were developed through the Speech Communication Association's Committee on Assessment and Testing. Before presenting them, however, two points regarding the conceptual view taken here are described.

The first point concerns the interrelatedness of communication skills. It is tempting to assume that skills learned through one mode of communication, such as writing, can be transferred easily to another mode, such as speaking. On this assumption, instruments and procedures suitable for assessing writing skill could seem to be suitable for assessing speaking. One might even go so far as to suggest that assessment of reading and writing skills is all that is necessary to assure achievement of communication competence. These assumptions and inferences are faulty. The best tests are those that assess behavior directly. A reading or writing test can assess reading or writing competencies in valid ways, but to base judgments about oral communication competencies on results from the same test is to make a dangerous inference. Assessment of communication skills must account for significant differences between oral and written language and hence for skills that are unique to oral communication.

The three distinctive features of oral communication identified by Brown, Backlund, Gurry, and Jandt (1979) are time, medium, and relationship. *Time* refers to the fact that oral communication is characterized by its immediacy. Time to look for the right words or phrases is limited and speech is impermanent. In contrast, the writer has time to choose words and phrases carefully and to edit them before submitting them to the receiver. Even then, response is not immediate, and it does not require the give and take of oral communication.

Medium refers to the difference in symbols used to communicate the message. The writer employs graphic symbols, whereas the speaker must rely on sound and nonverbal symbols. This difference creates the need for different skills. The writer must demonstrate skills in punctuating, spelling, and writing legibly to convey a message to readers. The speaker employs voice quality, volume, pitch, rate, intonation, stress, juncture, and bodily actions to communicate messages to a listener. The different media require different skills.

Relationship refers to the face-to-face directness of oral communication. The type of language and the tone that a speaker uses are different than those that the writer uses. Research has noted differences in the areas of abstraction, difficulty in comprehension, and psychogrammatical features.

These three distinctive features of oral communication emphasize the need for direct teaching and assessment of oral communication skills. Teachers do not automatically teach speaking when they teach writing, and they do not automatically assess competence in speaking skills when they assess competence in writing skills. This is true of many dimensions of communication knowledge or behavior.

The second point pertains to all testing. It concerns the predictive character of assessment. The determination of competence in oral communication is complex, as a large number of factors impinge on the interaction at any given time. Each student handles such situations with a different degree of success. Success depends on the student's knowledge of and skill in handling the purpose, the topic, the person or persons involved, and the time and place. To determine once and for all whether a student has achieved a given level of competence would require us to follow the student around and observe the student's performance in all kinds of situations.

Thus, no single assessment instrument or procedure can certify a student's levels of competence in oral communication in any definitive way. Faced with the limitations imposed by the situational character of communication behavior and by practical factors, we can only infer a given student's ability to communicate competently in situations beyond those directly assessed. This is both a strength and a weakness of assessment. It is a strength in that it fits well with the overall goals of competence-based education: to educate students who will function at least in some minimally competent manner inside and outside the classroom. It is a weakness in that one can never know for certain how competent a student is, and no testing procedure devised can give a definitive answer. This is a common problem of assessment, but it is important to recognize that assessment ultimately looks beyond demonstration of skill attainment in one setting to expectations that the skill will be used in future similar settings.

If we keep these two points in mind, criteria adopted by the Speech Communication Association (Crocker-Lakness, Manheimer, & Scott, 1991) for choosing assessment instruments may be helpful in guiding the selection of an assessment procedure or instrument. The criteria are organized into six areas—general, content, instrument selection, administration, frequency, and results use. The criteria are summarized in the following. (For the full text, please contact the Speech Communication Association.)

1. *General criteria.*
    a. Assessment should include consideration of knowledge, skills, and attitude of the person being assessed.
    b. Evaluation should not only reflect the judgment of the evaluator, but given the social nature of communication, should reflect the judgments of others within the communication context.

   c. Stimulus materials should require students to demonstrate skill as a speaker or listener and clearly distinguish speaking and listening from reading and writing. The foremost concern is that assessment instruments and procedures must involve students in oral communication acts.

   d. Assessment procedures should be sensitive to the effects of relevant physical and psychological disabilities on the assessment of competence.

   e. The assessment should be based in part on atomistic (specific behaviors) and holistic impressions.

2. *Content criteria.* Assessment should include assessment of both verbal and nonverbal aspects of communication and should consider competence in more than one communication setting. Assessment should include specialized knowledge related to the individual's areas of expertise.

3. *Instrument criteria.*

   a. Method of assessment should be consistent with skill being assessed.

   b. Performance skills must be assessed through actual performance.

   c. Instruments should be constructed as to allow for degrees of competence, rather than "pass/fail."

   d. Instruments and procedures should not discriminate on the basis of race, sex, religion, or national origin.

   e. The instruments should demonstrate appropriate levels of validity and reliability.

   f. The instruments should be suitable for the developmental level of the individual being assessed.

   g. Assessment instruments should be standardized and detailed enough so that individual responses will not be affected by an administrator's skill in administering the procedures.

4. *Instrument administration.*

   a. Assessment should protect the rights of those being assessed related to confidentiality of results.

   b. Use of the instruments for procedural decisions should, when feasible, be based on multiple sources of information.

   c. Individuals administering assessment procedures should have received sufficient training to make their assessment reliable.

5. *Assessment frequency.* Assessment should occur regularly through the educational careers of students.

6. *Use of assessment results.* Results of assessment procedures should be used in an ethical, nondiscriminatory manner for such purposes as diagnosing strengths and weaknesses, planning instructional strategies, certifications of students for entry or exit from programs, evaluating student achievement, screening students, counseling for academic and career options, and evaluation of the effectiveness of instructional programs.

These criteria can be particularly helpful in selecting an appropriate assessment procedure. No matter what the purpose of evaluation or assessment, it is critically important to make the selection with systematic care.

ISSUES OF VALIDITY, RELIABILITY, AND BIAS

After objectives and criteria have been clarified, attention can be turned to the quality of the data. Any testing program is no better than the data it gives. There are many factors that can distort the test results, giving the teacher an inaccurate picture of the student's skill. There are a few simple considerations that, when taken into account, can greatly increase the chances that the test results will be worthwhile.

The term *reliability* refers to the consistency with which a test measures what it is supposed to measure. One very important form of reliability is interrater reliability. We would hope that two or more raters, using the same scale, and looking at the same behaviors, would give a student the same score. Perfection is usually not possible, but they should be close. It would be useful for teachers to check with each other and compare ratings so that the ratings become more consistent and that they really are a rating of the skill and not the rater's preferences.

Another form of reliability that is useful to consider is temporal reliability. This is the stability of test scores over time. If a test produces one score the first time it is given, and a very different score when given again 3 days later, one has cause to doubt its reliability. A test must provide assurance that whatever is measured is not a one-time event. We can help ensure reliability by attempting to improve consistency between people using the test and by making sure that the test is consistent over time.

Validity refers to the necessity that a test measures what it is supposed to measure. This is where clear curriculum objectives apply. If objectives are clearly defined, it will be relatively easy to select or design a test that will tap those objectives. This is referred to as content or face validity. The usual reason for testing speaking and listening skills is to predict whether the student will be able to speak and listen effectively in real life or at least in situations other than those inherent in the test. We want to be able to predict whether or not a student will be successful. If we can predict certain results, then we know the test works.

Bias is the last of the factors considered here as a source of distortion in test results. Because the "rightness" of a response in a speaking and listening skill test depends frequently on the situation and the people in it, bias can be a real problem. The teacher or tester should work to remove the effects of cultural, racial, or sexual bias from the assessment procedure so that each student has an equal chance at being successful. Bias is described later in more detail, as it can easily distort the results of any assessment process, and it is a factor that many educators do not consider as closely as validity and reliability.

Teachers of speech communication have traditionally relied heavily on their own observations and subjective judgments of student development. At the same time, we know research on those subjective teacher judgments suggests there may be some important problems with the accuracy of those judgments (Rudman et al., 1980, Stiggins & Bridgeford, 1984). Further, we know that teachers are often not adequately trained in assessment and that, with a few exceptions, they are not provided with technical assistance to help them with their assessment efforts. This includes inadequate training in assessment. We know that there are many potential sources of bias in assessment (described later) that can creep into the educational testing and decision making process if the examiner is not trained to avoid cultural or sex bias. For these reasons, speech communication educators (and all educators) need to know about test bias and methods of overcoming it in assessing performance.

Bias in tests occurs when some characteristic of the test interacts with some characteristic of the test taker in such a way as to distort the meaning of the test score for a particular group or examinee (Shepard, 1980). Such distortions can lead to invalid assessment and inappropriate educational decisions when assessment items, procedures, or exercises are more familiar and understandable to members of one group—with its cultural and linguistic experience—than another group. Oral communication skill assessment procedures have to be particularly sensitive to cultural bias. In some cases, students in each group might be equally capable of performing competently on the test, but some language or experience factor extraneous to that skill intended to be measured might distort the results leading to invalid assessment.

In general, characteristics of assessment that may distort test scores and bias test results include ambiguous test items, items developed without attention to cultural differences, the test administration environment, and test scoring procedures. Ambiguous items are most problematic when individuals from diverse cultural groups differ in their assessment procedure familiarity and their ability to understand the objective of poorly designed items. Those who understand task requirements of tests due to prior experience will score higher, not because they know more, but because they have more highly developed test-taking skills.

Bias can occur in a procedure if subjective judgments play a role (as it does in virtually all communication assessment). This is particularly a problem in rating speaking skills. The potential for rater bias is a function of social experiences and attitudes of the rater, clarity and precision of the scoring criteria and standards, and the extent to which the scorer has internalized those standards. Backlund (1981) and Mead (1982) showed that training raters to apply specified scaling criteria increases the reliability of the assessment, but careful monitoring is needed to ensure the level is maintained. The training involves familiarizing the raters with the rating scale, and repeated trials with communication samples (a public speech, for example), so the raters begin to view the same behavior in the same way. Raters can be trained to rate behaviors reliably. However, when a program is under review, reliability becomes harder to achieve. In program review, rater bias can clearly have an impact on the quality of the evaluation.

Thus, with different levels of experience, comfort with testing, or tension due to evaluation anxiety across assessment situations, it is possible that the students' real competence will be misjudged. Reducing the possibility of test bias can be done, though it takes careful thought. Some suggestions include having minority group members carefully review test content and exercises, conducting technical test score or item analysis in order to identify differential patterns of examinee responses (Jensen, 1980), or using alternative modes of assessment as a means of reducing bias (Schmidt, Greenthal, Hunter, Berner, & Seaton, 1977).

COMMON TYPES OF ASSESSMENT PROCEDURES

A number of different procedures can be used to assess oral communication behavior. Because assessment usually involves both knowledge about and skill in the particular behavior, the most common procedures vary somewhat from the procedures found in most other academic subjects. The most common procedures are self-report instruments, written tests, interviews, and performance rating scales. As performance rating scales are the most commonly used in speech communication, they are described in greater detail.

Self-Report Instruments

Self-report instruments are particularly useful in gathering attitudinal and affective information about how students view communicative behavior—either their own, their professor's, or perhaps a department's. Obviously, self-report scales do not assess skills directly, but they can provide much valuable information about a student's attitude toward various types of communicative situations. Students may not respond truthfully to these scales and care may need to be taken to ensure reliable responses. Student self-report scales are particularly useful in determining the quality of an instructional program. Although student input is certainly not the only source in program review, students can give important information on factors such as (a) their own increased knowledge and comprehension, (b) their own changed motivation to subject matter and to learning, (c) their perceptions of teaching style indicators, and (d) their perception of the match between course material and testing. These are useful pieces of information in any program (or personal) evaluation.

However, students are not in a position to comment on items such as (a) quality of academic content, (b) justification for course content against eventual needs of the student and society, (c) quality of test construction, (d) professionalism of professor toward teaching, and (e) evidence of professor's out-of-class teaching related activities. Used appropriately, student self-report is a valuable tool in any assessment procedure. A key in this type of information gathering is the perception on the part of the students that their opinions *matter*. Properly used, self-report scales can generate valuable information about student achievement and program quality.

Oral Interviews

Oral interviews are not used extensively as they are very time consuming, but they can be very useful in testing certain types of skills. For example, the state of Massachusetts uses a one-on-one interview between teacher and individual students to rate speaking skill. If there are enough well-trained raters, this procedure can work quite well, but the key to success is the reliability of raters. The face-to-face contact between student and rater allows the rater to sample the student's ability directly. However, the interview is a contrived situation, it causes most students to experience a higher than normal level of anxiety, the procedure is time consuming, and its reliability is hard to establish.

Performance Rating Scales

Performance rating scales form the bulk of speaking skill assessment instruments. Performance tests are generally defined as those that require the student to apply previously acquired knowledge and skills to complete some performance task. A real-world or simulated exercise is presented, eliciting an original response by the student, which is observed and evaluated by the teacher. Performance tests have four important characteristics (Stiggins & Bridgeford, 1984). First, students are called on to apply the skills and knowledge they have learned. Second, performance involves completion of a prespecified task according to criteria in the context of real or simulated assessment exercises. Third, whatever task or product is required by the exercise, it must be observable and measurable. Fourth, the performance must be directly observed and rated by a trained, qualified judge.

There is a continuum of performance rating instruments. On one end are *obtrusive* procedures that ask a student to stand and speak (or perform in some way) and that rates them on specific criteria. Rating forms and the skills evaluated vary, but these are easy to use and construct. They can be constructed to fit most communication educational objectives, they make feedback to students relatively easy to give, and can be easily constructed to fit the criteria and objectives developed. They have some disadvantages:

The students being rated almost always feel some anxiety, reliability is hard to achieve, and in many cases only one student can be rated at a time.

The other end of the continuum is occupied by *unobtrusive* rating scales. A rater uses these scales, but students are unaware that they are being rated. Teachers can use such scales in a classroom setting during or after a class session to rate students' informal or conversational communicative behavior. This method has several advantages: A large number of students can be rated in a relatively short period of time; the speaking sample rated is natural, not made up or contrived; the method causes little anxiety; and the rating scale can be constructed to fit most speaking educational objectives. However, reliability is hard to establish, and the type of speaking behavior desired does not always appear naturally.

Speech communication educators have been using various forms of performance testing for years, particularly in public speaking ratings. Performance testing has been described in testing literature since the early 1950s, but it is only recently that the body of literature on performance testing has begun to be used to confirm the type of testing commonly used by speech communication professionals (see, for example, Stiggins, Backlund, & Bridgeford, 1985). Efforts to develop testing procedures for various forms of communication competence, more systematic and "acceptable" assessment procedures, and speaking, listening, interpersonal, and small group testing procedures for college students all can be strengthened by familiarity with the literature on methods to reduce bias in performance testing.

In theory, performance testing gives an excellent opportunity to reduce potential bias and other problems. For example, unlike traditional paper-and-pencil tests, performance procedures have far greater face validity; that is, the behaviors called for closely approximate the array of communication behaviors under examination. For example, in a performance assessment of speaking skills, a sample of actual behavior is far more likely to predict success in future speaking contexts than is a response to a multiple-choice question. In effect, the logical link between a sample of behavior and the criterion (future performance) seems stronger for the performance test than the logical link between objective paper-and-pencil test score (i.e., selecting the correct response to test items) and future performance.

It seems true that the well-developed performance test will exceed the well-developed objective test in validity when the purpose of the test is to measure the ability to apply knowledge to achieve some real-life objective. That similarity will make the test very believable. The concrete link between test behavior and criterion behavior in performance assessment can help the motivation of students to take the test seriously and do their best.

In addition, performance-based measures, which can be conducted unobtrusively, present the possibility of reducing evaluation anxiety. These can be very useful strategies in assessing communication skills in the classroom.

Given the potentially high validity of performance tests and the potential for dealing with several of the factors in testing associated with test bias, there is good reason to consider performance assessment as an effective tool in gathering effective information, in reducing the adverse impact of testing, and developing defensible information for any educational program.

If the reader is interested in reviewing some of the instruments developed for the assessment of oral communication skills, the sources listed in the reference section may be of use. (Further information can be found by contacting the Speech Communication Association.)

CONCLUSION

Assessing oral communication skills is not an easy task. If a department is attempting to assess the learning of its students as a means to gather information about the quality of the program, the problems compound. However, it clearly is possible to develop an assessment program that gathers useful, valid, reliable, and unbiased information. If the reader is already engaged in such a program or is contemplating starting one, here are some key points to keep in mind.

First, be very clear about the skills, objectives, or both that the assessment program will tap. The clearer skills and objectives are, the easier it becomes to select or develop appropriate methods. Second, evaluate possible instruments against clear criteria. This will help ensure that the instrument or procedure selected is the most effective. Third, do what is possible to ensure an optimum level of validity, reliability, and lack of bias. Fourth, plan the assessment procedure carefully so that the process itself does not interfere with its own effectiveness. With effective planning, it is possible to establish and maintain a useful and productive program to assess communication knowledge and skills.

The discipline of speech communication has made great strides in the development of assessment programs, but progress still needs to be made. However, the lessons learned thus far may be helpful to individuals who are working to establish new assessment programs.

REFERENCES

Backlund, P. (1981, November). *The development of a speaking screening test for in-coming freshmen: Inter-rater reliability.* Paper presented at the annual convention of the Speech Communication Association, Anaheim, CA.

Backlund, P., Gurry, J., Brown, K., & Jandt, F. (1982). Recommendations for assessing speaking and listening skills. *Communication Education. 31*(1), 9–18.

Brown, K., Backlund, P., Gurry, J., & Jandt, F. (1979). *Assessment of basic speaking and listening skills: State of the art and recommendations for instrument development.* Boston: Bureau of Research and Assessment, Massachusetts Department of Education.

Crocker-Lakness, J., Manheimer, S., & Scott, T. (1991). *Criteria for the assessment of oral communication: A national context*. Annandale, VA: Speech Communication Association.

Jensen, A. (1980). *Bias in mental testing*. New York: The Free Press.

Larson, C., Backlund, P., Redmond, M., & Barbour, A. (1978). *Assessing functional communication*. Falls Church, VA: ERIC/RCS and Speech Communication Association.

Mead, N. (1982, April). *Assessment of listening and speaking performance*. Paper presented at the National Symposium on Education Research, Washington, DC.

Rubin, D., & Mead, N. (1984). *Large scale assessment of oral communication skills: Kindergarten through grade 12*. Annandale, VA: Speech Communication Association.

Rudman, H., Kelly, J., Wanons, D., Mehrens, W., Clark, C., & Porter, A. (1980). *Integrating assessment with instruction*. Unpublished manuscript, Institute for Research on Teaching, Michigan State University, Ann Arbor.

SCA Guidelines: Can your students communicate effectively. (1985). Annandale, VA: Speech Communication Association.

SCA Guidelines: Communication competencies for teachers. (1988). Annandale, VA: Speech Communication Association.

SCA Guidelines: Essential speaking and listening skills for elementary school students (6th grade level). (1985). Annandale, VA: Speech Communication Association.

SCA Guidelines: Speaking and listening competencies for high school graduates. (1982). Annandale, VA: Speech Communication Association.

Schmidt, F., Greenthal, A., Hunter, J., Berner, J., & Seaton, F. (1977). Job sample vs. paper and pencil trades and technical tests: Adverse impacts and examinee attitudes. *Personnel Psychology, 30*(2), 187–197.

Shepard, L. (1980, November). *Definitions of bias*. Paper presented at the Johns Hopkins University National Symposium on Educational Research, Washington, DC.

Stiggins, R. J., Backlund, P. M., & Bridgeford, N. J. (1985). Avoiding bias in the assessment of communication skills. *Communication Education, 34*, 135–141.

Stiggins, R., & Bridgeford, N. (1984, April). *The nature, role and quality of performance assessment in the classroom*. Paper presented at the annual meeting of the American Educational Research Association, New Orleans, LA.

10

Public Speaking

Sherwyn P. Morreale
University of Colorado at Colorado Springs

In communication, as in other disciplines, educators and administrators are beginning to respond seriously to challenges associated with accountability. Directly related to such responses are concerns for reliable and valid evaluation and assessment of students' communication competencies and their abilities to perform orally. This chapter describes a public speaking performance assessment model that has been psychometrically tested and was developed based on the communication competency literature articulated by the communication discipline (Morreale, Moore, Taylor, Surges-Tatum, & Hulbert-Johnson, 1993).

The chapter begins by providing the reader a historical background on public speaking evaluation and a rationale for standardized speech assessment. Then *The Competent Speaker*[1] model is described including information on paradigm development and its use as an evaluative and pedagogical tool. The chapter concludes with a description of a pre- and postassessment program for the public speaking course and a discussion of other oral-competency-based methods and options for direct evaluation of students' progress. Those methods and options subsume evaluation of students' oral competency in four demains: cognition, behaviors, affect, and ethics. Concluding the chapter are recommendations for future directions for standardized assessment of public speaking.

HISTORICAL BACKGROUND TO PUBLIC SPEAKING EVALUATION

The evaluation and assessment of competency in public speaking have been topics of vital interest to scholars for decades, if not for centuries. The

---

[1]*The Competent Speaker*, and a manual for its use, contains detailed information on development, testing, training, and scoring, and can be purchased through the Speech Communication Association, 5105 Backlick Road, Building E, Annandale, VA 22003.

Aristotelian tradition postulated models for public oratory as early as 300 B.C. (Cooper, 1932). And no doubt, the sophists evaluated and provided feedback to their students regarding public performance as they taught on the hills of ancient Greece. Moving ahead by rhetorical leaps and bounds, public speech and its evaluation have been of concern to communication scholars throughout the 20th century. As early as the 1920s, Knower (1929) was probing the psychological ramifications associated with public speaking. In the next decade, Hayworth (1939) was concerned more with measuring aspects of public speaking. Norvelle (1947) further narrowed assessment to a comparison between specific types of college students, and Fotheringham (1956) developed a specific technique for measuring effectiveness in public speaking classes. Mulac (1974) examined the effects of the use of videotape on the acquisition of speech skills. That line of research was continued with Miles' (1981) finding that video self-critiquing favorably affected students' development of public speaking skills. Johnson and Szczupakiewicz (1987) examined whether the public speaking course is effectively preparing students with work-related public speaking skills. As might be expected, more recent research has focused on the application of advanced technology to public speaking. Cronin (1992), for example, investigated the effects of the use of interactive video in public speaking instruction. History's provision of evaluative studies such as these sets the stage on which current standardization attempts in public speaking evaluation are presented.

RATIONALE FOR STANDARDIZATION OF PUBLIC SPEAKING ASSESSMENT

An examination of recent scholarly literature reveals the degree to which communication competence and its assessment have become important to communication instruction (Backlund, 1990; Pearson & Daniels, 1988; Quianthy, 1990; Rubin, 1990; Spitzberg, 1988, 1993; Spitzberg & Cupach, 1989). Other empirical research specifically relates oral communication skills and competency to academic and professional success (Curtis, Winsor, & Stephens, 1989; Rubin & Graham, 1988; Rubin, Graham, & Mignerey, 1990). Considering the acknowledged importance of oral communication competency and the interest in it displayed by scholars and educators, a need exists to base instruction and assessment on a standardized and tested approach to public speaking.

Interestingly, despite the abundance of public speaking courses and the proliferation of speech evaluation forms of every kind, no standardized and psychometrically tested evaluation form has been available in the past. Nor has such a form been available that was grounded in the communication discipline's conceptualization of public speaking competency. *The Competent Speaker* was developed to address that need for a standardized and tested speech evaluation form.

A MODEL FOR PUBLIC SPEAKING COMPETENCY AND ASSESSMENT

Overview of the Instrument

The Competent Speaker speech evaluation form (Fig. 10.1) was developed to provide a statistically reliable and valid tool for the assessment of public speaking performance. The instrument was developed by a subcommittee of the Speech Communication Association's Committee on Assessment and Testing, which was charged to develop and test a competency-based speech evaluation form (Backlund, 1990). Development and testing extended over a 2-year period and involved representatives of 12 academic institutions from across the country.

The Competent Speaker is an instrument designed for evaluating public speaking skills. It focuses on the assessment of the verbal and nonverbal behaviors involved in competent public speaking—as opposed to knowledge about, or motivation to engage in, public speaking. The instrument can be used as a tool for several purposes: (a) evaluating informative and persuasive speeches in class, (b) testing-in or testing-out (placement) purposes, (c) instructing and advising students about preparing and presenting public speeches, and (d) generating assessment data for accountability-related objectives of academic institutions.

The instrument itself consists of eight public speaking competencies, four relating to preparation and four to delivery. For each of the eight competencies, specific performance standards and criteria are provided for three levels of performance: unsatisfactory, satisfactory, and excellent. Each competency is assessed with respect to appropriateness for the audience and occasion, so cultural and other biases are addressed. The eight competencies and their performance standards were derived from the most recent research on oral communication competency within the public speaking context.

Conceptualization of the Instrument

The instrument was derived from *SCA's Speaking and Listening Competencies for High School Graduates* (1982), *SCA's Communication is Life: Essential College Sophomore Speaking and Listening Competencies* (Quianthy, 1990), and the public speaking competencies contained in the Communication Competency Assessment Instrument (Rubin, 1982).

Scoring Procedure

As a tool for evaluating speeches, the instrument can be adapted to any numerical weighing system that serves the purposes of the evaluator and the particular speech event. For scoring purposes, the instrument acts as a ratio scale by using any numerical weighing system, between and within the eight competencies, that suits the rhetorical event being evaluated. For

SPEAKER'S NAME:_____ ASSIGNMENT:_____

EVALUATOR'S NAME:_____ DATE:_____/_____/_____

EIGHT PUBLIC SPEAKING COMPETENCIES	SPEAKING PERFORMANCE RATINGS		
	Unsatisfactory	Satisfactory	Excellent
Competency One: CHOOSES AND NARROWS A TOPIC APPROPRIATELY FOR THE AUDIENCE AND OCCASION Comments: **Assign Scoring Ranges:**	_____	_____	_____
Competency Two: COMMUNICATES THE THESIS/SPECIFIC PURPOSE IN A MANNER APPROPRIATE FOR AUDIENCE AND OCCASION Comments:			
Competency Three: PROVIDES APPROPRIATE SUPPORTING MATERIAL BASED ON THE AUDIENCE AND OCCASION Comments:			
Competency Four: USES AN ORGANIZATIONAL PATTERN APPROPRIATE TO TOPIC, AUDIENCE, OCCASION, & PURPOSE Comments:			
Competency Five: USES LANGUAGE THAT IS APPROPRIATE TO THE AUDIENCE, OCCASION, & PURPOSE Comments:			
Competency Six: USES VOCAL VARIETY IN RATE, PITCH, & INTENSITY, TO HEIGHTEN AND MAINTAIN INTEREST Comments:			
Competency Seven: USES PRONUNCIATION, GRAMMAR, & ARTICULATION APPROPRIATE TO THE DESIGNATED AUDIENCE Comments:			
Competency Eight: USES PHYSICAL BEHAVIORS THAT SUPPORT THE VERBAL MESSAGE Comments:			

General Comments: Summative Scores
                                               of Competencies:_____

FIG. 10.1. The Competent Speaker speech performance evaluation form.

example, assignment of 1 for unsatisfactory, 2 for satisfactory, and 3 for excellent, for each of the eight competencies, would result in a possible score range of 8 to 24 for a given speech.

Psychometric Reliability/Validity/Bias

The Competent Speaker was developed and tested carefully considering psychometric reliability, validity, and cultural biases. The following discussion includes the results of traditional as well as Rasch analyses of the tool.

Traditional Analysis. Interrater reliability testing with a variety of raters produced high and moderately high coefficients: (a) speech communication professionals generated an Ebel's coefficient of .92, (b) graduate teaching assistants utilizing the form generated a Cronbach's alpha of .76, and (c) community college speech instructors generated a Cronbach coefficient of .84.

In two convergent validity studies, results indicated that as speech scores on the speech evaluation form increased, (a) public speaking scores on the Communication Competency Assessment Instrument (CCAI; Rubin, 1982) also increased, and (b) public speaking scores on the Personal Report of Communication Apprehension (PRCA; McCroskey, 1970) decreased.

Two studies were conducted to investigate cultural bias. The first study, which examined interrater reliability of speech communication professionals and minority students, generated a Cronbach's alpha of .76. The second study, which examined actual speech evaluations in the classroom, investigated any significant differences in the use of the form by students of different ethnicity or gender. No significant differences in scores, by ethnic group (African-American, Anglo-American, Asian-American, Hispanic-American, or Native-American) or by gender, were found.

Rasch Analysis. This type of analysis produces results distinctly different from traditional statistical analysis. Rasch analysis allows the researcher to separate the elements under investigation and focus on one at a time. In this case the investigated elements are: (a) the items on the evaluation form, (b) the raters using the form, and (c) the speakers.

Using Rasch analysis, *The Competent Speaker* evaluation form was determined to be a valid, useful instrument with which to judge speeches. The analysis revealed no "misfitting" items; they all conformed to the pattern of expected responses. Additionally, raters were consistent in their understanding of each item and were not idiosyncratic in their responses. A comparison of minority student raters to speech teachers revealed no apparent bias in *The Competent Speaker* evaluation form. All the items maintained their placement and fit, which means the items are not being used differently by one group than the other. The use of the instrument is consistent, establishing confidence in its inherent fairness.

Training in the Use of the Form

Before using *The Competent Speaker* evaluation form to rate a public speaking performance, the evaluator first should thoroughly study the instrument itself and the eight competencies it contains. The evaluator also should become familiar with the descriptions of unsatisfactory, satisfactory, and excellent levels of performance for each competency presented in the criteria. After becoming familiar with the competencies and criteria, the evaluator should practice using the form with a training videotape of speeches exemplary of all three levels of competency. If more than one evaluator is being trained, then evaluators should rate speeches individually, compare their scores, and engage in discussion about those scores so that a satisfactory level of interrater reliability may be attained. Raters may, at their discretion, generate normative scores for speeches presented on videotape and use those scores for training purposes at their institutions.

Using the Form to Evaluate and Grade Speeches

In the actual use of the form to evaluate speeches, the evaluator may use any numerical weighing system for the three levels of competency that suits the particular context or course requirements. For example, the evaluator could: (a) examine the level of performance for each competency without assigning any numerical value to the competency—in other words, simply check off the level of performance; or, as indicated earlier, (b) assign 1 point for unsatisfactory, 2 points for satisfactory, and 3 points for excellent for each competency (in this case, the range of the grade for the speech would be from 8 to 24); or (c) for additional speeches, increase the assigned values to reflect the increasing level of importance or value of the particular speech; that is, for each competency, assign 2 points for unsatisfactory, 4 points for satisfactory, and 6 points for excellent (the range for the grade would be from 16 to 48); or (d) multiply the basic score of a speech (ranging from 8 to 24) by any number or fraction of a number to increase or decrease the total value of the speech.

In addition to using various numerical weighing systems for the three levels of competency, the evaluator also may consider differentially weighing the separate competencies, depending on the particular speech assignment. That is, certain competencies may be deemed more important than others in a given speech.

When actually evaluating a speech using the form, the rater(s) should always reference the standards and criteria for each competency. Those criteria, which follow, specifically describe the nature of unsatisfactory, satisfactory, and excellent for each competency.

Using the Form to Provide Instruction and Feedback

Prior to evaluating students' performances using *The Competent Speaker* form, the students may benefit immeasurably by the presentation of a lecture that provides an overview of the eight competencies. The instructor can supply any information and suggestions deemed relevant to the student's performance of that competency. Detailed presentation of the standards and criteria for each competency will provide the student with specific guidelines for the speech preparation process. Following the speaking performance, the eight competencies can act as a structure for providing evaluative feedback to the student. The instructor or speech rater may point out which competencies were the student's primary strength(s) and which ones may need more development. The specific standards and criteria for each competency follow.

EIGHT PUBLIC SPEAKING COMPETENCIES AND CRITERIA
FOR ASSESSMENT

Competency 1: Chooses and Narrows a Topic Appropriately for the Audience and Occasion

• *Excellent.* The speaker presents a topic and a focus that are exceptionally appropriate for the purpose, time constraints, and audience. (That is, the speaker's choice of topic is clearly consistent with the purpose, is totally amenable to the time limitations of the speech, and reflects unusually insightful audience analysis.)

• *Satisfactory.* The speaker presents a topic and a focus that are appropriate for the purpose, time constraints, and audience. (That is, the speaker's choice of topic is generally consistent with the purpose, is a reasonable choice for the time limitations of the speech, and reflects appropriate analysis of a majority of the audience.)

• *Unsatisfactory.* The speaker presents a topic and a focus that are not appropriate for either the purpose, time constraints, or audience. (That is, the speaker's choice of topic is inconsistent with the purpose, the topic cannot be adequately treated in the time limitations of the speech, and there is little or no evidence of successful audience analysis.)

Competency 2: Communicates the Thesis or Specific Purpose in a Manner Appropriate for the Audience and Occasion

• *Excellent.* The speaker communicates a thesis or specific purpose that is exceptionally clear and identifiable. (That is, there is no question that all of the audience members should understand clearly, within the opening few sentences of the speech, precisely what the specific purpose or thesis of the speech is.)

• *Satisfactory.* The speaker communicates a thesis or specific purpose that is adequately clear and identifiable. (That is, at least a majority of the audience should understand clearly, within the opening few sentences of the speech, precisely what the specific purpose or thesis of the speech is.)

• *Unsatisfactory.* The speaker does not communicate a clear and identifiable thesis or specific purpose. (That is, a majority of the audience may have difficulty understanding, within the opening few sentences of the speech, precisely what the specific purpose or thesis of the speech is.)

Competency 3: Provides Supporting Material Appropriate to the Audience and Occasion

• *Excellent.* The speaker uses supporting material that is exceptional in quality and variety. (That is, supporting material is unarguably linked to the thesis of the speech, and further is of such quality that it decidedly enhances the credibility of the speaker and the clarity of the topic.)

•*Satisfactory.* The speaker uses supporting material that is appropriate in quality and variety. (That is, supporting material is logically linked to the thesis of the speech, and is of such quality that it adds a measurable level of interest to the speech.)

•*Unsatisfactory.* The speaker uses supporting material that is inappropriate in quality and variety. (That is, supporting material is only vaguely related to the thesis of the speech, and variety is either too great or too little to do anything but detract from the effectiveness of the speech.)

Competency 4: Uses an Organizational Pattern Appropriate to the Topic, Audience, Occasion, and Purpose

•*Excellent.* The speaker uses an exceptional introduction and conclusion and provides an exceptionally clear and logical progression within and between ideas. (That is, the introduction clearly engages the audience in an appropriate and creative manner, the body of the speech reflects superior clarity in organization, and the conclusion clearly reflects the content of the speech and leaves the audience with an undeniable message or call to action.)

•*Satisfactory.* The speaker uses an appropriate introduction and conclusion and provides a reasonably clear and logical progression within and between ideas. (That is, the introduction clearly engages a majority of the audience in an appropriate manner, the body of the speech reflects adequate clarity in organization, and the conclusion reflects adequately the content of the speech and leaves a majority of the audience with a clear message or call to action.)

•*Unsatisfactory.* The speaker fails to use an introduction or conclusion and fails to provide a reasonably clear and logical progression within and between ideas. (That is, the introduction fails to engage even a majority of the audience in an appropriate manner, the body of the speech reflects lack of clarity in organization, and the conclusion fails to reflect adequately the content of the speech and fails to leave even a majority of the audience with a clear message or call to action.)

Competency 5: Uses Language Appropriate to the Audience and Occasion

•*Excellent.* The speaker uses language that is exceptionally clear, vivid, and appropriate. (That is, the speaker chooses language that enhances audience comprehension and enthusiasm for the speech, adding a measure of creativity that displays exceptional sensitivity by the speaker for the nuances and poetry of meaning.)

•*Satisfactory.* The speaker uses language that is reasonably clear, vivid, and appropriate. (That is, the speaker chooses language that is free of inappropriate jargon, is nonsexist, is nonracist, etc.)

•*Unsatisfactory* The speaker uses unclear or inappropriate language. (That is, the speaker chooses inappropriate jargon or language that is sexist, racist, etc.)

Competency 6: Uses Vocal Variety in Rate, Pitch, and Intensity (Volume) to Heighten and Maintain Interest Appropriate to the Audience and Occasion

•*Excellent*. The speaker makes exceptional use of vocal variety in a conversational mode. (That is, vocalics are exceptionally and appropriately well paced, easily heard by all audience members, and varied in pitch to enhance the message.)

•*Satisfactory*. The speaker makes acceptable use of vocal variety in a conversational mode. (That is, the speaker shows only occasional weakness in pace, volume, pitch, etc., thereby not detracting significantly from the overall quality or impact of the speech.)

•*Unsatisfactory*. The speaker fails to use vocal variety and fails to speak in a conversational mode. (That is, the speaker shows frequent weakness in controlling and adapting pace, volume, pitch, etc., resulting in an overall detraction from the quality or impact of the speech.)

Competency 7: Uses Pronunciation, Grammar, and Articulation Appropriate to the Audience and Occasion

•*Excellent*. The speaker has exceptional articulation, pronunciation, and grammar. (That is, the speaker exhibits exceptional fluency, properly formed sounds that enhance the message, and no pronunciation or grammatical errors.)

•*Satisfactory*. The speaker has acceptable articulation, with few pronunciation or grammatical errors. (That is, most sounds are properly formed, there are only minor vocalized disfluencies, and a few (1–2) minor errors in pronunciation and grammar.)

•*Unsatisfactory*. The speaker fails to use acceptable articulation, pronunciation, and grammar. (That is, nonfluencies and disfluencies interfere with the message, and frequent errors in pronunciation and grammar make it difficult for the audience to understand the message.)

Competency 8: Uses Physical Behaviors That Support the Verbal Message

•*Excellent*. The speaker demonstrates exceptional posture, gestures, bodily movement, facial expressions, eye contact, and use of dress. (That is, kinesic—posture, gesture, facial expressions, eye contact—and proxemic—interpersonal distance and spatial arrangement—behaviors and dress consistently support the verbal message and thereby enhance the speaker's credibility throughout the audience.)

•*Satisfactory.* The speaker demonstrates acceptable posture, gestures, facial expressions, eye contact, and use of dress. (That is, kinesic and proxemic behaviors and dress generally support the message, with minor inconsistencies that neither significantly distract from the speaker's credibility with the audience nor interfere with the message.)

•*Unsatisfactory.* The speaker fails to use acceptable posture, gestures, facial expressions, eye contact, and dress. (That is, kinesic and proxemic behaviors and dress are incongruent with the verbal intent and detract from the speaker's credibility with the audience, as well as distracting the audience from the speaker's message.)

A PRE- AND POSTASSESSMENT PROGRAM FOR THE PUBLIC SPEAKING COURSE

In addition to using a standardized approach to evaluating speeches, instructors may choose to assess the *impact* of a public speaking course on students. Typically, accountability-related assessment programs evaluate or measure three aspects of the curriculum: *process* (evaluated through observing behavioral and affective development, in-class learning assessment techniques, course evaluations, etc.), *outcomes* (evaluated through long-term tracking, job placement, surveys of graduates, etc.), or *impact* (evaluated through testing of cognitive learning, self-report questionnaires, etc.). One other approach to the assessment of actual impact of a course or curriculum on students is the pre- and postassessment approach. In such a program, selected assessment instruments are administered to students at the beginning and the end of any given course. Those tools are selected based on: (a) their proven psychometric reliability and validity, (b) the extent to which they are free of various cultural biases, and (c) the extent to which they assess or measure what the course is intended to impact.

A typical competency-based pre- and postassessment program for the public speaking course has been in place at University of Colorado, Colorado Springs (UCCS) for several years. That course requires that all students individually participate in both entrance (pre-) and exit (post-) interviews in an oral communication laboratory. These 1-hour interviews are conducted by a staff of graduate teaching assistants (GTAs) trained to administer the selected assessment instruments to students. The focus of the interviews is on both the assessment and the development of students' oral communication competencies. The instruments administered to the student in the pre- and postinterviews at UCCS are the Communication Competency Assessment Instrument (CCAI; Rubin, 1982), the Personal Report of Communication Apprehension (PRCA; McCroskey, 1970), and the Rosenberg Self-Esteem Scale (RSE; Rosenberg, 1965). Additionally, the student establishes personal goals for the public speaking course in the preinterview and reviews those goals in the postinterview.

The CCAI, administered one-on-one by the GTA to the student, assesses communication competency in the areas of public speaking, listening, interpersonal skills, and overall communication competency. Using the CCAI, GTAs are trained to evaluate a student's ability to:

1. Express ideas clearly.
2. Organize messages for understanding.
3. Express ideas concisely.
4. Express and defend point of view with evidence.
5. Use speaking voice effectively.
6. Communicate apprehension or anxiety.
7. Listen effectively.
8. Develop classroom communication and social skills.
9. Ask effective questions.
10. Give complete answers to questions.
11. Use appropriate words, pronunciation, and grammar.
12. Use appropriate nonverbal cues.

If an analysis of the CCAI scores indicates that the student requires further guidance in any area, the GTA is trained to direct and coordinate follow-up assistance.

Because the CCAI does not assess communication anxiety, the PRCA is administered to students. This diagnostic instrument explores apprehension in meetings, groups, conversations, public speaking, and overall apprehension. Students with higher than average levels of communication apprehension are encouraged to seek help in the form of the laboratory's individual assistance programs.

The RSE assesses the self-esteem level of the student. If the score derived from this diagnostic reflects low self-esteem, the student is referred to other student support services on campus.

Two of the three instruments (the PRCA and the RSE) are computer-administered and scored, providing immediate data for advising and statistical purposes. For purposes of consistency, the same GTA conducts the pre- and postinterviews with any given student. In the pretest interview, dialogue with the student concerns strengths and areas to consider to maximize the course experience. In the posttest interview with the student, at the conclusion of the course, progress and plans for future development of communication competencies are considered. These plans are based on a discussion with the student of differences in scores between the pre- and postinterview.

Results of the Pre- and Postassessment Program

Demographic data and results of the assessment process are collected from all three instruments during the entrance and exit interviews and entered into a database connected to the University's mainframe. At the conclusion of the course, those data are statistically analyzed. Results of the data analysis process are carefully reviewed by faculty and laboratory staff and are used for several purposes: (a) to provide advising to students to better develop their oral communication competencies, (b) to redirect course content and pedagogy to better meet the needs of all students, and (c) to provide evidence of the impact of the course on students, helping to address concerns regarding accountability and accreditation.

The results of the assessment process in the public speaking course for up to 2 academic years are reported in Tables 10.1, 10.2, and 10.3.

Table 10.1 presents the results of pre- and posttesting of the total population of students enrolled in the public speaking course for 1 academic year. Results indicate that students made significant improvement in all areas assessed. As expected, the most pronounced gains on subscores occurred in public speaking competency and in the reduction of public speaking apprehension. Dramatic changes also were noted in overall competency and overall reduction of communication apprehension. Of particular interest is the finding indicating that students also improved significantly on variables not specifically addressed by the course. For example, significant improvement is noted in students' listening skills, interpersonal skills, and perceived sense of self-esteem.

Table 10.2 compares pre- and postscores for the CCAI, PRCA, and RSE based on the gender of the total sample population for up to 2 academic years. Table 10.2 indicates that no gender differences were apparent; males and females both demonstrated significant improvement in regard to the variables assessed. Concerning ethnicity, some differences were indicated by Table 10.3, which compares pre- and postscores for the CCAI and PRCA based on the ethnicity of the total sample population for 2 academic years. Although overall improvement of the Anglo-American population as a group was positive, results suggest that more attention needs to be directed toward other ethnic groups. Obviously, the small sample size of the ethnic groups other than Anglo-American confounds the findings in this table. As the sample size of ethnically diverse students becomes larger, laboratory faculty will continue to monitor student progress and refine programs and curricula to better meet the needs of all students.

METHODS AND OPTIONS FOR EVALUATING STUDENTS' PROGRESS IN THE PUBLIC SPEAKING COURSE

In addition to examining the process and impact of the public speaking course on students using a technique such as pre- and postassessment, instructors may also directly evaluate students' progress in the course and provide feedback to students about that progress. To be comprehensive, the evaluation or assessment of students' progress can be based on a model of oral competency that focuses on the cognitive (knowledge), behavioral

TABLE 10.1
T Tests Comparing 1991–1992 Pre- and Postscores for Communication
Competency Assessment Instrument (CCAI), Personal Report
of Communication Apprehension (PRCA), and Self-Esteem.

Assessment Instrument	N	Mean	Std Dev	t Value	2-Tail Prob
CCAI Speaking	217			− 13.70***	.000
Pre		26.92	4.34		
Post		30.88	3.18		
CCAI Interpersonal	217			− 8.45***	.000
Pre		32.06	4.17		
Post		34.72	4.47		
CCAI Listening	217			− 8.26***	.000
Pre		14.57	3.05		
Post		16.49	2.51		
CCAI Overall Comm	217			− 12.38***	.000
Pre		72.73	9.40		
Post		81.24	8.00		
PRCA Group	224			3.53**	.001
Pre		14.62	4.87		
Post		13.20	5.98		
PRCA Meeting	224			7.09***	.000
Pre		16.01	5.06		
Post		13.92	4.36		
PRCA Conversation	224			7.77***	.000
Pre		14.25	4.03		
Post		12.25	4.41		
PRCA Public Speaking	224			16.41***	.000
Pre		20.60	4.99		
Post		15.66	4.23		
PRCA Overall Comm App	224			13.62***	.000
Pre		65.80	15.52		
Post		54.47	13.43		
Self-Esteem	144			− 7.04***	.000
Pre		32.17	4.86		
Post		34.35	4.00		

Note. An *increase* in scores on the CCAI and the Self-Esteem is positive and shows improvement, whereas a *decrease* in scores on the PRCA is positive and shows improvement.
*p < .05. **p < .01. ***p < .001.

(skills or performance), affective (feelings or motivation), and ethical (values) domains of communication (Morreale & Hackman, in press). Specifically, the students' progress or achievement in the public speaking course can be evaluated for each of the four domains/dimensions of oral communication using any of a variety of assessment techniques. For students to achieve in the four domains, they should be aware of and satisfy the valuative criteria for each domain, as selected by the course instructor. Instructors may judge which techniques or assessment methods will best evaluate students' progress for each of the four domains. Those techniques or methods, in many cases, are limited and determined by a variety of factors such as class size, time and labor limitations, and availability of technological equipment such as video cameras, players, computers, and so on. Those constraints aside, Table 10.4 presents an exemplary set of objectives for a public speaking course, conceptually describing each of the four domains of oral competency and providing representative valuative criteria that could be used for assessment of student progress for each domain.

TABLE 10.2
T Tests, by Gender, Comparing Pre- and Postscores for Communication Competency Assessment Instrument (CCAI) (1990–1992), Personal Report of Communication Apprehension (PRCA) (1990–1992), and Self-Esteem (1991–1992).

Assessment Instrument	N	Mean	Std Dev	t Value	2-Tail Prob
CCAI Overall					
Females	186			− 12.41***	.000
Pre		73.02	8.93		
Post		81.56	8.05		
Males	117			− 8.17***	.000
Pre		74.37	9.32		
Post		81.53	7.02		
PRCA Overall					
Females	215			13.77***	.000
Pre		65.59	16.13		
Post		53.93	13.95		
Males	128			9.62***	.000
Pre		62.48	14.88		
Post		52.38	12.90		
Self-Esteem Overall					
Females	87			− 6.28***	.000
Pre		31.46	4.90		
Post		34.00	4.25		
Males	57			− 3.42**	.001
Pre		33.25	4.63		
Post		34.88	3.56		

Note. An *increase* in scores on the CCAI and the Self-Esteem is positive and shows improvement, whereas a *decrease* in scores on the PRCA is positive and shows improvement.
*p < .05. **p < .01. ***p < .001.

TABLE 10.3

T Tests, by Ethnicity, Comparing 1990–1992 Pre- and Postscores for Communication Competency Assessment Instrument (CCAI) and Personal Report of Communication Apprehension (PRCA).

Assessment Instrument	N	Mean	Std Dev	t Value	2-Tail Prob
CCAI Overall					
African-American	13			− 2.57*	.025
Pre		75.62	9.39		
Post		80.15	6.56		
Anglo-American	258			− 13.20***	.000
Pre		73.75	8.84		
Post		81.65	7.64		
Asian-American	11			− 4.53**	.001
Pre		71.64	13.82		
Post		82.09	10.15		
Hispanic-American	17			− 4.27**	.001
Pre		70.24	8.90		
Post		79.18	7.74		
Native American[a]	4			− 1.95	.146
Pre		70.00	11.80		
Post		85.25	3.95		
PRCA Overall					
African-American	15			4.05**	.001
Pre		59.60	16.38		
Post		49.13	14.85		
Anglo-American	289			15.05***	.000
Pre		64.16	15.69		
Post		53.18	13.46		
Asian-American	12			2.72*	.020
Pre		72.75	19.76		
Post		59.08	12.67		
Hispanic-American	22			5.86***	.000
Pre		67.32	12.83		
Post		55.00	11.69		
Native American[a]	5			3.86*	.018
Pre		55.20	8.29		
Post		43.40	10.64		

Note. *Increases* in CCAI scores and *decreases* in PRCA scores are positive and show improvement.

[a]Native American scores for 1991–1992 only.

$*p < .05. **p < .01. ***p < .001.$

TABLE 10.4
Public Speaking Course Objectives and Valuative Criteria

1. *Cognitive Domain* (Knowing)
The student will be able to demonstrate knowledge and understanding of the theories and concepts related to academic inquiry and study in the areas of speech and thought, oral communication competency, and public presentation speaking.

Criteria
•Successful completion of a written or oral exam.
•Observable and informed participation in class discussion.
•Appropriate use and incorporation of theories and knowledge into in-class presentations.

2. *Behavioral Domain* (Doing)
The student will be able to demonstrate ability to organize thought(s) and use operational skills and communication behaviors and competencies necessary to communicate those organized thought(s) in a public presentation.

Criteria:
•Demonstrated ability to organize thoughts for presentation in outline form.
•Successful completion of in-class public presentations.
•Measurable improvement toward the achievement of personally set behavioral goals regarding communication behaviors and competencies.

3. *Affective Domain* (Feeling)
The student will be able to demonstrate, and attain measurable improvement in, the willingness and motivation to communicate thought(s) to other(s) in a public presentation.

Criterion:
A demonstrated increase in oral communication competency and decrease in communication apprehension, as assessed in the entrance and exit interviews.

4. *Ethical Domain* (Valuing)
The student will be able to demonstrate a defined personal set of ethics and values, in regard to communication competency, that takes responsibility for self, other(s), and relationship(s) and outcome(s) in communication interaction(s).

Criterion:
The development of a statement of personal ethics regarding public/presentational speaking and communication competency.

FUTURE DIRECTIONS FOR THE ASSESSMENT OF PUBLIC SPEAKING

The future for developing competency-based public speaking courses and for standardized speech evaluation processes and programs appears favorable, considering the proliferation of public speaking courses and the interest in accountability and standardized assessment programs. That being so, the procedures for standardized speech evaluation and for pre- and postassessment of the public speaking course presented in this chapter take on import.

Possible future directions for such assessment programs may vary under the influence of new media and educational technologies. For example, the speech evaluation form and criteria described in this chapter already are being adapted to include a computerized speech evaluation system. That software system will include a database of speech criticism comments that can be accessed by the rater while the student is speaking. The use of such a database, which provides immediate feedback to the student, could enhance that feedback in terms of depth and breadth.

In addition to innovative feedback techniques, each of the eight competencies that comprise *The Competent Speaker* speech evaluation form could be developed into a computer-assisted instructional (CAI) component. Then, when students experience difficulty with one of the eight competencies, they could be directed to the appropriate CAI component. Obviously this approach to instruction is not as labor intensive as past pedagogies, but neither is it as personal. CAI components could be developed to assist the student in speech preparation activities such as organizing and outlining the speech. Several interactive video and multimedia instructional tools on similar topics already have been developed and are available through their developers (Cronin, 1992). The computer also could be used to facilitate the pre- and postassessment program for public speaking courses. A variety of self-report instruments are amenable to non-labor-intensive computer administration.

The speech, the speech evaluation process, and the public speaking course are proudly grounded in a centuries-old rhetorical heritage. Yet that heritage is being interpreted in an era of new concerns—accountability, accreditation, assessment. The choice of the speech teacher is how to respond appropriately to these new concerns that pose a challenge for the future. Such appropriate responses should honor the rhetorical heritage of the past, interpreted anew for students in the contemporary public speaking course.

ACKNOWLEDGMENT

Contributions and editorial support for this chapter were provided by David A. Aldrich, University of Colorado, Colorado Springs.

REFERENCES

Backlund, P. (1990). *SCA Conference on Assessment of Communication Competency.* Denver, CO: University of Denver.

Cooper, L. (1932). The rhetoric of Aristotle: An expanded translation with supplementary *examples for students of composition and public speaking.* New York: Appleton.

Cronin, M. (1992, November). *The effects of interactive video instruction in constructing speaking outlines.* Paper presented at the annual meeting of the Speech Communication Association, Chicago.

Curtis, D., Winsor, J., & Stephens, R. (1989). National preferences in business and communication education. *Communication Education, 38*(1), 6–14.

Fotheringham, W. C. (1956, March). A technique for measuring speech effectiveness in public speaking classes. *Communication Monographs, 23,* 31–37.

Hayworth, D. (1939, November). Can public speaking be measured? *The Southern Communication Journal, 5,* 6–10.

Johnson, J. R., & Szczupakiewicz, N. (1987, April). The public speaking course: Is it preparing students with work related public speaking skills? *Communication Education, 36*(2), 131–137.

Knower, F. H. (1929, April). Psychological tests in public speaking. *The Quarterly Journal of Speech, 15,* 216–222.

McCroskey, J. C. (1970). Measure of communication-bound anxiety. *Speech Monographs, 37*(4), 269–277.

Miles, P. (1981). Student video self-critiques. *Communication Education, 30*(3), 280–283.

Morreale, S. P., & Hackman, M. Z. (in press). A communication competency approach to the introductory public speaking course. *Instructional Psychology.*

Morreale, S. P., Moore, M. R., Taylor, K. P., Surges-Tatum, D., & Hulbert-Johnson, R. (1993). *The competent speaker.* Annandale, VA: Speech Communication Association.

Mulac, A. (1974). Effects of three feedback conditions employing videotape and audiotape on acquired speech skill. *Speech Monographs, 41*(3), 205–214.

Norvelle, L. (1947). A comparison of the improvement of extension students with universal studies in a public speaking course. *Communication Monographs, 14,* 159–164.

Pearson, J. C., & Daniels, T. D. (1988). "Oh, what tangled webs we weave": Concerns about current conceptions of communication competence. *Communication Reports, 1*(2), 95–100.

Quianthy, R. L. (1990). *Communication is life: Essential college sophomore speaking and listening competencies.* Annandale, VA: Speech Communication Association.

Rosenberg, M. (1965). *Society and the adolescent self-image.* Princeton, NJ: Princeton University Press.

Rubin, R. B. (1982). *Communication competency assessment instrument.* Annandale, VA: Speech Communication Association.

Rubin, R. B. (1990). Communication competence. In G. M. Phillips & J. T. Wood (Eds.), *Essays to commemorate the 75th anniversary of the Speech Communication Association* (pp. 94–129). Carbondale: Southern Illinois University Press.

Rubin, R., & Graham, E. (1988). Communication correlates of college success: An exploratory investigation. *Communication Education, 37*(1), 14–27.

Rubin, R., Graham, E., & Mignerey, J. (1990). A longitudinal study of college students' communication competence. *Communication Education, 39*(1), 1–13.

Speaking and listening competencies for high school graduates. (1982). Annandale, VA: Speech Communication Association.

Spitzberg, B. H. (1988). Communication competence: Measures of perceived effectiveness. In C. H. Tardy (Ed.), *A handbook for the study of human communication: Methods & instruments for observing, measuring, & assessing the communication process* (pp. 67–105). Norwood, NJ: Ablex.

Spitzberg, B. H. (1993). The dialectics of (in)competence. *Journal of Social and Personal Relationships, 10*(1), 137–158.

Spitzberg, B. H., & Cupach, W. R. (1989). *Handbook of interpersonal competence research.* New York: Springer-Verlag.

11

Interpersonal Communication

Ellen A. Hay
Augustana College

Many published and "local" measures are available to assess interpersonal effectiveness. Measures have also been successfully developed by various departments to respond to their own conceptualizations of interpersonal competence. In order to enhance the assessment process in the future, professional associations, departments, and faculty members need to devise measures of the knowledge dimension, set standards for demonstration of interpersonal competence, create a bank of exemplar performances to reflect these standards, and follow sound assessment practices.

This chapter is organized around four questions: What are the challenges we face in designing assessment suitable to instruction in interpersonal communication? What are we trying to assess? How can we assess it? How might we do it better? Responses to these questions will offer perspectives on the outcomes, options, and resources that we have available when implementing assessment of interpersonal communication courses and programs.

WHAT CHALLENGES DO WE FACE IN ASSESSING INTERPERSONAL INSTRUCTION?

Assessment activities don't take a "rocket scientist" to implement. They require careful review of assessment options (means) available, and consideration of statements of intended student outcomes and resources available (usually small), as well as the specific requirements placed upon the department. There will never exist the perfect means of assessment. However, choices will need to be made and implemented based upon the department's judgment of the best means available at the time. (Nichols, 1991, p. 36)

Although Nichols' statement on conducting assessment demystifies the process, it is important to realize that this process is neither simple nor uncomplicated. Defining outcomes, generating options, and securing resources can be difficult and time consuming.

One of the biggest challenges that we face in communication, in fact, is designing assessment suitable to interpersonal communication. This occurs for a number of reasons. First, instruction in this subdiscipline encompasses a wide range of topics and issues, so defining the knowledge base is difficult. A cursory glance at the texts used in many courses indicates that topics in interpersonal communication instruction frequently include definitions of communication, models of communication, language acquisition, nonverbal communication, perception, self-concept, self-disclosure, relationship formation, development and termination, conflict, empathy, gender, family interaction, interviewing, listening, intimacy, emotions, communication climates, and intercultural communication. The vast array of topics makes assessment difficult. The topics are not all easily related to each other so assessment procedures can become lengthy and disjointed. Although there are undoubtedly commonalities in interpersonal instruction in colleges and universities across the country, many differences also exist in the choice and coverage of the aforementioned topics. Because discipline-based standards have yet to be articulated, differences in interpersonal instruction reflect the strengths, weaknesses, and biases of individual faculty members along with the varying departmental perspectives on the role and nature of interpersonal communication.

Second, although the development of interpersonal abilities does certainly occur in an interpersonal communication course, a variety of other settings and situations also promote the development of these abilities. Students who function as peer mentors or tutors, residence hall assistants, or organizational leaders regularly receive training in various aspects of interpersonal communication. Beyond any formal training, students in their everyday lives have a variety of interpersonal experiences from which they grow and develop. Because interpersonal abilities are developed in a variety of settings, it is more difficult to isolate the outcomes of a particular course or program.

Third, interpersonal abilities tend to be relationally specific. Abilities that are needed for friends are not the same as those needed for lovers, for family members, for acquaintances, for professional colleagues, and so forth. This is further complicated by time and context. Abilities and knowledge appropriate for one time and place may not be suitable for the next. It is, therefore, difficult to define a knowledge base or ability set that is applicable to these many different situations. As Spitzberg and Hecht (1984) noted in summarizing their model of relational competence:

> Person A is more likely to create impressions of appropriateness, and effectiveness and achieve functional outcomes if he or she is motivated to interact with person B in context C at time T; is knowledgeable about person B, context C and topical subject S; and is skilled behaviorally in enacting these knowl-

edge and motivation states. The importance and relevance of these components will be critical in influencing impressions of competence. (p. 576)

Even with these challenges, however, it is important to consider how
best to assess the development of knowledge, abilities, and motivations in
the interpersonal area. Departments of communication are facing considerable pressure to demonstrate the effectiveness of instruction. If a particular course of instruction does not have definable outcomes that can be
measured in some way, it could be considered suspect. The other more
positive advantage to developing appropriate assessment is that it helps to
inform the instructional process. It lets faculty know more about what they
are doing so that strengths can be maximized and weaknesses reduced.

WHAT ARE WE TRYING TO ASSESS?

The place to start assessment is at the end. Departments designing assessment plans need to first consider the outcomes of their courses and programs in interpersonal communication. Why do students take these
courses? What do we expect them to know when they finish the course or
program? What abilities do we expect students to develop during the
course or program? What attitudes do we expect them to develop? How do
interpersonal communication courses or programs tie into the goal and
mission statements for the department? Although questions such as these
seem fairly mundane at first glance, they are very complicated and difficult
to answer. Those who have tried to answer them can attest to their complexity. Fortunately there are a number of resources that might be beneficial
in beginning to articulate the goals and objectives of an interpersonal
course.

It might be helpful for interpersonal faculty to first discuss and agree
upon what they mean by a competent interpersonal communicator. Certainly, a number of views of competence have been articulated over the last
three decades. In summarizing the previous work in this area, Rubin (1990)
explained:

> In the interpersonal context, research has examined relational impressions
> formed by interactants and the interpersonal, prosocial skills that comprise
> interpersonal competence. Researchers. . .identified empathy, descriptive-
> ness, owning feelings, self-disclosure, and behavioral flexibility as compo-
> nents of interpersonal competence. Other researchers have developed similar
> schemas and add to this list qualities such as social relaxation, assertiveness,
> interaction management, altercentrism, expressiveness, supportiveness, be-
> havioral flexibility, immediacy, and control. (p.100)

Given the complexity in conceptualizing competence, interpersonal faculty may need to define exactly what they are seeking to address in their

instruction and develop statements of objectives that reflect their particular courses and/or programs, and tie these courses and programs into the overall mission of the department.

In operationalizing its conceptualization of interpersonal competency, interpersonal faculty might turn to the functional communication competencies that have been articulated for high school graduates (Bassett, Whittington, & Staton-Spicer, 1978) or the *Guidelines for Developing Oral Communication Curricula in Kindergarten Through Twelfth Grade* (SCA, 1991). Although these publications are primarily designed for younger students, they do provide models for articulating expectations that are relevant to interpersonal instruction.

Finally, the various interpersonal textbooks and instructor's manuals can be very helpful in defining the outcomes of instruction. For examples, textbooks such as *Interplay* (Adler, Rosenfeld, & Towne, 1989) introduce each new chapter with a listing of objectives for that chapter. Objectives such as these might be an effective starting point in defining intended outcomes.

Using the resources available, faculty need to develop clear, concise statements of outcomes. These statements should offer definable expectations of what students should know, do, and feel at the completion of a course or program in interpersonal communication. As noted in the *SCA's Criteria for the Assessment of Oral Communication* (Crocker-Lakness, Manheimer, & Scott, 1990): "Assessment of oral communication should view competence in oral communication as a gestalt of several interacting dimensions. At a minimum, all assessments of oral communication should include an assessment of knowledge, an assessment of skills, and an evaluation of the individual's attitude toward communication" (p. 3).

The following statements illustrate the types of objectives that need to be articulated and tied to the assessment of interpersonal communication.

At the completion of this introductory interpersonal communication course, students will be able:

Knowledge Dimension
- To explain the factors and forces that influence self-concept.
- To discuss the stages in relational development.
- To compare and contrast approaches to conflict resolution.

Ability Dimension
- To listen better.
- To use prosocial behaviors during an interaction with a classmate.
- To demonstrate how to initiate and encourage interaction with a classmate.

Attitudinal Dimension
- To express a greater willingness to engage in social interaction.
- To feel more confident about their interactional abilities.

Obviously after the outcomes have been identified the next and most important step is to design instruction that will allow students to realize these objectives. One of the significant benefits of the assessment movement has been the degree to which it has encouraged faculty to examine their instructional practices in light of stated outcomes and feedback from assessment techniques. Interpersonal instruction will continue to improve as we become more aware of what we are trying to do in our courses and how well we are succeeding.

WHAT MEANS ARE AVAILABLE FOR ASSESSING INTERPERSONAL INSTRUCTION?

In articulating outcomes and planning instruction, it is also important to plan for assessment. Departmental planning will help determine what forms of assessment should occur at the program level and which forms of assessment should be embedded within courses. An overall strategy can also be devised. Frequently, a pre/post approach is used to measure changes in knowledge, ability, and attitudes. Students complete a set of measures at the beginning of a course or program, and then again at the end. On other occasions, assessment occurs at the end of the course or program, and student performance must meet or exceed a predetermined level or standard. In implementing these strategies, interpersonal faculty have a number of measurement options. Faculty can select from a variety of published measures, or they can design their own. Most of the measures currently in use focus on the development of abilities and attitudes more than on knowledge acquisition.

Published Assessment Instruments

Several sources are helpful in identifying published measures from which to select assessment procedures. *Measures of Speech/Communication* (ETS, 1991), *the Handbook of Interpersonal Competence Research* (Spitzberg & Cupach, 1988), *the Handbook for the Study of Human Communication* (Tardy, 1988), and *Studying Interpersonal Interaction* (Montgomery & Duck, 1991) provide very complete listings and descriptions of various measures appropriate to interpersonal assessment.

The published measures seem best suited to assessing the ability and affective outcomes of instruction. Many of the instruments are self-reports where students appraise their own abilities in various interpersonal situations. Others are protocol for judging the abilities of interacts.

There are several measures that focus on overall communicative competence, which can provide information on interpersonal abilities (see Table 11.1). Undoubtedly the most widely known and used is the Communication Competency Assessment Instrument (Rubin, 1982), a portion of which requires that the student interact with the rater. The corresponding Com-

TABLE 11.1
Instruments for Assessing Overall Communication Competence

Source	Title	Items	Scale	Dimension Assessed
Ford & Wolvin (1993)	Basic Course Communication Competency Measure	24	7-point	Self-report of public speaking, interpersonal, interviewing, small group, and listening abilities and overall communication confidence.
McCroskey & McCroskey (1988)	Self-Perceived Communication Competence Scale	12	100-point	Self-report of competence in public speaking, large group, small group, and interpersonal situations with three different audiences.
Morreale, Morley, & Naylor (1993)	Communication Behaviors Inventory	170	7-point	Self-report of abilities in 26 situations that include public speaking, interpersonal, intrapersonal, and organizational contexts.
Rubin (1982)	Communication Competency Assessment Instrument	19 in 3 parts	5-point	Students present a speech, view a videotape, and discuss it with a trained rater who evaluates speaking, listening, and interpersonal abilities.
Rubin (1985)	Communication Competency Self-Report Questionnaire	19	5-point	Self-report of public speaking, interaction, and listening abilities.

munication Competence Self-Report Questionnaire (Rubin, 1985) asks students to self-evaluate their public speaking, interaction, and listening abilities. The Basic Course Communication Competency Measure (Ford & Wolvin, 1993) requires students to evaluate their public speaking, interpersonal communication, interviewing, group communication, and listening abilities, and level of confidence in classroom, family, social, and employment situations. The Self-Perceived Communication Competence Scale (McCroskey & Mc Croskey, 1988) has subjects consider their competence in four contexts (public speaking, large meeting, small group, and interpersonal) with three different types of receivers (stranger, acquaintance, and friend). The Communication Behaviors Inventory (Morreale, Morley, & Naylor, 1993), which is currently under development, also asks students about their behaviors in various interpersonal situations.

Other measures focus more exclusively on interpersonal communication competence (see Table 11.2). The Conversational Skills Rating Scale (Spitzberg & Hurt, 1987), the Relational Communication Scale (Burgoon & Hale, 1987), the Self/Alter-Rated Competence Scale (Cupach & Spitzberg, 1981), and the Communicative Competence Scale (Wiemann, 1977) can be used by a trained rater or a conversational partner in the evaluation of a student's interpersonal abilities. These measures can also be adapted to serve as self-assessments of abilities following an interaction. The instruments standardize evaluation of interaction abilities. They force raters to judge the effectiveness of particular interpersonal behaviors in specific situations. In using these instruments in an assessment program, faculty would select the ones that best fit its conceptualization of and instruction in competent interpersonal communication.

TABLE 11.2
Instruments for Assessing Overall Interpersonal Communication Competence

Source	Title	Items	Scale	Dimension Assessed
Burgoon & Hale (1987)	Relational Communication Scale	30	8-point	Self-report or observer rating of interaction abilities in relation to eight relational themes.
Cegala (1981)	Interaction Involvement Scale	18	7-point	Self-report of thoughts and behaviors during conversations with others to determine degree of involvement and participation.
Cupach & Spitzberg (1981)	Self/Alter-Rated Communication Scale	28	5-point	Self-report or observer rating of communicative competence elements such as other orientation, conversation skills, and self-centered behavior.
Daly, Vangelisti, & Daughton (1987)	Conversational Sensitivity Scale	36		Self-report of perceived awareness/sensitivity in various conversational situations.
Duck & Rutt (1991)	Iowa Communication Record	36	9-point multiple choice	Self-report of behaviors and conditions during a conversation lasting 10 or more minutes.
Duran (1983); Duran & Wheeless (1980)	Communicative Adaptability Scale	60	5-point	Self-report of social composure, wit, appropriate disclosure, and articulation.
Getter & Nowinski (1981)	Interpersonal Problem Solving Assessment Technique	46	open-ended	Presents 46 interpersonal problems to which the subject responds. Responses are evaluated on alternatives generated and response selected.
Lowe & Cautela (1978)	Social Performance Survey Schedule	100	5-point	Self-report or observer rating of the frequency of various social behaviors such as eye contact, facial expressions, and appropriate responses.
Riggio (1986)	Social Skills Inventory	105	9-point	Self-report inventory of social skills in areas such as emotional expressiveness, emotional control, and social sensitivity.
Spitzberg & Hurt (1987)	Conversational Skills Rating Scale	30	5-point	Self-report or observer rating of communication abilities such as altercentrism, composure, expressiveness, and interaction management during an actual or recalled interaction.
Wheeler, Reis, & Nezlek (1983)	Rochester Interaction Record	8	7-point	Self-report of intimacy, disclosure, quality, satisfaction, initiation, and influence during actual interactions.
Wiemann (1977)	Communication Competence Scale	30		Observer ratings of general communicative competence, affiliation, relaxation, flexibility, and empathy.

In addition to the aforementioned protocols that can be used in evaluating a student's interpersonal abilities during actual interactions, several other paper-and-pencil measures also focus on overall interpersonal communication competence. The Interpersonal Problem Solving Assessment Technique (Getter & Nowinski, 1981) presents students with 46 interpersonal problems to which they respond in an open manner. These responses are then evaluated by a trained rater. The Conversational Sensitivity Scale (Daly, Vangelisti, & Daughton, 1987), the Social Skills Inventory (Riggio, 1986), the Interaction Involvement Scale (Cegala, 1981), the Communicative Adaptability Scale (Duran, 1983; Duran & Wheeless, 1980), and the Social Performance Survey Schedule (Lowe & Cautela, 1978) are self-report measures with which students can evaluate their own interpersonal abilities. Each of these measures offers a slightly different view of interpersonal competence that would need to be matched to a program or course.

Another approach to measuring the development of interpersonal communication competence is for students to maintain an ongoing record of interpersonal encounters and their resulting behavior. The Rochester Interaction Record (Wheeler, Reis, & Nezlek, 1983) and the Iowa Communication Record (Duck & Rutt, 1991) are communication logs that encourage systematic recording and analysis of social interactions. Students and faculty can use these diaries at the end of an interpersonal course to identify patterns of behavior and areas of growth.

A number of self-report measures are also available to assess more specific interpersonal behaviors (see Table 11.3). If the outcomes of the course or program consider topics such as self-esteem, empathy, or nonverbal responsive, a battery of these measures that have a more specific focus might be suitable. For example, empathy might be measured using the Interpersonal Reactivity Index (Davis, 1980) or the LaMonica Empathy Profile (LaMonica, 1986). The Affective Communication Test (Friedman, Prince, Riggio, & DiMatteo, 1980) and the Self-Monitoring Scale (Snyder, 1974) evaluate student awareness and perceptions of nonverbal expressiveness during social interactions. The ability to encourage others to self-disclose can be measured with the Opener Scale (Miller, Berg, & Archer, 1983). Rosenberg's (1989) Self-Esteem Scale asks students to examine views of self. Assertiveness and aggressiveness can be evaluated using instruments such as the Verbal Aggressiveness Scale (Infante & Wigley, 1986), the Argumentativeness Scale (Infante & Rancer, 1982), or the College Self-Expression Scale (Galassi, DeLo, Galassi, & Bastien, 1974).

If listening receives significant attention in the interpersonal course or program, several instruments are available to assess listening ability (see Table 11.4). The Steinbrecher-Willmington Listening Test (Steinbrecher & Willmington, 1993), the Watson–Barker Listening Test (Watson, Barker, Roberts, & Johnson, 1991), and the Kentucky Listening Comprehension Test (Bostrom & Waldhart, 1985) have frequently been used to assess listening.

TABLE 11.3
Instruments Assessing Specific Interpersonal Communication

Source	Title	Items	Scale	Dimension Assessed
Davis (1980)	Interpersonal Reactivity Scale	28	5-point	Self-report of abilities in perspective taking, fantasy, empathetic concern, and personal distress.
Friedman, Prince, Riggio, & DiMatteo (1980)	Affective Communication Test	13	9-point	Self-report of nonverbal behaviors and emotional expressiveness during interpersonal interactions.
Galassi, DeLow, Galassi, & Bastien (1974)	College Self-Expression Scale	50	5-point	Self-report of assertiveness.
Infante & Rancer (1982)	Argumentativeness Scale	20	5-point	Self-report on the tendency to avoid or engage in argumentative situations.
Infante & Wigley (1986)	Verbal Aggressiveness Scale	20	5-point	Self-report on attacks to the self-concepts of others during influence situations.
LaMonica (1986)	LaMonica Empathy Profile	30	forced-choice	Self-report of nonverbal behavior, perception of feelings, listening, verbal responsiveness, respect, openness, honesty, and flexibility.
Miller, Berg, & Archer (1983)	Opener Scale	10	5-point	Self-report on the ability to encourage others to self-disclose.
Rosenberg (1989)	Self-Esteem Scale	10	4-point	Self-report of views of self.
Snyder (1974)	Self-Monitoring Scale	25	true/false	Self-report of awareness of nonverbal behaviors

All three measures have been norm referenced with fairly large populations that provide a basis for comparing student scores.

Several other measures may prove helpful in measuring the attitudinal dimension of student learning (see Table 11.5). The Interpersonal Communication Satisfaction Inventory (Hecht, 1978) and the Revised UCLA Loneliness Scale (Russell, Peplau, & Catrona, 1980) can tap the student's overall satisfaction with interpersonal relationships and interactions, whereas the Willingness to Communicate Scale (McCroskey & Richmond, 1987) considers motivation to interact with others in a variety of settings. More traditional measures of communication apprehension such as the PRCA-24 (McCroskey, 1982), the Communication Anxiety Inventory (Booth-Butterfield & Gould, 1986), the Classroom Apprehension about Participation Scale (Neer, 1987), and the Behavioral Assessment of Speech Anxiety (Mulac & Sherman, 1974) may also provide an indication of changes in attitudes toward interpersonal interactions. The Receiver Apprehension Test (Wheeless, 1975) could likewise yield information about the development of students' attitudes and motivations during interpersonal encounters.

TABLE 11.4
Listening Assessment Instruments

Source	Title	Items	Scale	Dimension Assessed
Bostrom & Waldhart (1985)	Kentucky Listening Comprehension Test	78	multiple choice	Four subscales measure short-term listening, short-term listening with rehearsal, interpretative listening, informative listening, and abilities to overcome distractions.
Steinbrecher & Willmington (1993)	Steinbrecher–Willmington Listening Test	55	multiple choice	Subjects answer questions about speeches, announcements, and conversations that they hear and view.
Watson, Barker, Roberts, & Johnson (1991)	Watson–Barker Listening Test	5 parts	multiple choice	Designed to measure short- and long-term listening.

TABLE 11.5
Attitudinal/Apprehension Assessment Instruments

Source	Title	Items	Scale	Dimension Assessed
Booth-Butterfield & Gould (1986)	Communication Anxiety Inventory	20	4-point	Self-report of apprehension following public speaking, dyadic, and small group situations.
Hecht (1978)	Interpersonal Communication Satisfaction Inventory	19	7-point	Self-report of satisfaction with communication behaviors during an actual or recalled interaction.
McCroskey (1982)	Personal Report of Communication Apprehension-24	24	5-point	Self-report of reactions and responses to public speaking, small group, and interpersonal situations.
McCroskey & Richmond (1987)	Willingness to Communicate Scale	20	100-point	Self-report of desire to communicate in group discussions, meetings, conversations, and speeches with strangers, acquaintances, and friends.
Neer (1987)	Classroom Apprehension about Participation Scale	20		Self-report of predisposition to participate in class discussion and overall confidence when doing so.
Russell, Peplau, & Catrona (1980)	Revised UCLA Loneliness Scale	20	4-point	Self-report of satisfaction with relationships.
Wheeless (1975)	Receiver Apprehension Test	20	5-point	Self-report of fears when receiving and processing information.

Obviously, there are a myriad of published measures that can be used in interpersonal assessment. The challenge for speech communication faculty is selecting those that can provide the most useful and relevant information. The program at the University of Colorado at Colorado Springs (Morreale et al., 1993) is an example of how such measures can be used. The students beginning interpersonal communication at UC–CS complete the Willing-ness to Communicate Scale (McCroskey & Richmond, 1987), and then after a 10-minute in-class interaction with a classmate, students complete the Conversational Skills Rating Scale (Spitzberg & Hurt, 1987) about them-selves and their partners. During an initial individual meeting with a graduate teaching assistant, these measures are discussed with the student and suggestions are made as to resources available for improvement in areas of weakness. The student and graduate teaching assistant set goals for improvement. The two measures are then repeated at the end of course, and a graduate teaching assistant again meets with the student individually to discuss progress made on these goals. In addition to providing faculty with an overall view of the development of their students, this approach also gives students an opportunity to consider the growth in their abilities. An approach similar to this could be used with the other measures already listed to reflect the goals and objectives of a particular course or program.

Locally Developed Instruments

Whereas some departments have chosen standardized, published mea-sures for their assessment programs, others have chosen to develop their own instruments. Departments and instructors that opt for this approach generally have started by turning their objectives into standards that clearly outline expectations in terms of demonstrated interpersonal behaviors. They next have created tests or, more commonly, authentic performance instruments to reflect these standards. Several examples serve to illustrate this approach to assessment.

One example of this approach is the program at the University of Missouri–Kansas City (Aitken & Neer, 1992). The faculty in this department first identified 12 competence areas (one of which was interpersonal com-munication) and then evaluated and redesigned the curriculum so that these goals were adequately addressed. A number of sources of information about student progress and performance were then identified or created to assess students at the start, middle, and end of the program. Students started to maintain portfolios of their progress in the program; forms for evaluating performance in each of the 12 competence areas were standard-ized so that feedback was more consistent, and a departmental test related to the 12 competencies was developed. The benefits of this assessment program are numerous as Aitken and Neer (1992) explained: "The process generated an attitude of faculty enthusiasm to collectively discuss and improve student learning. Departments at other colleges and universities can apply a comparable process to their particular situations. We found it exciting to actually define our own concept of effectiveness, which we then applied to curriculum development" (p. 283).

Another example of a locally developed approach was reported over a decade ago by Berryman-Fink and Pederson (1981) at the University of

Cincinnati. They defined four interpersonal skills as the focal point for the introductory interpersonal course and then created a 16-item test of hypothetical interpersonal situations that was used as a pretest and posttest for students in a basic interpersonal communication course. They reported significant gains in the scores from the pretest to the posttest.

In addition to paper-and-pencil measures, authentic performance-based instruments have been successfully created at a number of institutions. These require that faculty first define the elements of an effective performance and then articulate how such elements develop as the student acquires more refined knowledge, abilities, and attitudes. The "authenticity" of the assessments is related to the task used in the assessment stimuli. Authentic tasks require students to apply their knowledge and abilities to the solution of real-world problems. Such assessments are multidimensional and may involve functioning in a group, writing a proposal, or making a presentation. Such assessments may also occur over an extended length of time and may involve assembling an audiovisual or written portfolio. (For more information on alternative assessment in speech communication see Hay, 1993.)

In addition to focusing on the performance of particular abilities, authentic assessment also strives to involve the learners in the assessment process so they develop an awareness of their own growth. Zessoules and Gardner (1991) explained the advantages of authentic assessment:

> Though the goal of general education may not be to churn out professional choreographers, playwrights, scientists, or mathematicians, we hope that students will come to see themselves as active, thoughtful independent learners. Yet, standardized tests displace students from the process and responsibility of assessment. Instead, these tests subject students to evaluative measures whose norm-referenced, numerical scores cannot capture the kinds of reflective processes students engage as active learners generating work, tending ideas, and developing a way of thinking in a given domain. If authentic assessment is intended, as we think it should be, to reveal students' understandings, then we must find measures that capture the hidden aspects and processes that lie in, around, under, and behind students' work. (p. 54)

The University of Northern Colorado (Arneson, 1993) has adopted an authentic, performance-based approach for its courses in interpersonal communication, small group/organizational communication, and communication and influence. In interpersonal communication, students prepare for the assessment with a study guide that encourages them to review the assessment variables. Students then report to the assessment where they meet with others to discuss a topic previously chosen for its importance and relevance to students. During the assessment, students are evaluated on their impact of self, verbal/nonverbal effectiveness, and listening abilities. Standards at the advanced, intermediate, and basic levels have been defined to aid in identifying progress on each of the three abilities.

Another example of this performance-based approach comes from the University of Wisconsin–Oshkosh (Willmington, 1992). Faculty first defined interpersonal effectiveness in terms of empathy, self-disclosure, promoting interaction, physical involvement, vocal usage, language usage and listening. During a 5-minute structured interaction between a student and a trained initiator, various prompts are used so that the student has the opportunity to demonstrate the behaviors previously identified. Trained raters then evaluate these interactions. As Willmington (1992) explained, "there are those of us who believe that if a purpose of instruction is to develop proficiency as an interpersonal communicator, then as responsible instructors, we are compelled to assess students as actual performing communicators" (p. 2).

A third example of authentic assessment procedures comes from Alverno College in Wisconsin. Social interaction is defined as one of the eight competencies to be developed throughout the Alverno curriculum. Interaction abilities are assessed in several contexts and developmental levels. At the intermediate level of development, "The student is responsible for evaluating the effectiveness of her own and of others' interaction behavior in interpersonal and task-oriented interactions. As part of this evaluation process, she proposes changes in her own behavior and formulates a growth contract at the end" (Alverno Educators, 1983, p. C5L3). To accomplish this task, the student is videotaped or audiotaped in at least three different interactions. She then evaluates her contributions and those of others in each of these situations according to the interpersonal models and frameworks discussed in class. Finally the student writes a plan for further improving her interaction abilities. The written components of this assessment are kept in her departmental file and the taped components are added to her audio-visual taped portfolio. At graduation the student and her advisor have a complete record of her experiences at the college.

The faculty of Golden West College developed authentic means of assessing the interpersonal abilities of students in a variety of settings (Ratliffe, 1989). They defined seven essential competencies for their introductory interpersonal course: initiating and managing conversation, clarifying perceptions, using descriptive language, expressing emotions, using active listening, responding with relational feedback, and using assertive messages. For each competency, "Students are provided with skill sheets that consist of behaviorally descriptive statements of from five to nine specific skills components that must be included in a given demonstration in order to meet the minimum criteria" (Ratliffe, 1989, p. 6). Students can then demonstrate these abilities with a partner in the communication laboratory where they are assessed by a trained peer evaluator, in small groups during class, and in individual conferences with instructors. The Golden West faculty also adapted this approach to focus on peer and self-evaluation, and developed a format that fulfills their credit by examination option.

Obviously, authentic performance measures such as those described here provide the students and faculty with a more complete and accurate view of interpersonal abilities than a paper-and-pencil test might give. There are, however, clear disadvantages to this approach. O'Neill (1992) explained that performance assessment is "likely to be at least two or three times more expensive per student," that such measures require a considerable amount of time, and are open to questions of their psychometric capabilities (p. 18). Departments who are considering an authentic, performance-based approach need to be mindful of these drawbacks.

How Can We Make Interpersonal Assessment Better?

The previous section outlined several options available to speech educators as they plan and implement assessment programs. As we move beyond this beginning phase of assessment, and seek to refine our approaches to assessment, new challenges confront us.

One of these challenges is with regard to the knowledge dimension of interpersonal instruction. Most of the published instruments and locally devised performance tests focus on abilities and attitudes. If there is a body of knowledge that our students gain in completing courses in interpersonal communication, then we need to consider how best we can tap this knowledge. Which forms of measurement are best suited to evaluating interpersonal knowledge? Are the traditional multiple-choice examinations given during a course the best way to gain information on this dimension or are there other measures that we might construct and share that would encourage a higher level of thinking about the knowledge gained in an interpersonal class? How can we encourage students to analyze, evaluate, and synthesize the knowledge they have gained in their interpersonal courses? Although we undoubtedly do not need a national interpersonal test, a bank of testing options suitable to the knowledge dimension would be appropriate. For example, one option could be a set of interpersonal interactions either in writing or on videotape. The accompanying instructions would then ask the student to identify and evaluate critical behaviors in an interaction. Student responses could then be evaluated on the degree of sophistication reflected in their oral or written discussion of the interaction.

Second, through our professional associations and our departments, we need to articulate standards for evaluating interpersonal effectiveness. We have made progress in this regard in the public speaking area. We have measures such as *The Competent Speaker* (Morreale, Moore, Taylor, Surges-Tatum, & Hulbert-Johnson, 1992) that have isolated key public speaking behaviors at various levels. Now we need to expand this to other aspects of communication. What do we consider acceptable levels of knowledge and how should this knowledge be expressed? What do we consider an acceptable interpersonal performance? What attitudes do we expect our students to exhibit? These are serious questions that we need to answer.

Other professional organizations such as the National Council of Teachers of Mathematics, the American Association for the Advancement of Science, The National Council of Teachers of Social Studies, and the National Council of Teachers of English have all articulated performance standards for students at various levels (Herman, Aschbacher, & Winters, 1992). As a discipline and in individual departments, we need to consider our own standards for acceptable interpersonal interaction. Wolf, LeMahieu, and Eresh (1992) reinforced this when they noted:

> In short, nearly everywhere the wager is that American education can be galvanized by setting high standards and using new more probing assessments to hold districts, teachers, and students accountable. . . .The call is for all national disciplinary organizations to articulate clear, high standards for what students should know (content standards), and how well they should know it (performance standards). (p. 9)

Third, once we have defined our standards, we need to develop a bank of exemplar performances that exhibit these standards at various levels. We need to readily show students how these standards are evident at different levels of development. How does the interpersonal interaction of a beginning student differ from that of an advanced one? We should be able to show, for example, how appropriate self-disclosure, empathy, listening, and nonverbal cues are evident in a variety of different contexts. We should be able to offer models of written analyses or essays that reflect an advanced level of understanding. These examples reflect the standards and help to bring the standards to life. Wiggins (1991) explained:

> Quality is not an abstraction or a statistical artifact. Standards for rigor, precision, creativity, implied persistence, etc. are set by examples—samples of actual products/performances that exemplify the qualities we seek. Performance standards are empirically induced by a combination of research, observation and wise judgment. We "set" standards at the top of our scoring scale through the wise choices of "anchors"—samples of work that we believe to be genuinely excellent and apt models for emulation. Like the bullseye or prize-winning essay, a real standard supplies the essential element of effective self assessment—usable feedback—where I see for myself how my work compares with the standard setting work. (p. 7)

Fourth, following the practices of good assessment is crucial to assessment of interpersonal communication. (In addition to the aforementioned SCA assessment criteria, assessment planners might also consult the guidelines prepared by the Denver Conference Program Assessment Group, 1992.) We need to work from clearly defined outcomes, use multiple measures over an extended period of time, keep records of development, regularly share this information with students, and ask students to reflect on their learning. The outcomes of assessment should help to identify ways that interpersonal instruction and course offerings can be improved. One-shot, one-dimensional assessment adds little to faculty understanding and provides students with only limited understanding of their intellectual, skill, and attitudinal development. Sound assessment can provide a wealth of information, invigorate the faculty, and contribute to the development of lifelong learners.

Clearly, there are many obstacles to effectively assessing instruction in interpersonal communication. These obstacles, however, can be addressed by carefully articulating outcomes, and then selecting or designing measures to evaluate success in meeting the outcomes. Now that we have recognized the importance of assessment through books such as this, we can work as a discipline, in departments and as individuals to enhance the process, and ultimately improve the instruction that we offer in interpersonal communication. (For an assessment overview and sample assessment plan see Appendixes A and B.)

APPENDIX A: ASSESSMENT OVERVIEW: COURSES AND PROGRAMS IN INTERPERSONAL COMMUNICATION

Outcomes Component

What knowledge should students possess at the end of this course/program?	What abilities should students possess at the end of this course/program?	How motivated should students be to actually use interpersonal knowledge and abilities?

Instructional Component

How will essential knowledge be presented?	How will essential abilities be presented and practiced?	How will motivation be increased?

Assessment Component

How will knowledge be measured?	How will abilities be demonstrated?	How will motivation level be measured?

Feedback Component

What changes will be made in terms of choice and instruction in the knowledge dimension?	What changes will be made in terms of choice and instruction in the instructional dimension?	What changes will be made in terms of choice and instruction in the motivation dimension?

APPENDIX B: SAMPLE ASSESSMENT PLAN

Outcome	Instruction	Assessment
By the end of the course, the student will be able:	During the course, the student will:	At the end of the course, the student will:
To explain factors that influence self-concept such as looking-glass theory and social comparison theory.	Hear a lecture on self-concept. Discuss factors in relation to story, "Cypher in the Snow."	Respond to multiple-choice questions on self-concept
To list and explain five principles of appropriate self-disclosure.	Hear a lecture on self-disclosure. Complete and discuss Jourard's self-disclosure inventory.	Respond to multiple-choice questions on self-disclosure.
To use self-disclosure in an appropriate manner to build the relationship.	Participate in paraphrasing exercise.	Compare self-disclosure levels between a precourse assessment and postcourse assessment using the CSRS (Spitzberg & Hurt, 1987)
To be more willing to self-disclose.	Participate in trust-building exercises.	Compare precourse and postcourses on Willingness to Communicate Scale.
To explain the listening process.	Hear a lecture on listening.	Respond to multiple-choice questions on listening.
To be better listeners.	Complete various listening exercises and activities.	Compare a precourse standardized listening assessment with a postcourse retest.

Ultimately a detailed plan such as the one presented here allows faculty to tailor their assessment to the instruction that is offered in their department and their courses. In this case, the plan meant that certain assessments were administered on a pre-and postcourse basis so that levels of improvement could be determined. Other assessments such as the final multiple-choice examination were used only at the completion of the course.

Although initially very time consuming, course-by-course plans can be integrated to articulate the plan for the entire department. Most outside agencies that are now mandating assessment will be satisfied with departments that can articulate this kind of detailed approach. For the department itself, this approach can help to identify and correct weaknesses and provide further information for the planning of courses and programs. Because the assessment is tailored to the course or program, results provide much more relevant information.

REFERENCES

Adler, R. B., Rosenfeld, L. B., & Towne, N. (1989). *Interplay*. New York: Holt, Rinehart & Winston.
Aitken, J. E., & Neer, M. (1992). A faculty program of assessment for a college level competency-based communicator core curriculum. *Communication Education, 41*, 270–285.

Alverno Educators. (1983). *Faculty handbook on learning and assessment*. Milwaukee, WI: Alverno College.

Arneson, P. (1993). *Authentic exhibition assessment for speech communication*. Unpublished manuscript, University of Northern Colorado, Greeley, CO.

Bassett, R., Whittington, N., & Staton-Spicer, A. (1978). The basics of speaking and listening for high school graduates: What should be assessed? *Communication Education, 31, 9–17.*

Berryman-Fink, C. L., & Pederson, L. (1981). Testing the effects of competency based interpersonal communication course. *Southern Speech Communication Journal, 46, 251–261.*

Booth-Butterfield, S., & Gould, M. (1986). The communication anxiety inventory: Validation of state- and context- communication apprehension. *Communication Quarterly, 34, 194–205.*

Bostrom, R., & Waldhart, E. S. (1985). *Kentucky listening comprehension test*. Lexington: University of Kentucky Listening Research Center.

Burgoon, J. H., & Hale, J. L. (1987). Validation and measurement of the fundamental themes of relational communication. *Communication Monographs, 54, 19–41.*

Cegala, D. J. (1981). Interaction involvement: A cognitive dimension of communicative competence. *Communication Education, 30, 108–121.*

Crocker-Lakness, J. W., Manheimer, S., & Scott, T. E. (1990). *Criteria for the assessment of oral communication*. Annandale, VA: Speech Communication Association.

Cupach, W. R., & Spitzberg, B. H. (1981, February). *Relational competence: Measurement and evaluation*. Paper presented at the Western Speech Communication Association Conference, San Jose, CA.

Daly, J. A., Vangelisti, A. L., & Daughton, S. M. (1987). The nature and correlates of conversational sensitivity. *Human Communication Research, 14, 167–202.*

Davis, M. H. (1980). A multidimensional approach to individual differences in empathy. *JSAS Catalog of Selected Documents in Psychology, 1085.*

Denver Conference Program Assessment Group. (1992). Principles of speech communication program assessment. In E. Hay (Ed.), *Program assessment in speech communication* (pp. 8–11). Annandale, VA: Speech Communication Association.

Duck, S., & Rutt, D. P. (1991). Iowa communication record. In B. M. Montgomery & S. Duck (Eds.), *Studying interpersonal interaction* (pp. 44–49). New York: Guilford.

Duran, R. L. (1983). Communicative adaptability: A measure of social communicative competence. *Communication Quarterly, 31, 320–326.*

Duran R. L., & Wheeless V. E. (1980, November). *Social management: Toward a theory based operationalization of communication competence*. Paper presented at the Speech Communication Association, New York.

Educational Testing Service. (1991). *Measures of speech/communication*. Princeton, NJ: Author.

Ford, W. S. Z., & Wolvin, A. D. (1993). The differential impact of a basic communication course on perceived communication competencies in class, work, and social contexts. *Communication Education, 42, 215–223.*

Friedman, H. S., Prince, L. M., Riggio, R. E., & DiMatteo, M. R. (1980). Understanding and assessing nonverbal expressiveness: The affective communication test. *Journal of Personality and Social Psychology, 39, 333–351.*

Galassi, J. P., DeLo, J. S., Galassi, M. D., & Bastien, S. (1974). The college self-expression scale: A measure of assertiveness. *Behavior Therapy, 5, 165–171.*

Getter, H., & Nowinski, J. K. (1981). A free response test of interpersonal effectiveness. *Journal of Personality Assessment, 45, 301–308.*

Hay, E. A. (1993, November). *Alternative assessment in speech communication*. Paper presented at the Speech Communication Association Convention, Miami, FL.

Hecht, M. L. (1978). The conceptualization and measurement of interpersonal communication satisfaction. *Human Communication Review, 4, 253–264.*

Herman, J. L., Aschbacher, P. R., & Winters, L. (1992). *A practical guide to alternative assessment*. Alexandria, VA: Association for Supervision and Curriculum Development.

Infante, D. A., & Rancer, A. S. (1982). A conceptualization and measure of argumentativeness. *Journal of Personality Assessment, 46,* 72–80

Infante, D. A., & Wigley, C. J. (1986). Verbal aggressiveness: An interpersonal model and measure. *Communication Monographs, 53,* 61–69.

LaMonica, E. L. (1986). *LaMonica empathy profile.* Tuxedo, NY: XICOM.

Lowe, M. R., & Cautela, J. R. (1978). A self-report measure of social skill. *Behavior Therapy, 9,* 535–544.

McCroskey, J. C. (1982). *An introduction to rhetorical communication* (4th ed.). Englewood Cliffs, NJ: Prentice-Hall.

McCroskey, J. C., & McCroskey, L. L. (1988). Self-report as an approach to measuring communication competence. *Communication Education, 5,* 108–113.

McCroskey, J. C., & Richmond, V. P. (1987). Willingness to communicate. In J. C. McCroskey & J. A. Daly (Eds.), *Personality and interpersonal communication* (pp. 129–156). Newbury Park, CA: Sage.

Miller, L. C., Berg, J. H., & Archer, R. L. (1983). Openers: Individuals who elicit intimate self-disclosure. *Journal of Personality and Social Psychology, 44,* 1234–1244.

Montgomery, B. M., & Duck, S. (1991). *Studying interpersonal interaction.* New York: Guilford.

Morreale, S., Hackman, M., Ellis, K., King, K., Meade, P., & Tegtmeier, L. (1993, November). *Assessing communication competency in the interpersonal communication course: A laboratory-supported approach.* Paper presented at the Speech Communication Association Convention, Miami, FL.

Morreale, S. P., Moore, M. R., Taylor, K. P., Surges-Tatum, D., & Hulbert-Johnson, R. (1992). *The competent speaker.* Annandale, VA: Speech Communication Association.

Morreale, S. P., Morley, D. D., & Naylor, J. G. (1993). *The communication behaviors inventory.* Colorado Springs: University of Colorado at Colorado Springs.

Mulac, A., & Sherman, A. R. (1974). The behavioral assessment of speech anxiety. *Quarterly Journal of Speech,* 134–143.

Neer, M. R. (1987). The development of an instrument to measure classroom apprehension. *Communication Education, 36,* 154–166.

Nichols, J. O. (1991). *The departmental guide to implementation of student outcomes assessment and institutional effectiveness.* New York: Agathon.

O'Neill, J. (1992). Putting performance assessment to the test. *Educational Leadership, 49,* 14–19.

Ratliffe, S. A. (1989, November). *Strategies for assessment of the basic undergraduate interpersonal communication course.* Paper presented at a meeting of the Speech Communication Association, San Francisco.

Riggio, R. E. (1986). Assessment of basic social skills. *Journal of Personality and Social Psychology, 51,* 649–660.

Rosenberg, M. (1989). *Society and the adolescent self-image* (Rev. ed.). Middletown, CT: Wesleyan University Press.

Rubin, R. B. (1982). *Communication competency assessment instrument.* Annandale, VA: Speech Communication Association.

Rubin, R. B. (1985). The validity of the communication competency assessment instrument. *Communication Monographs, 52,* 173–75.

Rubin, R. B. (1990). Communication competence. In G. M. Phillips & J. T. Wood (Eds.), *Speech communication: Essays to commemorate the 75th anniversary of the Speech Communication Association* (pp. 94–129). Carbondale: Southern Illinois University Press.

Russell, D., Peplau, L. A., & Catrona, C. E. (1980). The revised UCLA loneliness scale: Concurrent and discriminant validity evidence. *Journal of Personality and Social Psychology, 39,* 472–480.

Snyder, M. (1974). Self-monitoring of expressive behaviors. *Journal of Personality and Social Psychology, 30,* 526–537.

Speech Communication Association. (1991). *Guidelines for developing oral communication curricula in kindergarten through twelfth grade*. Annandale, VA: Author.

Spitzberg, B. H., & Cupach, W. R. (1988). *Handbook of interpersonal competence research*. New York: Springer-Verlag.

Spitzberg, B. H., & Hecht, M. L. (1984). A component model of relational competence. *Human Communication Research, 10,* 575–599.

Spitzberg, B. H., & Hurt, H. T. (1987). The measurement of interpersonal skills in instructional contexts. *Communication Education, 36,* 28–45.

Steinbrecher, M. M., & Willmington, S. C. (1993). *Steinbrecher–Willmington listening test*. Oshkosh: University of Wisconsin, Oshkosh.

Tardy, C. H. (1988). *Handbook for the study of human communication*. Norwood, NJ: Ablex.

Watson, K. W., Barker, L. L., Roberts, C. V., & Johnson, P. M. (1991). *Development and administration of the Watson–Barker listening test*. New Orleans: Spectra.

Wheeler, L., Reis, H. T., & Nezlek, J. (1983). Loneliness, social interaction and sex roles. *Journal of Personality and Social Psychology, 45,* 943–953.

Wheeless, L. R. (1975). An investigation of receiver apprehension and social context dimensions of communication apprehension. *Speech Teacher, 24,* 261–268.

Wiemann, J. M. (1977). Explication and test of a model of communicative competence. *Human Communication Research, 3,* 195–213.

Willmington, S. C. (1992, October). *The validity and reliability of a performance test of interpersonal communication proficiency*. Paper presented at the meeting of the Speech Communication Association, Chicago.

Wiggins, G. (1991). *Toward one system of education: Assessing to improve, not merely audit*. Denver, CO: Education Commission of the States. (ERIC Document Reproduction Service No. ED 348 400)

Wolf, D. P., LeMahieu, P. G., & Eresh, J. (1992). Good measure: Assessment as a tool for educational reform. *Educational Leadership, 49,* 14–19.

Zessoules, R., & Gardner, H. (1991). Authentic assessment: Beyond the buzzword and into the classroom. In V. Perrone (Ed.), *Expanding student assessment* (pp. 47–71). Alexandria, VA: Association for Supervision and Curriculum Development.

12

Small Group Communication

Steven A. Beebe
Southwest Texas State University
J. Kevin Barge
Baylor University

Pedagogy and research document the importance of small group communication skills. Yet, despite the unchallenged importance of learning small group communication skills there have been few systematic efforts to identify and develop a valid and reliable measure of group competencies. This chapter identifies advantages of assessing group competencies and the issues that need to be addressed in order to develop a comprehensive group assessment tool. A review of research and small group assessment tools are presented. The first step in developing a group assessment instrument is to identify the purpose of the instrument. Small group competencies need to be identified and criteria for assessing the competencies should be formulated. Finally, the instrument should be developed and tested.

INTRODUCTION

Communicating in small groups has long been valued as an important skill. In ancient Greece, Socrates used the dialectical skill of using questions to search for truth, a systematic process that served as the foundation for today's courses in small group communication. We continue to teach students how to seek answers to questions, solve problems, and make decisions in small groups. Group communication skills are increasingly held in high esteem as corporate quality improvement programs, employee involvement efforts, and teamwork all hinge on individuals effectively communicating in small groups (Scholtes, 1988). The ubiquitous group meeting remains one of the most popular formats for making decisions and solving problems (Mosvick & Nelson, 1987). Yet, despite the unchallenged value of group deliberations, there have been few systematic efforts to identify the key competencies of working in groups.

Since the 1970s, communication educators have become increasingly interested in assessing communication competence. A lively discussion has ensued as to what communication competence is and how it can be assessed (Chomsky, 1965; Hymes, 1972; Larson, Backlund, Redmond, & Barbour, 1978; McCroskey, 1980, 1982, 1984; Rubin, 1984; Spitzberg, 1983). But many agree with Phillips' (1983) observation that "Defining 'competence' is like trying to climb a greased pole: Every time you think you have it, it slips" (p. 25).

A key participant in this discussion has been the Speech Communication Association's Committee on Assessment and Testing (CAT), which is undertaking a comprehensive effort to identify and assess communication competencies in several contexts. Rather than identifying an omnibus set of competencies for all communication contexts, the committee, supported by other scholars (Backlund, 1990; Hopper, 1983; Larson et al., 1978), has recommended that context-specific competencies be identified and that an instrument be developed to assess the competencies within each specific context. As stated by Backlund (1990), "No single communication assessment instrument can meet all of the objectives of effective assessment, and it would be unproductive to spend time and energy on developing such an instrument" (p. 1). Most researchers interested in assessing communication competence argue that it is context bound; behavior that is appropriate in one context may not be appropriate in another context. As noted by Larson et al. (1978), "To examine performance, we must include a discussion of the context in which the performance occurs" (p. 18). Yet, as Lumsden (1992) acknowledged, "Resources to assess all competencies in all communication contexts will be hard to find" (p. 6).

Several scholars have sought to develop competencies and assessment tools for specific communication contexts, of which public speaking and interpersonal communication appear to be the most popular (Rubin, 1984). Although several instruments have been designed to assess various group outcomes or a specific group member's behavior (e.g., Greenbaum, Kaplan, & Damiano, 1991; Kaplan & Greenbaum, 1989; Leathers, 1969; McCroskey & Wright, 1971), there have been few systematic efforts to identify and assess small group communication competencies. Members of CAT specifically identified small group communication as one of the contexts for identifying competencies: "As a minimum, assessment should occur in the one-to-many setting (e.g., public speaking, practical small group discussion . . .)" (Morreale, Moore, Taylor, Surges-Tatum, & Hulbert-Johnson, 1992, p. 3).

The purpose of this chapter is to review research that can aid in the search for group competencies, note challenges in seeking to identify and assess group competencies, identify assessment tools designed to measure group performance, and finally, suggest procedures for assessing group competence.

WHY ASSESS SMALL GROUP COMPETENCE?

It is evident that the emphasis on assessment in education is here to stay. Educational accrediting agencies, parents, politicians, and students are seeking measures that ensure educational accountability. Given the importance of communicating with others in small groups, it seems both wise and useful to strive to identify and assess key group member communication competencies. Such efforts will be of assistance to both educators and corporate human resource and development practitioners.

Assistance to Educators

Educators are increasingly being challenged to assess communication competence (Goulden, 1992). The Southern Association of Colleges and Schools (SACS) has made educational assessment of oral communication a criteria for accreditation (Fleuriet, 1993), as has the Western Association of Schools and Colleges (WASC; see chap. 3). Educational institutions are being required to identify valid and reliable measures to assess oral communication competence. Although SACS and WASC do not mandate course-specific assessment procedures, it is clear that colleges and universities seeking accreditation must be able to demonstrate how they can ensure that students have appropriate oral communication skills. Because it appears that assessment efforts in oral communication will increase, communication educators need to be involved in the process. As Smith and Hunt (1990) argued, "Assessment became a part of the mainstream of higher education without input from communication professionals and now we must catch up without benefit of having shaped the direction of the movement" (p. 3).

How are institutions using existing oral communication assessment measures? The answer to this question permits predictions as to how an assessment of group communication competencies will be used. Willmington (1983) found that schools with some form of oral communication assessment program made four key applications: (a) course exemption, (b)placement/screening, (c) class assessment, and (d) teacher certification. Willmington (1983) and Rubin (1984) found that public speaking was the most likely context for assessing oral communication competence and that the use of competency tests enhanced the educational process. A valid and reliable measure of small group communication competencies could serve similar purposes.

If an appropriate small group communication assessment measure could be developed, educators would have a useful diagnostic tool that could be used as a formative or summative measure of group communication competencies. First, a group assessment tool about which there is widespread agreement and use could help standardize the key competencies taught and evaluated in group communication courses. A review of group communication teaching resources reveals some agreement about topics discussed (Warnemunde, 1986), yet there appears to be little consensus in the identification of core group communication competencies. An assessment tool, based on research-supported group competencies, could help shape the objectives of group communication instruction. Although standardization is not an inherent advantage of developing an assessment instrument, curriculum consensus could help identify a core of competencies that instructors could customize.

Second, identifying competencies and assessment measures can also have direct applications to student learning about small group communication. Kelly, Kuehn, and McComb (1990) offered support for the value of identifying and measuring group competence. They concluded:

> To teach competent [group] performance, we must also train our students to recognize competence, and the need for it. Communication competence consists of knowing what to do, how to do it, and when to do it; students should leave the group discussion course able to judge competence themselves. They must also be able to recognize incompetent behavior in others, and act to effectively manage incompetent behavior to the group's benefit. Managing incompetence may not always achieve great success, but it is the only course of remedial action. Any set of communication competence skills should include standards for recognizing incompetence and a behavioral repertoire useful in managing incompetence. (p. 71)

Developing a consensus among educators about the core small group competencies can help instructors develop increased consistency in teaching key group communication behaviors. Core competencies can also help instructors identify group communication behaviors that are typically incompetent. As a postcourse measure, students could be assessed as to their mastery of key group communication competencies. Being able to document their competence in key group communication behaviors should enhance students' group practice and eventual employability.

Assistance to Corporate Human Resource Development

Corporate assessment centers, becoming increasingly useful to organizations (Papa & Graham, 1991), could utilize an assessment tool for measuring group competence to help identify key behaviors useful for job performance. Although a comprehensive survey of organizational group measurement instruments by Greenbaum, Kaplan, and Damiano (1991) identified 19 instruments that measure various aspects of task-oriented group behavior, none of the instruments appear to measure a group member's competence. A review of brochures of market training materials reveals that many instruments claim to identify and assess group member effectiveness (e.g., *Group Development Assessment* and *Intergroup Diagnostic Survey* [Jones & Bearly, 1993a, 1993b] and *Team Communication Inventory*

[Glaser, 1993]). Little, if any, support is offered to document the validity and reliability of such instruments. Developing a psychometrically sound measure of group communication competence could ensure that key group competencies are identified and assessed. An instrument that assesses group communication competence could be of value to personnel directors and others who need to assess group communication competence.

CHALLENGES TO ASSESSING SMALL GROUP COMPETENCE

The advantages of developing an instrument to assess small group competence are clear, yet several obstacles pose difficulties for developing a comprehensive assessment instrument. In general, these obstacles revolve around a set of methodological and conceptual issues. To assess small group competence, it is important to develop a method that can evaluate whether one is a competent communicator in a group setting. The development of such a method requires researchers to conceptualize what counts as a communication skill, as well as decide what form the measuring instrument will assume. Numerous questions exist regarding group communication competence, and at least four issues must be addressed to form a basis for any assessment of group communication competence.

Question 1: What Is a Group Communication Skill?

This question appears to be a deceptively simple one to answer. Yet, as Phillips (1983) observed, trying to define competence is like trying to climb a greased pole. It is a process marked by careful forward progress that is punctuated by sliding back to the original starting point, or in some instances even behind one's initial start. To define clearly what is meant by a *skill*, one must differentiate among competing definitions of a skill, as well as distinguish a skill from such related terms as *knowledge, motivation,* and *competence.*

Skills have traditionally been differentiated according to three levels (Spitzberg & Hurt, 1987). The *molecular level* of skills equates skills with either the performance or nonperformance of a specific behavior. For example, it may be necessary for group members to use alignment moves to establish coherency in the group discussion (Poole, 1985; Poole & Doelger, 1986). A group communicator would be classified as skilled if he or she was able to produce the actual behavior. At a slightly higher level of abstraction, a number of molecular skills may be grouped together at a *molar level.* Functionalist approaches to group communication exemplify this approach (e.g., Hirokawa, 1988a; Hirokawa & Rost, 1992). Most functionalist approaches to group discussion (e.g., Hirokawa, 1988a) maintain that groups will make effective decisions if they perform the following key functions:

1. Establish operating procedures.
2. Define and analyze the problem.
3. Generate and develop solutions.
4. Evaluate solutions.

Researchers using a functionalist approach typically code individual messages as instances of one of these categories. The emphasis is not the variety of linguistic forms or the manner in which the message is phrased but whether the message fulfills the specified function. This allows several different kinds of molecular behaviors to be grouped in the same function. Skill at the *process level* looks beyond the function, analyzing the cognitive and behavioral processes that lead up to performance. For example, assessing a group member's skill at managing difficult personalities would involve examining the cognitive processes that led to the classification of that person as difficult, considering alternative tactics and techniques of how to handle the person, and selecting the interaction behaviors and strategies used to manage the person.

Researchers must also determine how they wish to associate skill to such related concepts as knowledge, motivation, and competence. For some researchers, skill is synonymous with knowledge, motivation, and competence. McCroskey (1982) contended that competence is knowledge and that overt behaviors are not a sign that person is skilled or possesses the needed skills. From his viewpoint, a person who has the ability (knowledge) to perform a behavior but chooses not to is still skilled, because that person could perform the needed behavior if so inclined. Landy and Becker (1987) argued that motivation is indexed by behavior; therefore, skilled behavior becomes a sign of motivation. Spitzberg (1983) contended that skill represents a concept distinct from motivation, knowledge, and competence. From his perspective, a skill is the performance of a molecular behavior, such as asking a question or offering an idea. His formulation can be specified in the following equation:

Competence = F(Motivation x Knowledge x Skill)

For Spitzberg (1983) competence is an evaluation or impression that others attribute to an individual. It is more likely that people will be perceived as competent if they are motivated, have the knowledge regarding what to do, and are able to produce the desired behavior. In Spitzberg's formulation, the concepts of competence, motivation, knowledge, and skill represent interrelated but distinct concepts.

Question 2: What Are the Criteria for Competent Small Group Communication?

Evaluative standards must guide any assessment of communicator competence. The problem of assessing an individual's competence in a group is similar to the challenge of assessing the quality of a group decision. Gouran (1990) observed that there have traditionally been three major methods for assessing group decision outcomes. First, a *procedural model* assumes that effective decisions will be reached if a set of procedures, decision techniques, or agendas are followed. Decision quality is equated with a group's ability to successfully follow a procedure. Second, an *outcomes model* proposes that a decision is effective if it produces a desired and intended result. The consequences of the decision, not the group processes that achieved them, are most important in assessing decision quality. High-quality decisions are distinguished by a high number of positive as opposed to negative consequences. Third, an *appropriateness model* incorporates elements of both the procedural and outcomes model. Given the nature of the group decision-making situation, a decision may be viewed as appropriate if it is warranted by the group's charge and is based on warranted rational inferences and reasons. Finally, a *task model* is based on the assumption that behaviors can be analyzed and described by explicating specific skills. The skills necessary to perform the task are identified and described so that others may perform the essential functions. These competing models of group decision making provide some insight into how researchers may go about assessing an individual's communication competence within a small group.

Procedural Model. One approach would be to identify those behaviors (e.g., procedures) that characterize effective communication within a group and simply to measure the degree to which an individual performs them. The presence or absence of a behavior would be the cue to whether an individual was skilled. Researchers operating from such a model would need to engage in a two-step process: Identify relevant communication behaviors, and then record the frequency of their occurrence in the group dialogue. Such an approach can be seen in the group leadership emergence literature, in which researchers attempt to identify how features regarding the quantity of talk (Mullen, Salas, & Driskell, 1989) and elements of discourse such as task and relational behavior (Eagly & Karau, 1991) relate to leadership emergence. This approach, however, suffers from two key problems. First, a consensus must occur regarding what constitutes the relevant and competent behaviors. As illustrated later, little consensus exists regarding competent communicative behaviors. Second, such an approach assumes that the frequency of performing a behavior is associated with levels of competence. Yet, in small groups, there are times when being silent is much more competent than saying anything. Moreover, issues of timing are neglected. It is not the quantity of discourse that an individual contributes to the discussion that is most important to creating perceptions of competence, it is the timing of when the individual decides to make a contribution to the discussion and its appropriateness to the ongoing discussion that is critical to perceptions of competence. Therefore, the assumption that increased frequency of a particular communicative act will lead to increased perceptions of competence may be invalid.

Appropriateness Model. To manage the faulty assumption that the quantity of discourse is related to competence, an alternative approach based on evaluating the quality of communication has been proposed. It still follows a procedural model in that it attempts to isolate those behaviors relevant in the situation, but rather than being evaluated according to frequency, they are evaluated according to appropriateness and effectiveness (Spitzberg, 1983). Appropriateness regards whether the communication fits into the existing culture or set of relationships that exist among group members. Effectiveness references whether the skill allows the communicator to achieve a desired goal. From this perspective, researchers examining an entire episode or piece of discourse would evaluate the communicator on the appropriateness and effectiveness of certain specified behaviors. For example, Spitzberg (1988) used a Conversational Rating Scale, on which he listed various behaviors and had conversational participants rate the degree to which they evidenced appropriate or inappropriate behavior. Similarly, group researchers could either rate or have group participants rate one another on the quality (e.g., appropriateness and effectiveness) of their discourse.

Outcomes Model. An alternative approach to assessing an individual's group communication competence is based on the outcomes model. Having identified the desired outcomes of group interaction, researchers could see whether individuals created those outcomes. For example, one outcome of the competent communicator may be that the particular individual assumes a leadership role. Outcomes such as perceived status and power, centrality in the group's network, or a group member's perceptions of deviance and conformity could also serve as end states for the competent communicator. A competent communicator's performance could also be associated with creating higher levels of group cohesion and satisfaction (Barge & Hirokawa, 1989). The difficulty with such an approach, however, is that the fine-grained details of the communicative process are ignored at the expense of identifying desirable outcomes.

Task Model. Consistent with the appropriateness model, a task approach to assessing skill and competency has been suggested. Using this approach, researchers must initially identify the requirements of the task and divide the task into its component parts. Subsequently, researchers must isolate the kinds of skills required to complete each task and subtask.

Task typologies may be based on the kinds of questions that must be addressed, such as fact, conjecture, value, or policy (Beebe & Masterson, 1994); the underlying dimensions of tasks, such as coordination requirements (Hirokawa, 1988b, 1990); or the additive, conjunctive, or disjunctive nature of tasks (Steiner, 1972). One starting point for group researchers may be to identify the kinds of tasks or problems that groups encounter and attempt to isolate skills that allow them to manage a particular task. From this perspective, competency could be assessed according to the degree to which individuals exhibit skills that allow them to manage the task or obstacle. For example, Hirokawa (1988b) observed that when a decision task has a single solution, is fairly simple, and does not require the cooperation of all group members, all that is required in a group is that an individual announce the correct answer and another individual confirm it. On the other hand, when the task has multiple solutions, is difficult, and requires the cooperation of all group members, skills aimed at coordinating information, reasoning through alternatives, and evaluating decisions become important. A task contingency approach would attempt to identify those problems groups have and correlate the skills needed to manage them successfully. An alternative task approach would be to identify the skills that are required for the group to manage different phases of group development. Andersen (1988) suggested that group member competence could be organized around the five typical phases that groups go through, as identified by Tuckman and Jensen (1977). The forming, storming, norming, performing, and adjourning group phases could provide a useful framework for discussing group member competency behaviors.

Question 3: What Is the Appropriate Unit of Analysis for Group Communication Competence?

Groups are made up of unique individuals who come together to form an identity that transcends their individual identity. As such, the individual performance of a group member is linked to the overall group performance. This interlinking of different people increases the complexity of group communication. The possible number of interactions calculated by Bostrom (1970) illustrates the problem:

Number in the group	2	3	4	5	6	7	8
Interactions possible	2	9	28	75	186	441	1,056

More people mean greater potential for interaction, and with greater interaction come greater challenges in coordinating the collective activity of individuals.

The complexity of the group communication context is further augmented by the inextricable link between the individual performance of a group member and the performance of the group, and by the long-acknowledged interaction between the behavior of the group and the group outcomes. Cattell (1948) discussed *group syntality*, Shaw (1976) identified a *group personality*, Janis (1971) coined the term *groupthink*, and Campbell (1958) used the term *entativity* to describe the degree to which a group is a unique entity to which members feel that they belong, rather than a less cohesive gathering of people with separate identities. Kelly, Kuehn, and McComb (1990), in summarizing the challenge of attempting to assess individual group behavior, affirmed, "group behavior is more than the sum of the behavior of the individuals" (p. 72). The behavior of an individual in a small group is influenced by choices made by others in the group. The effect the group has on individual performance is thus a challenge when attempting to identify and assess individual competence. What is the relationship between individual and group competence? Does competence need to be assessed at an individual level or at a group level?

One alternative for assessing group competence is to use the *individual as the unit of analysis*. From such a perspective, researchers focus on the communicative abilities and skills of the individual group member and develop or adapt a classification system to determine whether the individual performed particular behaviors that were deemed competent. Such a system would facilitate the view that an individual can be competent within an incompetent or dysfunctional group.

A second alternative is to utilize the *group as the unit of analysis*. It makes sense to argue that a group can only act competently if all of its members contribute in a meaningful fashion. One individual cannot make a difference to group outcomes; outcomes rely on the collective interaction of all group members. In examining the relationship of leadership to group productivity, Barge (1989) found that it was the collective behavior of all group members, rather than the individual behavior of the group leader, that directly influenced group productivity. This finding suggests that competence should be assessed at a group level, as opposed to an individual level. Rather than focus on the individual abilities or skills of the group members, the interlacing of these skills and abilities to form a group become the central indicators of competence.

A middle-ground conception that simultaneously recognizes the importance of both the individual and collective group activity may be provided by viewing *competence as a systemic concept*. From this perspective, the competence must be assessed not from either an individual or group perspective, but must be viewed as the fit between an individual and the group, as well as the fit between the group and the larger organization of which it is a part. What this means is that an individual's competence must be assessed in the context of the group's goals and objectives, as well as its culture. An individual may only be viewed as competent if they are able to align their actions with others in such a way that facilitates the group's accomplishing its goals and is consistent with the group's culture. In a pragmatic sense, this means that an individual's behavior is viewed situationally within the confines of the group's task and culture. An individual cannot be competent or incompetent apart from the group that provides the means by which the individual's competence can be judged. Similarly, a group's overall competence can only be assessed in terms of its relationship within the context of the larger organization.

Question 4: What Is an Appropriate Method for Measuring Group Communication Competence?

There are many methods for measuring communication competence, and extensive reviews are provided elsewhere (Cohen, Serdlik, & Smith, 1992; Spitzberg & Cupach, 1989). Given the variety of methods and assessment tools, three key choices face researchers who seek to measure communication competence.

Should Competence Measures Assess Fundamental Predispositions or Overt Behaviors? Competence measures can be developed that tap into individuals' fundamental predispositions or attitudes toward competence. These tools are particularly useful in helping determine selection and evaluation of potential group members (Ancona & Caldwell, 1992). Although such measures may be linked to overt behavior performance, the primary emphasis is on identifying those cognitive orientations, drives, and motives that allow individuals to succeed in groups.

A second option is for researchers to concentrate on systems that evaluate an individual's or group's behavior through surveys and questionnaires. For example, Schultz (1986) had group members rate one another using a series of semantic differential scales measuring different communication functions. Rather than use surveys or questionnaires, researchers may use behavioral coding schemes, in which actual group dialogue is observed and then categorized. Interaction analysis becomes the primary mode for observation and assessment.

Should Self-Report or Other-Report Measures Be Used?
Particularly when using surveys as the means for assessing competence, one must ask whether the self-perceptions of the individual or group being studied should serve as the primary data or whether more objective external observers' perceptions should be privileged. A common warning against self-report measures is that they may be inaccurate and do not mesh with the perceptions of others (Cohen et al., 1992). Although this a legitimate concern, whether or not to use self-report measures depends on the conceptualization of skill a researcher selects. If skill is conceived of as knowledge and does not necessarily have to be manifested during dialogue, then self-report measures may be the only means by which to tap into the individual's knowledge level. Conversely, if skill is defined as overt behavior, other reports may be particularly useful.

How Can Issues of Timing and Sequencing Be Measured? If   an in-dividual's communication competence is measured by his or her ability to sequence communication, then methods that only tap into the presence or absence of a communicative act or the frequency and intensity of a communication act are inadequate. Methods must be employed that can assess the adaptive nature of an individual's communication. There are several ways to meet this challenge. First, for researchers employing a questionnaire methodology, the response set for the questions could be changed from words that measure intensity or frequency (e.g., *very frequently, frequently, not frequently/infrequently*, etc.) to a response set that uses appropriateness and effectiveness as key markers. The shift in response set is significant because it breaks the tie between frequency and competency. An individual may be competent and act appropriately when saying little during a discussion. Second, researchers may employ a role-play methodology to assess an individual's competence. Such a methodology typically entails having individuals role play a specific task and presenting these individuals with different obstacles that frustrate achieving the task. This allows researchers to get beyond the first response that individuals may give in trying to achieve a task, and to see whether they are capable of adapting their communication. Many times, the first response individuals give is not a good indicator of their competence because it may be highly scripted. By posing obstacles to the standardized response, the researcher can then see the breadth and depth of the repertoire the individual can use to manage the situation. The relative importance of including elements of timing and sequencing in competence is a direct function of the conceptual choice one makes in deciding what to count as a skill.

THE SEARCH FOR SMALL GROUP COMPETENCE

Having discussed general issues related to communication competencies, as well as advantages of and challenges to identifying and assessing small group communication competence, we now review pedagogy and research that provides support for the identification and assessment of group communication competencies. Three areas of small group communication may provide useful insights into the kinds of competencies group members may require: pedagogy, research, and assessment of group outcomes.

Pedagogy

As Kelly and Phillips (1990) noted, "If teachers are to perform their pedagogical mission, they must first identify what skills are to be taught. Scattered through texts in small group discussion are suggestions about what students ought to do to be effective group members" (p. 6). A content analysis of selected small group communication texts identifies the key topics presented. Kerr (1990) conducted a word count of nine widely used small group communication texts in an effort to identify trends in the amount of attention given to small group communication principles and skills. As reported in Table 12.1, she found the most consistently covered topics include defining small group communication, group communication theories and models, roles, cohesiveness, conflict management, interpersonal communication, problem-solving agenda, and leadership. Her results are generally consistent with the survey conducted by Warnemunde (1986), which found that leadership, problem-solving patterns, conflict management in groups, and group roles were the most frequent topics covered in small group communication classes, as determined by the number of class periods devoted to each topic.

Most small group communication educators organize group member behavior into task and relationship dimensions. Behaviors associated with the group task involve helping the group make a decision, solve a problem, or perform its assigned task. Relationship behaviors are those that help manage attitudes and feelings group members have toward one another. Small group communication textbooks are replete with suggested task, procedural, and relationship skills in small groups. Few efforts have been made, however, to develop or identify a comprehensive taxonomy of small group communication competencies.

Dewey's (1910) reflective thinking sequence remains an important launch pad for most of the task competencies small group communication textbook authors recommend. Although other formats have been developed (e.g., single question, ideal solution, RISK), most are derivative from the problem-to-solution sequence of activities Dewey identified. It was not until the 1940s that academicians in speech, sociology, and psychology began developing courses in group behavior. Courses in speech focused on principles and skills that would enhance the quality of group discussion and group leadership. Dewey's reflective thinking pattern, along with research and critical thinking skills, were key content areas included in speech courses. The social science perspective focused more on personality and individual group characteristics; of key interest was how group behavior contrasted with the problem-solving behaviors of the individual. Psychologists also became increasingly interested in group therapy and sensitivity training.

A series of essays from speech communication researchers and educators, beginning in the 1970s, suggested specific directions for small group communication research. Bormann (1970), Mortensen (1970), Larson (1971), and Gouran (1970) advocated that speech communication research and pedagogy should be directed to task-oriented groups that solve problems and make decisions. Consequently, small group communication research in speech communication has focused on the communication behaviors that explain and predict effective problem solving and decision making. In summarizing the focus of speech communication literature, Cragan and

TABLE 12.1
Word Count Content Analysis of Group Communication Texts

	Barker, Wahler, Cegala, & Kibler (1983)	Beebe & Masterson (1990)	Bormann (1975)	Brilhart (1982)	Cragan & Wright (1980)	Fisher (1974)	Patton & Giffin (1978)	Verderber (1982)	Wood, Phillips, & Pedersen (1986)
Definition of small group communication	942	748	2,138	1,392	1,426	3,462	633	96	1,250
Small group theories/models	3,704	685	6,993	3,616	3,818	4,068	1,792	1,092	2,880
Types of small groups	6,590	2,094	2,868	5,141	3,685	801	–	660	1,531
Needs/goals the small groups satisfy	5,275	3,372	5,755	4,165	2,860	–	736	–	288
Types of discussion techniques	1,973	2,784	1,934	4,307	4,802	–	–	1,807	–
Roles	2,659	1,957	7,264	2,964	904	5,844	1,262	1,788	288
Norms	–	1,116	3,635	3,591	610	2,549	1,727	1,224	1,368
Status	570	885	470	1,464	–	1,716	451	–	–
Consensus	695	1,781	–	1,083	509	572	–	900	138
Cohesiveness	2,302	765	9,357	1,226	667	2,151	1,781	600	864
Groupthink	1,208	3,290	–	678	–	584	4,586	774	3,132
Conflict	2,714	2,339	389	1,821	689	10,442	4,018	4,644	3,468
Trust	–	3,430	–	405	805	648	1,353	–	–
Interpersonal communication	6,463	6,433	300	19,174	11,288	882	8,356	3,684	936
Problem-solving agenda	3,744	1,935	620	1,809	2,642	7,941	24,685	20,951	30,785
Researching/preparing for discussion	1,351	2,920	14,754	6,265	2,972	–	–	4,188	–
Types of reasoning	2,646	704	2,556	–	2,180	–	–	4,188	–
Leadership (general)	7,494	6,808	12,729	14,406	10,081	13,178	1,656	9,072	5,050
Theories/perspectives of leadership	1,436	5,637	2,721	2,720	4,994	5,834	566	4,932	738
Behaviors/responsibilities of leaders	6,058	–	–	8,452	3,580	5,776	1,100	4,140	1,107
Planning/leading meetings	3,739	874	1,083	5,569	1,507	4,997	–	3,396	1,188
Observing/evaluating/improving small groups	262	4,212	7,089	4,057	–	7,831	10,888	3,027	–

Wright (1980) noted, "Of the last hundred pieces of research on small group communication produced by speech communication scholars, the majority focused on the specific communication behaviors that occur during small group discussions" (p. 10).

Aitken and Neer (1992), in suggesting a competency-based core curriculum for communication departments in higher education, offered some recommendations for decision-making competence. Although not specifically explicating small group competence, their suggestions clearly have implications for task-oriented small group deliberations:

> Decision-making competence includes knowledge of: reflective thinking processes, rhetorical sensitivity, argumentation methods, decision emergence, task process activities, relational activities, topic focus, listening, critical thinking processes and developmental decision-making. The competent decision-maker is able to determine the most appropriate methods by which to communicate effectively, while applying various communication competencies to the decision-making process. (p. 270)

Taking a more holistic perspective, Ford and Wolvin (1993) identified the following competencies for the small group communication component of a basic hybrid speech communication course:

> Completing tasks in a small group situation.
> Interacting with others in a small group situation.
> Listening to others in a small group situation.
> Feeling comfortable communicating in a small group situation. (p. 220)

They were able to demonstrate that these group communication competencies could be identified and assessed. The assessment, however, was a self-report of "perceived competence" for these and 20 other items, that were designed to measure respondents' perceptions of their communication competence. Even though there are only a handful of efforts to identify and assess small group competency, at least there is a point of departure.

Group Research

Compared to the contexts of public speaking, voice and articulation, listening, and interpersonal communication, there has been little effort to identify core small group communication competencies. As Jarboe (1990) summarized, "The diversity of content that can fall under the rubric of small group communication is vast" (p. 15). In developing the assessment instrument for public speaking competencies (Morreale et al., 1992), CAT was able to draw on several studies and conference reports in which individuals and teams had attempted to identify key public speaking competencies. The small group communication context has received little attention.

Historically, the study of small groups has focused on issues of group discussion and how discussion can be utilized in making decisions. In fact, much of the group research conducted since the 1950s has focused on how discussions can be better organized to facilitate quality decision making (Frey, in press). Whether group researchers have focused on identifying the qualities of good meeting agendas (Mosvick & Nelson, 1987) or the key functions that lead to high-quality decision making (Hirokawa, 1988a), the focus has been on organizing discussion to make better decisions. Despite a diversity of opinion regarding what constitutes appropriate decision making, Janis (1989) provided a good summary of the functions skilled communicators may need to perform during discussion. Decision makers should, both individually and as a group:

1. Survey a wide range of objectives to be fulfilled, taking account of the multiplicity of values that are at stake.
2. Canvas a wide range of alternative courses of action.
3. Search intensively for new information relevant to evaluating the alternatives.
4. Assimilate and take account of new information or expert judgments to which they are exposed, even when the information or judgment does not support the course of action initially preferred.
5. Reconsider the positive and negative consequences of alternatives originally regarded as unacceptable before making a final choice.
6. Examine carefully the costs and risks of negative consequences that could flow from the alternative that is preferred.
7. Make detailed provisions for implementing and monitoring the chosen course of action, with special attention to contingency plans that might be required if various known risks were to materialize. (pp. 30–31)

The link between these key communication behaviors and group decision-making outcomes has been the basis for the functional approach to groups (Gouran, Hirokawa, Julian, & Leatham, 1993; Hirokawa, 1985, 1988a, 1990).

For competent group communicators, this means that they should attempt to master the kinds of messages that facilitate group decision making, as well as become skilled at implementing a variety of discussion or meeting management procedures to guide the group. The former is represented by Barge's (1990) study to identify specific kinds of messages that facilitate the decision-making process. He found that facilitative messages had four distinct qualities:

1. Facilitative messages critically assess the positive and negative aspects of potential solutions.

2. Facilitative messages structure and encourage participation.
3. Facilitative messages motivate others by offering encouragement and showing respect for diverse viewpoints.
4. Facilitative messages alert group members to the importance of other organizational constituencies.

The latter approach is represented by empirical work that summarizes the value of such discussion techniques as Nominal Group Technique, Delphi Technique, or brainstorming as it relates to assisting groups in generating, evaluating, and implementing ideas (Janis, 1989; Poole, 1985).

The dominant research trends in small group communication have typically focused on decision-making activities. Wyatt (1993a, 1993b) contended that such an approach devalues other important areas of small group communication and, by implication, the kinds of communication skills required by small group communicators. She argued that small group research has been male dominated, with a focus on identifying task (e.g., decision making), as opposed to relational aspects of group life. Moreover, in identifying forms of task communication, she contended that the male-dominant view misclassifies as relational communication the ways that women perform task functions through stories and narratives.

Although the dominant focus of small group communication competence has been on task communication, as indicated by the emphasis on decision making, most small group researchers and texts recognize that group communication contains both task and relational elements. Warnemunde's (1986) discovery that the top-ranked topics for most small group communication courses were leadership, problem-solving patterns, conflict management, roles and stages in group formation, and group development, reflects this balance in task and relational communication. In one of the few studies to look explicitly at competency in small groups, Barge and Hirokawa (1989) contended that communication skills can be broken down into two classes: task and relational. Task competencies are similar to the ones previously identified and include skills at establishing operating procedures, analyzing the problem, generating solutions, evaluating solutions, and implementing solutions. Relational skills concern the managing of the interpersonal climate and the structuring of roles within the group. Skills such as interaction management, expressiveness, other orientation, and relaxation are designated as key skills that build constructive group climates and systems of organizing.

Although research examining needed communication behaviors and skills has provided needed insight into group processes, current research is limited by the emphasis on the internal as opposed to external workings of groups. Ancona (1987) argued that most group studies have been conducted using laboratory groups that strip away the hierarchical and historical context that most groups find themselves in. Putnam and Stohl (1990) argued that group researchers must consider the embedded nature of groups. Simply, most groups exist across time and within a hierarchical context. For example, work teams are embedded in the larger organizational structure and, as a result, must not only manage the internal relationships among group members, but also manage the group's boundary with the larger organization. Ancona (Ancona, 1990; Ancona & Caldwell, 1988) argued that effective groups must monitor their boundary and at times must promote themselves to the larger organization and at other times must carefully insulate the group from pressures from the outside organization.

What is the implication of embeddedness for the content of group communication competencies? One implication is that the competent group communicator may need to be able to do more than simply make decisions, manage conflict, and provide feedback. The competent communicator must also be able to perform boundary management activities such as gatekeeping, networking, and public relations, in order to serve up a positive image of the group to the larger organization and simultaneously protect the group from pressures and obstacles created by the larger organization. A second implication is that our core conceptualization of communication skills should include skills that are useful for simultaneously managing the internal and external dynamics of groups. For example, Barge (1994) contended that the following communication skills are critical for leaders to manage groups successfully:

1. *Networking.* The establishment of relationships with others within and outside the group. Networking is predominantly concerned with the acquisition and collection of information.

2. *Data splitting.* A skill that assists group members in attuning to the fine-grained details of a situation. Many times group members use pre-existing scripts or rules of thumb to guide how they formulate a problem. Data splitting is intended to counteract the biases associated with such practices and become more critical of new information and its relationship to the existing scheme of organizational activity.

3. *Decision making.* These are skills associated with selecting among alternative solutions. They include skills related to analyzing problems and to generating, evaluating, and implementing solutions.

4. *Relational management.* As groups perform their work, they create a system of roles and rules that guide the interaction. When groups create an organizing system, conflicts and disputes will arise. Relational management involves managing the interpersonal relationships among group members. Feedback and negotiation skills become critical to creating effective interpersonal relationships.

These skills can be used to manage both the internal dynamics of the group and the boundary of the group within the parent organization.

Small Group Assessment Tools

A variety of methods have been developed by educators and researchers to measure various aspects of group member behavior (Bales & Cohen, 1979; Greenbaum et al., 1991;   Kaplan & Greenbaum, 1989; Leathers, 1969; McCroskey & Wright, 1971). Small group communication textbooks also include numerous group measurement instruments that reflect the diversity in measuring various aspects of group member behavior (e.g., Beebe & Masterson, 1994; Galanes & Brilhart, 1994). Kelly, Kuehn, and McComb (1990) suggested, "There is no hard-and-fast rule available for the evaluation of discussion outcomes" (p. 7). Reviewing the various efforts to assess group behavior leads to the unprofound conclusion that there is little agreement as to which group behaviors should be assessed.

One research team systematically reviewed, categorized, and evaluated organizational group behavior instruments. Greenbaum et al. (1991) selected organizational group measurement tools published between 1950 and 1990. Although they found almost 200 instruments, only 40 were supported with reliability data. Further, only 19 instruments were supported by factor analysis. The researchers categorized the 19 instruments by level of analysis (environmental, group, individual member, and task) and, using a systems theory paradigm, also categorized the instruments by stages (input, process, output, and feedback). Resulting in a 16-cell categorization framework.

Of particular interest to our search for small group competencies are those instruments that measured individual group member behavior, especially individual input, output, and process variables. But, a review of the instruments summarized reveals no general consensus as to key input variables validly and reliably measured in organizational settings.

A study that evaluated three instruments designed to measure work group effectiveness (Kaplan & Greenbaum, 1989) found several differences in the factors the instruments measured. All three instruments measured some aspects of task performance, influence, satisfaction and knowledge, and creativity. Two instruments measured member relations, and one of the three instruments measured participation, intergroup interaction, and feedback. Again, this study suggests that existing measurement tools have considerable variety in measuring group behavior and outcomes.

In addition to instruments designed to measure group behavior in organizational settings, measurement instruments and assessment tools of various aspects of group communication behavior are included for classroom application in most group communication texts. We compared a sample of these measurement instruments for consistency in method and content. We categorized the instruments into those that measured group outcomes (e.g., cohesiveness, satisfaction, decision quality) and those that measured individual group member behavior (e.g., participation). Table 12.2 reports a summary of the measurement instruments that measure

TABLE 12.2
Group Outcomes Assessment Tools

Source	Title	Items	Scale	Dimensions Assessed
Anderson (1992)	Group Processing Evaluation	12	Open-ended	Appropriate size, room arrangement, adequate breaks, training strategy, leaders, participants, withdrawn & dominant, conflicts/disagreements, resolution, improve group dynamics
Baird & Weinburg (1977)	Goldman Study of Group Morale	20	5-point	Individual motives, interpersonal relations, homogeneity of attitude, leadership
Barnlund & Haiman (1960)	Leadership Rating Scale	22	7-point	Initiating discussion, organizing group thinking, clarifying communication, summarizing and verbalizing agreements, resolving conflict, stimulating critical thinking, encouraging criticism, balancing abstract and concrete thought, climate making, regulating participation, overall leadership
Beebe & Masterson (1990)	Post-Meeting Reaction Sheet	9	Open-ended	Understanding of purpose, social climate, participation by members, conflict, work through agenda, suggestions for improvement
Bormann & Bormann (1988)	Checklist—After the Meeting	9	Open-ended	Adequate preparation, clear purpose, permissive social climate, nonverbal communication, stay on agenda, sound conclusions, leadership, follow-up plans, improvements
Brilhart (1986)	Post-Meeting Reaction Form	8	3-point	Goals of the discussion, atmosphere, organization of discussion, leadership style, preparation, willingness to speak, results, willingness to work again
		8	10-point	Adequacy of communication, opportunity to speak, climate of acceptance, interpersonal relations, leadership, satisfaction with role, quality of product
		10	7-point	Leader—preparation, organizing and guiding discussion, participation, style, Encounters—discussion, sharing feelings, supportiveness, specificity, responsibility
		7	Open-ended	Feelings about meeting, strong points, weaknesses, future changes, like/dislike about meeting, what was learned, approve/disapprove of leader
Cathcart & Samovar (1984)	Task Orientation Checklist	4	3-point	Appropriateness of task, strategy, information processing, decision proposal
Cragan & Wright (1986)	Wright Group Satisfaction Index	12	7-point	How the group feels about itself
	Group Evaluation Form	10	5-point	Definition/limitation/analysis of problem, information sharing, suffrage of problem, establishment of criteria, evaluation of solution, group productivity/cohesion/leadership
Festinger & Katz (1953)	Conference Rating Scale	8	10-point	Understandability, opportunity to communicate, ego involvement, urgency, importance, formality, supportiveness, pleasantness

Source	Title	Items	Scale	Outcomes Assessed
Gulley & Leathers (1977)	Rating Scale for Evaluating Group Decision	4	5-point	Quality of decision, decision based on discussion, member agreement, member satisfaction and commitment
	Productivity Rating Instrument	5	7-point	Effectiveness, feasibility, creativity, significance, comprehensiveness
Jensen & Childberg (1991)	Return-Potential Model of Group Norms	# in group	Chart	Speaking turns
Kell & Corts (1980)	Group Member Satisfaction Form	10	5-point	Effective definition of purpose, efficiency, comfortableness, free expression, participation in discussion, contributions, dominant member, preparation, effective discussion
Klopf (1989)	Post-Meeting Reaction Form	6	3-point	Satisfaction, organization, leadership styles, preparation, participation, willingness to work in group again
	Group Discussion Evaluation	7	5-point	Nature of problem, causes of problem, best solution, implementing solution, organization of discussion, oral performance
Patton & Giffin (1978)	Rating Scale of Decision-Making Behavior	6	5-point	Degree of concern, effort to reach understanding, analyzing problems, impelling and constraining forces, analysis, valid information secured
	Checklist of Questions for Evaluating Decision-Making Behavior	12	Checklist	Mutual concerns, member concerns, complementarity, superordinate goals, existing conditions, impelling and constraining forces, valid information, possible approaches, criteria for evaluation, reasonable predictions
Potter & Anderson (1976)	Effectiveness of Private Discussion	5	Open-ended	Togetherness, share equally in discussion, orderly steps toward goal, improvements, suggestions for future
	Group Climate	12	5-point	Pleasantness, security, cohesion, purposefulness, objectivity, involvement, cooperativeness, communicativeness, permissiveness, productivity, flexibility, integrativeness
	Evaluation of Discussion: Goal Achievement	10	Open-ended	Purpose, suitability of topic, hidden purposes, reconciliation of hidden purposes, systematic steps, accomplishments, skills and attitudes, maintenance/task functions, suggestions
Ross (1989)	Problem-Solving Process Scale	11	5-point	Member concerns, problem analysis, goal defined, valid information, possible solutions, criteria, predictions, consensus, orderly process
Seashore (1990)	Seashore Index of Group Cohesiveness	3	Checklist	Feel like part of group, moving to another group, compare with other groups, get along with other members, stick-togetherness, help others
Verderber (1982)	Decision Analysis	6	Open-ended	Clear group goal, consideration of key issues, quality information, full discussion of data, decision defensible, likely to work

group outcomes, identifying the number of items in the instrument, the type of scale used, and key outcomes assessed. Although this summary of instruments does not claim to be exhaustive, it does provide a representative sample of the various approaches used to measure group outcomes.

Most of the measures reported in Table 12.2 seek to assess the quality of such group variables and outcomes as climate, cohesiveness, organization, participation, decision quality, solution quality, variables, and leadership appropriateness. Survey results suggest a lack of consistency in measurement approaches. There is considerable variation in the number of items of the measures, type of scale, and the dimensions assessed. This variation provides further evidence that there is no consensus as to approaches or dimensions of measuring group outcomes.

Table 12.3 summarizes measurement instruments that seek to assess individual group member behavior. Rating scales or assessment measures that measure individual group member behavior were identified, and the following was noted about each instrument: number of items, type of scale or measurement employed, and individual group member attributes assessed. Results of the survey point to the variation in methods and group member attributes assessed.

The results of this review of survey instruments further document the challenge of developing an assessment measure of group competencies. There appears to be little consistency in what small group educators deem appropriate to assess. Whereas there is some consistent interest in identifying leadership behavior, relationship skills, and contributions that help the group complete the task, the assessment outcomes measured vary widely.

PROCEDURES FOR ASSESSING SMALL GROUP COMPETENCIES

Having identified challenges, advantages, issues, and previous efforts involved in assessing small group communication, we now offer a suggested course of action for developing an assessment tool. We suggest five key steps based on the successful efforts of those who have developed an assessment tool of the public speaking context (Morreale et al., 1992): (a) identify the purpose of the instrument, (b) identify small group communication competencies, (c) identify criteria for assessing the competencies identified, (d) develop the instrument, and (e) test for the validity and reliability of the instrument.

Instrument Purpose

The purpose of an instrument designed to measure small group communication competency could be threefold: (a) It could be used as a teaching tool to evaluate the attainment of small group communication competencies taught in the classroom, (b) it could be used as a pre- or posttest of small group communication competencies in a basic or small group communication course, and (c) it could be used to assess small group communication competencies in vocational settings (e.g., personnel selection and evaluation).

Identify Competencies

As summarized earlier, compared to public speaking and other communication contexts, there have been relatively few efforts to identify competencies of the small group communicator. Careful study and synthesis of the small group communication research and pedagogy is needed to develop a theory- and practice- grounded list of group competencies.

In developing competencies for the public speaking context, conferences have been convened and several committees and individual researchers have nominated key competencies; from ensuing discussion has emerged a general consensus (Morreale et al., 1992). In interpersonal contexts, a priori competency items, identified after reviewing research and pedagogy, have sometimes been presented to the subject for self-assessment (Duran, 1983; Spitzberg, 1983; Spitzberg & Cupach, 1984). Another method of identifying competencies is to ask subjects what they perceive as attributes of effective and ineffective communicators. Schrader (1989) asked 660 university students to identify characteristics of the best and worst communicators they knew. Out of a total of 70 attributes suggested, using statistical analysis, Schrader identified 39 items that best discriminated between perceptions of effective and ineffective communicators. A similar approach could be used to identify small group competencies.

We suggest that the identification of competencies be based on three information sources. First and foremost, group communication competencies should be based on research-tested communication behaviors. Second, because one of the purposes of the assessment measure is to evaluate student mastery of competencies taught in group communication classes, the competencies assessed should be consistent with the goals of small group communication educators. Finally, competencies should be anchored in the small group communication behaviors valued in the workplace.

The small group communication competencies identified in the as yet untested group communication evaluation instrument included at the end of this chapter represent a first effort to identify critical small group competencies (see Appendix A). We emphasize that the instrument is not supported by quantitative analysis. It is the result of our efforts to begin distilling the multitude of group communication variables into a manageable number of key competencies. These competencies were selected by the authors based on the criteria we suggest. Research that identified the function of group communication (Barge, 1990; Barge & Hirokawa, 1989;

TABLE 12.3
Individual Group Member Assessment Tools

Source	Title	Items	Scale	Outcomes Assessed
Bales (1970)	Tabulation for IPA Data	12	Tabulation sheet	Friendliness, dramatizes, agrees, gives suggestions/opinions/information, asks for information/opinions/suggestions, disagrees, shows tension, seems unfriendly
	Bales Interaction Categories	12	Chart	Social-emotive areas: positive and negative; task area: neutral
Brilhart (1986)	Verbal Interaction Diagram	# of members	Diagram	Frequency and direction of participation
	Discussion Rating Scale	5	5-point	Organization of discussion, equality of opportunity to speak, cooperative group orientation, listening to understand, evaluation of ideas
	Behavioral Functions of Discussants	21	Checklist	Behavioral functions
	Discussion Participation Evaluation Scale	15	5-point	Preparation, contributions, comments, speaking skills, frequency of participation, nonverbal responses, listening skills, open-minded, discussion skills, contributions, respect toward other members
	Assertiveness Rating Scale	8	3-point	Getting the floor, expressing opinions/personal desires, sharing information, voice, posture/movements, eye contact, overall manner
	Leader Rating Scale	31	5-point	Personal style, preparation, procedural and interpersonal leadership techniques
	Self-Rating Scale for Problem-Solving Discussion Leaders	20	Yes/no	Preparation, discussion skills, listening skills, encouragement in group
Burgoon, Heston, & McCroskey (1974)	Sample Tally Sheet	12	Checklist	Shows solidarity/tension release, agrees, gives suggestion/opinion/orientation, asks for orientation/opinion/suggestion, disagrees, shows tension/antagonism
Cathcart & Samovar (1984)	Discussant Functions	21	Checklist	Group task functions, maintenance functions, self-centered functions
Gulley (1960)	Gulley System for Evaluating Leadership	9	5-point	Knowledge of group process, knowledge of problem, reasoning ability, respect for others, language and speech skills, guiding/regulating/introducing/ending the discussion
Gulley & Leathers (1977)	Running Record of Efficiency of Group Productivity	# in group	5-point	Unrelated topics, helped leader, new solutions, contributions
Harnack, Fest, & Jones (1977)	Feedback-Eliciting Evaluation Form	22	4-point	Communication skills, observation skills, problem-solving skills, morale-building
Kell & Corts (1980)	Flip Chart	# of members	Chart	Flow of discussion
	Individual Member Power/Status Chart	5	Chart	Line graph depicting one participant's power/status
	Leadership/Followership Form	10	5-point	Introductory procedures, preservation of process, sequence order, encouragement of all participants to contribute, keeping the group on time, discouraging/calming overzealous participants, avoiding/minimizing tangents, clarifying/restating ambiguous points, providing transitions, providing internal summaries, summation procedures

Source	Title	Items	Scale	Outcomes Assessed
Klopf (1989)	Participant Rating Scale	5	5-point	Substantive contributions, contribute to group procedures, cooperative attitude, speaking skills, value to group
	Learning Group Discussion: Critique of Participant	6	Checklist	Participation, group developmental progress, use of learning group format, practice of roles, factors of interaction, overall effectiveness
	Problem-Solving Discussion: Critique of Participant	6	Checklist	Participation, group developmental progress, use of learning group format, practice of roles, factors of interaction, overall effectiveness
	Learning Group Discussion: Critique of Chairperson	6	Checklist	Procedural functions, group developmental process, use of learning group format, chairperson's participation, factors of interaction, overall effectiveness
	Problem-Solving Discussion: Critique of Chairperson	6	Checklist	Procedural functions, group developmental process, use of problem-solving format, chairperson's participation, factors of interaction, overall effectiveness
	Self-Assessment of Discussion Skills	35	3-point	Discussion skills
		42	7-point	Participant in group discussion, listener, task participant, chairperson, researcher, preparing to discuss
	Learning Group Participation and Development	16	5-point	Self-evaluation of participation
		6	5-point/ Checklist	Participation of members, group developmental progress, use of learning format, practice of roles by members, factors of interaction, overall effectiveness
	Personal Group Feedback	15	Open-ended	Feelings as a group member, characteristics that have helped/hindered group, best/most distressing part of group, perceptions of group members
Leathers (1969)	Feedback Rating Instrument	8	7-point	Deliberateness, relevancy, atomization, fidelity, tension, ideation, flexibility, digression
Pfeiffer & Jones (1969)	Task/Performance Questionnaire	35	5-point	Task skills, group relationship skills
Potter & Anderson (1976)	Effectiveness of Individual Participants	6	Open-ended	Preparation, analytical skills, communication with group, contributions to discussion, aid in building permissive atmosphere, value to group
Ross (1989)	Ross Discussion Evaluation Form	# of members	Checklist	Task contributions, procedural behavior, relational effectiveness, team-building efforts, overall effect
	FORN Group Report	12	4-point	Seems friendly, dramatizes, agrees, gives suggestion/opinion/information, asks for information/ opinion/suggestion, disagrees, shows tension, seems unfriendly
Stogill & Coons (1957)	Stogill–Coons Leader Behavior Description Questionnaire	10	Checklist	Initiation, membership, representation, integration, organization, domination, communications up and down, recognition, production
Verderber (1982)	Member Analysis	# of members	Open-ended	Preparation, presentation, negative roles
	Leadership Analysis	# of members	Open-ended	Preparation to lead, leading the group
	Interaction Analysis	# of members	Diagram	The number of times a person speaks, pattern of interaction, relationship of leader to group
	Interaction Analysis-Roles	# of members	Diagram	The number of times a person speaks, pattern of interaction, relationship of leader to group (each comment is labeled)

281

Hirokawa, 1985, 1988b, 1990; Hirokawa & Rost, 1992) proved very useful in documenting the competencies nominated. A review of group communication texts (see Tables 12.1, 12.2, and 12.3) and the work of Kaplan and Greenbaum (1989), which tested the reliability of assessment instruments used to measure group communication behavior in the workplace, were also useful in confirming the competencies selected. Clearly, statistical analysis is needed to begin evaluating the soundness of the competencies identified.

Identify Criteria for Assessing Small Group Communication Competencies

After competencies have been identified, decisions need to be made about how to determine what constitutes competency attainment. If, for example, the ability to generate solutions to a problem was identified as a group member competency, what criteria would be applied to determine whether someone has demonstrated this behavior successfully? Viewed from the cognitive domain, what knowledge about group communication competencies is the minimal knowledge needed to demonstrate competency?

Decisions also need to be made as to whether atomistic, holistic, or both approaches will be used. Goulden (1992) documented the confusion that has occurred in the assessment literature when these two terms are used. She urged those seeking to assess communication behaviors to have a clear understanding of the general approach to be used. Drawing on a definition offered by Lloyd-Jones (1977), she defined the atomistic approach as "evaluations that have as their goal the evaluation of parts or specific traits of a product/performance with no attempt to produce a single, comprehensive rating of it" (p. 260). The holistic evaluation "applies when the evaluator's viewpoint is that the product/performance should be evaluated as a whole" (p. 260). Goulden's (1992) work will be helpful to those seeking to develop new assessment instruments.

Develop The Instrument

Once criteria for assessing competencies have been identified, the assessment instrument may then be designed. Goulden (1992) offered the following menu of assessment techniques: "traditional written tests, self-report instruments, and the dominant approach, product/performance assessment of student speaking behaviors by external raters using rating scales" (p. 258). Morreale et al. (1992), whose *The Competent Speaker* assessment instrument evaluates a student performing a speech, recommended that "speaking and listening skills must be assessed through actual performance in social settings (speaking before an audience, undergoing an interview, *participating in a group discussion*, etc.) appropriate to the skill(s) being assessed" (p. 3, italics added). Similarly, assessing an individual's group communication competence would call for observations of an individual participating in a small group. Of critical importance to the assessment process would be the specific task the group members would be asked to assess. An effective task for group members to tackle should be realistic and appropriately challenging. Given the importance of the behavioral domain of learning, an instrument would undoubtedly include a list of competencies that a rater could use to determine whether or not the competencies were exhibited by the participant.

Test the Validity and Reliability of the Instrument

Of paramount importance is the confirmation of the validity and reliability of any assessment instrument. Assuming that raters are involved in evaluating whether group members did or did not demonstrate selected group competencies, raters would need training to ensure valid and reliable evaluations occur. Following the procedures used in the development of *The Competent Speaker* (Morreale et al., 1992) videotapes of persons communicating in a small group could be selected that would illustrate various levels of the group competencies selected for evaluation. Raters could then be asked to become familiar with the criteria for assessing competency, observe videotapes of individuals demonstrating various levels of competency, and then evaluate videotapes to assess competency. Reliability coefficients could then be obtained to measure interrater reliability. Special care should be taken with any assessment instrument to ensure that the instrument is free of culture and gender bias (Stiggins, Backlund, & Bridgeford, 1985). Reliability data could be collected from both minority assessors and assessees to document that the instrument is not culturally biased.

The validity of the instrument could be demonstrated in several ways. Face validity could be established by linking the competencies identified with research conclusions that support the inclusion of the competencies. Similarly, competencies could also be linked to concepts presented in small group communication texts. In addition, group competencies identified could be evaluated by individuals in organizational settings for the relevance to work settings. The ultimate test of the validity and reliability of an instrument is demonstrated in its use and application.

CONCLUSION

Group communication skills are important. Courses in small group communication are a well-established component of the communication curriculum. Corporate training and development programs continue to teach people how to solve problems, make decisions, work in committees, and develop teamwork skills. Yet, despite the importance of learning small group communication skills, systematic efforts to identify and assess key small group competencies have been limited.

Many challenges have kept educators from developing a comprehensive assessment of small group communication competencies. Basic issues as to what constitutes a group communication skill, how to identify the criteria for a competent small group communicator, how to identify the appropriate unit of analysis for group competence, and challenges in selecting methods of assessing group competence need to be addressed before a valid and reliable assessment instrument can be developed. There is little consensus among educators and researchers as to what constitutes small group competence, as evidenced by analyzing both group textbooks and existing group assessment instruments.

Despite these obstacles, there are distinct advantages to forging ahead in the development of an instrument to assess small group competencies. Such an instrument would be valuable to educators increasingly sensitive to the need to document that learning has occurred. It would also be useful to corporate training programs that seek to confirm that employees have mastered critical skills that can enhance efficiency and effectiveness. Clearly identifying the purpose of the instrument is the first step in developing an assessment tool. Next, small group communication competencies supported by research need to be identified. Finally, the criteria for assessing the competencies should be formulated, and the instrument should be developed and tested for validity and reliability.

The development of an assessment tool will not be easy. The interactive, process nature of group communication provides challenges for the development of a psychometrically sound tool. Yet developing such an instrument can be of great value as we seek to understand how to enhance the abilities of communicating with others in small groups.

APPENDIX A: SMALL GROUP COMMUNICATION COMPETENCIES

Eight Small Group Competencies	Number of Occurences	Satisfactory or Unsatisfactory Evaluation	Comments: Rationale for Evaluation
Group Task Competencies			
Competency One: Defines and analyzes problems and issues that help orient the group to the task at hand.			
Competency Two: Participates in the establishment of the group goal and appropriately identifies criteria for assessing the quality of the group outcome.			
Competency Three: Identifies solutions or alternatives to appropriately manage the problems or decisions the group considers.			
Competency Four: Evaluates the solutions or alternatives identified by group members.			
Competency Five: Helps the group stay on the task, issue, or agenda the group is discussing.			
Group Relational Competencies			
Competency Six: Seeks to manage disagreements and conflict.			
Competency Seven: Provides appropriate supportive comments to other group members.			
Competency Eight: Helps manage interaction and appropriately invites other to participate.			

A *satisfactory evaluation* means the evaluator concluded that the display or nondisplay of the competency was appropriate given the needs and goals of the group.

An *unsatisfactory evaluation* means the evaluator concluded that the display or nondisplay of the competency was inappropriate given the needs and goals of the group.

REFERENCES

Ancona, D. G. (1987). Groups in organizations: Extending laboratory models. In C. Hendrick (Ed.), *Annual review of personality and social psychology: Group and intergroup processes* (pp. 207–231). Beverly Hills, CA: Sage.

Ancona, D. G. (1990). Outward bound: Strategies for team survival in an organization. *Academy of Management Journal, 33*(2), 334–365.

Ancona, D. G., & Caldwell, D. F. (1988). Beyond task and maintenance: Defining external functions in groups. *Group and Organizational Studies, 13,* 468–494.

Ancona, D. G., & Caldwell, D. F. (1992). Demography and design: Predictors of new product team performance. *Organization Science, 3*(3), 321–341.

Aitken, J. E., & Neer, M. (1992). A faculty program of assessment for a college level competency-based communication core curriculum. *Communication Education, 41,* 270–286.

Andersen, J. (1988). Communication competency in the small group. In R. S. Cathcart & L. A. Samovar (Eds.), *Small group communication reader* (pp. 450–458). Dubuque, IA: Brown.

Anderson, K. (1992). *To meet or not to meet.* New York: National Press.

Backlund, P. (1990). *SCA conference on assessment of communication competency.* Denver, CO: University of Denver.

Baird, J. E., Jr., & Weinburg, S. B. (1977). *Communication: The essence of group synergy.* Dubuque, IA: Brown.

Bales, R. F. (1970). *Personality and interpersonal behavior.* New York: Holt, Rinehart & Winston.

Bales, R. F., & Cohen, S. P. (1979). *SYMLOG: A system for the multiple level observation of groups.* New York: The Free Press.

Barge, J. K. (1989). Leadership as medium: A leaderless group discussion model. *Communication Quarterly, 37*(4), 237–247.

Barge, J. K. (1990, November). *Task skills and competence in group leadership.* Paper presented at the annual meeting of the Speech Communication Association, Atlanta, GA.

Barge, J. K. (1994). *Leadership: Communication skills for organizations and groups.* New York: St. Martin's Press.

Barge, J. K., & Hirokawa, R. Y. (1989). Toward a communication competency model of group leadership. *Small Group Behavior, 20,* 167–189.

Barker, L. L., Wahler, K. J., Cegala, D. J., & Kibler, R. J. (1983). *An introduction to small group communication: Groups in process.* Englewood Cliffs, NJ: Prentice-Hall.

Barnlund, D. C., & Haiman, F. S. (1960). *The dynamics of discussion.* Boston: Riverside Press.

Beebe, S. A., & Masterson, J. T. (1986). *Communicating in small groups: Principles and practices* (2nd ed.). Glenview, IL: Scott, Foresman.

Beebe, S. A., & Masterson, J. T. (1990). *Communicating in small groups: Principles and practices* (3rd ed.). Glenview, IL: Scott, Foresman/Little, Brown.

Beebe, S. A., & Masterson, J. T. (1994). *Communicating in small groups: Principles and practices* (4th ed.). New York: Harper Collins.

Bormann, E. G. (1970). The paradox and promise of small group research. *Speech Monographs, 37,* 211–217.

Bormann, E. G. (1975). *Discussion and group methods: Theory and practice.* New York: Harper & Row.

Bormann, E., & Bormann, N. (1988). *Effective small group communication* (4th ed.). Minneapolis, MN: Burgess.

Bostrom, R. (1970). Patterns of communicative interaction in small groups. *Communication Monographs, 37,* 257–258.

Brilhart, J. K. (1982). *Effective group discussion* (4th ed.). Dubuque, IA: Brown.

Brilhart, J. K. (1986). *Effective group discussion* (5th ed.). Dubuque, IA: Brown.

Burgoon, M., Heston, J. K., & McCroskey, J. (1974). *Small group communication: A functional approach.* New York: Holt, Rinehart & Winston.

Campbell, D. T. (1958). Common fate, similarity, and other indices of the status of aggregates of persons as social entities. *Behavioral Science, 3,* 14–25.

Cathcart, R. S., & Samovar, L. A. (1984). *Small group communication: A reader* (4th ed.). Dubuque, IA: Brown.

Cattell, R. B. (1948). Concepts and methods in the measurement of group syntality. *Psychological Review, 55,* 48–63.

Cattell, R. B. (1951). New concepts for measuring leadership, in terms of group syntality. *Human Relations, 4,* 161–184.

Chomsky, N. (1965). *Aspects of the theory of syntax.* Cambridge, MA: MIT Press.

Cohen, R. J., Serdlik, M. E., & Smith, D. K. (1992). *Psychological testing and assessment.* Mountain View, CA: Mayfield.

Cragan, J. F., & Wright, D. W. (1980). *Communication in small group discussion: An integrated approach.* St. Paul, MN: West.

Cragan, J. F., & Wright, D. W. (1986). *Communication in small group discussion* (2nd ed.). St. Paul, MN: West.

Dewey, J. *(1910). How we think.* Boston: DC Heath.

Duran, R. L. (1983). Communicative adaptability: A measure of social communicative competence. *Communication Quarterly, 31,* 320–326.

Eagly, A. H., & Karau, S. J. (1991). Gender and the emergence of leaders: A meta-analysis. *Journal of Personality and Social Psychology, 60*(5), 685–710.

Festinger, L., & Katz, D. (Eds.). (1953). *Research methods in the behavioral sciences.* New York: Holt, Rinehart & Winston.

Fisher, B. A. (1974). *Small group decision making.* New York: McGraw-Hill.

Fleuriet, C. (1993). *The oral communication competency dilemma: A documentary analysis of the fulfillment of the oral communication competency requirement by universities and colleges accredited by the Southern Association of Colleges and Schools.* Unpublished doctoral dissertation, University of Texas, Austin.

Ford, W. S. Z., & Wolvin, A. D. (1993). The differential impact of a basic communication course on perceived communication competencies in class, word, and social contexts. *Communication Education, 42,* 215–223.

Frey, L. R. (in press). Remembering and 're-remembering': A history of theory and research on communication and group decision-making. In R. Y. Hirokawa & M. S. Poole (Eds.), *Communication and group decision-making* (2nd ed.). Newbury Park, CA: Sage.

Galanes, G. J., & Brilhart, J. K. (1994). *Communicating in groups.* Madison, WI: Brown.

Glaser, R. (1993). *Team communication inventory.* King of Prussia, PA: Organization Design and Development, Inc.

Goulden, N. R. (1992). Theory and vocabulary for communication assessments. *Communication Education, 41,* 258–269.

Gouran, D. S. (1970). Response to 'the paradox and promise of small group research.' *Speech Monographs, 37,* 218.

Gouran, D. S. (1990). Evaluating group outcomes. In G. M. Phillips (Ed.), *Teaching how to work in groups* (pp. 125–196). Norwood, NJ: Ablex.

Gouran, D. S., Hirokawa, R. Y., Julian, K. M., & Leatham, G. B. (1993). The evolution and current status of the functional perspective on communication in decision-making and problem-solving groups. In S. Deetz (Ed.), *Communication yearbook 16* (pp. 573–600). Newbury Park, CA: Sage.

Greenbaum, H. H., Kaplan, I. T., & Damiano, R. (1991). Organizational group measurement instruments: An integrated survey. *Management Communication Quarterly, 5,* 126–148.

Gulley, H. E. (1960). *Discussion, conference, and group process* (2nd ed.). New York: Holt, Rinehart & Winston.

Gulley, H. E., & Leathers, D. G. (1977). *Communication and group process: Techniques for improving the quality of small-group communication* (3rd ed.). New York: Holt, Rinehart & Winston.

Harnack, R. V., Fest, T. B., & Jones, B. S. (1977). *Group discussion: Theory and technique* (2nd ed.). Englewood Cliffs, NJ: Prentice-Hall.

Hirokawa, R. Y. (1985). Discussion procedures and decision-making performance: A test of a functional perspective. *Human Communication Research, 12,* 203–224.

Hirokawa, R. Y. (1988a). Group communication and decision-making performance: A continued test of the functional perspective. *Human Communcation Research, 14*(4), 487–515.

Hirokawa, R. Y. (1988b, April). *The role of communication in group decision-making efficiacy: A tasking-contingency perspective.* Paper presented at the annual meeting of the Central States Speech Association, Schaumburg, IL.

Hirokawa, R. Y. (1990). The role of communication in group decision-making efficacy: A task-contingency perspective. *Small Group Research, 21*(2), 190–204.

Hirokawa, R. Y., & Rost, K. (1992). Effective group decision-making in organizations: Field test of vigilant interaction theory. *Management Communication Quarterly, 5,* 267–288.

Hopper, R. W. (1983). Expanding notions of competence: Implications for elementary speech programs. *Speech Teacher, 20,* 29–35.

Hymes, D. H. (1972). On communicative competence. In J. B. Pride & J. Holmes (Eds.), *Sociolinguistics* (pp. 15–53). Harmondsworth, England: Penguin.

Janis, I. L. (1971). Groupthink. *Psychology Today, 5,* 43–46, 74–76.

Janis, I. L. (1973). *Victims of groupthink.* Boston: Houghton Mifflin.

Janis, I. L. (1989). *Crucial decision: Leadership in policymaking and crisis management.* New York: The Free Press.

Jarboe, S. (1990). What we know about individual performance in groups: Myths and realities. In G. M. Phillips (Ed.), *Teaching how to work in groups* (pp. 13–49). Norwood, NJ: Ablex.

Jensen, A. D., & Childberg, J. C. (1991). *Small group communication theory and application.* Belmont, CA: Wadsworth.

Jones, J. E., & Bearly, W. L. (1993a) *Group development assessment.* King of Prussia, PA: Organization Design and Development, Inc.

Jones, J. E., & Bearly, W. L. (1993b). *Intergroup diagnostic survey.* King of Prussia, PA: Organization Design and Development, Inc.

Kaplan, I. T., & Greenbaum, H. H. (1989). Measuring work group effectiveness. *Management Communication Quarterly, 2,* 424–448.

Kell, C. L., & Corts, P. R. (1980). *Fundamentals of effective group communication.* New York: MacMillan.

Kelly, L., Kuehn, S., & McComb, M. (1990). Evaluating how individual performance affects group outcomes. In G. M. Phillips (Ed.), *Teaching how to work in groups* (pp. 66–83). Norwood, NJ: Ablex.

Kelly, L., & Phillips, G. M. (1990). Introduction: Teaching how to make groups work. In G. M. Phillips (Ed.), *Teaching how to work in groups.* Norwood, NJ: Ablex.

Kerr, C. (1990). *An analysis of small group communication texts.* Unpublished manuscript, Southwest Texas State University, Department of Speech Communication.

Klopf, D. W. (1989). *Interacting in groups: Theory and practice* (3rd ed.). Englewood, CA: Morton.

Landy, F. J., & Becker, W. S. (1987). Motivation theory reconsidered. In L. L. Cummings & B. M. Staw (Eds.), *Research in organizational behavior, 9* (pp. 1–18). Greenwich, CT: JAI.

Larson, C. E. (1971). Speech communication research on small groups. *The Speech Teacher, 20,* 89–107.

Larson, C., Backlund, P., Redmond, M., & Barbour, A. (1978). *Assessing functional communication.* Falls Church, VA: Speech Communication Association.

Leathers, D. G. (1969). Process disruption and measurement in small group communication. *Quarterly Journal of Speech, 55,* 287–300.

Leathers, D. G. (1972). Quality of group communication as a determinant of group product. *Speech Monographs, 35,* 171.

Lloyd-Jones, R. (1977). Primary trait scoring. In C. R. Cooper & L. Odell (Eds.), *Evaluating writing: Describing, measuring, judging* (pp. 33–68). Urbana, IL: National Council of Teachers of English.

Lumsden, D. (1992, October). *What lies ahead? Problems and politics of assessment in speech communication*. Paper presented at the annual conference of the Speech Communication Association, Chicago, IL.

McCroskey, J. C. (1980). On communication competence and communication apprehensions: A response to Page. *Communication Education, 29*, 109–111.

McCroskey, J. C. (1982). Communication competence and performance: A research and pedagogical perspective. *Communication Education, 31*, 1–8.

McCroskey, J. C. (1984). Communication competence: The elusive construct. In R. N. Bostrom (Ed.), *Competence in communication: A multi-disciplinary approach* (pp. 259–268). Beverly Hills, CA: Sage.

McCroskey, J. C., & Wright, D. W. (1971). The development of an instrument for measuring interaction behavior in small groups. *Speech Monographs, 38*, 335–340.

Morreale, S. P., Moore, M. R., Taylor, K. P., Surges-Tatum, D., & Hulbert-Johnson, R. (1992). *The competent speaker: Speech evaluation form*. Annandale, VA: Speech Communication Association.

Mortensen, C. D. (1970). The status of small group research. *Quarterly Journal of Speech, 56*, 304–309.

Mosvick, R. K., & Nelson, R. B. (1987). *We've got to start meeting like this! A guide to successful business meeting management*. Glenview, IL: Scott, Foresman.

Mullen, B., Salas, E., & Driskell, J. E. (1989). Salience, motivation, and artifact as contributions to the relation between participation and rate and leadership. *Journal of Experimental Psychology, 25*(6), 545–559.

Papa, M. J., & Graham, E. E. (1991). The impact of diagnosing skill deficiencies and assessment-based communication training on managerial performance. *Communication Education, 40*, 368–384.

Patton, B. R., & Giffin, K. (1978). *Decision-making group interaction* (2nd ed.). New York: Harper & Row.

Pfeiffer, J. W., & Jones, J. E. (1969). *Structured experiences for human relations training*. Iowa City, IA: University Associated Press.

Phillips, G. M. (1983). A competent view of 'competence.' *Communication Education, 32*, 25–36.

Poole, M. S. (1985). Task and interaction sequences: A theory of coherence in group decision-making interaction. In R. Street & J. Capella (Eds.), *Sequence and pattern in communicative behavior* (pp. 206–224). London: Edward Arnold.

Poole, M. S., & Doelger, J. (1986). Developmental processes in group decision-making. In R. Hirokawa & M. Poole (Eds.), *Communication and group decision-making* (pp. 35–62). Beverly Hills, CA: Sage.

Potter, D., & Anderson, M. P. (1976). *Discussion in small groups: A guide to effective practice*. Belmont, CA: Wadsworth.

Putnam, L. L., & Stohl, C. (1990). Bona fide groups: A reconceptualization for groups in context. *Communication Studies, 41*, 248–265.

Ross, R. S. (1989). *Small groups in organizational settings*. Englewood Cliffs, NJ: Prentice-Hall.

Rubin, R. B. (1984). The validity of the communication competency assessment instrument. *Communication Monographs, 52*, 173–185.

Scholtes, P. R. (1988). *The team handbook: How to use teams to improve quality*. Madison, WI: Joiner Associates.

Schrader, D. (1989, May). *Toward a conceptual refinement of interpersonal communication competence: An analysis of subjects' conceptions of adept and inept communicators*. Paper presented at the annual meeting of the International Communication Association, San Francisco, CA.

Schultz, B. (1986). Communication correlates of perceived leaders in the small group. *Small Group Behavior, 17*, 51–65.

Seashore, S. (1954). *Group cohesiveness in the industrial work group*. Ann Arbor: University of Michigan Institute for Social Research.

Shaw, M. L. (1976). *Group dynamics*. New York: McGraw Hill.

Smith, R. M., & Hunt, G. T. (1990). Defining the discipline: Outcomes assessment and the prospects for communication programs. *ACA Bulletin, 72*, 1–4.

Spitzberg, B. H. (1983). Communication competence as knowledge, skill, and impression. *Communication Education, 32*, 323–329.

Spitzberg, B. H. (1988). Communication competence: Measures of perceived effectiveness. In C. H. Tardy (Ed.), *A handbook for the student of human communication: Methods and instruments for observing, measuring, and assessing communication processes* (pp. 67–106). Norwood, NJ: Ablex.

Spitzberg, B. H., & Cupach, W. R. (1984). *Interpersonal communication competence*. Beverly Hills, CA: Sage.

Spitzberg, B. H., & Cupach, W. R. (1989). *Handbook of interpersonal competence research*. New York: Springer-Verlag.

Spitzberg, B. H., & Hurt, H. T. (1987). The measurement of interpersonal skills in instructional contexts. *Communication Education, 36*, 28–45.

Steiner, I. D. (1972). *Group process and productivity*. New York: Academic Press.

Stiggins, R. J., Backlund, M., & Bridgeford, N. J. (1985). Avoiding bias in the assessment of communication skills. *Communication Education, 34*, 135–141.

Stogill, R. M., & Coons, A. E. (Eds.). (1957). *Leader behavior: Its description and measurement*. Columbus: Ohio State University.

Tuckman, B. N., & Jensen, M. A. C. (1977). Stages of small-group development revisited. *Group and Organizational Studies, 2*, 419–427.

Verderber, R. F. (1982). *Working together*. Belmont, CA: Wadsworth.

Warnemunde, D. E. (1986). The status of the introductory small group communication course. *Communication Education, 35*, 389–396.

Willmington, C. (1983, November). *Assessing oral communication performance skills*. Paper presented at the annual meeting of the Speech Communication Association, Washington, DC.

Wood, J. T., Phillips, G. M., & Pedersen, D. J. (1986). *Group discussion: A practical guide to participation and leadership*. New York: Harper & Row.

Wyatt, N. (1993a). *Intergroup diagnostic survey*. King of Prussia, PA: Organization Design and Development, Inc.

Wyatt, N. (1993b). Organizing and relating: Feminist critque of small group communication. In S. P. Bowen & N. Wyatt (Eds.), *Transforming visions: Feminist critiques in communication studies* (pp. 51–86). Cresskill, NJ: Hampton.

13

Organizational Communication

Pamela Shockley-Zalabak
Ruth Hulbert-Johnson
University of Colorado at Colorado Springs

A review of the practice of assessing organizational communication competency within organizations suggests that no comprehensive framework exists for either describing communication competency or determining how or at what level it should be assessed. The same is generally true for most organizational communication curricula. This absence of a competency framework contributes to the difficulty of developing assessment methods that are both meaningful and useful. This chapter proposes a competency framework that is broad in nature and capable of adaptation to a variety of specific course objectives. The chapter concludes with a description of assessment methodologies appropriate for the proposed framework.

ORGANIZATIONAL COMMUNICATION COMPETENCY

Quintilian's ideal of the "good man speaking well" is not as far removed from contemporary concepts of organizational communication competency as history might suggest. Research conducted with business and industry to identify those skills specifically needed for success as an organizational member consistently describes the need for broad-based communication capabilities with an emphasis on ethical behaviors (Curtis, Winsor, & Stephens, 1989; DiSalvo, Larsen, & Seiler, 1976; Staley & Shockley-Zalabak, 1985). DiSalvo et al. (1976), for example, surveyed business administration graduates (1969–1973) from a Midwestern university who were employed in a variety of businesses and industries. Survey participants identified listening, persuading, advising, instructing, and small group problem solving as the top five skills for career success. These same respondents also identified skills they wished they had been taught at the university. Those skills included listening, public speaking and presentational skills, writing, small group leadership and problem solving, human relations, and persuasion and attitude theory. DiSalvo et al. (1976) concluded "it is now our [communication professors] responsibility to take the idea of accountability seriously in order to ensure that students are trained in, and competent in, the communication skills suggested by those currently occupying positions in organizations and businesses" (p. 275).

In later work, DiSalvo (1980) surveyed 25 studies describing the need for communication skills in organizations. He discovered a contemporary good communicator theme with today's organizations needing people who can listen, write, persuade others, demonstrate interpersonal skills, gather information, and exhibit small group problem-solving expertise.

Curtis et al. (1989) continued the investigation of skills needed for job attainment and job success and courses helpful in career planning by surveying 1,000 personnel managers employed in a variety of organizations. Results indicated a strong emphasis on communication skills. "It is noteworthy to mention that three out of the top four factors and six of the top nine are communication skills or attributes" (Curtis et al., 1989, p. 10). Specifically, those skills that were identified as helping individuals attain employment were (in descending order): oral/speaking communication, listening, enthusiasm, written communication skills, technical competence, appearance, poise, work experience, résumé, and specific degree held. Those skills listed by personnel managers needed for job success were (in descending order): interpersonal/human relations, oral/speaking, written, persistence/determination, enthusiasm, technical competence, personality, work experience, dress/grooming, and poise. Once again communication skills were among the top three. Respondents additionally identified those courses that should be taught at the university level for future managers: written communication, interpersonal communication, management, public speaking, ethics in management, personnel management, financial management, computer programming, marketing, and mathematics. Again, communication courses were among the top five (Curtis et al., 1989). The MIT commission (Berger, Dertouzos, Lester, Solow, & Thurow, 1989) lent further support to these findings when it concluded that the effective use of modern technology requires involved and responsible people to develop capabilities for planning, judgment, collaboration, and analysis of complex systems. In other words, organizations in our information society need flexible and creative people who have diverse and well-developed communication abilities.

In sum, research since the 1970s (as had previous work) establishes the centrality of the communication discipline to identified organizational communication needs. Less clear, however, are answers to the question of how the discipline does and should respond.

DEFINITIONS OF COMMUNICATION COMPETENCE

Researchers differ in how they define communication competency. Some believe people are competent if they know what is appropriate in a specific situation, whether that behavior actually occurs or not. A student, for example, who realizes that class participation is required for a high grade may choose not to participate, yet the student can be considered competent because of the knowledge or awareness of the appropriate behavior. Other researchers extend the competency concept beyond knowledge of appropriate behaviors to include actual language performance and the achievement of interpersonal goals. The student, from this latter perspective, must not only recognize appropriate participation behaviors but also participate in order to demonstrate communication competency. A report of the Subcommittee of the Educational Policies Board (1993) of the Speech Communication Association summarized much of the discipline's current thinking about communication competency:

> Oral communication competence involves the ability to see the relationship between context and meaning, the ability to choose effective messages through, in part, anticipating the consequences of communication choices. Competent communicators, therefore, adapt to the requirements of the context in which they find themselves while, at the same time, maintaining their individual identities and individual goals. Communication competence involves the awareness of and ability to enact behavioral alternatives appropriately. A communicator must have the flexibility to adapt alternatives to the demands of a particular situation and the individuals involved in the communication interaction. (Spitzberg & Cupach, 1984, p. 1; see also McCroskey, 1982; Phillips, 1983; Spitzberg, 1983)

Organizational communication competence has received far less academic attention than the previously discussed research might indicate. Jablin et al. (1989) conducted an extensive literature review in this area and suggested that although this is an important issue to both organizational scholars and practitioners, little research has been specifically directed to this domain: "The handful of investigations that have explored the construct in the organizational setting have typically adapted applications of communication competence developed for the study of interpersonal communication relationships" (p. 1).

These findings suggest further research in this area is needed, and that possibly a different kind of definition and methodology is needed specifically for organizational communication competence. One reason for a different perspective was articulated by Jablin and his colleagues (1989) when they suggested organizational members already have a minimum level or threshold of communication competence due to education and the selection and retention processes inherent in organizational life.

A review of the sparse organizational communication competency literature that does exist provides two broad perspectives not unlike the perspectives in the general communication competency work. The first perspective perceives competence as performance or skills and the second views it as social cognition/symbolic interaction (Jablin et al., 1989). A definition as developed by Jablin et al. (1989) encompasses both these perspectives. Organizational communication competence is defined as: "The set of abilities, henceforth termed resources, which a communicator has available for use in the communication process. These resources are acquired via a dynamic learning process and take the form of interrelated subsets of communication skills, henceforth termed capacities, and strategic knowledge of appropriate communication behavior" (p. 9). There are two issues regarding this definition that should be articulated. First, this definition does not mean just individuals within any given organization. The communicator may be the organization as a whole. Second, this definition is not unlike the previously discussed general communication competence definition, which does not include effectiveness as a necessary component (McCroskey, 1982; McCroskey & McCroskey, 1988).

Rubin (1990) also reviewed the organizational communication competence literature. Her review reflects Jablin et al.'s (1989) comments that much organization literature perceives organizational communication competence as a sum of the individual parts (the people). Rubin suggested there are three broad skill areas individuals in organizations must possess to be perceived competent. These include: listening and being able to understand instructions, speaking in the sense of using grammatical and syntactic rules correctly, and human relations skills that include conflict management, cooperation, and perspective taking. Rubin further identified more explicit skills from the literature in which organizational interactants must be competent. These include advising, persuading, instructing, business writing, telephone, interviewing, and cognitive differentiation. Finally, Rubin suggested future research in this area needs to explore theory and measurement issues. Without a strong theoretical foundation, measurement issues will be problematic with the potential for disagreement with each new assessment instrument developed.

ASSESSING ORGANIZATIONAL COMMUNICATION COMPETENCY

The review of the organizational communication competency literature suggests that no comprehensive framework exists for either describing communication competency or determining how, whether, or at what level it should be assessed. It is not surprising, therefore, that assessment practices related to organizational communication competence are mostly without theoretical foundation and adapted from other domains of the discipline such as interpersonal and public speaking. Indeed, Phillips (1983) explicitly questioned "whether competency/skill research is worth the effort" (p. 25). He argued competency is a potential that is difficult to measure or assess: "Thus, if competence is potential, we can never know it. If skill is a sign of associated competence, we must argue the connection without confirming it" (p. 26).

Phillips (1983) suggested there have been three methods of assessing competence: self-report, observation, and success or failure of individuals. He argued there are several explanations besides incompetence for any given individual's failure to meet the criteria for competence. First, the stimulus (question or scenario) did not trigger retrieval in the individual's brain. Second, the respondent misunderstood what was asked. Third, there may be disagreement between researcher and subject as to what the requirements are in the situation. Finally, the subject simply prefers not to respond. In the classroom, Phillips (1983) suggested that teachers of speech communication too often base teaching methodologies on educational mythology about what is effective or ineffective. "Teachers *believe* their methods work and they are probably right, but specific connections between teaching method and performance outcome are hard to make" (p. 29). Phillips further defined the problem for communication professors as one of connecting real-world activities to those in the classroom. Further, he argued educators are able to evaluate effective classroom performance, but are not as effective at understanding how classroom criteria relate to the real world. To close the gap between classroom and real-world activities, educators should follow a protocol by which: "1. We. . .connect speech behaviors with goal accomplishment. 2. We must find ways by which to discover performance deficits. 3. We must discover methods to meet perceived deficits. 4. We must integrate learned skills into natural state performance" (p. 33). In other words, we must teach skills that will assist the student in achieving life goals.

There are few instruments currently available for assessment of organizational communication competence (Monge, Bachman, Dillard, & Eisenberg, 1982). Some assessment procedures have converted interpersonal communication competence instruments for organizational use, but much may be sacrificed in the conversion process. For example, Monge et al. (1982) argued attempts to force organizational communication competence onto the Procrustean bed of interpersonal competence are problematic:

> However, in attempting to apply past work on interpersonal competence to organizational research a problem arises: many of the. . .specified skills lose their importance. . . .Since the majority of organizational communication relationships are non-interpersonal, rather than interpersonal or intimate. . .the sort of skills that should be considered relevant are those that facilitate interaction between persons occupying role positions. (p. 507)

This position suggests the interpersonal communication competence literature has marginal relevance with regard to organizational competence where the focus should consider roles individuals fulfill. As an alternative, Monge et al. (1982) suggested encoding and decoding as the relevant areas for investigation of organizational competence. They developed a 12- item scale wherein 7 items assessed encoding factors and 5 items assessed decoding factors. This instrument was designed to be used with superior–subordinate dyads wherein each person assessed the other's competence. Lamude and Daniels (1990) converted Rubin's (1982) Communication Competency Assessment Instrument (CCAI) from a trained rater context at the tertiary level to a paper-and-pencil instrument they purported measures communication competence of managers. Again the dependence on other competency domains is evidenced with the first 7 of the 19 items converted from items previously utilized by a trained rater evaluating students' public speaking skills.

In addition to theoretical issues, communication competence in organizations has become increasingly important as resources dedicated to the understanding and training of organizational members have become a larger portion of organizational expenditures. DeWine (1987), for example, cited a Carnegie Foundation report: "U.S. companies today are training and educating nearly 8 million people (close to the total enrollment in American's four-year colleges and universities) at a cost of $40 billion a year" (pp. 113–114).

There are a multiplicity of instruments available to organizational practitioners when developing training and assessment programs. Shockley-Zalabak and Hulbert-Johnson (1993), as part of an assessment project under the auspices of the Committee on Assessment and Testing of the Speech Communication Association, reviewed 63 instruments widely utilized in business, industry, and government to assess the organizational communication competencies of organizational members and organizational communication patterns of organizations as a whole. That review indicated organizational practitioners have a plethora of instruments from which to select assessment tools. With rare exceptions, these instruments generally do not assess organizations at the macro level (see Adler, 1989b; Cochran, 1989; Daly, McCroskey, & Falcione, 1976; Doppelt, 1978; Falcione, 1974c; Goldhaber & Rogers, 1979; Greenhaus, 1985; Guion, 1978b; Hellweg & Andersen, 1989; McCroskey, Jensen, Todd, & Toomb, 1972; McCroskey & McCain, 1974; McDermott & Faules, 1973; Schmidt, 1978), but conceptualize organizational communication competence as residing within various individuals or factors of organizational life, and therefore, assess competence at the micro level. For example, organizational climate and culture are measured in two instruments (see Parsons, 1992b; Sippola, 1992). Five instruments reviewed assess conflict styles as an indicator of competence (see Konovsky, Jaster, & McDonald, 1989; Landry, 1978a; Putnam & Wilson, 1982; Shockley-Zalabak, 1988; Thornton, 1989b; Weider-Hatfield, 1988; Wilson & Waltman, 1988; Womack, 1988).

Additionally, stress and coping skills have been measured as they relate to organizational communication competence (see Benson, 1992; Downs, Driskill, & Wuthnow, 1990). Another component of organizational life presumed to assess competence has been teamwork and group processes (see Aleamoni, 1992; DeVito, 1985; Erchul, 1989; Fitzpatrick, 1978; Kirsch, 1992; Lachar, 1992; Lifton, 1985; Motowidlo, 1978b; Schutz, 1992; Thayer, 1978; Wiggins, 1989).

By far the most frequently assessed organizational members and components have been managers and managerial styles. Shockley-Zalabak and Hulbert-Johnson (1993) reviewed 31 instruments that specifically conceptualized this component as indicative of communication competence (see Adler, 1989a; Bernardin, 1989; Bernardin & Pynes, 1989; Borman, 1978a, 1978b; Carbonell, 1985; Dipboye, 1978a, 1978b; Dixon, 1989; Dobbins, 1985a, 1985b; Geisinger, 1992; Guion, 1978b; Gutenberg, 1985; Harmon, 1989; Kanungo, 1989; Katkovsky, 1992; Kavanagh, 1978; Kehoe, 1992; Korman, 1978a, 1978b; Kozma, 1992; Landry, 1978b; McIntyre, 1985; McReynolds, 1989; Motowidlo, 1978a; Mueller, 1989; Owens, 1985; Parsons, 1992a; Porterfield, 1992; Saunders, 1992; Sauser, 1992; Schoenfeldt, 1989; Taylor, 1978; Thornton, 1985, 1989a; Waller, 1992a, 1992b).

The previous discussion of assessment instruments would appear to indicate that organizational practitioners have a plethora of well-developed instruments from which to choose when designing organizational selection, placement, and training protocols. But on review of the 63 instruments, Shockley-Zalabak and Hulbert-Johnson (1993) found that far too often instruments have been developed without adequate attention to providing information regarding rationale, psychometric data, and developmental processes. Specifically, reviewers have expressed concern for inadequate information regarding theoretical rationale underpinning any given instrument (see Borman, 1978a; Guion, 1978a; Thayer, 1978). An often-discussed issue regarding assessment instruments is the lack of adequate reliability and validity studies (see Bernardin, 1989; Gutenberg, 1985; Kanungo, 1989; Korman, 1978a, 1978b; Lachar, 1992; McIntyre, 1985; Waller, 1992b). Indeed, on review of one instrument, Thornton (1989a) declared "No student in my undergraduate class on tests and measurements, and certainly no graduate student in my class on psychometric theory and test construction would pass the course if he or she turned in such deficient reports of test construction efforts and data to support the instrument" (p. 459). A third concern regarding many instruments is the lack of reported normative data and procedures utilized to derive what normative data are provided. That is not to say that all instruments suffer from the lack of psychometric testing and reporting; there are stellar examples of manuals furnishing clear administration instructions, normative data, theoretical rationale, and psychometric testing (see Dipboye, 1978a; Wiggins, 1989). But organizational practitioners too often must make assumptions regarding the appropriate use for and the reliability and validity of the selected instrument.

Taken as a whole the review of academic literature and assessment practices in organizations supports the conclusion that no comprehensive framework exists for either describing organizational communication competency or determining how or at what level it should be assessed. This lack of definitional clarity poses important challenges to those attempting to develop assessment and accountability models for organizational communication curricula. The remainder of this chapter proposes a broad organizational communication competency framework capable of adaptation to a variety of specific course objectives. The chapter concludes with a description of several assessment methodologies appropriate for the proposed framework.

A PROPOSED FRAMEWORK FOR A COMPETENCY-BASED ORGANIZATIONAL COMMUNICATION CURRICULA

Littlejohn and Jabusch (1982) proposed a particularly useful definition of communication competency for organizational communication curricula. They suggested that communication competency is the "ability and willingness of an individual to participate responsibly in a transaction in such a way as to maximize the outcomes of shared meanings" (p. 29). This definition requires not only knowledge of appropriate behaviors but also motivation to engage in communication that results in mutual understanding. In other words, communication competency involves our personal willingness and ability to communicate so that our meanings are understood and we understand the meanings of others. Regardless of differences in perspectives, organizational communication competency relates to message encoding and decoding abilities—the process of communication initiation and consumption.

Littlejohn and Jabusch (1982) contended that competency arises out of four basic components—process understanding, interpersonal sensitivity, communication skills, and ethical responsibility. Process understanding refers to the cognitive ability to understand the dynamics of the communication event. Interpersonal sensitivity is the ability to perceive feelings and meanings. Communication skill is the ability to develop and interpret message strategies in specific situations. The ethical component of competency is the attitudinal set that governs concern for the well-being of all participants in taking responsibility for communication outcomes. Finally, Littlejohn and Jabusch believed that competence comes from the interaction of three primary elements—theory, practice, and analysis.

Staley and Shockley-Zalabak (1985) and Shockley-Zalabak (1988, 1991) modified and expanded the Littlejohn and Jabusch approach for specific application to organizational communication curricula. Specifically Shockley-Zalabak (1988, 1991) proposed a framework for developing organizational communication competency, which includes knowledge, sensitivity, skills, and values. Knowledge is described as the ability to understand the organizational communication environment. Knowledge competencies can be developed through the exploration of the interactive, process nature of human communication. Curricula developing knowledge competencies address major theoretical approaches for the study of organizational communication and explore the roles of individuals in organizations. Sensitivity competencies are described as the ability to accurately sense organizational meanings and feelings. Sensitivity competencies are developed through the study and practice of leadership, conflict management, and a variety of other related subjects. Sensitivity competencies are developed through exposure to and experiences with cultural diversity, racism, and the changing work force. Skill competencies are described as the ability to accurately analyze organizational situations and to initiate and consume organizational messages effectively. Skill competencies can be developed through analysis and practice opportunities. Specifically, analytical skills can be developed by applying knowledge and sensitivity competencies to case studies and individual organizational experiences. Problem-solving and conflict-management skills are frequent curriculum topics. Finally, value competencies are described as the importance of taking personal responsibility for effective communication. Value competencies can be developed through discussion of personal responsibility for participation in organizational communication. Ethical dilemmas relating to organizational communication and the importance of values to organizational culture are frequent topics. Organizational communication competency, therefore, is best understood as a complex interaction of knowledge, sensitivity, skills, and values.

This proposed framework can be adapted to the basic course in organizational communication as well as to more advanced topics. Staley and Shockley-Zalabak (1985) provided a detailed description of a curriculum utilizing this framework. Specifically, the concept or organizational communication competency as an integration of knowledge, sensitivity, skills, and values has been utilized in courses with titles as diverse as Leadership, Conflict Management, Business and Professional Communication, Team/Group Processes, Intercultural/International Business, Business and Professional Presentations, and Internship.

METHODS OF ASSESSMENT FOR ORGANIZATIONAL COMMUNICATION CURRICULA

Those who conceptualize curriculum assessment as a rigid process of improving test scores at the expense of learning raise important concerns for assessment of organizational communication curricula. First, what are the goals of assessment, who should establish these goals, and for whom is assessment intended? Second, how can reliable and valid assessment processes be developed? Finally, can assessment processes inform curricula development as opposed to simply monitoring curricula implementation? This chapter does not pretend to fully answer these questions, but it proposes assessment strategies designed to integrate assessment methodologies into the processes of curricula development, implementation, and revision; to provide assessment feedback to students; and to meet institutional accountability needs.

Goals and Levels of Assessment

Curricula development should be conceptualized as the beginning of the assessment process. Content choices, teaching strategies, course levels, and requirements all represent basic decisions about what is important, how students learn, and what students should accomplish based on exposure to specific information. Course design, therefore, provides guidance for developing the goals for a broad assessment process. Specifically, what types of assessments benefit students in providing feedback on individual performance, what types of assessments benefit faculty in course design and revision, and what types of assessments assist the institution in communicating accountability to its various constituencies? Answers to these questions not only vary by course, but reflect student and institutional differences. These questions, however, suggest the importance of multiple goals and levels for assessment based on student, faculty, and institutional needs.

Reliability and Validity of Assessment

Assessment processes have been appropriately criticized for inattention to issues of reliability and validity. The review of organizational practices in assessing communication competency is an example of the scant attention paid to determining whether organizational assessments are meaningful and useful. Given the breadth and diversity in organizational communication curricula coupled with the lack of precise measurement instruments, the issue of reliability and validity (and the related issues of meaning and use) of assessment methodologies takes on particular importance. As most faculty involved in the teaching of organizational communication would agree, no singular method for curricula assessment currently exists that meets generally accepted reliability and validity standards, whether the goals of assessment are singular or multiple. The complexity of the curricula, the importance of multiple goals and levels for assessment, and the diversity of institutional needs suggest that once assessment goals have been established, multiple methods best contribute to meaningful and useful assessment. Regardless of methods selected, a primary task of assessment planners is attention to broad issues of reliability and validity, as well as meaning and use of the methods chosen.

Much assessment has been viewed as monitoring or accounting for the products of education. As business and industry have experienced, this inspection mentality is both expensive and contributes less to quality than proponents would desire. Assessment methodologies should be selected for their capability to provide information that guides curricula development and revision as well as communicates the quality of curricula to external constituencies. The use of assessment as pedagogy generally improves our abilities to address issues of reliability and validity.

Methods of Assessment

Given the aforementioned responses to extremely complex and important questions, we present the following assessment methodologies for consideration. We again want to reinforce that the selection of specific methodologies should be based on a theoretical framework of communication competency from which assessment goals have been established. The communication competency framework we have chosen—knowledge, sensitivity, skills, and values—is the basis for the design and selection of the following methodologies. These methodologies currently are utilized at the University of Colorado at Colorado Springs for curriculum design and revision, student assessment, and as part of the universitywide state-mandated accountability report. These strategies, however, can be utilized with other theoretical conceptions of competency and in combination with additional methodologies (see Table 13.1).

The Community Panel. Annually a community panel composed of communication professionals reviews a portfolio of materials from organizational communication students. These materials include research papers, training designs, theory-based case analyses, and other materials as appropriate. The portfolio materials represent a range of organizational communication courses and feature work from students of varying ability levels. Panel members are provided an evaluation instrument to assess quality of the work and have opportunities for narrative comments. Panel members additionally are asked to identify emerging needs within their professions. The composition of the panel changes each year. Data are compiled by the department's methodologist and statistician and distributed to all faculty engaged in organizational communication instruction. Data also are included in the department's accountability report. This methodology addresses knowledge and skill components of communication competency.

The Internship Program. The student internship program is an assessment opportunity that contributes to student and faculty understanding of the application of curricula to organizational problems and situations. The course design for the internship program becomes part of the assessment

TABLE 13.1
Strengths and Weaknesses of Organizational Communication Assessment Methodologies

Method	Strengths	Weaknesses
Community panel	Provides external assessment Assesses practical applications of curricula Identifies emerging needs Builds institutional/community relationships Provides curricula design information Provides data for institutional accountability	Limited awareness of student capabilities Limited awareness of institutional resources Potential to assess in terms of short-term needs Limits reliability of assessments
Internship program	Provides a summary evaluation of student capabilities Provides students assessment feedback and identifies development opportunities Assesses practical applications of curricula Builds institutional/community relationships Provides faculty feedback on adequacy of graduates Provides curricula design information Provides data for institutional accountability	Limited awareness of student capabilities May assess organizational fit more than overall competency of individual intern May assess organizational more than academic needs Limits reliability of assessment
Student goals and organizational communication instrumentation	Provides individual student feedback Indivudualizes instruction Improves pedagogy	Provides no data for institutional accountability Frequently exhibits reliability and validity concerns Provides limited input for curricular design
Senior course	Provides summary information for curricula design Provides individual student feedback Individualizes instruction Provides data for the panel or other institutional reports Provides portfolio materials	Presents reliability and validity concerns Does not reflect assessment for those not graduating from particular programs May reflect instructor as opposed to programmatic assessment
Computer-based tracking systems	Provides student population characteristics important for curricular design Provides data for department and institutional accountability Provides quantifiable data Provides data for curricula design	Limited usefulness for specific course design Limited validity for quality assessments Potential for quantifiable data to eliminate factors such as resources from accountability
Survey of graduates	Provides longitudinal evaluation of educational experience Promotes relationships between student experiences and practical applications of learning Provides information for curriculum design Provides feedback on emerging needs Builds relationships between alumni and institution Provides data for institutional accountability	Provides information only from those completing program Potential for short-term need identification Limited awareness of resource constraints Present reliability and validity concerns
External review team	Provides professional assessment external to the department or institution Provides input to institution administration Provides curriculum design innovations	Potentially a political process Presents reliability and validity concerns Often conducted without focused goals

process for the curriculum. Internship data provide information for curriculum design and revision and for institutional reporting requirements. Student interns are supervised by an organizational communication faculty member. Each intern is asked to establish, in conjunction with the organizational supervisor, a set of goals for the internship. The faculty supervisor must approve the goals prior to the initiation of the internship. The student intern participates in weekly internship seminars with university faculty and other student interns to discuss organizational experiences and progress toward goals. Organizational supervisors have at least one personal conference with the faculty supervisor and are provided, toward the end of the internship, evaluation instruments to specifically assess the intern's accomplishments and overall capabilities. Interns also complete a self-assessment on the same dimensions and write a concluding paper describing the internship experience. Students review with faculty the organizational assessment of their performances and conclude their learning with an exit interview with the faculty supervisor. The internship experience potentially provides students with assessments of communication competency in all four components— knowledge, sensitivity, skills, and values. Department faculty are presented overall results relative to knowledge and skills demonstrated by students, and the department's institutional report includes overall data.

Student Goals and Organizational Communication Instrumentation. Several organizational communication courses lend themselves to student goal setting and the careful selection and administration of instruments commonly utilized in business and industry such as the Myers–Briggs Type Inventory. Course design can include individualized student goal setting at the beginning of a course sequence and utilize instrumentation as a point of discovery and learning for students. When goal setting and instrumentation are utilized, students have an opportunity to evaluate at the end of the course sequence their individual progress toward goals and assess additional areas for development. This method can be developed for in-course presentation or utilized with the resources of laboratories or learning centers. Although all four competency components can be addressed with this methodology, sensitivity, skills, and values components are particularly appropriate. This methodology provides assessment information directly to students and indirectly contributes to course development. No specific information from this process is included in institutional reports. The methodology can be included in institutional reports as an example of ongoing pedagogy that individualizes instruction and provides inputs for course design.

Senior Course. The advanced organizational communication course can be utilized as a capstone course, important for overall curriculum assessment. Content and assigned projects can be developed to reflect a summation of the experiences of the curricula and provide direct assessment to students of their accomplishments. The course provides materials appropriate for inclusion in the panel review methodology described previously and the projects in the course provide faculty with significant insight into the cumulative knowledge, sensitivity, skills, and values of students. The course can serve an assessment function only if the curriculum is designed to integrate and synthesize across course offerings. The capstone course provides information for student assessment, course design, and, through the use of the panel method, institutional reporting. The course provides assessment opportunities in all four competency components.

Computer-Based Tracking Systems. Many institutions regularly track a variety of characteristics of their student populations. This tracking includes but is not limited to describing incoming freshman, dropout rates, progress toward degrees (grade point averages, course loads, etc.), course selection, and graduation rates. Care should be taken that this information is not presented as a quality assessment of any specific curriculum, although indicators such as grade point average and graduation rates invite that evaluation. Tracking information frequently is utilized as part of institutional accountability. Tracking data are much less frequently utilized by faculty to better understand student populations and design curriculum appropriate for their needs. We recommend including tracking data in broad assessment processes in order to continuously monitor characteristics of the student population important for course design.

Survey of Graduates. Many departments have the opportunity to continue contact with graduates or students who transfer to other institutions by utilizing alumni lists or departmental records. Surveys of graduates can support assessment goals by determining how graduates perceive their education, by describing activities in which graduates are engaged, and by determining what graduates believe to be most useful in their education and what they wish they had experienced as part of a given program. This method, as well as several other of the methods mentioned, can be applied to a variety of types of curricula, but is especially appropriate for organizational communication where students are expected to make ready relationships between academic material and their work in organizations. Again, based on assessment goals, it is possible to development information about all four of the competency components. Findings from graduate surveys are useful to faculty in curriculum development and revision and in general institutional reporting.

External Review Teams. Many institutions require external program review consisting of review by peer faculty in related departments, review by faculty in the communication discipline who are from other institutions, and administrative review. Although frequently viewed negatively, effective external program reviews can be utilized to strengthen course development, provide direction for resources, and provide input to institutional reports. Again, external reviews are more likely to become a constructive part of curricula assessment if a theoretical framework supported by specific program goals is utilized for the review.

CONCLUSION

The methodologies described in this chapter are not the only methodologies that have potential for organizational communication curricula assessment. They are, however, among the most likely methods to support multiple goals and levels of assessment. Many departments and organizational communication faculty select methodologies that best support the goals of particular programs. Other faculties and departments continue to resist assessment requirements, often with important and valid arguments about the misuse of assessment. This latter group, however, faces a future where others external to the discipline may select the methods by which the organizational communication course or program will be evaluated.

If an instructor is teaching an organizational communication class and is either required or feels compelled to develop an assessment strategy, based on our previous discussion, we would recommend the following. First, establish course objectives based either on a competency framework or a clear articulation of the goals of a particular course. Second, identify the levels of assessment appropriate for the course. We recommend at a minimum that students are provided assessment feedback and that the assessment strategy selected guide future development of the course. Third, select assessment methodologies appropriate for both course objectives and levels of assessment. Finally, determine how the assessment strategies selected will contribute to the broad assessment and accountability processes of the department and institution.

In sum, this chapter described the general lack of a theoretical framework for organizational communication competency assessment. A framework for competency assessment—knowledge, sensitivity, skills, and values—was proposed and methodologies appropriate for assessment described. Regardless of the theoretical perspective taken or specific methodologies, the recommendation is made for multiple goals, levels, and methods for assessment. As such, assessment is most appropriately understood as an integral part of the process of developing excellence in organizational communication curricula.

REFERENCES

Adler, S. (1989a). Review of the Management Styles Questionnaire. In J. C. Conoley & J. J. Kramer (Eds.), *The tenth mental measurements yearbook* (pp. 461–462). Lincoln: University of Nebraska.

Adler, S. (1989b). Review of the People Performance Profile. In J. C. Conoley & J. J. Kramer (Eds.), *The tenth mental measurements yearbook* (pp. 609–610). Lincoln: University of Nebraska.

Aleamoni, L. M. (1992). Review of the Team Process Diagnostic. In J. J. Kramer & J. C. Conoley (Eds.), *The eleventh mental measurements yearbook* (pp. 919–920). Lincoln: University of Nebraska.

Berger S., Dertouzos, M., Lester, R., Solow, R., & Thurow, L. (1989). Toward a new industrial America. *Scientific American, 260*(6), 39–47.

Benson, P. G. (1992). Review of the Survey of Organizational Stress. In J. J. Kramer & J. C. Conoley (Eds.), *The eleventh mental measurements yearbook* (pp. 905–906). Lincoln: University of Nebraska.

Bernardin, H. J. (1989). Review of the Management Appraisal Survey. In J. C. Conoley & J. J. Kramer (Eds.), *The tenth mental measurements yearbook* (pp. 457–459). Lincoln: University of Nebraska.

Bernardin, H. J., & Pynes, J. E. (1989). Review of the Managerial Style Questionnaire. In J. C. Conoley & J. J. Kramer (Eds.), *The tenth mental measurements yearbook* (pp. 463–465). Lincoln: University of Nebraska.

Borman, W. C. (1978a). Leadership Evaluation and Development Scale. In O. K. Buros (Ed.), *The eighth mental measurements yearbook* (Vol. 2, pp. 1751–1752). Highland Park, NJ: Gryphon.

Borman, W. C. (1978b). Management Relations Survey. In O. K. Buros (Ed.), *The eighth mental measurements yearbook* (Vol. 2, pp. 1754–1756). Highland Park, NJ: Gryphon.

Carbonell, J. L. (1985). Review of Supervisory Inventory on Communication. In J. V. Mitchell, Jr. (Ed.), *The ninth mental measurements yearbook* (Vol. 2, pp. 1501–1502). Lincoln: University of Nebraska.

Cochran, L. (1989). Review of the People Performance Profile. In J. C. Conoley & J. J. Kramer (Eds.), *The tenth mental measurements yearbook* (pp. 610–611). Lincoln: University of Nebraska.

Curtis, D. B., Winsor, J. L., & Stephens, R. D. (1989). National preferences in business and communication education. *Communication Education, 38,* 6–14.

Daly, J. A., McCroskey, J. C., & Falcione, R. L. (1976, April). *Homophily-heterophily and the prediction of superior satisfaction.* Paper presented at the International Communication Association Convention, Portland, OR.

DeVito, A. J. (1985). Review of Myers–Briggs Type Indicator. In J. V. Mitchell, Jr. (Ed.), *The ninth mental measurements yearbook* (Vol. 2, pp. 1029–1032). Lincoln: University of Nebraska.

DeWine, S. (1987). Evaluation of organizational communication competency: The development of the communication training impact questionnaire. *Journal of Applied Communication Research, 15*(1–2), 113–127.

Dipboye, R. L. (1978a). Leader Behavior Description Questionnaire. In O. K. Buros (Ed.), *The eighth mental measurements yearbook* (Vol. 2, pp. 1742–1747). Highland Park, NJ: Gryphon.

Dipboye, R. L. (1978b). Leadership Behavior Description Questionnaire-Form 12. In O. K. Buros (Ed.), *The eighth mental measurements yearbook* (Vol. 2, pp. 1747–1751). Highland Park, NJ: Gryphon.

DiSalvo, V. S. (1980). A summary of current research identifying communication skills in various organizational contexts. *Communication Education, 29,* 283–290.

DiSalvo, V., Larsen, D. C., & Seiler, W. J. (1976). Communication skills needed by persons in business organizations. *Communication Education, 25,* 269–275.

Dixon, D. D. (1989). Review of the Problem-Solving Decision-Making Style Inventory. In J. C. Conoley & J. J. Kramer (Eds.), *The tenth mental measurements yearbook* (p. 665). Lincoln: University of Nebraska.

Dobbins, G. H. (1985a). Review of Professional and Managerial Position Questionnaire. In J. V. Mitchell, Jr. (Ed.), *The ninth mental measurements yearbook* (Vol. 2, pp. 1213–1214). Lincoln: University of Nebraska.

Dobbins, G. H. (1985b). Review of Supervisory Practices Inventory. In J. V. Mitchell, Jr. (Ed.), *The ninth mental measurements yearbook* (Vol. 2, pp. 1503–1504). Lincoln: University of Nebraska.

Doppelt, J. E. (1978). Minnesota Satisfaction Scales. In O. K. Buros (Ed.), *The eighth mental measurements yearbook* (Vol. 2, pp. 1686–1687). Highland Park, NJ: Gryphon.

Downs, C. W., Driskill, G., & Wuthnow, D. (1990). A review of instrumentation on stress. *Management Communication Quarterly, 4*(1), 100–126.

Erchul, W. P. (1989). Review of The Schutz Measures: Elements of Awareness (Research ed.). In J. C. Conoley & J. J. Kramer (Eds.), *The tenth mental measurements yearbook* (pp. 727–728). Lincoln: University of Nebraska.

Falcione, R. L. (1974). The factor structure of source credibility scales for immediate superiors in the organizational context. *Central States Speech Journal, 25,* 63–66.

Fitzpatrick, R. (1978). Survey of Organizations: A machine-scored standardized questionnaire instrument. In O. K. Buros (Ed.), *The eighth mental measurements yearbook* (Vol. 2, pp. 1527–1528). Highland Park, NJ: Gryphon.

Geisinger, K. F. (1992). Review of the Managerial Competence Index. In J. J. Kramer & J. C. Conoley (Eds.), *The eleventh mental measurements yearbook* (pp. 502–503). Lincoln: University of Nebraska.

Goldhaber, G., & Rogers, D. (1979). *Auditing organizational communication systems: The ICA audit.* Dubuque, IA: Kendall/Hunt.

Greenhaus, J. H. (1985). Review of Personal Performance Problems Inventory. In J. V. Mitchell, Jr. (Ed.), *The ninth mental measurements yearbook* (Vol. 2, pp. 1160–1162). Lincoln: University of Nebraska.

Guion, R. M. (1978a). Minnesota Satisfaction Questionnaire. In O. K. Buros (Ed.), *The eighth mental measurements yearbook* (Vol. 2, pp. 1677–1680). Highland Park, NJ: Gryphon.

Guion, R. M. (1978b). Personnel Relations Survey. In O. K. Buros (Ed.), *The eighth mental measurements yearbook* (Vol. 2, pp. 1760–1761). Highland Park, NJ: Gryphon.

Gutenberg, R. L. (1985). Review of Power Management Profile. In J. V. Mitchell, Jr. (Ed.), *The ninth mental measurements yearbook* (Vol. 2, pp. 1179–1180). Lincoln: University of Nebraska.

Harmon, L. W. (1989). Review of the Management Inventory on Modern Management. In J. C. Conoley & J. J. Kramer (Eds.), *The tenth mental measurements yearbook* (pp. 460–461). Lincoln: University of Nebraska.

Hellweg, S. A., & Andersen, P. A. (1989). An analysis of source valence instrumentation in the organizational communication literature. *Management Communication Quarterly, 3*(1), 132–159.

Jablin, F. M., Cude, R. L., Wayson, K. W., House, A., Lee, J., & Roth, N. L. (1989, May). *Communication competence in organizations: Conceptualization and comparison across multiple levels of analysis.* Paper presented at the annual convention of the International Communication Association, San Francisco.

Kanungo, R. N. (1989). Review of the Power Base Inventory. In J. C. Conoley & J. J. Kramer (Eds.), *The tenth mental measurements yearbook* (pp. 651–652). Lincoln: University of Nebraska.

Katkovsky, W. (1992). Review of the Leatherman Leadership Questionnaire. In J. J. Kramer & J. C. Conoley (Eds.), *The eleventh mental measurements yearbook* (pp. 465–466). Lincoln: University of Nebraska.

Kavanagh, M. J. (1978). Supervisory Behavior Description. In O. K. Buros (Ed.), *The eighth mental measurements yearbook* (Vol. 2, pp. 1763–1766). Highland Park, NJ: Gryphon.

Kehoe, J. F. (1992). Review of the Managerial Assessment of Proficiency MAP. In J. J. Kramer & J. C. Conoley (Eds.), *The eleventh mental measurements yearbook* (pp. 500–502). Lincoln: University of Nebraska.

Kirsch, S. K. (1992). *MBTI Team building program: Team member's guide.* Palo Alto, CA: Consulting Psychologists.

Konovsky, M. A., Jaster, F., & McDonald, M. A. (1989). Using parametric statistics to explore the construct validity of the Thomas–Kilmann Conflict Mode Survey. *Management Communication Quarterly, 3*(2), 268–290.

Korman, A. K. (1978a). Management Style Diagnosis Test, second edition. In O. K. Buros (Ed.), *The eighth mental measurements yearbook (Vol. 2*, pp. 1756–1757). Highland Park, NJ: Gryphon.

Korman, A. K. (1978b). Styles of leadership and management. In O. K. Buros (Ed.), *The eighth mental measurements yearbook* (Vol. 2, pp. 1762–1763). Highland Park, NJ: Gryphon.

Kozma, E. J. (1992). Review of the Management Style Inventory. In J. J. Kramer & J. C. Conoley (Eds.), *The eleventh mental measurements yearbook* (p. 495). Lincoln: University of Nebraska.

Lachar, B. (1992). Review of the Teamness Index. In J. J. Kramer & J. C. Conoley (Eds.), *The eleventh mental measurements yearbook* (pp. 929–931). Lincoln: University of Nebraska.

Lamude, K. G., & Daniels, T. D. (1990). Mutual evaluations of communication competence in superior–subordinate relationships: Sex role incongruency and pro-male bias. *Women's Studies in Communication, 13*(2), 39–56.

Landry, F. J. (1978a). Conflict Management Survey. In O. K. Buros (Ed.), *The eighth mental measurements yearbook* (Vol. 2, pp. 1741–1742). Highland Park, NJ: Gryphon.

Landry, F. J. (1978b). Leadership Evaluation and Development Scales. In O. K. Buros (Ed.), *The eighth mental measurements yearbook*, (Vol. 2, pp. 1752–1753). Highland Park, NJ: Gryphon.

Lifton, P. D. (1985). Review of The FIRO Awareness Scales. In J. V. Mitchell, Jr. (Ed.), *The ninth mental measurements yearbook* (Vol. 1, pp. 577–579). Lincoln: University of Nebraska.

Littlejohn, S. W., & Jabusch, D. M. (1982). Communication competence: Model and application. *Journal of Applied Communication Research, 10*(1), 29–37.

McCroskey, J. C. (1982). Communication competence and performance: A research and pedagogical perspective. *Communication Education, 31*, 1–7.

McCroskey, J. C., Jensen, T., Todd, C., & Toomb, J. K. (1972, November). *Measurement of the credibility of organization sources.* Paper presented at the Western Speech Communication Association Convention, Honolulu, HI.

McCroskey, J. C., & McCain, T. A. (1974). The measurement of interpersonal attraction. *Speech Monographs, 41*, 261–266.

McCroskey, J. C., & McCroskey, L. L. (1988). Self-report as an approach to measuring communication competence. *Communication Research Reports, 5*(2), 108–113.

McDermott, P. J., & Faules, D. F. (1973). Context effects on the measurement of organizational credibility. *Central States Speech Communication Journal, 24*, 189–192.

McIntyre, R. M. (1985). Review of Supervisory Practices Inventory. In J. V. Mitchell, Jr. (Ed.), *The ninth mental measurements yearbook* (Vol. 2, pp. 1504–1506). Lincoln: University of Nebraska.

McReynolds, P. (1989). Review of the Problem-Solving Decision-Making Style Inventory. In J. C. Conoley & J. J. Kramer (Eds.), *The tenth mental measurements yearbook* (pp. 665–666). Lincoln: University of Nebraska.

Monge, P. R., Bachman, S. G., Dillard, J. P., & Eisenberg, E. M. (1982). Communicator competence in the workplace: Model testing and scale development. In M. Burgoon (Ed.), *Communication yearbook* (Vol. 5, pp. 505–527). Newbury Park, CA: Sage.

Motowidlo, S. J. (1978a). Management Transactions Audit. In O. K. Buros (Ed.), *The eighth mental measurements yearbook* (Vol. 2, p. 1757). Highland Park, NJ: Gryphon.

Motowidlo, S. J. (1978b). Survey of Organizations: A machine-scored standardized questionnaire instrument. In O. K. Buros (Ed.), *The eighth mental measurements yearbook* (Vol. 2, pp. 1528–1530). Highland Park, NJ: Gryphon.

Mueller, D. J. (1989). Review of the Communications Profile Questionnaire. In J. C. Conoley & J. J. Kramer (Eds.), *The tenth mental measurements yearbook* (pp. 201–202). Lincoln: University of Nebraska.

Owens, W. A. (1985). Review of Power Management Inventory. In J. V. Mitchell, Jr. (Ed.), *The ninth mental measurements yearbook* (Vol. 2, pp. 1178–1179). Lincoln: University of Nebraska.

Parsons, C. K. (1992a). Review of the Management Styles Inventory. In J. J. Kramer & J. C. Conoley (Eds.), *The eleventh mental measurements yearbook* (pp. 495–496). Lincoln: University of Nebraska.

Parsons, C. K. (1992b). Review of the Survey of Organizational Climate. In J. J. Kramer & J. C. Conoley (Eds.), *The eleventh mental measurements yearbook* (pp. 902–903). Lincoln: University of Nebraska.

Phillips, G. M. (1983). A competent view of "competence." *Communication Education, 32*, 25–36.

Porterfield, W. D. (1992). Review of the Leatherman Leadership Questionnaire. In J. J. Kramer & J. C. Conoley (Eds.), *The eleventh mental measurements yearbook* (pp. 466–468). Lincoln: University of Nebraska.

Putnam, L. L., & Wilson, C. E. (1982). Communicative strategies in organizational conflicts: Reliability and validity of a measurement scale. In M. Burgoon (Ed.), *Communication yearbook* (Vol. 6, pp. 629–652. Beverly Hills, CA: Sage.

Rubin, R. B. (1982). Assessing speaking and listening competence at the college level: The communication competency assessment instrument. *Communication Education, 31*, 19–32.

Rubin, R. B. (1990). Communication competence. In G. M. Phillips & J. T. Wood (Eds.), *Speech communication: Essays to commemorate the 75th anniversary of the Speech Communication Association.* Carbondale: Southern Illinois University.

Saunders, D. M. (1992). Review of the Management Interest Inventory. In J. J. Kramer & J. C. Conoley (Eds.), *The eleventh mental measurements yearbook* (pp. 493–494). Lincoln: University of Nebraska.

Sauser, W. I., Jr. (1992). Review of the Manager Profile Record. In J. J. Kramer & J. C. Conoley (Eds.), *The eleventh mental measurements yearbook* (pp. 496–497). Lincoln: University of Nebraska.

Schmidt, F. L. (1978). Managerial Style Questionnaire. In O. K. Buros (Ed.), *The eighth mental measurements yearbook* (Vol. 2, pp. 1758–1760). Highland Park, NJ: Gryphon.

Schoenfeldt, L. F. (1989). Review of the Communications Profile Questionnaire. In J. C. Conoley & J. J. Kramer (Eds.), *The tenth mental measurements yearbook* (pp. 202–203). Lincoln: University of Nebraska.

Schutz, W. (1992). Beyond FIRO-B—Three new theory-derived measures—Element B: behavior, Element F: feelings, Element S: self. *Psychological Reports, 70*, 915–937.

Shockley-Zalabak, P. (1988). Assessing the Hall Conflict Management Survey. *Management Communication Quarterly, 1*(3), 302–320.

Shockley-Zalabak, P. (1991). *Fundamentals of organizational communication: Knowledge, sensitivity, skills, values.* New York: Longman.

Shockley-Zalabak, P., & Hulbert-Johnson, R. (1993, November). *Oral communication competency and its assessment in organizations: Approaches, instruments, and methods.* A paper presented at the Speech Communication Association Convention, Miami Beach, FL.

Sippola, B. C. (1992). Review of the Survey of Organizational Culture. In J. J. Kramer & J. C. Conoley (Eds.), *The eleventh mental measurements yearbook* (pp. 903–905). Lincoln: University of Nebraska.

Spitzberg, B. H. (1983). Communication competence as knowledge, skill, and impression. *Communication Education, 32*, 323–329.

Spitzberg, B. H., & Cupach, W. R. (1984). *Interpersonal communication competence.* Beverly Hills, CA: Sage.

Staley, C. C., & Shockley-Zalabak, P. (1985). Identifying communication competencies for the undergraduate organizational communication series. *Communication Education, 34*, 156–161.

Subcommittee of the Educational Policies Board. (1993, November). *Oral communication in the undergraduate general education curriculum.* Paper presented at the annual meeting of the Speech Communication Association, Annandale, VA.

Taylor, R. N. (1978). Management Transactions Audit. In O. K. Buros (Ed.), *The eighth mental measurements yearbook* (Vol. 2, pp. 1757–1758). Highland Park, NJ: Gryphon.

Thayer, P. W. (1978). Process diagnostic. In O. K. Buros (Ed.) *The eighth mental measurements yearbook* (Vol. 2, pp. 1680–1681). Highland Park, NJ: Gryphon.

Thornton, G. C. (1985). Review of Professional and Managerial Position Questionnaire. In J. V. Mitchell, Jr. (Ed.), *The ninth mental measurements yearbook* (Vol. 2, pp. 1214–1215). Lincoln: University of Nebraska.

Thornton, G. C. (1989a). Review of the Management Appraisal Survey. In J. C. Conoley & J. J. Kramer (Eds.), *The tenth mental measurements yearbook* (pp. 459–460). Lincoln: University of Nebraska.

Thornton, G. C. (1989b). Review of the Rahim Organizational Conflict Inventories. In J. C. Conoley & J. J. Kramer (Eds.), *The tenth mental measurements yearbook* (pp. 676–677). Lincoln: University of Nebraska.

Waller, N. G. (1992a). Review of Supervisory Communication Relations. In J. J. Kramer & J. C. Conoley (Eds.), *The eleventh mental measurements yearbook* (pp. 896–897). Lincoln: University of Nebraska.

Waller, N. G. (1992b). Review of Supervisory Human Relations. In J. J. Kramer & J. C. Conoley (Eds.), *The eleventh mental measurements yearbook* (pp. 897–898). Lincoln: University of Nebraska.

Weider-Hatfield, D. (1988). Assessing the Rahim Organizational Conflict Inventory II (ROCI-II). *Management Communication Quarterly, 1*(3), 350–366.

Wiggins, J. S. (1989). Review of the Myers–Briggs Type Indicator. In J. C. Conoley & J. J. Kramer (Eds.), *The tenth mental measurements yearbook* (pp. 536–538). Lincoln: University of Nebraska.

Wilson, S. R., & Waltman, M. S. (1988). Assessing the Putnam–Wilson Organizational Communication Conflict Inventory. *Management Communication Quarterly, 1*(3), 367–388.

Womack, D. F. (1988). Assessing the Thomas–Kilmann Conflict MODE Survey. *Management Communication Quarterly, 1*(3), 321–349.

14

Assessment in Theatre Programs

Mark J. Malinauskas
Gary T. Hunt
Murray State University

Assessment in theatre programs, because of the field's fine arts tradition, presents unique challenges. This chapter provides the reader an overview of theatre education assessment and considers important issues including the role of professional organizations, a rationale for undertaking assessment, the practical steps in carrying out an assessment plan, and the assessment of general education theatre courses. This chapter's discussion includes a variety of assessment strategies including the use of capstone experiences, exit interviews, and alumni surveys.

INTRODUCTION

National efforts to develop broad profiles of information about academic program quality have become a reality for most institutions of higher education. Often the composition of these profiles is determined by individuals who are not part of the staff of the university. Legislators and bureaucrats in statewide coordinating offices and discipline leaders, who usually have their offices inside the Washington Beltway, often determine what we in higher education must do as we attempt to respond to calls for *assessment* of student outcomes in higher education. The guidelines, parameters, and the assessment agenda are often determined by individuals who, although very interested in their respective disciplines, have had no direct administrative experience in providing the data requested through assessment mandates. It is within this confusing assessment framework that administrators in higher education must function. Often administrators perceive that they must respond to requests for data that are well removed from their daily activities of running an academic program.

The material presented in this book provides practical information designed to enable a faculty member or an administrator to respond to assessment mandates. Much of the material presented, however, deals with the communication disciplines. Assessment in interpersonal or mass communication is a difficult task. But, there is a common thread to both of these areas. They both rely on either social science or critical theoretical perspectives. Courses within these disciplines stress a balance of theory and practice. Further, the two areas have been moving in similar directions as the result of the development of large "umbrella" departments and the presentation of research at common conventions such as at the International Communication Association and the World Communication Association. Except in highly applied journalism courses, assessment models for courses in theory of mass communication, communication theory, and communication research methods will usually look pretty much alike.

However, there remains one field in the broad communication discipline that is quite different from either mass or interpersonal communication: theatre. Because of the aesthetic and fine arts traditions, the theatre faculty of a department or college will likely be forced to depart from a classical social science orientation stressing quantitative data gathering in the development of their assessment models. Such fine arts topics as criticism, performance, and artistic growth and development guide the assessment models in theatre. These topics would probably not be addressed in the assessment models in interpersonal and mass communication courses.

ISSUES INVOLVING ASSESSMENT

Because of the uniqueness of theatre when it is a part of the communication program, several issues emerge. As an introduction, we feel that these issues must be addressed early in a chapter on assessment.

Fine Arts Versus Liberal Arts Mission

Unlike most communication programs, which have already decided that they are a liberal art, the debate about the mission is still raging in theatre. Perhaps the best index about on which side a department falls in this debate is the degree that the unit elects to offer. *The Handbook of the National Association of Schools of Theatre* (NAST, 1992) is quite specific in outlining what differentiates a "professional" Bachelor of Fine Arts degree from a "liberal arts" Bachelor of Arts degree. According to NAST, the accrediting body in theatre, the BFA students must earn 65% of their total course credit in theatre studies. For the BA, the standard is usually that from one third to one half of the total course credits should be in theatre. The BA is usually a general degree, covering several broad areas. In the BFA on the other hand, students can *specialize* (NAST's term) in such areas as acting and set design.

Assessing the BFA demands great attention to the details of the specialization. Although BFA programs are widely represented throughout the country, our belief is that the BA program is the primary degree at most comprehensive and liberal arts institutions and it is our primary focus in this chapter. However, we recognize that the universities hoping to "professionalize" their offerings in theatre will eventually seek to confer the BFA degree.

Performance

Regardless of degree offered, theatre students are expected to have some experience in performance. Performance can be broadly defined to include acting, design/technology, playwriting, and directing. According to NAST (1992), the "excellence of work in the theatre produced by students is the best determinant of the adequacy of performance studies offered by an institution" (p. 54). How a department treats performance is necessarily an important component of its assessment program. Certainly, in highly professional programs, performance becomes critical. However, in liberal-arts-oriented programs, faculty may elect not to emphasize performance, choosing instead to stress the thinking, speaking, and writing skills traditionally associated with a liberal arts program. Such departments are likely to emphasize the history, theory, and criticism of theatre. Our point here is not that one view of performance is more valid than the other. Rather, it is that a faculty of theatre must carefully reflect on the relative weight of performance in its assessment model.

Developing an assessment program that emphasizes performance will mean extensive use of videotape, peer and outside review, and a rigorous adherence to the professional standards of the discipline. In assessing liberal arts programs such measurement techniques as critical essays, senior projects, and exit interviews can be used. Obviously, as has been suggested throughout the book, a program's assessment model should follow naturally from the type of academic unit it has defined itself to be and from its unit's mission statement.

General Education

The theatre unit is likely to have a component within the university's general education program. This can be viewed as both an opportunity and a challenge as far as assessment goes. The challenge stems from the need to standardize assessment models on campus. Usually this implies working within a broad interdisciplinary committee and employing the methods that are developed through and approved by this committee. The opportunity presents itself through the chance to develop broad data about the theatre discipline from a broad cross section of students. Once the theatre faculty has agreed on the curricular objectives about content covered and skills sought from students in the the general education program, the assessment process should enable the faculty to develop specific paper-and-pencil instruments to determine whether or not the program has successfully produced students who can demonstrate the requisite skills. We consider further the general education issue later in this chapter.

Administrative Concerns

Because of the experiential aspects of theatre education, unique challenges are presented to administrators. For example, in the best of all assessment worlds, students, on entering the program, would acquire a videotape that would stay with them until they graduate. Cuttings of performances, samples from stage designs, and other aspects of their educational work could be added to the tape as appropriate. Faculty comments would be integrated into the tape as well. At the end of the student's career, the tape would be a record of accomplishments. The question comes, for the administrator, about how many resources can be expended in actuating any type of assessment model. Such practical issues as faculty time, storage space, and the cost of production must all be considered by administrators. Because the focus of so many theatre programs must be on individual skill development, the challenges of how to group the data to assess an entire program become significant. We return to this point later in the chapter. We believe that these administrative issues must be addressed before a theatre unit begins the process of program assessment.

The Role of Professional Organizations in Theatre and in Assessment

Although the movement to assess student outcomes has been a legislative agenda since the mid-1980s (Hunt, 1990), it is our belief that departments have been somewhat slow to respond to these mandates; but, even slower has been the response of the professional organizations. There are several key professional theatre organizations. (For a complete listing of addresses, see Appendix A.) Probably the most important is NAST. It is this body that professionally accredits theatre programs. Going for professional accreditation is one way to assess the quality of a university's theatre. Standards and guidelines established by NAST outline specifically what must be done to achieve professional accreditation. As of late 1993, 88 universities had achieved professional accreditation. The International Council of Fine Arts Deans (ICFAD) established a task force on measurable outcomes for all of the fine arts. This group, made up of deans of colleges of fine arts, is interested in establishing sets of potential outcomes for all of the fine arts disciplines taught in higher education. There are several other professional organizations with interest in the theatre. The Southeastern Theatre Conference, Inc. (SETC) is a body of theatre faculty and professionals that sponsors annual meetings. Several programs at recent conventions have been devoted to assessment. The Theatre Division of the Speech Communication Association also sponsors annual programs dealing with theatre education.

The membership of the Association for Communication Administration (ACA) is made up of departments and colleges of communication, many of which have units in theatre. The ACA conducts an annual meeting that often features programs on assessment. Two publications of the ACA that will be helpful to theatre programs in building assessment models are *Handbook for Theatre Department Chairs* (Whitmore, 1988) and *Directory of Theatre Programs* (Whitmore, 1991). Another theatre organization is the Association for Theatre in Higher Education (ATHE), which publishes two periodicals: *Theatre Journal* and *Theatre Topics*. Both occasionally publish articles related to assessment.

ASSESSMENT IN THEATRE

Prior to instituting an assessment strategy, it is imperative that theatre faculty reach consensus on the particular competencies that comprise the intended learning outcomes for the student matriculating in the program. Obviously, a careful examination of the institutional mission, its avowed purpose, and its instructional objectives is required before phrasing desired educational results. Most universities require some background in aesthetics as a component of their general education requirements. The rationale is that arts and language form the basis for coming to an understanding of the way in which humans think, act, and feel which, in turn, leads to the development and formation of cultures and civilizations. At some institutions the arts are incorporated into a humanities curriculum. In still others, they are a part of a fine arts curriculum that includes art, music, theatre, and dance. Rather than attempt to present an assessment model that addresses the global issue of aesthetics or the varying types of assessment instruments available to all the arts, we have elected to dwell on the theatre unit where it exists as a singular department or is a unit within a department of speech communication. As a result, our discussion is specifically geared to identifying a model for use by theatre faculties as they prepare to document an accreditation report, or to provide a raison d'etre for their existence within an institutional framework as to their instructional effectiveness; and to assist in clarification and identification of values as they fine tune a curricular program.

A necessary first step in determining the formulation of an assessment strategy is the need to review the standards suggested by the professional associations that govern the discipline. In this regard, the Association for Theatre in Higher Education (ATHE, 1990) adopted and endorsed a policy statement in 1990. Although an extensive document, it is extremely useful for offering broad guidelines and categorizing what it considers to be the three foremost value-added outcomes of theatre education. These fall in the realms of knowledge, skills, and attitudes.

The knowledge category reflects what might be termed a historical perception of the discipline in its multifaceted dimensions; that is, the unique means by which theatre is created (acting, directing, technical theatre, design, playwriting) in points of time. In the skills area, the Association materials identify creative and interpretive acts, as well as motor skills, as they are displayed in actual theatrical practice. The delineation of attitudinal skills addresses the nurturing of a personal value system that embraces such concepts as social responsibility and respect for the discipline and profession of theatre.

The NAST (1992) Handbook offers a broad-based standard for undergraduate degrees in theatre. It indicates that the graduate in theatre from a liberal arts program should display "the knowledge and skills required of a performer, creator, teacher, theorist, and historian" (p. 49). As suggested earlier, the value of the NAST guidelines is the differentiation it offers in liberal arts degrees in theatre from specific professional programs, such as the BFA degree in acting or design/technology. Here the guidelines become relatively specific (e.g., a knowledge of the history of furniture) rather than the broad generic comments applied to the liberal arts theatre major.

Because the ATHE document provides the greatest opportunity for theatre units to tailor and gear their assessment strategy to the mission and purposes of the university in which they are located, it is best to focus on their plan for purposes of this chapter. The three outcomes ATHE identifies (knowledge, skills, and attitudes) parallel, to some degree, the elements Gardner identified for monitoring and assessing aesthetic growth (Brandt, 1987). Gardner provided a useful broad framework for us to consider in the assessment process. The elements Gardner identified are: production, perception, and reflection. *Production,* for Gardner, is a result of students actually doing theatre rather than simply engaging in a verbal and analytic approach that he said characterizes a traditional means of arts education. Gardner attempted to assess artistic thinking and making by employing his theory of multiple intelligences. Perception in this order implies developing abilities to see, hear, and discriminate performance possibilities in a more sophisticated fashion. Reflection allows for development of a value system providing for a hierarchical scale of aesthetic merit.

The Gardner approach is an attempt to measure growth as a result of actual experience with arts activities. It is particularly suitable to the arts because it is focused and proceeds from what might be termed *internal activity* (emanating from the subject) rather than *external activity* (information laid on and then tested by an outside auditor). Theatre, especially, lends itself to this manner of assessments, for the typical curriculum involves training in the three domains of learning—affective, cognitive, and psychomotor. Devising a single instrument that combines a test of outcomes in all three domains does not appear to be a productive possibility. One can, however, develop information from the several categories of instruments that are available. We look at these instrument categories and the advantages and disadvantages later in this chapter.

Those who have been calling for assessment in the schools—legislators and taxpayers—are interested in looking at percentages and statistics as the concrete demonstration of classroom results. In addition, a Gallup (1980) poll indicates the public is interested in reading figures that measure the cognitive domain rather than the remaining two. As a consequence, it behooves the theatre unit to supply data and information from the area that the public and state legislatures value. Indeed, educators are divided as to the possibility of creating an instrument that focuses solely on the affective domain. Oliva (1982) wrote, "Affective measures are both difficult to identify and extremely difficult—often impossible—to measure" (p. 362). There is some question whether or not the affective domain is an appropriate area to be tested for another reason. Kratwahl and others who amplified study of the affective domain appear to limit their definition to development of emotions, feelings, beliefs, and values (Kratwahl, Bloom, & Mosia, 1964). The key word, of course, is the manner in which emotions, feelings, and beliefs are *developed*. Theatre training in the affective area is concerned with the skill of displaying emotion from an acting viewpoint. From the director's perspective, it is fostering emotional display in others and discerning the appropriate degree of emotional intensity to be displayed. In each case, so many factors are operating in the performance process, it is difficult to make an objective judgment and assessment of appropriate affect display. Indeed, the continuing debate in performance training as to which system is most appropriate for acting and directing training (that is, internal approach vs. external approach vs. combined internal/external affect display in performance) lessens the possibility of creating a valid instrument to measure outcomes in the affective domain.

Because it would be folly to pursue this avenue, faculties are left with the choice of the cognitive domain for designing, testing, and validating intended learning outcomes. Whereas the ATHE and NAST documents are helpful in identifying what to assess in content and contextual categories, it is left to theatre units to develop institutional unit instruments in the areas of skills and participation. Here it may be possible to devise scales that can yield numerical data. As an example, the method in which an individual can manipulate pitch, tempos, and vocal intensity can be measured and documented. This is possible by the use of contemporary technology through the use of oscilloscopes and other such devices. Such basic and simplistic skills as a demonstration of stage geography and body position are easily assessed. Clear speech and the absence of regionalisms are equally capable of being discerned. Judging the degree to which one can "project one's self believably in word and action into imaginary circumstances, evoked improvisationally or through text" (NAST, 1992, p. 54) becomes problematical because it is highly subjective and hinges on the level of experience and background of the individual auditors. A 10-year faculty member will likely be in disagreement with the first-year faculty member in evaluating and weighting the numerous variables evident in the performing process. Clearly, tangible data that is credible and verifiable is necessary in establishing an assessment scheme. Let us then turn our attention to an established schema that has been universally endorsed.

Bloom (1956), in his highly regarded *Taxonomy of Educational Objectives*, ordered learning into six categories (see Table 14.1 and 14.2). Tests can be designed that phrase questions to cover both the general education classes offered by the theatre unit and the entire major. Before examining some sample questions, let us review the learning behaviors that each of Bloom's categories yields.

The first category, knowledge, asks students to recall previously existing learned materials. In theatre, for the general education course as well as the required major courses, elicited information may cover any number of areas. Tables 14.3 and 14.4 give sample questions and are based on Bloom's taxonomy in the cognitive domain.

Knowledge questions simply ask individuals to remember information (Metfessel, Michael, & Kirsner, 1969).

Comprehension questions ask students to reorganize material in order to demonstrate they understand the meaning of materials.

TABLE 14.1
Knowledge (Remember)

Objective	Questions
To define	Define *stage apron.*
To identify	Who wrote *The Cherry Orchard?*
To recall	What year did the Astor Place Riots occur?
To recognize	What are the parts of an ellipsodial reflector?

TABLE 14.2
Comprehension (Understand)

Objective	Questions
To illustrate	Give an example of "realistic drama" and explain why you classify it in this manner.
To rephrase	Francis Fergusson says the theme of *The Cherry Orchard* is "the suffering of change." What do you think he means by this?
To compare	How are Williams' *The Glass Menagerie* and Miller's *Death of a Salesman* similar?
To contrast	Contrast the visual effects of a fresnel instrument with that of a ellipsodial instrument.

TABLE 14.3
Application (Problem Solution)

Objective	Questions
To classify	What elements of empressionism do you find in Chekov's *The Cherry Orchard*?
To apply/employ	Apply the structure of *Freytag's Pyramid* to the opening scene of *The Glass Menagerie*.
To develop	Create a simple scene that shows a beginning.
To use	Generate a lighting design for a set using the Bellman "key and fill" system.

TABLE 14.4
Analysis (Logical Order)

Objective	Questions
To detect	What is Chekov saying about class struggle in *The Cherry Orchard*?
To discriminate	Does the author of *The Glass Menagerie* appear to favor one character over another? Why do you believe this?
To identify	How do socioeconomic conditions impact on the Loman family?
To deduce	What evidence does Othello have that seems to justify his actions?

Application, the third element of the taxonomy, offers questions that require students to use previously learned material to solve problems in new situations (see Table 14.3).

The fourth element identifies the principle of *analysis,* questions that require students to break an idea into component parts for logical analysis (see Table 14.4).

Synthesis questions require students to combine existing knowledge and ideas into a statement or idea that is new to them (see Table 14.5).

The last element asks students to make *evaluations* or *judgments* based on a set of their own criteria or that of another (see Table 14.6).

Gardner's views on learning appear to presuppose some student mastery within the framework of the Bloom taxonomy. The degree of sophisticated learning becomes evident in the process of creation (Gardner's production step). Consequently, we conclude that Bloom's final taxonomic objective becomes the springboard from which Gardner launched his views on artistic assessment. When one considers possible instrument categories to which the given taxonomy can be applied, it is apparent that knowledge questions, for example, are appropriate to multiple-choice type testing, which usually occurs in general education or survey courses.

TABLE 14.5
Synthesis (Create)

Objective	Questions
To design	Design a floor plan for *The Glass Menagerie*.
To propose	Memory plays a significant role in *The Cherry Orchard*. Can you identify an American play in which the same can be said?
To write	Create a monologue on the order of the opening speech of *The Glass Menagerie* in which you inform us of the current social milieu and your family's place in it.
To diagram	Provide a parallel diagram of the family relationships that are evident in *King Lear*.

TABLE 14.6
Evaluation (Judge)

Objective	Questions
To assess	Assess the merits of the playwright's use of memory in *The Cherry Orchard* and *The Glass Menagerie*. Which playwright uses the technique to greater effect?
To appraise	Create a review for a performance of *The Glass Menagerie*.
To judge	Does *The Glass Menagerie* as a literary work justify awarding a Pulitizer prize to the author?
Compare/contrast	Tennessee Williams and Arthur Miller are noted playwrights. Which of the two do you favor and why?

APPLICATION OF THE TAXONOMY

The general education courses are those we addressed earlier designed to meet the core requirements of an institution. Survey courses are those required courses of a historical or period orientation designed to acquaint the student with the developmental nature of the theatre discipline.

Some institutions gather assessment data for both types of courses by administering a pretest at the entering point of matriculation in the course. At the conclusion of instruction, a posttest is offered over the same materials. A sample question in the pretest general education course would be the correct identification of Thespis as the first recognized actor. The survey course might ask the student to recall that deWitt was the Dutch traveler credited with making the contemporary drawing of the interior of the Swan Theatre. Some version of these samples is included in the posttest in order to determine value added. The value to employing pre- and posttesting is that as a check of knowledge outcomes it is an easy and relatively simple device. Tests can be computer scored with printouts yielding percentage of correct responses along with standard deviation. Retaining documentary evidence can be performed by a secretary or student worker, thereby involving little faculty time, aside from the original design, for administration and collection of data. Unfortunately, higher order skills are not tested. Consequently, the value of the data for assessment purposes may be called into question. This does not mean, however, that simple knowledge questions are not valued in an assessment scheme because the information disclosed by these instruments is readily quantifiable and forms the basis for the process-oriented learning behaviors of the higher skills.

COLLECTING ASSESSMENT DATA IN GENERAL EDUCATION

To resolve the difficulty of collecting data from a single realm, some institutions in their general education classes design curricula where simulations and performances are used. This technique, if employed, presupposes the class size of the survey course is of a manageable quantity. Our institution has adopted a unique solution to the size problem by enrolling approximately 90 students in its theatre appreciation class. The entire class meets in plenary session on the first day of instruction, at which time they are introduced to the three faculty assigned to the course. Faculty are teaching specialists in one of three areas: dramatic theory/criticism, performance, or design/technical theatre. At the plenary session, students are assigned to a rotational pool or letter category to match one of the teaching areas. Thus, Student 1 may be assigned to Pool A and will receive instruction over 10 class periods in dramatic theory/criticism. Student 2 is assigned to Pool B and receives performance training. Similarly, Student 3 meets with Instructor C and receives instruction in design/technical theatre. The plenary session also includes administration of a pretest. At the conclusion of the 10th class period, students are tested on the materials covered in the section. Students then rotate into another pool category. Thus, the dramatic theory/criticism section moves on to study performance, and so on. Aside from being tested in course-specific multiple-choice exams, a project is assigned for completion in each section. In the dramatic theory/criticism section, for example, students are expected to write a short scenario with a beginning, a middle, and an end. They also write a critique of a studio or main stage theatrical presentation. The project for students in performance is to perform in an open scene after having written a character profile that develops the physical, social, psychological, and moral characteristics of the character. The students are first videotaped in a stand-up reading of the scene. They do not have discussion benefit or practice any performance techniques prior to the exercise. The tape is viewed by the students, after which an initial discussion is held in which performance techniques are discussed and demonstrated. Succeeding sessions develop practice with the element of choice in demonstrating the verbal and nonverbal aspects of performance. Students are asked to incorporate these devices in their rehearsal for the final scene. The character analysis, referred to earlier, is created as an ongoing process. The rehearsed material is given as a final performance and is again videotaped. A final evaluation involving the entire class and instructor concludes the process. This is a crucial assessment device, for it provides observable and, in most cases, demonstrable growth. The theatre design/technical theatre section assigns creation of a set rendering or model for a script that will be produced on the university's main stage season for the semester. In this way, students are able to make individual comparisons with the fashion and manner in which a professional theatre designer solved the problems of dramatic metaphor and scenic concept. These pedagogical approaches in the basic course allow for each taxonomic category to be operational, thereby assuring a holistic course assessment. An added benefit includes the creation of what might be termed a miniportfolio for the student by virtue of the fact that the students have engaged in three Gardner production projects and have also completed the perception and reflection aspects of his scheme. If the individual decides to continue work in a theatre curriculum, this can be referenced as a record of growth development.

The idea of "capturing growth over time so that students can become informed and thoughtful of their own histories as learners" (Wolf, 1987, p. 25), is the engine that drives the assessment plan in the theatre unit at our university. Earlier in this chapter, reference was made to the Gardner approach to monitoring aesthetic growth. His ideas have been employed in an assessment system titled ARTS PROPEL, which was a project funded by the Rockefeller Foundation and set in place at the Pittsburgh City School System. The PROPEL project suggests a multidimensional strategy to weigh production, perception, and reflection. In PROPEL students found: (a) what characterized their individual work (they were able to see a "personal signature" develop); (b) what, in their works, changed with time; and (c) what remains to be done (Wolf, 1987, p. 28). In order to assure a global awareness for the student and in order to provide significant assessment data that not only address Bloom's taxonomy, but also Gardner's theory of multiple intelligences, the assessment techniques for the major suggest themselves.

ASSESSMENT IN MAJOR PROGRAMS

Preparing a plan to assess the major is dependent on the time and personnel available to provide follow-through over a 4-year period. It can be elaborate if it employs each of the following methods suggested. Or, it can be a selective model that furnishes sufficient data to assist the student in personal growth and the department in weighing its effectiveness.

Entrance Interview

Employing a videotaped interview at the onset of enrollment in the major accomplishes several purposes. Aside from yielding information on personal background, it is a significant indicator of the amount and degree of preparatory background the student brings to the major. It has been our experience that the status of theatre programs at the secondary level is a mixed assortment from highly developed programs (performing arts schools) to the "Let's put on a play" mentality of amateur producing groups. This is, as such, an indictment of local school districts and also state educational systems, which have forsaken arts and theatre education in the elementary and secondary curriculum. Most students, we have found, have little or no formal training in dramatic literature, its historic development, and its place on the contemporary scene. Knowledge of performance theory is nonexistent. Performance skills are perhaps the best developed. This is a result of the individual's participation on high school speech teams. Although a national thespian society has called for the institution of advanced placement testing, the idea has received little acceptance at the college and university level. Consequently, the entrance interview is, at present, the best barometer for screening, advising, and counseling incoming students. Depending on the types of information solicited in the questioning period, an interview allows for assessment of the individual's ability to apply what has been previously known. Similarly, as the person articulates insights gained from previous experience, competency in analyzing, synthesizing, and evaluating information becomes apparent. Although the questions utilized in the interview can be general in nature, some tailoring of materials should occur in order to examine the individual's level of sophistication. The taped record should become a part of the student's permanent file and be deposited with the advisor of record. Although it is possible to question the necessity of offering entrance interviews, the information obtained is not only a valuable resource in coming to know the student and individual needs, it is a useful device to group students according to ability, which is especially desirable for performance courses, in which case the interview should be accompanied by a simple audition.

Portfolio

Maintaining a portfolio package is crucial to the success of any viable assessment program (see chap. 6). Contents of the package may vary; however, the following items are likely materials for inclusion:

Personal Journal. Entries need not be made on a daily basis. Rather it should hold substantive items that reflect and respond to student achievements, attempts, and failures. These reflective statements become the motivators for the individual to phrase personal goals and objectives. They also tend to limit the personal frustrations inherent in any disciplined study. In a sense, this personal instruction allows for the recognition of obstacles and the construction of strategies to overcome them. As such, the journal becomes a healthy form of intrapersonal communication.

Videotape of Performance Projects Including Monologues and Short Scenes. This record should include on-camera commentary by the performance instructors addressing level of proficiency and items to be pursued in order to further develop performance skills.

Copies of Course-Specific Examinations as Reference for the Capstone Experience and/or Comprehensive Examination. This may be a difficult task to complete because some instructors jealously guard copies of examinations and prohibit students from retaining the examination. Where possible, the student may simply self debrief and note the salient aspects of the examination. Scores should be retained, as well as copies of semester grade reports.

All Written Creative and Research Projects. Retention of project material is an exceptional manner for the student and evaluator to judge evolution of literary ability in both the creative and synthetic modes. Use of literary devices becomes apparent, as does a mastery of grammatical and structural fundamentals.

Clippings to Mirror the Student's Focus in the Major. A design student, for example, may include room designs from magazines, recent construction techniques, and items that contain unique blends of color, and so on. Directorial candidates may include reviews of productions, plot outlines, playwright biographies, and so forth.

Diligent collection of these materials will yield a thorough and complete indication of a student's work. It provides a splendid opportunity for the student to reflect on what has been done and what remains to be achieved. Shared with a mentor/advisor, it allows for objective evaluation and counseling. The mentor/advisor preparing to evaluate the portfolio has a chronological portrait of the subject. The data can be grouped according to the Bloom taxonomy or Gardner's elements. Because the information provided is both quantitative and qualitative, a credible and principled document emerges.

Course-Specific Examinations

Ideally, each course examination administered should contain questions that test the cognitive skills of students in each taxonomic category. Uniform application of this throughout the curriculum should allow students to become habituated to the process. Uniform application also provides unity to the pedagogic devices employed by the teaching faculty.

Performance and Production Activity

Because the liberal arts theatre major presumes developing skills in the activity of theatre, it is presumed the student will seek out opportunities to exercise a personal pattern of maximum exposure to the cocurricular theatrical production activity of the department. This may be in performance, production, design, or the various management positions available to the student. Documentation of such work should be the responsibility of the student and placed in the portfolio. Occasionally, some departments have invited outside evaluators to comment on the work of individual faculty as they may be considered for merit increases, tenure, or promotion. In such cases, the outside adjudicator should be encouraged to comment directly on student work where that work is apparent and evident. Certainly, if a faculty director is having a production critiqued by a guest, oral and/or written commentary on the performance skills of the student actors should be elicited and encouraged. Our institution has engaged in this practice with benefit to faculty, students, and the administration.

When outside evaluation is financially infeasible, every effort should be made to secure funding for theatre units to participate in the American College Theatre Festival (ACTF). Appearance at state, regional, and national events assures evaluation by schooled and highly skilled theatre adjudicators who have a wealth of experience in the judicious offering of critical commentary. Frankly, ACTF adjudicators represent the best the entire discipline has to offer in this practice.

Capstone Experiences

The concluding educational activity for undergraduates should reflect the breadth and depth of the curricular transcript. Some institutions have adopted the comprehensive model as the standard to mark termination of undergraduate study and to provide an overall academic assessment. Comprehensives, which may be oral, written, or both, have the advantage of providing a common expectation of all students. Unfortunately, this system yields selective questions and offers a spotty sampling. Some institutions have employed a senior seminar in which case studies are explored and discussed. This results in the production of a minithesis, of which a final assessment is an oral examination. Again, this method minimizes the synthesis of information and process development and gives little opportunity for performance training to be evaluated. Our institution requires all theatre students to produce and direct a piece of dramatic literature. Work on this venture is documented in a very specific fashion. The eventual product is a formatted director's book that relates work done in several categories. It is viewed as incorporating the entire scope of assessment techniques by allowing for demonstration of cognitive skills, the production of a theatrical product, perception as to its impact, and reflection as to its effectiveness. The requirements for a completed director's book are listed in Appendix B. As a culminating experience, the production of a play prompts the individual to bring together all of the course-specific experiences learned in the areas of the liberal arts theatre experience: dramatic theory/criticism, performance, design/technical theatre, and administration. Assessment can be accomplished in a variety of fashions. The entire faculty may grade the project, a selected faculty committee including representatives from outside the discipline may be involved, or an outside expert may be engaged to review the materials and provide commentary.

Exit Interviews

This videotaped session permits comparison with the entrance interview if such material exists. Obviously, the same or similar interrogatives should be employed in order to make a valid comparison and evaluative standards used in the initial interview should be applied (see chap. 8).

Alumni Survey

This technique provides for a global assessment of the curricular program that can direct faculty to make program adjustments. (A sample of an alumni questionnaire is Appendix C.) The intention of such surveys is to provide sophisticated and mature response as a recollection of experience. Potential drawbacks include responses from individuals who are disenchanted with their current status and have an "axe to grind" or glowing reports from individuals enjoying successful career endeavors. In either case, samplings and returns often do not justify the effort and expense of this device. A more appropriate tool for "programmatic assessment" would be to employ the good office of NAST and/or ATHE to identify disinterested observers to perform such duties.

Incorporating any or all of these assessment methods must be a deliberate and determined objective. Each institutional and theatre unit mission must be given careful consideration prior to setting in place a viable assessment scheme. When it is in place, however, the scheme will result in materials to ensure continual monitoring of the instructional program's effectiveness. It proves to the student that evaluation is not only an instructor's responsibility, but also a matter of individual responsibility. The conclusive and convincing data gathered in the process should placate even the most skeptical and wary agent of an accrediting body.

APPENDIX A: THEATRE ORGANIZATIONS

National Association of Schools of Theatre (NAST)
NAST National Office
11250 Roger Bacon Drive
Suite 21
Reston, VA 22090
(703) 437-0700

International Council of Fine Arts Deans (ICFAD)
P.O. Box 1772
San Marcos, TX 78667-1722
(512) 245-3387/2651

Southeastern Theatre Conference (SETC)
William Rackley
Department of the Dance and Theatre
University of North Carolina–Charlotte
Charlotte, NC 28223
(704) 547-4473

Speech Communication Association (SCA)
SCA National Office
5105 Backlick Road #E
Annandale, VA 22003
(703) 750-0583

Association for Communication Administrators (ACA)
5105 Backlick Road #F
Annandale, VA 22003
(703) 750-0583

Association for Theatre in Higher Education (ATHE)
Patricia Angotti
ATHE
THEeatre SERVICE
Box 15282
Evansville, IN 47716
(812) 474-0549

APPENDIX B: COMPLETED DIRECTOR'S BOOK
REQUIREMENTS

This project should be looked upon as an extended research paper. As such, it should reflect sophisticated scholarship and be cast in proper grammatical fashion in a unified whole. The entire text is to be typed copy.

The objective of the director's book is dual in nature:

1. It should be designed to assist the director in discovering the meaning of the play and in finding a way to project that meaning to an audience.
2. It assists future researchers in arriving at a knowledge of the directorial approach employed while giving an imaginary visual approximation of the production.

Note: A director's book is created as an ongoing process; it is not completed at the end of a production. It must be written as the director is working on the show. Items that should be included in the director's book and that should be tabbed and labeled as such are:

Part 1

Tab 1 Reasons for the choice of the play.

Tab 2 Background material and research, of the author, comparisons with other works, readings or biographies, etc. Critical commentary on the chosen play.

Tab 3 A statement of the theme or meaning of the play as interpreted by the director. A statement on the unique form and style of the production. A statement of the through line of action for the play and each major character's relation to it (e.g., Chekov's *The Cherry Orchard*, "to show the suffering of change").

Tab 4 An analysis of each of the major characters of the play from a physical, social, psychological, and moral dimension.

Tab 5 The plot of the play.

Part 2

Tab 1 The text of the play (cut and edited). Reasons for deletions are appropriate. Blocking of the scenes. The Director's Book should include the three column analysis indicating intentions, adjustments, and action. This is placed adjacent to the text.

Tab 2 A ground plan of the set to scale.

Tab 3 Notation on the use of technical elements within the text—separate pages for props, costumes, music, light cue sheets, equipment, set-up charts, and so on.

Tab 4 Photographs of selected scenes.

Part 3

Tab 1 Rehearsal log, listing rehearsal objectives and manner to achieve them.

Tab 2 An objective assessment detailing the effectiveness of the experience and the knowledge gained.

Tab 3 Bibliography and use of source materials.

This is the desired sequential presentation of the material to be included in the Director's Book. It should be submitted no later than 1 week after the production. If, for any reason, a segment cannot be completed, the reason should be documented and the degree of activity to complete the requirement should be noted. The completed Director's Book becomes the property of Murray State University Theatre for archival purposes.

APPENDIX C: ALUMNI SURVEY

Note: This alumni survey was modeled after one developed by the Department of Music at Murray State University under the direction of Dr. Roger Reichmuth. The authors appreciate Dr. Reichmuth and his colleagues allowing us to borrow heavily from their departmental survey form.

Murray State University Program in Theatre Alumni Assessment

1. Please indicate the date, relevant minor and years to complete your degree below.

Semester & Year Conferred   Academic Minor (if any)
No. of years to Complete Degree

2. Please circle the numbers below which represent your opinions regarding the following areas:

	Low Quality			High Quality	
a. Overall quality of the MSU theatre program	1	2	3	4	5
b. Quality of your academic major	1	2	3	4	5
c. Quality of your academic advisement in the MSU theatre program	1	2	3	4	5
d. Quality of general education courses outside of theatre	1	2	3	4	5
e. Quality of your theatre courses	1	2	3	4	5

3. Please list the full-time positions you have occupied since graduating from MSU and the number of years in each position. (If you have never held a full-time position in theatre, please skip to Question 4.)

Position/Institution/Location   Year(s) (e.g.,1986–1989)

4. If you have never been employed in a full-time theatre position, please list the part-time positions you have occupied since graduating from MSU. (Skip this question if you answered Question 3.)

Position/Institution/Location   Year(s) (e.g.,1986–1989)

5. Please circle the numbers below which best represent your opinions regarding the quality of instruction at Murray State University in the following areas (if you did not have any classes in a specified field, circle N.O. for "No Opinion"):

	Low Quality				High Quality	
Theatre History	1	2	3	4	5	N.O.
Directing	1	2	3	4	5	N.O.
Theatre Literature	1	2	3	4	5	N.O.
Acting	1	2	3	4	5	N.O.
Technical Theatre	1	2	3	4	5	N.O.
Theatre Management	1	2	3	4	5	N.O.

6. Please describe any courses that you think should be added for theatre majors at MSU.

7. Please list any courses you were required to take that you think should not be required.

8. Do you feel that the breadth of your studies prepared you adequately for doing your final directing project?

Yes   No

9. To what degree were your project advisors or committee members helpful?

Not at all helpful   Very helpful
1   2   3   4   5

10. How important were the following elements in your decision to attend Murray State University?

	Not Important			Very Important	
a. Location	1	2	3	4	5
b. Cost of tuition	1	2	3	4	5
c. Recommendation of a teacher/acquaintance	1	2	3	4	5
d. Scholarship/financial aid	1	2	3	4	5
e. Quality of education	1	2	3	4	5
f. Reputation of the theatre program	1	2	3	4	5
g. Presence of a particular faculty member	1	2	3	4	5
h. Other reasons (specify)	1	2	3	4	5

11. Do you feel you had adequate opportunities to perform in the following situations:

Main Stage Productions	Black Box Productions	Off-Campus Productions
Yes	Yes	Yes
No	No	No

12. What was the general influence of these performance opportunities on your career development?

	No Influence			Great Influence	
Main Stage	1	2	3	4	5
Black Box	1	2	3	4	5
Off-Campus	1	2	3	4	5

13. Would you recommend the theatre program at Murray State University to someone considering the study of the theatre?

Yes   No

14. How well did the theatre program prepare you in the following areas:

	Little Preparation			Great Preparation	
a. To communicate well orally	1	2	3	4	5
b. To communicate well in writing	1	2	3	4	5
c. To understand interpersonal differences	1	2	3	4	5

d. To appreciate the arts	1	2	3	4	5
e. To work effectively in small groups	1	2	3	4	5
f. To understand cultural differences	1	2	3	4	5
g. To display leadership	1	2	3	4	5

15. Do you have any comments or suggestions regarding the theatre program at Murray State University?

Name:
Address: Phone #:
City: State: Zip:

Thank you for filling out this survey. Please return it in the enclosed envelope or mail it to:

Alumni Assessment
Department of Speech Communication and Theatre
Murray State University
1 Murray ST
Murray, KY 42071

REFERENCES

Association for Theatre in Higher Education. (1990). *Assessment guidelines for theatre programs in higher education*. Evansville, IN: Author.

Bloom, B. (Ed.). (1956). *Taxonomy of educational objectives: Goals, handbook I: Cognitive domain*. New York: Longman.

Brandt, R. (1987). On assessment in the arts: A conversation with Howard Gardner. *Educational Leadership, 45*(4), 30–34.

Gallup, G. (1980). The 12th annual Gallup Poll of the public attitudes toward the public schools, *Phi Delta Kappa, 62*(1), 41–42.

Hunt, G. (1990). The assessment movement: A challenge and opportunity. *ACA Bulletin, 72*(2), 5–8.

Kratwahl, D., Bloom, B., & Mosia, B. (Eds.). (1964). *Taxonomy of educational objectives: The classification of educational goals, handbook II: Affective domain*. New York: Longman.

Metfessel, W., Michael, W., & Kirsner, D., (1969). Instrumentation of Bloom's and Kratwahl's taxonomies for the writing of the educational objective. *Psychology in the Schools, VI*(3), 227–231.

NAST. (1992). *Handbook of the National Association of Schools of Theatre*. Reston, VA: Author.

Oliva, P. (1982). *Developing the curriculum*. Boston, MA: Little, Brown.

Whitmore, J. (Ed.). (1988). *Handbook for theatre department chairs*. Annandale, VA: Association of Communication Adminstrators.

Whitmore, J. (Ed.). (1991). *Directory of theatre programs*. Annandale, VA: Association of Communication Adminstrators.

Wolf, D. (1987). Opening up assessment. *Educational Leadership, 45*(4), 24–29.

15

Using Accreditation for Assessment

Joanne Easley Arnold
University of Colorado, Boulder

Although some argue that the accreditation process is too costly in time and money; that it is often outdated, rigid, and inappropriately prescriptive; and that it typically fails to address the effectiveness of instructional programs, most observers believe accreditation is here to stay. With thoughtful changes to encourage institutions themselves to define their goals and missions, to move toward more flexible standards, to serve better and more openly the public interest, and—above all—to examine student outcomes, the benefits of accreditation to academic programs and their institutions will outweigh the costs. Here, a systematic approach to measuring instructional outcomes is outlined, beginning with laying intended course outcomes against a grid of Accrediting Council on Education in Journalism and Mass Communication (ACEJMC) accreditation standards, filling the gaps through curriculum development, and defining ways to express objectives and measure hoped-for outcomes.

INTRODUCTION

The most straightforward starting place for thinking about measures of student outcomes is with accrediting standards. Indeed, one could argue that such a starting place is the most obvious way to construct a coherent instructional program and the most useful basis for assessment.

Assessment and *accreditation* are joined in this case to help individual instructional units identify strengths, discover areas for improvement, and enhance communication with a variety of important constituents. It is not the purpose here to discuss in depth the approaches taken by higher

333

education commissions in Louisiana and Tennessee and elsewhere to use accreditation as a measure for performance funding and program continuance. For detailed discussions of state or regional mandates that require accreditation, see Hebert and Thorn (1993, p. 58), Banta (1985), and chapter 3. Rather, this chapter, after a discussion about accredition in general, looks at accreditation as defined by the ACEJMC.

Accreditation as a Valid Factor

It is not the primary purpose here to argue for or against accreditation. The debate continues on its own, particularly as institutions find themselves in financial straits and as the public calls for greater accountability. The process of accreditation is too costly in both time and money, many say. It has been suggested that with six regional accreditation bodies and some 90 specialized accreditation agencies, a large research university could conceivably be the regular subject of as many as 30 accreditation studies, all with time and money attached (Jaschik, 1991, pp. A21–22; Leatherman, 1991, pp. A1, A22). At the same time, the public calls for evidence that institutions are offering instructional programs that work, and the accreditation process is acknowledged to offer at least some of that evidence. Pointing out that accreditation should be included in performance funding, Neel (1986) said, "Accreditation is simple and straightforward for an institution to report, and it is easy for the state coordinating agency to interpret. As an indicator of at least a minimum level of quality, *especially if measures of student outcomes are included*, the inclusion of accreditation in standards for performance funding is acceptable" (p. 58, italics added).

Most agree that accreditation has pushed many institutions to address and correct major problems, whether they be library acquisitions, class sizes, classroom space, or safety hazards. Because they are often underfunded, with little budgetary flexibility, small institutions are thought to be the greatest beneficiaries of these kinds of results of accreditation in that the accreditation requirement may provide needed muscle for improved program support.

Many Programs Are Beneficiaries

Academic departments, schools, and colleges within larger institutions, too, have reaped benefits that have been prompted by the specialized accreditation process. Most obvious are increased allocations for underfunded, understaffed programs. Substandard and marginal facilities and equipment have been improved. An increase in allocations for library purchases has been typical.

Accrediting teams look at faculty salaries and often their recommendations have influence in improving below-average compensation. That is, when accrediting teams find program shortcomings that are the result of underfunding, their informed suggestions to chief academic officers often result in improvements for those programs.

Accreditation studies also have the important potential to discover inappropriate administrative arrangements. They can examine the appropriateness of search processes, seek evidence of balance and diversity, and assess the effectiveness of faculty governance. Their examination can lead to improvements that otherwise would be difficult to address.

Obviously, the accreditation process aims at the improvement of instruction, and it is the improvement of instruction, through the measurement of student outcomes, that this chapter examines in depth later.

Doubts About Accreditation

Many believe accreditation is in trouble. In 1992, the U.S. Congress very nearly removed the restriction that only students attending accredited institutions could receive federal financial aid. Severing student aid eligibility from institutional accreditation could be disastrous for the accreditation process. In 1993 the Council on Postsecondary Accreditation voted to disband, noting its inability to speak effectively about accrediting issues and its failure to bring together disparate accrediting agencies.

Some critics of accreditation claim that money and time spent for the privilege of being accredited could be much better spent improving programs. They claim that the rules for accreditation are often outdated and rigid, that criteria are geared to large research universities and are less applicable to small programs, and that standards are inappropriately prescriptive. In fact, Cheryl Lovell (1993) of the National Center for Higher Education Management Systems warned that if the accrediting process is not part of the fabric of the institution—"the heart of the management process"—efforts and subsequent results are often found wanting. She urged institutions to view the process as a cycle where information gained during the accrediting study serves as the focus for future institutional (or departmental) goals and objectives. The overarching concept should be the necessary institutional support to improve student learning.

In a nutshell, critics ask, does accreditation improve academic programs? Do accredited mass communication programs, for example, graduate better journalists? Does national certification really ensure that better teachers are trained by schools of education? The answers are mixed.

Growing Criticism of Higher Education

In the face of such growing criticism and real threats to the accreditation process, both regional and specialized accrediting agencies are responding by encouraging institutions themselves to define their goals and missions and by moving toward more flexible standards.

Ralph A. Wolff (1993), executive director of the Accrediting Commission for Senior Colleges and Universities of the Western Association of Schools and Colleges, is one of many who believe that accreditation must change. Writing in the *Chronicle of Higher Education*, Wolff suggested that "everyone involved in the process needs to refocus on standards and criteria for demonstrating educational effectiveness. Even the most prestigious institutions will need to address *how much students are learning* and the quality of student life" (p. 81, italics added). Higher education must attend more seriously and carefully to public concerns about the effectiveness of colleges and universities. Accreditation should look at such public concerns as student attrition, teaching effectiveness, and student learning. "Higher education is too important to society to be left solely in the hands of educators" Wolff (1993, p. 81) claimed.

A New Approach to Accreditation

To develop that new approach for accrediting, Wolff suggested a model with at least four characteristics:

1. *Consciously serving the public interest.* In the future, institutions must focus the process so that it serves the public as much as it serves colleges and universities.

2. *Developing a new definition of accountability.* Each institution would be required to set and maintain performance standards in important basic skills against which it would be measured.

3. *Serving as a voice for quality.* Accrediting agencies are credible resources that are able to gather and make public information about the effectiveness of colleges and universities.

4. *Making the process public.* For the public to understand this self-regulation system, it must be visible and accountable. Indeed, some regional accrediting bodies have already become more public about their work and its results. Some have become more open in publicly reporting sanctions against colleges. Three of the six have policies allowing public observers, and one—the Southern Association of Colleges and Schools—not only allows outsiders to observe, but actually encourages their participation.

As accreditation moves inexorably toward openness and accountability, it will answer questions the public is most concerned about. It will observe and publicly report on program effectiveness. It will answer questions about completion time for degree programs, performance standards in basic skills, dropout rates, teaching quality, and student learning. Some questions are easy to answer. Others, like those about student learning, are not.

Accreditation standards serve well as a starting place to look at student learning. They provide a rational, valid, and thoughtful place to begin an assessment of instructional outcomes.

OUTCOMES AND ACCREDITATION STANDARDS

The primary usefulness of outcome measurement is diagnostic. Assessing outcomes against an informed set of standards leads to program improvement: Units discover what they are doing well and can do more of it; they discover what they are doing less well and can improve.

And contrary to oft-repeated fears that commissions, legislatures, and trustees will use assessment information to punish and diminish units with disappointing outcome results, evidence suggests that their patient understanding is more to be expected. Indeed, disappointing outcome results have been known to highlight the underfunding of essential program elements and argue successfully for increased resources. At the unit level and for individual instructors, outcomes assessment answers the right question: Are students learning what we think we are teaching? Here is a hypothetical description of a broadcast program:

> *Broadcast:* The broadcast program offers two options, news and production/management. The news option seeks to provide students with the understandings and skills they need to do broadcast writing, reporting, editing, and performing and to present the news with balance, fairness, and accuracy. The production/management option seeks to provide students with the understandings and skills they need to work successfully in the technical and management operations of broadcast media. Each option teaches basic understandings and fundamental skills in the other. Both options emphasize the necessity to work ethically, to appreciate the unique role of the press in a democracy, and to respect the legal environment of broadcast media. The program seeks to prepare students not only for successful entry-level experiences in broadcast journalism, but also for productive lifelong professional careers.

How do we know as a unit if we are doing that?

The Outcomes-Accreditation Grid

With a grid that lists accrediting standards as outcome goals on the horizontal side and course offerings on the vertical, one can get a quick initial view of a program's potential for instructional effectiveness. One sees then, which courses serve to address which outcome goals (see Fig. 15.1). The curriculum standards of the ACEJMC will serve here as a useful approach for those academic units accredited by ACEJMC, those aspiring to accreditation, and those who are neither but will look at the standards as a thoughtful list of instructional goals they may amend for their own use if they wish. Educators in other fields will find this model analogous and appropriate to their own disciplines.

The accrediting council's goals have evolved from the best thinking of experienced mass communication educators over a period of nearly five decades. Frances C. Volkmann (1992), chairwoman of the Commission on

COURSE	Competence/English	Writing	Reporting	Editing	Visual Communication	Layout/Design	History	Law	Ethics	Mass Communication Theory	Sequence Technology	Gather/Organize Info for Specialty
1001 - Intro. Journalism							√	√	√	√		
2100-News Writing	√	√	√	√				√	√		√	√
3102-Photogrpahy					√	√	√	√	√		√	√
3552-Editing	√	√	√	√		√		√	√		√	√
3771-History	√	√					√	√	√	√		
4201-International	√	√					√	√	√	√		
4651-Law	√	√					√	√	√	√		√
4831-Pub. Design				√	√	√		√	√		√	√
3403-Prin. Advertising	√	√			√	√	√	√	√	√	√	√
3463-Copy/Layout	√	√		√	√	√		√	√	√	√	√
4403-Campaigns	√	√					√	√	√	√	√	√
3604-Broadcast News	√	√	√	√			√	√	√		√	√
3644-Broadcast Prod.				√	√	√		√	√		√	
4644-Station Mgmt.		√					√	√	√		√	

FIG. 15.1. Accrediting standards/curriculum offerings.

Institutions of Higher Education of the New England Association of Schools and Colleges, suggested that "the pressure to change, to improve, to meet a set of educational . . . standards that have been carefully articulated not by governments or religious or other bodies *but by peers* is one of the most important features of the accreditation process" (p. 3, italics added).

The ACEJMC standards emphasize a curricular balance between journalism and mass communication courses and courses in the liberal arts and sciences, taught by departments in other disciplines. Assessment in these general education courses is most typically done by those departments themselves; however, one easily administered national test, the ACT COMP short form, is considered well suited for measuring general education outcomes (Humphreys, 1986, p. 65).

The ACEJMC (1991) curriculum standards suggest, among other goals, that students should learn to "gather, analyze, organize, synthesize, and communicate information in a format appropriate to their areas of specialization" (p. 9).

Further, the ACEJMC says competence in the correct use of the English language should be mastered and demonstrated. Other accreditation standards declare that students should learn basic skills and master writing, reporting, editing, visual communication, layout, design, and "other fundamental techniques appropriate for such specialties as advertising, public relations, and broadcasting" (p. 9). In addition, the association says, students should learn from "philosophical instruction in such areas as history, law, ethics, and mass communications theory" (p. 9).

CURRICULUM DEVELOPMENT: FILLING IN THE GAPS

With these standards, the grid helps identify the extent to which their curriculum covers the potential achievement of each goal. With an examination of course goals, individual courses can be attached to various standards, and units can discover what is being taught, when, and in which courses. This is curriculum development. It starts with program goals, designs a curriculum intended to meet each of those goals, and defines ways to assess students' actual learning, the outcome of instructional efforts.

Outcomes to be assessed, then, can flow from these accreditation standards and goals and from curriculum objectives—usually proposed by faculty curriculum committees, sequence faculty planners or faculty committees of the whole. Curriculum objectives flow to course goals, expressed by instructors in their course syllabi.

And when a faculty member declares in the syllabus, "The goal of this course is to . . . ," how does he or she know if that goal is achieved?

Outcome measures inform individual faculty members. They surely need to know, as they are helping to fill their crucial spot in a coherent program, that they are actually teaching what they think they are teaching. Faculty measures learning all the time—with quizzes, exams, class discussions, term papers, and the like. The fulfillment of curriculum goals obviously emanates from faculty members as they plan a course and answer the critical question, "What do I want students to *learn*? What is the purpose of the course?"

DEFINING OBJECTIVES AND OUTCOMES

Fulfilling curriculum goals begins when the faculty member writes a "perfect" syllabus that includes, among other information, the objectives of the course (see chap. 5). Students should be informed at the outset, according to Sharon Rubin (1985), assistant dean for undergraduate studies at the University of Maryland, where the course leads, intellectually and practically: "Students should be able to find out what they will know by the end of the course, and also what they will be able to do better afterward than before" (p. 56). That is, what will be the outcome for the student? What will the student learn? It is a statement of intended outcomes. Thus, syllabi of all course offerings should reflect in their statements of course objectives at least some of the instructional goals of the department.

An efficient and comprehensive approach to designating objectives based on accreditation standards is to divide them into two categories: knowledge and skills. This division fits comfortably with ACEJMC's ideal balance between "practical skills" and "the more philosophical aspects."

Each specialty or major within a larger academic unit (commonly called a *sequence*) can then describe measurable objectives: What do we want our students to be able to do? What do we want them to know? Interestingly, units going through this process often discover surprising consensus and coherence. Appendix A offers a sample objectives statement.

Objectives by sequence are typically written by sequence faculty. To be useful for outcome assessment, they must be measurable. They should be expressed simply. They need say only what we want students to be able to do and what we want them to know as the result of our instruction. Through examining outcomes, we can assure a far more coherent program.

Sequences find many shared goals that cut across all specialties; for example, knowledge of the nature and functions of contemporary mass media; knowledge of the Constitutional provisions relating to freedom of the press and speech; ability to write correctly, concisely, interestingly, and so forth.

On the other hand, many are sequence specific; for example, knowledge of the economics of broadcast production, knowledge of electronic media organizations, ability to use equipment to shoot and edit broadcast materials, and others.

The possibilities for measures are virtually endless. They might include such measures as conventional academic exams, standardized tests like GRE subject exams, ACT's Proficiency Examination Program tests, ACT's College Outcomes Measures Project assessment, or custom-developed standardized exams (see chap. 16). They might be the examination of student performance in "capstone" courses (see chap. 7), comprehensive papers assessed by faculty other than those teaching the courses, or portfolios collecting a student's work examined by professionals in the field (see chap. 6). Appendix B is an example of measures for a single objective.

Each unit can best design its own measures, based on the availability of testing resources and the nuances of goals that may be peculiar to that particular unit or student body (see Calhoun, 1986; Ewell & Lisensky, 1988). Ewell (1990) offered helpful advice. He suggested four primary considerations in designing assessments in the academic major:

1. *Comprehensiveness*: Assessment procedures should cover knowledge and skills taught throughout the program's curriculum.
2. *Multiple judgments*: Assessment procedures should involve more than one source of evidence or involve multiple judgments of student performance.
3. *Provision of diagnostic information*: Assessment procedures should provide information on multiple dimensions of student performance; that is, they should yield more than a single summative grade.
4. *Directness of assessment*: Assessment procedures should involve at least one type of evidence based on direct observation or demonstration of student capacities; that is, they should involve more than simply a self-report.

ASSESSMENT PAYS AT MANY LEVELS

Outcomes assessment based on accrediting standards allows units to measure themselves against a goal system to which they subscribe—at a minimum, one they respect. Units demonstrate the seriousness of their intent and their good faith effort to reflect those standards by using them as outcome goals to be measured. And outcome assessment pays off in program planning, curriculum development, and enhanced credibility.

Measuring outcomes allows us to think in terms of sequences and at the same time requires us to think about our program as whole, with informed acknowledgment of the contributions of each sequence to the mission of the program.

An understanding of our teaching successes allows us to be honest with students, parents, legislators, and trustees. We can describe our programs to foundations, funders, and academic administrators in concrete terms, not wishful platitudes. How empowering it is to be able to say, "Our students can do A, B, and C. Our graduates know X, Y, and Z," and support those claims with data (see Appendix C).

Perhaps we should stipulate here that we probably cannot measure everything we teach and students learn, but let us measure that knowledge and those skills we can. We will know that much more about what we are doing and why. As we have seen, outcome measures are intended to demonstrate what and how much our students have learned. Those are good things to know. And in this precarious world of litigious students and parents and run-amok legislatures, they are essential to know. Departments can begin with their own grid reflecting ACEJMC instructional standards or their own version of a similar set of standards, as seen in Fig. 15.1.

What follows from the grid, then, is a picture of which standards are being addressed and which are not. We learn which objectives have a chance of being met and which do not. This picture informs curriculum planning and adjustment, suggesting where courses need to be added or current course content expanded. Once that view is clear, the department can enumerate instructional goals, both departmentwide and sequence specific, examples of which are shown in Appendix A.

Next, departments should describe how they will measure outcomes. In most cases, some data are already available. Departments that already use exit interviews should glean outcome information from those (see chap. 8). Sometimes outsider evaluations of interns are routinely gathered and that information can be useful. Some institutions regularly survey students and alumni, and those results are almost always applicable to outcomes assessment.

Units may want to start slowly with the new measurement of only one or two outcomes at a time. Appendix B suggests ways to measure a single outcome, ability to perform in a professional setting.

Finally, once an assessment is made, the unit should report the results, as in Appendix C, to whomever should receive them: perhaps the chief academic officer of the institution and the unit head or dean, and certainly the department's faculty. When results are highly positive, as they often are, departments like to highlight them in alumni newsletters. Certainly, as Lovell (1993) suggested, the information gathered during accreditation studies and outcomes assessments becomes the obvious focus of future outcomes objectives. For further discussion see Appendix D.

APPENDIX A: DEPARTMENT GOALS

Department of Journalism

Department Goals Statement

The Department of Journalism seeks to assure that its graduates have a strong grounding in the liberal arts and possess the knowledge and skills of the profession necessary not only for successful entry-level performance but also for lifelong careers of ever-increasing responsibility and influence.

Instructional Objectives for All Journalism Majors

Knowledge:

1. Knowledge of the nature and functions of contemporary mass media.
2. Knowledge of the history of national and international mass communication.
3. Appreciation for the unique role and responsibility of mass communication in a democracy.
4. Knowledge of the Constitutional provisions relating to freedom of the press and expression.

5. Knowledge of the laws controlling and supporting freedom of the press and expression.
6. Knowledge of the formation and influence of public opinion.
7. Understanding of social responsibility and media ethics.

Skills:

1. The ability to gather information from records and by asking questions.
2. The ability to write correctly, concisely, and interestingly.
3. The ability to perform in a professional setting.

Sequence-Specific Instructional Objectives

Broadcast Majors (Television and Radio)

Knowledge:

1. Knowledge of the economics of electronic media production.
2. Knowledge of structure and organization of electronic media organizations in the United States and abroad.
3. Understanding of the principles of electronic media production.
4. Knowledge sufficient to evaluate electronic media performance.
5. Knowledge of issues and controversies surrounding the effects of electronic news, information and entertainment in society.

Skills:

1. Ability to write general news pieces as well as specialized report packages.
2. Ability to use equipment to shoot and edit broadcast materials.
3. Ability to develop, write, and produce general information and entertainment programs, both short and long form, such as documentaries, panel discussions, and sporting events.
4. Ability to synthesize complex material and present it through the electronic media in an easy-to-understand manner.
5. Ability to present news and information in an appropriate and acceptable manner through radio and television.

News-Editorial Majors (Print)

Knowledge:

1. Knowledge of the structure and organization of print media in the United States and abroad.

2 Knowledge of the economics of print media organizations.

3. Knowledge sufficient to evaluate print media performance.

Skills:

1. Ability to report with accuracy, fairness, and balance.
2. Ability to write general news pieces as well as specialized reports.
3. Ability to correct and perfect story manuscripts for publication.
4. Ability to execute appropriate publication design.

Advertising Majors

Knowledge:

1. Understanding of the relationship of advertising to the presentation of news and entertainment.
2. Knowledge of the organization of the advertising industry.
3. Understanding of research techniques applicable to the industry.
4. Knowledge of how advertising programs are planned and evaluated.
5. Understanding of the principles of advertising writing and design.
6. Knowledge of the principles of advertising campaign planning.
7. Knowledge of issues and controversies surrounding the effects of the industry in society at large.

Skills:

1. Ability to analyze a communication problem to determine if it is amenable to solution through advertising.
2. Ability to analyze a communication problem and to present succinct arguments for recommendations.
3. Ability to develop a comprehensive written plan for the solution of a communication problem.
4. Ability to present complex material persuasively using oral, visual, and written forms.

APPENDIX B: SAMPLE MEASURES OF THE OBJECTIVE ABILITY TO PERFORM IN A PROFESSIONAL SETTING

1. The Department will submit to a panel of three expert broadcast professionals videotapes of three editions of its live cable news program—written, produced, directed, and performed by advanced broadcast students in their capstone courses.

2. The Department will submit to a panel of three expert newspaper professionals three issues of its student newspaper—written, edited, designed, promoted, and supported by news editorial students.

3. The Department will ask a panel of at least three expert advertising professionals to assess the presentation of its advanced advertising students in the American Advertising Federation's Regional Student Advertising Competition.

All expert judges will be asked to evaluate students' work by their own professional standards.

APPENDIX C: ASSESSING OBJECTIVES/OUTCOMES

DEPARTMENT OF JOURNALISM
1992–1993 Assessment Report
Goal Assessed: Ability to Perform in a Professional Setting

Methods Used:

Evaluation of Broadcast Sequence. Three professional broadcasters independently reviewed videotapes of three representative editions of the live cable news program, "The Campus Report," which is written, directed, and performed by advanced broadcast students.

Evaluation of News-Editorial Sequence. Three professional journalists independently reviewed three issues of "The Campus Voice," which is written, edited, designed, and promoted by news-editorial students.

Evaluation of Advertising Sequence. A panel of advertising professionals assessed the presentation of advanced advertising students in the American Advertising Federation's District Student Advertising Competition.

Evaluation of All Sequences. As a new measure for 1992–1993, evaluations by professional work supervisors for the Department's interns were analyzed, tabulated, and assessed.

Validation. In each case, students evaluated are typical of their cohorts, because the activities are capstone and involve at one time or another virtually all majors.

The Broadcast sequence evaluators were:

xxxxxx xxxxxxxx, News Producer. KPIX-TV, San Francisco.
xxxxxx xxxxxxxx, News Producer, WLOX-TV, Biloxi, MS.
xxxxxx xxxxxxxx, Executive Producer, WSMV-TV, Nashville, TN.

The News-Editorial sequence evaluators were:
xxxxxxxx xxxxxx, Reporter, Rocky Mountain News, Denver, CO.
xxxxxx xxxxxxx, Section Editor, Daily Camera, Boulder, CO.
xxxxxx xxxxxxx, Editor, Sentinal Newspapers, suburban Denver.

The Advertising sequence evaluators were:
Judges in the AAF district competition: xxxx xxxxx, xxxxxx xxxxx, xxxxx xxxxxx and xxxx xxxx—all marketing and advertising professionals.

Outcomes Assessment

The Broadcast sequence evaluators agree the Department is providing an excellent and rare opportunity for its Broadcast students. Applying the same standards they use to evaluate their own newscasts, evaluators note the work is very good. They praised many stories and noted the high quality of reporters and anchors. Evaluators suggested needed improvement in writing and flow. They also noted a need for more and better graphics. 1992–1993 evaluations show marked improvement over 1991–1992.

The News-Editorial sequence evaluators reported that "The Campus Voice" is interesting, well written, comprehensive, and balanced—professionally done. Design is acceptable, following standard rules. Grammar, spelling, and style are excellent. Evaluators praised the addition of the Focus page, devoted to in-depth articles. Critics agreed that in some cases stories needed to be better researched, more fact based, and better organized. They suggested improvements in photography, page layout, and editorial page design.

The Advertising sequence evaluators judged advertising students the best in district competition, noting that their work is highly professional and praiseworthy. They noted that students think strategically as well as executionally. The Department's emphasis on integrated marketing communication set students apart because they understood the necessity of taking into consideration all of the target audiences and all of the different ways these audiences can be reached and motivated. Students' presentation skills were unusual and outstanding. Students' weakest area was developing media plans.

All Sequences: The quality of on-the-job work by 89 students in all sequences was assessed by their professional internship supervisors. The single summary measure, *Career potential*, was tabulated for all 89. On the following scale—Excellent, Very Good, Good, Average, Below Average, and Poor—the results were as follows: Excellent, 52; Very Good, 22; Good, 10;

Average, 5; Below Average, 0; Poor, 0. Thus, 58% were considered excellent; 83% were considered either excellent or very good.

A sampling of internship assignments indicates such diverse responsibilities as the City of Norwood, *Entertainment Tonight* in Los Angeles, the Associated Press, IBM, the Washington offices of Senator Tim Wirth and Rep. Tom Petri, all four major Denver television stations, PBS, newspapers in . . . the Woodward Health Center—and some 75 other intern employers all over the country.

Comments from intern employers support the Department's reading that students are being prepared to perform well in professional settings: "On behalf of the entire staff, I wish to express our deepest appreciation to the Department for developing students as outstanding as Mr. xxxx." "I don't know what I'll do without xxxx." "There are only a few soon-to-be college grads who have what it takes to begin newsroom work immediately upon graduation. Xxxxx is one of the few. She is a testament to the effectiveness of your program."

These results are taken to mean that students in all sequences are performing in an admirably professional way.

Program Changes

Broadcast faculty will emphasize instruction and experience in writing, flow, and delivery. The Department will seek resources to improve the extent and quality of graphics.

News-Editorial faculty will encourage comprehensiveness in reporting and urge redesign of the editorial page to create a better sense of coherence. They will insist that photography be improved. Emphasis will be on tighter writing and better organization of stories. Classroom instruction in reporting, design, and photography will reinforce these improvements as well.

Advertising faculty will continue to orient undergraduate advertising instruction toward integrated marketing communication and will build more rigor into the media planning course. The faculty also propose a new course in marketing communication skills that will focus on writing and presenting.

APPENDIX D: RECOMMENDED READINGS

Aper, J. P., & Hinkle, J. P. (1992). State policies for assesssing student outcomes: A case study with implications for state and institutional authorities. *Journal of Higher Education, 62*(5), 539–555.

Astin, A. W. (1974). Measuring the outcomes of higher education. In H. Bowen (Ed.), *Evaluating institutions for accountability.* San Francisco: Jossey-Bass.

Astin, A. W. (1979). Student-oriented management: A proposal for change. In *Evaluating educational quality: A conference summary* (pp. 3–18). Washington, DC: Council on Postsecondary Accreditation.

Astin, A. W. (1990). Educational assessment and educational equity. *American Journal of Education, 98*(4), 458–493.

Astin, A. W. (1992). Values, assessment, and academic freedom: A challenge to the accrediting process. *NCA Quarterly: A Publication of the North Central Association, 67*, 295–306.

Banta, T. W. (Ed.). (1986). *Performance funding in higher education: A critical analysis of Tennessee's experience.* San Francisco: Jossey-Bass.

Banta, T. W. (Ed.). (1988a). *Implementing outcomes assessment: Promise and perils.* New Directions for Institutional Research (Serial No. 59). San Francisco: Jossey-Bass.

Banta, T. W. (Ed.). (1988b). *Student outcomes assessment: Promise and pitfalls.* New Directions for Institutional Research (Serial No. 47). San Francisco: Jossey-Bass.

Banta, T. W., & Pike, G. R. (1989). Methods for comparing outcomes assessment instruments. *Research in Higher Education, 30*(5), 455–469.

Bowen, H. R. (Ed.). (1974). *Evaluating institutions for accountability.* San Francisco: Jossey-Bass.

Ewell, P. T. (1983a). *Information on student outcomes: How to get it and how to use it: Executive overview.* Boulder, CO: National Center for Higher Education Management Systems.

Ewell, P. T. (1983b). Program reviews: Inputs and outputs. *NCHEMS Monograph 5.* Boulder: National Center for Higher Education Management Systems.

Ewell, P. T. (1985a). *Assessing educational outcomes.* New Directions for Institutional Research (Serial No. 47). San Francisco: Jossey-Bass.

Ewell, P. T. (1985b). Transformation leadership for improving student outcomes. *NCHEMS Monograph 6.* Boulder, CO: National Center for Higher Education Management Systems.

Ewell, P. T. (1991). *Benefits and costs of assessment in higher education: A framework for choicemaking.* Boulder, CO: National Center for Higher Education Management Systems.

Halpern, D. (Ed.). (1987). *Student outcomes assessment: What institutions have to gain.* New Directions for Institutional Research (Series No. 39). San Francisco: Jossey-Bass.

Jacobi, M., Astin, A., & Ayala, F. (1987). *College student outcomes assessment: A talent development perspective.* College Station, TX: Association for the Study of Higher Education.

Lenning, O. T. (Ed.). (1976). *Improving educational outcomes.* New Directions for Higher Education. Boulder, CO: National Center for Higher Education Management Systems.

Muffo, J. A. (1992). The status of student outcomes assessment at NASULGC member institutions. *Research in Higher Education, 33*(6), 765–774.

Pace, C. R. (1979). *Measuring outcomes of college.* San Francisco: Jossey-Bass.

Romney, L. C., Bogen, G., & Micek, S. (1979). Assessing institutional performance: The importance of being careful. *International Journal of Institutional Management in Higher Education, 3*, 79ff.

Terenzini, P. T. (1989). Assessment with open eyes: Pitfalls in studying students outcomes. *Journal of Higher Education, 60*(6), 644–664.

Young, K. E., Chambers, C. M., & Kells, H. R. (1983). *Understanding accreditation.* San Francisco: Jossey-Bass.

REFERENCES

Accrediting Council on Education in Journalism and Mass Communications (ACEJMC). (1991). *Accredited journalism and mass communications education 1991–92.* Lawrence, KS: Author.

Banta, T. W. (1985). Use of outcomes information at the University of Tennessee, Knoxville. In P. T. Ewell (Ed.), *Assessing educational outcomes* (pp. 19–32). San Francisco: Jossey-Bass.

Calhoun, W. H. (1986). Measuring achievement in the major field. In T. W. Banta (Ed.), *Performance funding in higher education: A critical analysis of Tennessee's experience* (pp. 73–83). Boulder, CO: National Center for Higher Education Management Systems.

Ewell, P. T. (1990). *ASJMC administrators' workshop on outcomes assessment: Support materials*. Boulder, CO: National Center for Higher Education Management Systems.

Ewell, P. T., & Lisensky, R. P. (1988). *Assessing institutional effectiveness*. Washington, DC: Consortium for the Advancement of Private Higher Education.

Hebert, E., & Thorn, D. (1993). Accreditation as a tool of accountability and incentive. *Journalism Educator, 47*(4), 55–62.

Humphreys, W. L. (1986). Measuring achievement in general education. In T. W. Banta (Ed.), *Performance funding in higher education: A critical analysis of Tennessee's experience* (pp. 61–71). Boulder, CO: National Center for Higher Education Management Systems.

Jaschik, S. (1991, March 13). Education dept. accreditation panel thrust into midst of some of higher education's most volatile issues. *Chronicle of Higher Education*, pp. A21–22.

Leatherman, C. (1991, September 18). Specialized accrediting agencies challenged by campus officials. *Chronicle of Higher Education*, pp. A1, A22.

Lovell, C. D. (1993, November). *Meeting our responsibility for student outcomes assessment: Part 1*. Paper presented at the National Association for Student Personnel Administrators Annual Conference, Boston, MA.

Neel, C. W. (1986). Accreditation as a performance indicator. In T. W. Banta (Ed.), *Performance funding in higher education: A critical analysis of Tennessee's experience* (pp. 55–60). Boulder, CO: National Center for Higher Education Management Systems.

Rubin, S. S. (1985, August 7). Professors, students, and the syllabus. *Chronicle of Higher Education*, p. 56.

Volkmann, F. C. (1992, October). *Regional accreditation and general education: An emphasis on accountability*. Paper presented at the annual conference of the National Association for General and Liberal Studies, Columbus, OH.

Wolff, R. A. (1993, June 9). Restoring the credibility of accreditation. *Chronicle of Higher Education*, pp. 1–2B.

16

Exit Examinations for the Media Major

Susan Tyler Eastman
Indiana University

Departments of mass communication employ about 15 different types of assessment to measure either their students' individual achievement or the curriculum and teaching. Of these, exit examinations for seniors have raised the most apprehension nationwide. This chapter reports the results of a national survey of 276 4-year colleges and universities teaching mediated communications under such departmental titles as mass communication, radio-television, broadcasting, telecommunications, and mass media. Results (response rate exceeded 82%) showed that 94% of media departments do not use exit tests, and that most of the 6% that do use them to measure improvements in curriculum and teaching, not individual student achievement. And even when individual student outcomes are the goal, few schools make passing exit tests a requirement for graduation. Conclusions drawn from surveys and interviews with media faculty suggest a 10-part assessment decision-making model to guide other faculty and administrators in setting an assessment course.

INTRODUCTION

Should Media Departments Be Testing Their Majors?

Testing students as they leave school to find out what they know is an idea with immediate appeal. After all, higher education successfully uses comprehensive or preliminary exams to test what graduate students know, so that model could be applied to university undergraduates. Indeed, the U.S. Department of Education's Goal 5.5 calls for assessment of the communication skills of all college graduates, a task many schools have taken on (see chap. 1). Ervin (1988) called for "journalism and mass communication departments to band together to create a specialized examination that [would] be administered uniformly on the undergraduate academic level" (p. 22). Kittross (1989) drew attention to a diagnostic test for graduate students entering Michigan State University (first described by Baldwin & Surlin, 1970). Kittross asserted that this exam could easily "be converted to a final check of the knowledge (if not the skills) level of graduating seniors" (p. 31) and might eventually lead to a standardized nationwide instrument. Pushing the social science research model one step further, educators could even test students as they enter (a *pretest*) and before they leave (a *posttest*), subtract, and plausibly presume the gain is what students learned in school (Wolf, 1989). Such tests could be used to weed out the few students who sneak through the system without learning enough, however much enough is, and such tests could be used to compare schools and even teachers on how well they educate. Unfortunately, or perhaps quite fortunately, such testing has fallen far short of expectations in successfully measuring acquired student knowledge, and has far exceeded expectations about cost.

Why Is Assessment an Issue Now?

We are living in the age of assessment. The idea of assessing achievement—in the sense of measuring, comparing, ranking, and judging—schools, teachers, curricula, and teaching methods is an outgrowth of the philosophy of *accountability* (see chap. 1). Increasingly, both government and the public are trying to find ways to hold the recipients of public funds responsible for what they do with that money. In the case of education, government officials and the public want assurance that students are indeed being educated. No longer does a college degree automatically guarantee employment and high earnings. Too many cases of high school graduates who cannot read and college graduates who cannot spell have waved a big red flag at the cow of education. Concern about the quality of undergraduate teaching in light of rapidly increasing tuition costs is forcing universities and colleges to justify themselves. The public now mistrusts education and educators, and, in response, governments seek to hold colleges and universities accountable. They want a warranty on education.

Even respected scholars deplore the achievements of present-day higher education on the undergraduate level. John Wallace (1985) for example, Professor of Philosophy and administrator at the University of Minnesota, decried "(a) the lack of purposiveness in undergraduate education and (b) widespread failure to achieve the learning outcomes we profess for undergraduate education" (p. 3). And sensation-mongering books such as *Profscam* outrage the public and press.

In theory, more or better assessment is an appealing response to these complaints. Assessing what is achieved can improve curricula, motivate teachers, motivate students, and can, if positive outcomes are demonstrated, silence the unbelievers. On the other hand, Ernst Benjamin (1990), general secretary of the American Association of University Professors, objected to this idealization: "Assessment promotes a misdiagnosis of the problems of undergraduate instruction. The deficiencies of undergraduate instruction are not due primarily to poor teaching and will not be remedied by improving the teaching of individual instructors. Rather, the problems of undergraduate instruction are systemic and are best summarized as inadequate 'involvement in learning'" (p. B2).

Even so, when assessment has been mandated by state legislators or university administrative fiat, the question often becomes *what type of assessment*. In spite of persuasive arguments from prestigious educational associations, among them the American Association of University Professors (1990), in favor of multiple assessment measures rather than standardized outcomes testing, states such as New Jersey, Oklahoma, Tennessee, and Illinois have decreed quantifiable outcomes testing for general education and in the major, and Texas, Colorado, Virginia, Missouri, Louisiana, and Kentucky have instituted economic or accreditation pressures with similar effects. Tennessee, for example, has tied a portion of higher education funding (called *performance funding*) directly to explicit demands for quantitative tests in major fields. The Tennessee Higher Education Commission (1992) specified that campuses may use either an externally developed test (from an approved list) or a test developed locally in accordance with its guidelines. Florida, Georgia, and South Dakota also have established statewide assessment. Several of these states have espoused the "value added" approach, requiring state-supported colleges and universities to demonstrate how much their students have gained since entering college. However, Boyer, Ewell, Finney, and Mingle (1987) pointed out that "most of the newer statewide programs, on the other hand [excepting Tennessee], are explicitly avoiding the 'rising junior' or 'value-added' approaches typified by these early entrants" (p. 3).

What Is Accreditation's Role?

Higher education's accreditation bodies are also getting into the act by demanding that universities document their students' academic achievement as a criterion for accreditation (see chap. 3). The North Central Association, for example, requires universities to have "clear and publicly stated purposes," show how they have organized their resources to achieve these purposes, and demonstrate ongoing progress in accomplishing these purposes (Allison, 1993, p. 6). Such general requirements can be met through documentation of student and faculty recruitment and retention practices, financial audits and budgeting procedures, safety and space allocations, library acquisitions, and academic degree program viability. Only the last of these has any faint connection with the major, and even there, accrediting agencies have traditionally been more directly concerned with the addition, reduction, or elimination of departments and programs than with student outcomes achievement, although indirectly, all these factors affect how well the faculty teaches. However, beginning in the 1990s, accrediting associations turned their attention to assessment in general education and the major (see Eshelman, 1990).

How Do Schools Define Assessment?

Assessment at its best is about both learning and teaching. According to Indiana University's Associate Dean of the Faculty Barbara Wolf (1989):

> [Assessment] is about expanding student accomplishments rather than homogenizing them. It is about empowering teachers and learners to determine explicit expectations and to know whether they are being met. In the process, there is change and, as other institutions are beginning to show, there is refinement in curricular design and improved student performance. Implicit in these effects is the relationship of assessment to improved faculty performance in the teaching arena. (p. 5)

Many administrators of large research institutions call for increased integration of research and teaching, seeing that as a means of empowering undergraduate education in the competition for scarce resources (Wallace, 1985). However, one monumental review of more than 2,500 pieces of research on higher education showed that students "make statistically significant gains in factual knowledge and in a range of general cognitive and intellectual skills" in college, but change little in values and beliefs (Pascarella & Terenzini, 1991, quoted in Lewis, 1992, p. 46). Given the broad goals of most institutions, reflected in requirements for humanities as well as science courses and increasing numbers of ethics courses, these results are discouraging. And the public, the business community, and state officials responsible for funding higher education are demanding an accounting of what schools do.

Is Testing the Right Type of Assessment?

Objections to outcomes testing are legion. Nielsen and Polishook (1990), for example, claimed: "Despite their superficial appeal, such schemes are as likely to harm as enhance the educational process, and their results are as likely to confuse as inform" (p. A14). Students do not start with the same knowledge, ability, and skills, never have the same formal and informal learning experiences when in school, and gain different things even from the same lessons. Students differ too much from one another and what they learn is too diffuse and too diverse to ever be captured meaningfully in standardized tests. Such tests seem to measure mostly one's ability to perform well on future similar tests, the traditional (but unloved) fare of college course examinations. Thus, proposals to institute standardized pretests and posttests to measure what students learned in school look like sieves. Many teachers contemplate more standardized testing with despair. They justifiably complain such tests fail to measure much of anything worth measuring about their students (Eastman, 1987). Goals such as developing cognitive skills, adding to intellectual capacity, developing creative capacity, and enhancing depth of appreciation and understanding lie beyond quantitative measurement (Nielsen & Polishook, 1990).

Ironically, along with calls for assessment, faculty can hear the clarion call for improving our schools, in part by moving away from standardized tests of facts and definitions toward a focus on qualitative and affective learning and increased application of concepts and skills. The dangers of "teaching to the test," fostering intellectual conformity, and the invitation to concentrate on the trivial and devalue the controversial and unmeasurable have been widely touted. Indeed, the challenge of multiculturalism moves colleges and universities further away from core curricula and thus further from common bodies of knowledge about which to test (Chase, 1990).

Some objections to outcomes testing recede if testing efforts are focused only on cumulative learning in the major field of study. After all, college students are relatively mature, and the body of knowledge in the upper division major is relatively fixed, some say. Is it not possible to measure what students know about media (radio-television? telecommunications? broadcasting?) as they enter as first-year students, or whenever they indicate interest in the major, and then test them again as graduating seniors to assess what they have learned? Could we not adopt the graduate-student model and give minicomprehensive exams to senior undergraduates to see if they have learned enough to deserve to graduate? (And further, to see if some departments and some teachers teach better than others?) Raising Kittross' implied question, is it appropriate to measure undergraduate outcomes with tests designed for entering graduate students? Would we be testing for the same things?

What Can This Chapter Tell Me?

The topic of outcomes assessment has relevance for all communication programs, whether in media, speech, or theatre. This chapter focuses solely on the field of media because so little has been written about it. It summarizes the key issues and describes appropriate types of major outcomes assessment. Then the chapter reports the results of a nationwide study of electronic communication departments on the subject of exit examinations, analyzes the tests that some colleges and universities now use, and finally proposes a model of what can and cannot be effectively achieved in this arena by media departments. The chapter's conclusions, however, have importance for educators and students in all communication fields.

WHAT IS KNOWN ABOUT ASSESSMENT IN THE MEDIA MAJOR?

Experts in the assessment field conclude that small liberal arts colleges can effectively tackle across-the-board assessment in general education, whereas large research universities should undertake assessment at the departmental level (Magner, 1989). However, according to the bibliography maintained by the Assessment Resource Center at the University of Tennessee, more than 40 fields lack national exams, including, to no one's surprise, communications and journalism.

Ervin (1988) summarized the advantages of national testing instruments for the major as (a) saving faculty time, (b) providing norms for comparison, and (c) theoretically resolving questions of credibility and validity (although others, such as Baker, 1986, argued that point). He contrasted the advantages of local instruments as (a) reflecting the local curriculum, (b) serving as a valuable tool for planning and curricular revision, and (c) involving faculty input (and by implication, their support). However, Ervin (1988) noted that both objective and essay tests require time and resources, commodities in short supply in media departments. Objective tests provide only limited coverage of content, and text constuction and constant rewriting are costly; essay tests take longer and are much harder to grade according to any standard guidelines.

What Dangers and Costs Come with Exit Testing?

Carol Schneider, Executive Vice President of the Association of American Colleges, efficiently pointed to faculty's two main concerns: "Faculty members in general are suspicious of and resistant to efforts to develop cumulative assessments of students' learning in the major, partly because they are wary about the uses to which assessment findings will be put, especially in state systems, and partly because of the predictable costs in faculty time and energy" (Wolf, 1989, p. 8).

At publicly supported universities, the very real danger arises of having quantitative student assessments twisted into measures of teaching achievement, thus affecting retention, promotion, and salary setting. For media departments, this can be particularly acute because they typically operate under enormous pressure to accommodate more students relative to the size of faculty and facilities than older departments; curricula are often interdisciplinary in nature and rapidly changing, not lending themselves to easy understanding by more traditional faculty; media faculty's research and teaching is usually widely varied in content, methods, and philosophical approach, making mutual agreement on evaluation of achievements difficult to achieve. Moreover, media attracts relatively little by way of grant money compared to the hard and social sciences. But typically, the larger, traditional departments can best spare the faculty to sit on tenure and promotion committees (and are the departments that many deans look to first). Thus, assessment in the major carries more threat to faculty in media departments than in the traditional fields.

At universities adopting responsibility-center management (RCM) and responsibility-center budgeting (RCB), the threat of financial impact becomes particularly critical if the department resides in an arts and sciences college rather than a school or college of communication. In theory, units of the university are designated *responsibility centers* and control their own income (tuition and other funds) and expenses (salaries and facilities). In practice, both large units with large budgets and those generating outside income in the form of grants and patent royalties tend to be in a better position than either small units or those without outside revenues (where electronic media departments typically fall).

Furthermore, locally devised instruments are extremely time consuming as they usually require psychometric expertise and extensive pilot testing, presuming that the faculty could agree on what to test for. For large universities, the process from start up at the university level to initial data collection at the departmental level is estimated at 3 to 5 years. Too often departments have rushed into commitments entailing exit exams without allowing for the years that proper pilot testing necessitates and without the expertise in psychometrics that developing recognized reliability and validity measures requires. Of course, expertise can be hired, but repeated testing of several classes of graduating seniors cannot be rushed.

Some hair-raising data are available on the costs of cumulative testing. These costs include the measurement instrument, its administration (proctoring if needed), the statistical analysis of results (and sometimes data entry), and coordination or supervision of assessment activities. In mass communication departments, which are small compared to many traditional university departments such as history, English, and biology, administration, analysis, and coordination probably can be handled by graduate students or faculty. This usually will involve a budget for hiring the students or released time for the faculty. But the enormous cost lies in developing locally specific examinations. They are estimated to require over $3,000 per exam (Wolf, 1989, p. 10), an amount far beyond the reach of many departmental budgets.

How Do Faculty Define the Field?

One problem arises in considering departments of journalism and departments of communication in the same breath. The former tend toward applied professional education; the latter contain some with the same goal (in, say, television production) and many others with more in common with departments of humanities or social science and little direct concern with professional job preparation (see Blanchard & Christ, 1993; Eastman, 1985; Gomery, 1985; Limberg, 1987; Porter & Szolka, 1991; Sterling, 1985; Webster, 1989). Although professional journalists have loudly criticized the way colleges and universities prepare future journalists (consider the *Roper Report, Electronic Media Career Preparation Study*, 1987), no such constituency exits for the broader field of electronic communication and its fellows, radio-television, telecommunications, and so on.

Ervin (1988) found that 39% of journalism schools responding to his survey utilized outcomes assessment, but their definitions of what was appropriate ranged from ordinary assignments and grades to course evaluations concerned with the worth of the instructor and course to, in a very few cases, standardized exit testing. In the late 1980s, a few media departments experimented with the ACT, the Cooperative English Exam (COOP), or the general portion of the GRE, but recognized their inappropriateness for measuring major achievement in broadcasting, journalism, radio-television, telecommunications, and so on.

How Do Faculty Define Test Content?

Finally, but perhaps most significant, is the issue of *what to test* within the major. The interdisciplinary field of mass communications subdivides itself into departments focusing on production and application, business and management careers, critical studies and aesthetics, broadcasting to the exclusion of alternate technologies or, conversely, telecommunications, downplaying traditional broadcasting. Only a few telecommunications departments give telephone more than lip service. Furthermore, the field encompasses departments of journalism with a few mass communication courses and departments excluding all journalism. The range in size of schools, number of faculty, number of students, and number and kinds of courses is almost beyond counting (Robinson & Kamalipour, 1991). A single national test seems impossibly visionary.

But even on the local level, students at a large university have programs within the major as diverse as the overall departments already described. Indiana University, for example, divides its undergraduate offerings into the four areas of Management and Strategies; Design and Production; Technology, Economics, and Policy; and Society and Culture, but permits as many as a dozen specialties within the broad classifications to accommodate differing student goals and abilities. In contrast, Grambling State University divides its major into Visual Communications, Public Relations, Broadcast Production, News Editorial, and Broadcast News. Some students have well-defined job goals; others are uncertain or concerned more with breadth of education than immediate employment. Moreover, many students graduate without wholly fulfilling any track as specific classes may be unavailable, overenrolled, or conflicting in scheduled time, and following a plan is voluntary anyway. Thus, devising a test to measure the learning of such diverse seniors on more than the most superficial level seems impractical.

Moreover, information in the media field does not hold still. The key facts and concepts for students a decade ago are no longer quite so important (consider reregulation of broadcasting) or may even be reversed (consider the industry's reversal from the principle of scarcity necessitating program parsimony to the expectation of immense channel capacity as a result of digital compression). Even the main entities in the field are not now who they were a decade ago. Repeated revolutionary transformations of assumptions, theories, and practices so characterizes the fundamentals of electronic media that the experiences of such disciplines as history, English, and sciences provide little guidance. Textbook author F. Leslie Smith (1980) bemoaned quick changes in broadcasting; think how much more sweepingly the industry has changed and continues to change now.

But perhaps the most serious issue is the tightening pressure for professionalism, defined increasingly as vocationally oriented programs at many small and midsized colleges and universities. Benjamin (1990) outlined this danger: "[Testing] would encourage students' tendency toward excessive specialization and vocationalism and diminish the opportunity major provides for independent and analytical inquiry" (p. B1).

What Are the Ethical Risks?

Based on a 1989 survey of 91 schools with membership in the Association of Schools of Journalism and Mass Communication for Education (ASJMC), Eshelman (1991) outlined five ethical dangers associated with exit testing. Indeed, he indicted outcomes assessment because of the risk of creating untenable situations for faculty and administrators, and his conclusions apply to a wide range of major departments.

The first ethical risk is that departments can be coerced into adopting meaningless tests lacking all educational validity in response to political pressure. One such test Eshelman described consists of 25 questions from each of several mass communication courses; students are not required to pass the test and have no incentive to study for it. He also made the second point that standardized tests cannot measure the creative skills that are essential parts of the artistic and craft components of journalism and broadcast education, and thus most exit testing measures little of value, although departments must, in the academic way of things, make claims for the validity of tests.

Eshelman went on to make the third point that the answers to the questions used in many standardized tests often can be bought on the street, reporting examples from major newspaper investigations of test buying. Eshelman's fourth ethical criticism relates to "teaching to the test" (p. 20), the strategy of teaching students what they need to know to pass. A fifth danger occurs when departments are pressured to show improvement in average scores; tests can be refined by eliminating difficult questions and substituting easier ones, thus raising average scores as desired. None of these practices is educationally and morally sound, and compelling or coercing departments into exit testing reflects administrators' and legislators' misunderstandings about the nature of the learning process and the goals of undergraduate education.

How Do Faculty React?

Having more than a small inkling of these concerns, most faculty, especially in interdisciplinary fields such as communications, initially resist the idea of exit examinations and often succeed in postponing serious developmental efforts for many years, even when such testing is mandated at the state or university level. Ervin (1988) quoted one administrator's candid response: "These standardized tests provide easy scoring but the questions asked did not report how much his graduates had learned, but the GRE satisfied the Provost; if it satisfies his interest, we don't want to rock the boat" (p. 22). However, it should be noted that Schneider (quoted in Wolf, 1989) concluded that "faculty members who participate in assessments of students' cumulative learning are frequently both enlightened and engaged by the findings" (p. 8). Whether such a conclusion is warranted for media-related fields is unknown.

Some kind of assessment in the major, however, is mandated in many states, by accrediting associations, and by some universities. Moreover, it can bring rewards in terms of reallocation of university resources and reaccreditation. For those with sincere commitment to teaching, one key purpose for assessing students' cumulative learning is to find out whether content, skills, and attitudes are indeed integrated, an explicit or implicit goal of most major programs. Moreover, assessment, at its best, can show how the learning process can be enhanced or streamlined (Wolf, 1989). In addition, it can become an opportunity for imaginative integrative approaches as in the hypercard applications being developed by Professor David Brain for the field of sociology at New College at the University of South Florida (Wolf, 1989, personal communication, September 23, 1992).

OUTCOMES ASSESSMENT OPTIONS?

In addition to overall program review, nearly a dozen kinds of outcome assessment within the major field can be identified. Many of these focus on knowledge of content, but they are largely indirect measurements, test only in one narrow area, or are not suited to administration at the pregraduation level.

Standardized Curricula

One form of assessment within the major is standardizing the curriculum in order to give every student approximately the same academic preparation, presumably the best preparation that educators can devise. Speakers at recent Broadcast Education Association conventions have argued for and against proposals for specific core courses to standardize the media field. For proponents, the argument turns on identification of fundamentals that all media students "should know"; on the negative side, opposing any national curriculum, the argument is that the goals and faculty resources of departments vary so widely that commonalities beyond the introductory course content (already embodied in several widely used textbooks) are impossible.

Leaving aside other schools, another form of standardized curricular design is the *core program* within a single department. Some faculties identify concepts, theoretical arenas, and skills specific to the major that they require of all majors (Schwalbe, 1991). Having a core of courses required of all majors implies that this body of knowledge and skills is essential for the degree. Regular course testing and graded assignments have traditionally been presumed to account adequately for command of this knowledge. Indeed, several instructors may use the same examinations across many sections of the same course. However, in most media departments, core courses occur at the entry level (or lower division) rather than senior level. Thus, having a core can simultaneously imply a standard body of knowledge but not be amenable to exit testing because the core courses generally are taken 2 or even 4 years before graduation. Both students and faculty perceive some unfairness about testing material covered several years prior to the exam. Moreover, questions on introductory material do not approach what is meant by cumulative or comprehensive testing in the major.

Moreover, there is wide disagreement on what constitutes an appropriate core. Dates (1990) for example, argued for a grounding in history, ethics, and communication theory; others speak up for industry studies (Kamalipour, 1992) or production, or a mix (Carroll, 1987). The *Roper Report (Electronic Media Career Preparation Study*, 1987) fired up debate about the required and optional curriculum. However, a department with a set of core courses has at least taken the first step toward identifying a common body of knowledge. Whether this knowledge is, and even ought to be, retained in testable form until near graduation is an open question.

Whether very large, diverse departments can or should have a well-defined core of courses depends, at least in part, on whether they are within a college of communication or a college of arts and sciences. In the first circumstance, they must replace a basic liberal arts curriculum, and a strong core consisting of several courses is an appropriate tool for structuring that learning experience. In the second situation, the curriculum largely serves as an upper division major, and its very diversity limits its ability to require both breadth and depth.

Observation

Another method of finding out what and perhaps how much students are learning in the major is to directly observe classes. Although this can provide a realistic assessment of student abilities, it best suits production and performance classes when the purpose is evaluating *student* learning. Observing in large lecture classes can provide considerable information about teaching and tell something about how much the students are paying attention and interacting, but provides little information about how much factual and conceptual knowledge they have gained. And of course, regular, systematic observation of all classes carries the price tag of enormous demands for more of faculty's already limited time and energy.

Peer Review

External review by faculty from other institutions is widely used to assess the quality and viability of programs (see Schwalbe, 1991, for one report of assessment in a communications department). Typically, established senior faculty with expertise in the department's specialties and in program evaluation are invited to spend a couple of days reading reports, listening to presentations, and asking questions about a department and its faculty, curriculum, finances, and students, ultimately preparing a written assessment of the department's strengths and weaknesses, its reputation, and the field's likely future. Such assessments are useful in setting goals for departments and criteria for allocating resources to meet needs and goals, but tell little about what and how much students are learning. Such assessments depend on the assumption that an academically strong faculty, adequate facilities and budget, and a curriculum consistent with that of most similar programs will provide an ideal learning environment, and thus learning will take place. Although these are reasonable, even practical assumptions, they are a long way from precise measures of students' cumulative learning.

Rising Junior Exams

One counterpart to cumulative examinations is the entrance exam, a test administered to second-semester sophomores or low juniors as a requirement of admittance to the program. Few 4-year schools utilize such tests in the communications-related departments, but many employ a cutoff grade in either prerequisite or entry-level classes. Indiana University's Telecommunications Department, for example, for many years required all majors and minors to achieve an average grade of C in two lower division introductory courses surveying the history, regulation, economics, programming, technology, and social effects of the electronic media.

A variant on the rising junior exam at a 4-year college is the cumulative exit examination given at the end of 2 years at a community or 2-year college. Such a test measures introductory material and what might be gained in a 2-year major program. These tests need not face the immense diversity of individual programs that characterize 4-year curricula.

Production Skill Tests

Many departments measure the ability of their undergraduates to handle television or radio equipment. Called production, equipment, or operations tests, such tests are often administered in order to certify some students to utilize expensive video equipment away from the classroom or to permit certified students to operate a radio station without direct supervision. Although these are certainly a form of assessment, they are rarely applied to all students and are generally not a graduation requirement.

Writing Skills Tests

Another type of requirement necessitates passing a writing skills test administered by the department, sometimes taken before or during major studies or just prior to graduation (Meeske, 1980). At schools such as San Francisco State University, the test becomes a requirement for upper division status and thus enough school time remains for remedial writing help before course work is completed. As a graduation requirement, however, a writing test has little diagnostic value and must be considered an exit exam intended to uphold the honor of the department or university in the eyes of the external world by awarding degrees only to students with minimal writing skill.

Internships

Still another method of assessing student application and integration of learning is the industry internship (see chap. 8). This provides qualitative rather than quantitative measures of student learning and focuses on the outcome of application in a limited situation (normally a few weeks with limited responsibility at one station). For a broader assessment of cumulative learning we must look elsewhere.

Portfolios and Résumés

Requiring students to assemble a portfolio of their course work, often accompanied by a professional résumé, is an option for professionally oriented departments. Portfolios can include demonstration video or audiotapes, student essays and reports, and copies (or photographs) of course project materials (see chap. 6). Programs in which most students concentrate on television production (or journalism) may find formal faculty evaluation of such a portfolio in an interview before graduation an appropriate measure of each student's achievement. The interview, usually with two or three faculty, can be utilized to help students plan their professional future, as well as evaluate the students' self-presentation in the interview and in the portfolio. New Mexico State University, for example, requires a "commercial résumé videotape" of all broadcast journalism and broadcast production majors.

Senior Seminars

A capstone course intended to help students synthesize preceding course work and apply it to their own futures is often called a *senior seminar* (see chap. 7). Generally limited to 25 or fewer students, a senior seminar typically hinges on a unifying theme such as professional ethics, or a contemporary event such as the quadrennial national elections, and themes may vary from year to year or instructor to instructor. Another approach to the capstone course is to require advanced student projects, such as research studies or advertising campaigns, and usually include in-class presentations.

Senior Theses

Undergraduate student research projects can be formalized as senior theses (see chap. 7). These may be minitheses if students have sufficient methodological background, or they can be highly polished student papers, typically achieved after many individual conferences with the teacher and many rewrites.

Exit Interviews

Asking majors questions at the time they graduate is useful to provide feedback on courses and faculty. Called *exit interviews*, written questionnaires or oral interviews with graduating seniors are useful for getting a sense of student perceptions and satisfactions—or misperceptions and dissatisfactions (see chap. 8). But such exit reports do not provide measures of knowledge gained during course work. In addition, gaining more than a nonrandom sampling of student opinion just before graduation is difficult because no penalty can be attached to noncompletion or nonattendance. Results tend to be more useful as tipoffs for departmental curricular or procedural problems, and, where positive about individual faculty, as ammunition for supporting tenure and promotion cases.

Senior Orals

Oral examinations or interviews can be required in combination with any other outcome measure or given as the sole assessment tool (in addition to grades). Faculty generally find oral tests difficult to grade and tend to pass nearly all students, but one-on-one contact provides a chance to explore a student's strengths and weaknesses and share the faculty's assessment in a setting that drives the message home. More typically, orals partake more of interviews than tests with the aim of aiding the student to define entry-level and long-term professional goals.

BAM Certification

In the early 1980s, the Research Committee of the Broadcast Education Association proposed two levels of voluntary testing on the procedures, content, and uses of audience research (Fletcher, 1981, 1982). Certification was intended to assure broadcast managers and others in the industry that students who passed the test had the skills and knowledge necessary to become users and analysts of syndicated and custom audience ratings reports (Level 1) or had the advanced research skills necessary to those who design, conduct, and report audience studies (Fletcher, 1982). The proposal was worked on for several years, but did not catch on for several reasons, among them that multischool pretesting demonstrated the huge, and perhaps irreconcilable, range in ways of teaching audience research, and also predictable resistance from both students and universities to having outsiders recertify achievements that already appeared to have been completed satisfactorily on student transcripts. The proposal was put aside pending more standardization of teaching and finally made moot by changes in the attitudes toward audience ratings.

Exit Examinations

Finally, we come to content-intensive exit examinations in the major, generally comprehensive tests given just before graduation that must be passed to obtain the degree. At their best, exit examinations mix factual and conceptual knowledge with application questions and allow for imaginative and creative responses; such exit tests are essay style and open ended. In practice, most such tests employ machine-scored multiple-choice questions. Such exams have some appeal in academic fields with a stable body of knowledge—or in which there is general agreement on what must be learned and retained.

In fields such as biology, history, and English, for example, considerable experimentation has been undertaken with some success in developing written tests that measure at least part of what undergraduates must be familiar with in order to justify a degree. The most respectable tests have a written essay component as well as electronically scored items, increasing their reliability but substantially jacking up the time and effort needed for analysis. One science professor noted that the cost depends on the goal: If the purpose is to evaluate the faculty's teaching, a random sample of students could be tested quite economically; if, however, the purpose is to evaluate individual students, then two concerns arise: low levels of faculty interest and administrative suspicion that outcomes testing magnifies problems, not successes. In Indiana University's Biology Department, it was found that a careful analysis and comparison of final course exams in a single, key required course was more profitable for the faculty and students than a large exit exam.

To date, no national exit tests have been developed for 4-year mass communication departments, and few local tests are perceived as successful by the faculties using them. Some 2-year colleges use rising-junior examinations, but they usually focus on basic general education skills or production equipment skills. Decisions to adopt exit testing depend on the key factor of the testing's goal (to measure students or faculty), what would be done with the results, whether tests would be standardized on common course work or individualized, and whether passing such a test would be required for graduation. The remainder of this chapter reports the results of a national study of media departments and then synthesizes the findings in relation to current scholarly knowledge of major outcomes assessment.

WHAT ARE OTHER MEDIA DEPARTMENTS NOW DOING?

Because rumors of widespread exit testing persist without hard evidence of the number of schools attempting such exams and their successes and failures, and because increasing numbers of media departments were feeling pressure to begin quantifiable major assessment, in Fall 1992 a national mail survey was conducted of the 276 institutional members of the Broadcast Education Association (BEA) with undergraduate mass communication programs. Its purpose was to find out exactly which schools now utilize exit examinations. The BEA encompasses virtually all colleges and universities with extensive course work or major fields of study in such areas as mass communications, radio-television (with or without film), telecommunications, broadcasting, communication arts, many speech communication programs with a mass media component, and journalism (if the unit is not oriented solely toward the print media). The BEA Directory was a more appropriate sampling frame than the Mass Communication Division mailing lists of either the ICA or SCA, because they generally attract the more research-oriented faculties, and this study focused on teaching programs. Similarly, the AEJMC directory includes too many schools with only a print media orientation, whereas most departments taking a broader look at mass communications would very probably belong to the Broadcast Education Association. Altogether, departments with 57 different titles responded to the survey.

How Was the Data Collected?

To identify schools using some form of exit exam, all 276 4-year institutional members listed in the annual *BEA Directories* of 1990–91, 1991–92, and 1992–93 were mailed a brief questionnaire. Cross-checking multiple directories allowed for schools that had failed to renew their membership in time for inclusion in the most recent (1992–93) directory. After defining (broadly) exit examinations, the questionnaire asked only if the department/division/program was now using, planned to use, or had formerly used any form of exit examination for majors. Exact department titles were also requested, and each questionnaire was coded to identify some schools for follow-up interviews. The survey form was kept very simple to encourage quick response and because academic experience suggested that very few schools would have such a test and those that did would vary widely in type and motivation.

How Were the Interviews Collected?

Drawing on the mail survey results, interviewers telephoned the department or division chair or head, or failing that, the faculty member who was the BEA representative, at all departments responding that they utilized some sort of exit examination. Based on pilot interviews (Banta & Schneider, 1986), interviewers inquired about the type of exit assessment (exit test, interview, senior seminar, senior thesis, portfolio, etc.), whether the state or the university or college mandated major assessment and of what type, and how the results of the major assessment were utilized (to evaluate students or curriculum and teaching). If a test was reported, interviewers asked whether it was objective or essay style, what kinds of items it included (facts and concepts, applications, skills, affective questions), how it was developed, who revised it and graded it, when it was administered, how it was pretested and validated, and whether students had to pass it to graduate. A copy of the test, if there was one, and permission to quote from it were solicited. When tests once used were referred to, the interviewer asked why a test was no longer being used. When a test was presently being used, the interviewer asked if the faculty in the department were generally satisfied with its effectiveness and appropriateness. Open-ended and informal telephone interviews were utilized because academic experience suggested that departments would vary widely from one another and not fit easily codifiable patterns.

What Were the Results of the Mail Survey?

Altogether, 226 questionnaires were received from 4-year BEA member departments, an 82% response rate. Not surprisingly, by far the overwhelming number of schools did not use an exit test, had not used one in the past, and had no plans for using one in the future. Survey results, confirmed by telephone, revealed that 94% of departments did not use any kind of exit test in the mass communication major, and only 6% did (14 schools). Many schools, however, reported using some other form of major outcomes assessment, such as portfolios, equipment competency tests, senior theses, or senior seminars. As Table 16.1 shows, only 4% of schools reported that they planned to adopt exit testing in the near future. Moreover, there were only 2 reports of discontinued tests.

What Were the Results of the Interviews?

From individual interviews, two distinct approaches to exit testing in the major emerged. One approach addresses the question of whether the students *collectively* are learning through a comprehensive outcomes test, thus demonstrating, presumably, whether the department has been doing its job of effective teaching; such testing is sometimes voluntary, and passing is *never* tied to graduating. The other approach measures *individual student achievement*, and passing is *usually* tied to graduation for each student.

Of the 14 schools giving exit tests in the major as of Fall 1992, 10 departments give written examinations that students need not pass or, in some cases, even take. These are used to assess the curriculum or respond to state-mandated requirements for assessment in the major. Five departments give multiple-choice tests, one gives a half objective/half essay test, three give essay tests (one a case study), and one is an oral.

For example, the Communication Department at the University of Tennessee at Chattanooga maintains a battery of multiple-choice questions based on its core courses and gives a 100-item test the day before final exams start. The test is voluntary and students do not have to take it to graduate, but attendance is very good. Occasionally refreshments are provided and local radio personalities attend, giving the event a social character that draws students. After a pilot test, items were evaluated by a testing expert from the School of Education. The test provides empirical data on the department's teaching to show annual improvement, needed because the

TABLE 16.1
Results of Survey of BEA Member Schools

	Number of Schools
Do not use an exit test	212
Discontinued a former test	2
Planning to adopt a test	8
Presently use an exit test	14
Did not respond	50
Total	$N = 276$

state has adopted a formula for funding based on performance assessment. The department chair also thought the testing helped to keep required courses in focus and had improved testing within courses.

The Broadcasting Department at the University of Tennessee at Knoxville also gives an annual 60-item comprehensive test in the major (all multiple-choice) to all seniors, again to demonstrate improvement to the state's Higher Education Commission. Students must take the test (as part of the capstone course) but passing is not required for graduation; students are told "not to study and do not take the test very seriously." The items were reviewed by the University's assessment office and faculty at other universities for validity and are not changed from year to year. It is presumed that test scores are used to compare media teaching across state-supported schools.

The Communication Department at East Tennessee State University tests only on the two common courses in the major curriculum, an introductory course and a mass communication law course, and all students' scores are summarized for administrative use. For individual assessment, students complete a practicum or a senior project.

Grambling State University in Louisiana gives a university-wide test developed at Princeton that tests English and general knowledge and is required for graduation. The Mass Communication Department also gives an objective test with items customized for each of four concentrations and items on the common core. The test helps the faculty to keep track of each senior's progress. It is not used to evaluate the department or the teaching, only aid the student.

The Communications Department at Bethany College in West Virginia requires a 12-hour essay examination (broken up over 3 days), supplemented by a 1-hour oral. Grading is pass/fail, but passing is not required for graduation. Questions are changed annually. Exit testing in the major is required by the college, and the department chair reported liking such testing because it was a synthesizing learning experience that required students "to pull everything together," to unite and relate knowledge gained in seemingly disparate courses.

The Department of Journalism and Radio-TV at Murray State University in Kentucky gives each student a take-home case-study test in the student's concentration area (such as advertising, public relations, production management). Papers are graded pass/fail on content and pass/fail on style, but the scores do not affect graduation. Instead, two faculty summarize all students' strengths and weaknesses in each area for the department's benefit in improving the curriculum.

At Colorado State University's Speech Communication Department, the faculty gives an annual test on all areas of communication, including electronic media (as well as argumentation, rhetoric, and speech). Participation by students is voluntary, and the results are used to demonstrate to the state legislature what the department does, in response to a state assessment mandate.

The Communications Department at the University of La Verne in California conducts an oral test and portfolio examination with each senior prior to graduation. The test is not formal enough to grade and is used mostly to allow students to demonstrate what they have learned, give feedback on their departmental experiences, and receive guidance on the portfolio and job preparation.

In response to pressure from South Dakota's state legislature and the university administration, Black Hills State College gives a mostly objective test that students need not pass to graduate. The results are used to evaluate the department and its teaching. The Mass Communication faculty constructs the test and gives it every fall and spring. Media studies is part of a comprehensive unit encompassing speech, theatre, modern languages, art, and mass communication.

Augusta College in Georgia gives its students in the Broadcast/Film Department an internally generated objective test that includes both track-specific items and general communication skill questions. Students are required to take the test, but it need not be passed to graduate. The test serves as an advising and curriculum tool when a pattern of deficiencies emerges. The test is given at the end of the fall quarter within the senior seminar and graded by the main faculty in each area. The test was instituted by the department.

Of the 14 aggregate schools presently using an exit test, only 4 give written examinations that majors must pass to graduate. One is an objective-style multiple-choice exam, and three are essay examinations.

Like all other departments at the University of Tennessee at Martin, the Communications Department requires its majors to pass an objective-style test. The University also requires a pretest/posttest on general education given in the freshman and senior years. If an increase in the average scores is shown, the University qualifies for the state's performance funding. Only a posttest is required for departmental majors, and Communications gives it within its senior seminar. The test is intended as an inventory of common (50%) and specialized (50%) course work. The core consists of seven courses (21 credits) and represents half the major; the specialized tracks are broadcasting, journalism, and public relations. In addition to using the test as a requirement for graduation, the faculty averages the students' numerical scores to track the department's progress from year to year. The chair reported that the faculty was generally dissatisfied with the test and considering supplementing it with a portfolio evaluated by the faculty.

At the University of Arkansas, Little Rock, the Radio-TV Department has begun exit testing using an essay exam. The faculty negotiated 10 concepts and questions based on them to form a pool from which exam questions are drawn. The test is graded pass/fail by five faculty. One special value of the concept-pool approach to the department is its guidance for part-time faculty. It has also helped to standardize the content of the department's seven required courses. This assessment process was developed in proactive response to indirect pressure from deans and accrediting bodies, in part to forestall more rigid state requirements. Such testing is acknowledged to involve a lot of extra work.

Kutztown University in Pennsylvania conducts an essay test within a required senior seminar (graded by the course professor but constructed by all faculty and changed every semester). The test deals with the major subject areas of production and law and is graded pass/fail. It is given every semester and summers. At least some of the faculty are "not thrilled now" by the test.

Xavier College of Louisiana utilizes a two-part test in the communications major, the first part of which is an essay test and the second part a television equipment practicum requiring problem solving (it includes editing a news story). The essay test itself divides into comprehensive questions on mass communications (80%) and focused questions on core courses (20%). The 3-hour written essay portion is given on a Saturday in spring and fall, and it is graded pass/fail. The faculty claims to have learned a great deal about the program's strengths and weaknesses from these tests and are now revising the curriculum. They are, however, considering reducing the essay test to only 50% of the exit requirement and adopting a two-step portfolio/résumé requirement: Each student would initially prepare a portfolio at the sophomore level and then revise it at the senior level to show progress.

Beyond the 14 schools already described, another 8 schools reported that they planned to adopt an exit test. Most have opted for multiple-choice exams.

At San Jose State University, the Radio-TV-Film area (which is part of a larger department that includes Dance and Drama) has been preparing for the last 2 years a comprehensive multiple-choice test to be administered in one of four senior-level required courses. The test will cover all the department's major broadcasting areas (corporate video, production, writing, and social/historical/political communication), but at least initially, students will be required to take the test, but not to pass it to graduate. The department is also weighing the possibility of administering the test at the rising junior level so as to have both pretest and posttest results. Having outcome assessment was mandated by the University's trustees, in response to state legislative initiatives, accreditation association pressure, and grade inflation, but the type of assessment depends on the program's nature (Dance and Drama, for example, are adopting portfolios).

The Communication Department at Sangamon State University in Illinois is also planning to institute a multiple-choice pretest/posttest to provide empirical data on what its students learn. Separate tests will be developed in the department's three areas of mass media systems, meaning systems, and interpersonal and organizational systems. At least at the beginning, students will not have to pass the test to graduate, but it is expected that the data may eventually affect salaries and other faculty concerns down the road. Quantitative assessment in the major in Illinois is being driven by legislative budget reductions and threats to cut entire departments to save money. The University mandated quantitative outcomes assessment for all major programs to stave off these threats.

At Southeastern Louisiana University, the Communication and Theatre Department is planning an objective-style test as part of a three-prong outcomes assessment process that includes skills testing (covering talking and reading, perhaps on a randomly selected subset of students), attitudinal questions asking about the curriculum and courses, and cognitive test items on content in the major, but probably restricted to the core courses (which include one mass communication course). There will be no questions in production or any other specialty. The test will be voluntary and passing will not be required to graduate. Assessment here, as at other schools in Louisiana, is being driven by the accreditation process.

Several other schools, including West Texas State University, the University of Southwestern Louisiana, Jacksonville State University in Alabama, Amarillo College in Texas, and the University of Central Oklahoma, have less definite plans for exit testing, in three cases for multiple-choice tests, and in two cases for essay or part-essay tests.

Only two schools reported having once had an exit test that they no longer have. The Communications Department at De Pauw University in Indiana had a test in the early 1980s. It involved a Saturday morning written component and an oral component, but it was dropped because it took too many faculty to manage it as the number of majors grew from 30 to 150. The Communications Department of Loyola University of New Orleans also reported having a multiple-choice exit test until 1988. At that time, the University required an exit test in each major, but the departments were not allowed to flunk anyone. It was dropped when cooperation on the part of students and faculty ebbed.

ARE THERE ALTERNATIVES?

Some schools have come down on the side of nonquantitative outcomes assessment. At least four schools, among them Eastern Connecticut State University and University of North Dakota, plan to adopt portfolios as an outcome assessment tool, and many are already using them. Southern Illinois at Edwardsville plans to assess majors by means of a major paper on their learning and internship. Other schools with a production orientation utilize an equipment competency test, sometimes combined with a content test or a project or a portfolio. Still other schools have adopted a senior project, either in the research or applied arena, as at Walla Walla College, Southern Illinois University at Carbondale, Cedarville College, De

Pauw University, or La Sierra University. Many schools the researchers talked with, however, were still weighing their options.

WHAT DID MEDIA FACULTY PREDICT?

Some schools still had a year or two to get an assessment plan in place. In Oklahoma, for example, the class of 1996 will be the first to undergo testing on their 4 years of education. In Detroit, however, Wayne State University insisted that all departments begin major assessment by the end of 1992–93. Although Louisiana schools are under strong pressure to begin outcomes assessment as part of the accreditation process, one chair claimed that "severe budgetary problems—to the point of financial exigency—will forestall action." Other chairs felt the opposite way: Greater pressure on legislators to divide up a shrinking pie of state funding will lead to increased insistence on outcomes assessment to justify allocations.

Several chairs reported their faculties as "very resistant" to outcomes assessment in the major. One typical comment was, "We would like to have a comprehensive test and oral, but my faculty says 'where's the time?'!" Another chair pointed out, "If a student completes a curriculum designed to prepare him or her for a particular profession, I don't think giving a test later (or a practicum course) can be any more effective as an indication of ability and achievement than the grades already given in classes." One respondent from a North Carolina school was outraged: "Such exams are *not* used on this campus in any way. I can't imagine our administration *allowing* such, much less encouraging it." Another South Carolina respondent agreed: "Winthrop University has been and is a leader in assessment in South Carolina and the Southeast for several years; one firm principle we have is 'NO EXIT EXAMS,' although a few departments have unwisely attempted them."

Another chair said, "We're facing a general expectation in the university; there is no requirement, but we're going to have to be accountable." Another said, "The Regents are mainly interested in posttests, in evaluating the effectiveness of the university." Higher administration are attempting to find means of proving that they do a good job, or if they do not, it is because they do not have enough money. They want positive data that are reasonably credible to help them make a case; they do not really want, in most cases, evidence of weakness. Thus departments might consider putting aside their own need for curricular feedback in favor of testing student achievement. But most faculty are rather idealistic; they will accept useful measurement tools administered credibly that give them feedback. They will be unable to accept proforma testing that measures nothing, but can be manipulated to show ever-increasing total scores.

The experience of Loyola University of New Orleans warns us that faculty and students may eventually rebel against tests that are not required for graduation if other reinforcement is not forthcoming. The experience of Eastern Tennessee State in turning an optional test into a social occasion suggests one happy option.

The issue of lawsuits bothers some faculty. The chair of the Department of Mass Communication at Bemidji State University raised these questions on behalf of his faculty: "Would a student be denied graduation if he/she failed the exit exam? What would it say about the quality of instruction if a student didn't pass—especially a last-quarter senior? What action would be taken if the student didn't pass? Could the student file suit against the university?" He pointed out that Bemidji was working instead to stiffen entrance requirements and screen students before they come into the program. Many departments do that, of course, and find it useful, but entrance exams do not address the same issues as outcomes assessment.

WHAT DID THE TESTS REALLY LOOK LIKE?

In this study, 10 departments currently using an exit examination shared a copy of the test with the researcher. Half of the exit exams were objective and half were essay and short answer. The objective tests ranged from a low of 60 to a high of 150 multiple-choice or true–false items, but typically had 100 items. One short-answer and definitions test focused solely on audio and video production. Another essay test called "comprehensive" focused solely on an internship experience. Three additional essay tests varied from analysis of a single case study to a dozen short essays.

The sample of five objective and five essay and short-answer tests is too small for any quantitative analysis, but a few comments from students seem appropriate. A small honors class was asked to examine the tests and rate each one for *scope*, *difficulty*, and *fairness*.

First, the quality of the objective questions was generally weak. These students found four of the five quantitative tests too easy: three 100-item multiple-choice tests because they covered too much territory too superficially, another specialty-only test too limited to be sufficiently difficult. They likened the questions in the so-called comprehensive tests to those used in large, lower division survey classes and felt that this was inappropriate knowledge to test on several years later. On these four tests, they judged many questions poorly constructed (and testing experts would agree). The fifth quantitative test was thought to involve too much professor-specific or book-specific memorization and too little analytic thinking, but it was judged significantly better than the others. However, it remained a test of introductory material, not a student's specialization.

Here are some examples of elementary, trivial, and poorly constructed multiple-choice items drawn from several schools' tests. Dozens of questions were pointed out as general knowledge information (at least among young people) or of the "easy guessing" type that required no information learned in school. Surprisingly, one school made it clear that some questions on a graduation test came from a course entitled "Introduction to Mass Communication." Questions 1–3 are the types considered too basic (in media studies) for graduation testing:

1. The signal for VHF, UHF, and FM
   a. is sent in digital mode.
   b. travels by microwave.
   c. travels primarily through the ground.
   d. bounces off the ionosphere.
   e. travels in a straight line.

2. The largest share of advertising revenue goes to
   a. radio.
   b. newspapers.
   c. television.
   d. magazines.
   e. direct mail.

3. The Sullivan decision provided
   a. a definition of libel.
   b. a definition of malice.
   c. a definition of negligence.
   d. a definition of a public figure.
   e. a distinction between public figures and private persons.

Questions 4–6 are were evaluated as too trivial for graduation testing. Question 4 was pointed out as the sort of general knowledge unrelated to major studies that does not belong on any test. Questions 5 and 6 were noted as simply unimportant information.

4. An album that has sold 500,000 copies and a single record that has sold one million is considered
   a. gold.
   b. platinum.
   c. silver.
   d. brass.

5. Appropriation consists of
   a. stealing another person's money.
   b. using a person's name, reputation, or likeness for commercial purposes without consent.
   c. destroying a person's reputation.
   d. trespassing on someone else's property in order to cover the news.
   e. writing a news story about a person without permission.

6. *Harlem Book of the Dead* is by
   a. James Van der Zee.
   b. Avedon.
   c. Gordon Parks.
   d. Karsh.

Questions 7–9 were pointed out as examples of exceptionally poor questions. Question 7 is the type that all students would answer *a* to because no other answer is viable. Questions 8 and 9 were considered "insulting" test items that underestimate young people. Testing experts would also point out that five full answers should be included for each question to reduce the odds for guessing and that "all of the above" and its counterpart "none of the above" are to be avoided:

7. Theory Z of management assumes that employees are:
   a. to participate fully in the running of the company.
   b. not to be trusted under any conditions.
   c. not creative and have to be heavily supervised.
   d. to be paid bare minimum.

8. Nonverbal communication consists of
   a. sign language.
   b. hand waving.
   c. smiles.
   d. all of the above.

9. Printed or written defamatory material is
   a. gossip.
   b. slander.
   c. libel.
   d. none of the above.

An example of a test questions they found fair, of sufficient difficulty, and requiring either important factual knowledge or analytic thinking was in Question 10.

10. The media of this nation increasingly are owned by large corporations rather than independent owners. Many view this trend as a threat to
    a. the law of large numbers.
    b. equal access rules.
    c. a free marketplace of ideas.
    d. the fairness doctrine.
    e. recent FCC rulings on exclusivity.

Second, the honors students found marked bias toward different subject areas even in tests appearing to be "comprehensive." One 100-item test, for example, favored regulation and policy (55 items) over all other subject areas (45 items). Another favored public relations even within the core portion of the questionnaire. Others tended to favor the history of the field.

Third, the evaluating students preferred specialty tests over basic industry information. They thought tests given at graduation time should concentrate on material learned in upper division specialty classes, not lower division introductory material. They thought testing library skills (how to interpret a bibliographic reference) at graduation was rather useless (it belonged at a much lower level), but they approved of English language proficiency segments in tests even at the senior level. Items on grammar, word choice, and correct usage were approved.

And, not surprisingly, these honors students uniformly thought the essay tests (or essay items at the end of mixed tests), requiring application to real-world situations, to be the best measures of what students had learned. However, even these test items varied from superficial to meaningful in the students' view. They liked best case-study questions such as the following, but most case studies (in the sample sent to us) proved to relate to news journalism (even when they were called "public relations" or "radio/television" questions).

11. The editors of [student newspaper] would like to improve the paper in terms of the stories it covers and its layout and graphics. Before doing that, they are eager to know what students think about the paper and what they would like to see included in [newspaper name] in the future. You volunteered to do a scientific survey of student opinions. Describe in detail the steps you would take to determine the students' opinions.

12. All journalists, broadcasters, public relations consultants, and advertising executives are faced with ethical decisions daily. Review the differing ethical principles that may arise. Remember to link the ethical principles very explicitly to your examples. Accurate illustration of the principles you raise should be your main aim.

In sum, these honors students judged most multiple-choice questions as tests of test-taking skills rather than accumulated knowledge and ability to integrate and synthesize. They found most objective test items too basic, often trivial, and too often poorly constructed. Short answer or essay questions were usually better for demonstrating writing and thinking skills, but they were also unsatisfactory (in terms of scope, level, and fairness) when they measured memorized subject matter.

Exit testing, if it must occur, should focus on students' writing, research, and analytic skills, not memorized material. Individualized or small group tests should be constructed that match the subject area of each student's interests as much as possible, rather than using the same test for all students. Differences in subject matter are irrelevant to measurement (but important for motivating students to do their best). Evaluation should focus on the student's ability to apply knowledge and skills and avoid rote learning of facts and measurements of objective test-taking skills.

WHAT CONCLUSIONS CAN BE DRAWN AND WHAT QUESTIONS MUST I ASK ABOUT MY DEPARTMENT?

At its start, this chapter promised a model for action. To develop one, the author drew on what other schools are doing and plan to do and what other faculty, as well as the author, think ought to be done. This model is phrased as a series of sometimes-controversial statements.

1. *How to assess depends on whether the goal is preparing students or measuring students.* In such states as Tennessee, Oklahoma, and Illinois, legislators now require plans for quantifiable measurements of teaching and learning, commonly called *outcomes assessment,* but faculty have some leeway. What becomes crucial in deciding whether to implement any test is the department's goal: Is the purpose of major assessment to measure the individual students' achievements or to measure the department's achievements?

If the goal is to measure individual *student* achievement as a precursor to granting a degree, tests often are the poorest option. Tests must, by their very nature, be standardized, and if required for graduation, often must be quantifiable and legally defensible. Yet educators recognize that multiple-choice tests are weak tools for measuring anything but the most basic factual material. They rarely succeed in measuring students' ability to integrate their learning, synthesize seemingly unrelated ideas, apply skills and knowledge in new situations, theorize about causes or impacts, demonstrate analytic or creative thinking, and so on. Indeed, objective tests tend to devalue what is important about education—the creative, controversial, and immeasurable—and foster what is trivial, valueless, and measurable. Interviews with departments required to assess their majors reveal widespread adoption of several alternatives to testing, including senior seminars, senior theses or projects, and portfolios/résumés. These options appear more credible and efficacious for measuring the individual student's achievement in the major.

If the goal is to assess the *department's* achievements in teaching, a test may be appropriate. As the interviews show, testing students on content learned in the major may be initially useful in providing feedback to the faculty about weaknesses and strengths of course work, curriculum, and teaching. The results of tests can be compared over time to demonstrate improvements in curriculum. However, on the negative side, eventually such testing can have an undesirable impact on courses as faculty quite naturally begin "teaching to the test." Moreover, in small departments where who teaches what course is well known, the results of such testing can readily have impact on merit evaluations and salary increases. Such a danger is less apparent in large departments where several individuals teach the same course.

2. *Whether to test depends on resources available.* Small departments with 10 or 20 graduating seniors may be able to muster sufficient resources, to write, administer, and grade individually customized tests. They can take account of the specific courses each individual has completed and design measures that allow students to show their strengths as well as weaknesses. For such departments, essay tests, oral examinations, and portfolios of work can get students to display their ability to integrate, synthesize, and apply their course work. Large departments, graduating anywhere from 50 to 200 or more students annually, on the other hand, lack the faculty time and commitment for anything but objective tests, and because these exams seem to test the wrong things, they should avoid exit testing entirely.

3. *If testing is used, incentives are needed to get both students and faculty to take the test seriously.* Faculty need explicit rewards for devoting more of their scarce time and energy to assessment, beyond what they already do. Students need immediate rewards for participating in assessment, and purely negative "rewards" (such as "you will not graduate if you don't pass") are, the educational literature teaches, wholly undesirable and will have long-term negative effects on the students' (and thus the public's) view of college. Indeed, academia may already be suffering from this problem.

4. *If testing is used, examine students on what they have studied recently in their specialties.* Some faculty presume that, to be fair, a test must concentrate on what students have in common, the department's required or core course work. However, in many departments, most required courses are completed in lower division, sometimes as first-year students; it is hardly appropriate educationally to test on that material 2 or 4 years later, nor would such a test tell educators anything they want to know.

5. *Avoid the pretest/posttest trap.* Too many academics, facing too many demands and pressures, see the pre-/posttest paradigm as a way out of the "testing to show improvement" dilemma. However, not only will such tests reveal nothing of value, their content will creep insidiously into the curriculum, eventually resulting in the worst sort of "teaching to the test." For the most cynical faculties, such tests can easily be manipulated in highly unethical fashion to demonstrate so-called improvement.

6. *Choose a test based on the department's curricular goal(s).* If the department's central mission is to prepare its students for graduate study, then utilizing the general section of the Graduate Record Exam (GRE) or Michigan State's test for entering graduate students makes some sense. If the mission is to prepare students for the broadcasting work force, then portfolios make sense. If the mission is broad and the curriculum will have

varied outcomes for different groups of students, then no single tool is appropriate.

7. *Puncture the myth of the nationally normed test.* Media departments are too diverse in orientation and goals to ever have national standardized outcomes tests. Even statewide, departments do and should vary to reflect the specialties of the faculty. Not all schools need teach the same things; indeed, fostering clones by standardizing communications curricula across schools wastes precious resources and fails to make the full range of options available to students. Moreover, nationally normed tests apparently are weak tools for all fields, even the sciences. As knowledge has proliferated, so has specialization in curricula within all university departments.

8. *If testing is for the department's benefit, test at intervals.* One option for avoiding many of the negative side effects of testing is to not test every year. Testing majors at 3- or 5-year intervals minimizes the likelihood of the curriculum being driven by the test and individual faculty salaries being tied to test results. Furthermore, testing with the goal of assessing the department need not be required of all students; large departments can test random samples, if sufficient common course work is taken. Or they can develop tests administered only to those in a specific emphasis or track, varying which track to test from year to year.

9. *Insist that legislators pay the cost of developing local measurement tools.* Even within one large department, students take a wide diversity of programs of study and the facts and concepts of the field change with unparalleled frequency. In addition, any test must be constantly rewritten to avoid breaches of security, and multiple-choice test items should have evaluation by testing experts to avoid charges of bias. Testing must be viewed in light of pressures for multiculturalism. The sum total of customization to meet individual student needs, re-evaluation of test items to keep pace with industry changes, and development and testing of new questions will have a prohibitively high cost. Most media departments are understaffed, underfunded, and overrun with students. They must have financial help before taking on new tasks.

10. *Consider the underlying purpose of undergraduate education before buying into the idea of assessment.* Is the learning of content the goal of undergraduate education or is it demonstrating the ability to learn? Does the faculty aim to pour concepts and facts into the receptacle of students' minds? Or are they much more concerned about imparting the reading, writing, investigating, and thinking skills essential to learning through the student's professional and personal life? If you come down, as I do, on the side of *learning how to learn* as the central purpose of undergraduate education, then assessing cumulative knowledge seems profoundly counterproductive and a wicked waste of scarce resources, indeed, even a bit surreal.

CONCLUSION

Do not misunderstand. I am not opposed to assessment. Indeed, we assess students all the time and should do it more efficiently and effectively. I am opposed to objective tests that foster a misapprehension about what education *is* and *is not*. I have a great horror of giving in to those legislators, trustees, higher education officials, and even colleagues who want to reduce education to something simple, an in–out process. For me, education is an ongoing process of growth and expansion, fostering the abilities of learning how to learn, responding creatively to one's environment, thinking, and imagining. Especially at the undergraduate level, we must resist the narrow idea that our job is to prepare students for the job market. What that job market will be tomorrow is unknown, and what the rest of our students' lives will be is unknowable.

REFERENCES

Allison, T. M. (1993, April). *Regional accrediting association requirements: Developing outcomes statements.* Paper presented to the Broadcast Education Association, Las Vegas, NV.

American Association of University Professors.(1990). Mandated assessment of educational outcomes: A report of Committee C on College and University Teaching, Research, and Publication. *Academe, 76*(6), 34–40.

Baker, E. L. (1986, October 25). *Critical validity issues in the methodology of higher education assessment.* Paper presented to the Education Testing Service Invitational Conference, New York.

Baldwin, T. F., & Surlin, S. H. (1970). A tool for graduate student advising. *Journal of Broadcasting, 14*(4), 449–454.

Banta, T. W., & Schneider, J. A. (1986, April). *Using locally developed comprehensive exams for majors to assess and improve academic program quality.* Paper presented at the American Educational Research Association, San Francisco.

Benjamin, E. (1990, July 5). The movement to assess students' learning will institutionalize mediocrity in colleges. *Chronicle of Higher Education,* pp. B1–B2.

Blanchard, R. O., & Christ, W. G. (1993). *Media education and the liberal arts: A blueprint for a new professionalism.* Hillsdale, NJ: Lawrence Erlbaum Associates.

Boyer, C. M., Ewell, P. T., Finney, J. E., & Mingle, J. R. (1987). Assessment and outcomes measurement: A view from the states. *AAHE Bulletin, 40*(4), 14.

Carroll, R. (1987). No "middle ground": Professional broadcast education is liberal education. *Feedback, 28*(2), 10–11.

Chase, W. M. (1990, November–December). "The real challenge of multiculturalism (is yet to come)." *Academe, 76*(6), 20–23.

Dates, J. L. (1990). The study of theory should guide the curriculum. *Feedback, 31*(3), 10–11.

Eastman, S. T. (1985). Directions for telecommunications. *Feedback, 27*(3), 23–27.

Eastman, S. T. (1987). A model for telecommunications education. *Feedback, 28*(2), 21–25.

Electronic media career preparation study. (1987, December). New York: Roper Organization.

Ervin, R. F. (1988, October). Outcomes assessment: The rationale and implementation. *ASJMC Insights,* 19–23.

Eshelman, D. (1990, December). *Outcomes assessment and discipline specific accreditation in mass communication: An analysis.* Paper presented at the Administrator's Workshop of the Association of Schools of Journalism and Mass Communication, New Orleans, LA.

Eshelman, D. (1991, April). *Outcomes assessment strategies: Implications for broadcast education.* Paper presented to the Courses and Curriculum Division of the Broadcast Education Association, Las Vegas, NV.

Fletcher, J. E. (1981). A proposal for voluntary certification. *Feedback, 21*(1), 17–18.

Fletcher, J. E. (1982). BAM exams: Screeners for broadcast managers. *Feedback, 22*(1), 15.

Gomery, D. (1985). Radio, television *and* film: The state of study in the 1980s. *Feedback, 27*(4), 12–16.

Kamalipour, Y. R. (1992). Broadcast education vs. vocational education. *Feedback, 33*(1), 2–3.

Kittross, J. M. (1989). Six decades of education for broadcasting . . . and counting. *Feedback, 30*(4), 30–42.

Lewis, L. (1992, July–August). Review of Ernest T. Pascarella and Patrick T. Terenzini's *How college affects students: Findings and insights from twenty years of research. Academe, 78*(4), 44–47.

Limberg, V. E. (1987). Administrative structures and program orientation in broadcast communications curriculum. *Feedback, 28*(3), 22–28.

Magner, D. K. (1989, February 1). An expert on 'assessment' wants the concept to become universal. *Chronicle of Higher Education,* p. A13.

Meeske, M. D. (1980). Testing R-TV-student writing skills. *Feedback, 21*(2), 22–23.

Nielsen, R. M., & Polishook, I. H. (1990, April 11). Taking a measure of assessment. *Chronicle of Higher Education,* p. A14.

Pascarella, E. T., & Terenzini, P. T. (1991). *How college affects students: Findings and insights from twenty years of research.* San Francisco: Jossey-Bass.

Porter, M. J., & Szolka, P. (1991). Broadcasting students' perspectives of a liberal arts education. *Feedback, 32*(2), 18–21.

Robinson, W. L., & Kamalipour, Y. R. (1991). Broadcast education in the United States: The most recent national survey. *Feedback, 32*(2), 2–5.

Schwalbe, T. (1991). Program review: A time for change. *Feedback, 32*(3), 22–24.

Smith, F. L. (1980). 'So, you wanna write a book . . .!' *Feedback, 21*(2), 8–11.

Sterling, C. H. (1985). The meaning in the name. *Feedback, 27*(3), 13–14.

Tennessee Higher Education Commission. (1992, July 1). *Performance funding standards, 1992–1993 through 1996–1997.* Knoxville, TN: Author.

Wallace, J. (1985, October). *What undergraduates learn: The role of assessment in large research universities.* Paper presented at the National Conference on Assessment in Higher Education, sponsored by the American Association for Higher Education, Columbia, SC.

Webster, J. (1989). Media study in a time of technological change. *Feedback, 30*(3), 20–24.

Wolf, B. L. (1989, November 28). *The assessment initiative at Indiana University-Bloomington.* Unpublished paper, Indiana University, Bloomington, IN.

Author Index

Richmond, V. P., 245, 246, 247, *255*
Riggio, R. E., 243, 244, 245, *254, 255*
Roberts, C. V., 244, 246, *256*
Robinson, W. L., *382*
Rodrigues, R. J., 20, *29*
Rogers, D., 296, *307*
Rogers, E. M., 34, 35, *55*
Rogers, J. S., 19, 21, 27
Rogers, J. T., 58, *86*
Romney, L. C., *348*
Rosenbaum, J., 21, *29*, 82, *200*
Rosenberg, M., 228, *236*, 244, 245, *255*
Rosenfeld, L. B., 240, *253*
Ross, R. S., 277, 281, *289*
Rost, K., 261, 282, *288*
Roth, N. L., 293, 294, *307*
Rothblatt, S., 44, *55*
Rowland, W. D., Jr., 170, *179*
Rubin, A. M., 35, *55*
Rubin, D., 208, *217*
Rubin, R. B., 35, *55*, 220, 221, 223, 228, *236*, 239, 241, 242, *255*, 258, 259, *289*, 294, 296, *309*
Rubin, S. S., 340, *349*
Rudman, H., 212, *217*
Russell, C., 123, 124, *129*
Russell, D., 245, 246, *255*
Rutt, D. P., 243, 244, *254*
Ryan, M. P., 116, 128, *129*
Rydell, S., *154*

S

Salas, E., 263, *289*
Samovar, L. A., 276, 280, *286*
Saunders, D. M., 297, *309*
Sauser, W. I., Jr., 297, *309*
Schafer, W., 114, 117, 118, 120, 121, 122, 125, 128, *129*
Schilling, K. L., 17, 22, 26, *29*
Schilling, K. M., 17, 22, 26, *29*
Schmidt, F. L., 296, *309*
Schmidt, F., 213, *217*
Schneider, J. A., 367, *381*
Schoenfeldt, L. F., 297, *309*
Scholtes, P. R., 257, *289*
Schrader, D., 279, *289*
Schultz, B., 267, *289, 309*
Schutz, W., 297, *309*
Schwalbe, T., 361, 362, *382*
Scott, T. E., 209, *217*, 240, *254*
Seashore, S., 277, *289*
Seaton, F., 213, *217*
Seiler, W. J., 291, 292, *306*
Seldin, P., 90, *112*
Serdlik, M. E., 267, *2867*

Shaw, M. L., 266, *290*
Shepard, L., 212, *217*
Sherman, A. R., 245, *255*
Shockley-Zalabak, P., 291, 296, 297, 298, 299, *309*
Simmons, C. E., 34, *54*
Simmons, H. L., 65, 66, *85*
Simosko, S., *154*
Sims, S. J., 6, 13, 14, 17, *29*, 36, 37, 39, 40, *55*, *86*
Sippola, B. C., 296, *309*
Slark, J., 19, *28*
Smellie, D. C., 156, 157, *178*
Smith, D. K., 267, *287*
Smith, F. L., 359, *382*
Smith, R. M., 259, *290*
Snyder, M., 244, 245, *255*
Solow, R., 292, *306*
Southern Association of Colleges and Schools Commission on Colleges, 58, 59, 60, 76, 79, *85, 86*
Spady, W. G., 76, 77, *86*
Speech Communication Association, 12, *26*, 207, *217*, 221, *236*, 240, *256*, 287, 293, *309*
Spitzberg, B. H., 220, *236*, 238, 241, 243, 247, *254, 256*, 258, 261, 262, 264, 267, 279, *290*, 293, *309*
Staley, C. C., 291, 298, 299, *309*
Stark, J. S., 16, *29*
Staton-Spicer, A., 240, *254*
Steinbrecher, M. M., 244, 246, *256*
Steiner, I. D., 265, *290*
Stephens, R. D., 220, *236*, 291, 292, *306*
Sterling, C. H., 358, *382*
Stiggins, R., 114, 115, *129*, 212, 214, 215, *217*, 283, *290*
Stogill, R. M., 281, *290*
Stohl, C., 273, *289*
Strengthening the ties that bind, 33, 44, 45, *54*
Stufflebeam, D., 10, *28*
Sullivan, M., 181, *200*
Surges-Tatum, D., 219, *236*, 250, *255*, 258, 271, 278, 279, 282, 283, *289*
Surlin, S. H., 352, *381*
Sweet, S. D., 43, *54*
Swezey, R., 118, 120, *130*
Sykes, C., 31, *55*
Szczupakiewicz, N., 220, *236*
Szolka, P., 358, *382*

T

Tankel, J. D., 34, *53*
Tardy, C. H., 241, *256*

Subject Index

250, 252, 267, 269, 276–277, 281,
291, 298, 316, 360, 372
aesthetic sensibility, 46, 51, 159
apprehension (instruments), 246
dimensions, 76, 240–241
leadership capacity, 46, 51, 159
motivation of continued learning, 46, 51,
159
scholarly concern for improvement, 46,
51, 159
questionnaire/insturments, 80, 82, 246,
276–277, 281

B

Behavior(al), 77, 90, 115, 208–209, 230–231,
255
criteria, 90, 208, 210
domain (public speaking), 230–231, 234
and educational effectiveness, 7
instruments, 242–243, 245–246, *see also*
The Competent Speaker
and interpersonal communication, 239,
240, 242–244, 247, 249, 250, 255
objectives, 118–119
organizational, 291, 293, 295, 298, 309
procedures, 213–216
professional, 46, 51, 159
and psychomotor learning, 157–158
small group, 258–290
teaching, 90–93, 104–105
theatre, 313, 318–319, 321
Bias (cultural, gender, test), 120, 274, 283,
290, 376, 380 *see also* Assessment
and diversity, Minority
and advisory boards, 191
and oral communication, 203, 205, 211–
213, 215–217
and public speaking, 221–224, 228
Bloom's *Taxonomy of Educational Objectives*,
48–49, 53, 156–157, 178, 317–320,
322, 324, 332
Broadcast Education Association, 40, 182,
361, 366,
certification from, 365
directories, 367
Broadcasting outcomes
examples, 68–80, 146–151, 342–347
Budget(ing),
and accreditation, 334, 353
and exit examinations, 357
incentive funding, 13
performance funding, 13
and portfolios, 152
process, 13
program, 36, 50, 61, 357, 362, 372–373
responsibility center (RCB), 357

C

Campaign for Genuine Accountability in
Education, 14
Campus Trends, 15, 16
Capstone Courses, 21, 70, 79, 155–179, 325–
326, 340, 364, 369
advantages, 166–169
course description, 173–174
disadvantages, 169–170
oral presentation, 164, 166–167, 169
objectives, 174
portfolio, 164, 166–167, 169
requirements, 174–176
senior thesis, 164, 166–167, 169, 177–178
senior project/orals, 164, 166–167, 169,
176–177
Capstone experiences, *see* Assessment, Capstone courses, Theatre education
Carnegie Corporation, 10, 132
Carnegie Forum on Education and the
Economy, 10
Carnegie Foundation 114, 160, 164, 165–166,
179, 296
Carnegie National Board for Professional
Teaching Standards (NBPTS), 10
Carnegie outcomes, 44, 45
Carnegie Report, 159, 163
Center for the Study of Higher Education
(Pennsylvania State University),
10
Central Michigan State University Prior
Learning Assessment Team, 141,
142–143
Classroom
assessment
formal, 117–122
informal, 122–123
research, 122–123, 129
syllabus, 115–116
Classroom assessment techniques (CATs),
122
Cognitive
abilities, 119, 156–157, 298, 372
differentiation/domains/dimensions,
76–77, 156, 230, 234, 240, 254,
282, 294, 316–318
drives/motives/orientations, 267
learning/knowledge, 82, 155–160, 166–
167, 228, 316, 355
limitations/weaknesses, 135, 138
objectives/outcomes, 15, 76
processes, 262
skills, 9, 48, 156, 324–325, 354–355
taxonomies, 48, 178
College Basic Academic Subjects Exam
(CBASE), 13